Formal Theories
of
Visual Perception

Formal Theories
of
Visual Perception

Edited by

E. L. J. Leeuwenberg and H. F. J. M. Buffart

Psychology Department
Katholieke Universiteit
Nijmegen, The Netherlands

JOHN WILEY AND SONS
Chichester · New York · Brisbane · Toronto

Library of Congress Cataloging in Publication Data:

Main entry under title:

Formal theories of visual perception.

Includes index.
1. Visual perception—Addresses, essays, lectures.
I. Leeuwenberg, Emanuel Laurens Jan. II. Buffart, H. F. J. M.
BF241.F63   152.1   77-12441
ISBN 0 471 99586 X

Photoset and printed in Malta
by Interprint (Malta) Ltd

List of Contributors

A. A. BLANK — Department of Mathematics, Carnegie-Mellon University, Schenley Park, Pittsburgh, Pennsylvania, U.S.A.

H. F. J. M. BUFFART — Department of Experimental Psychology, University of Nijmegen, Nijmegen, The Netherlands

T. CAELLI — Department of Psychology, University of Melbourne, Parkville, Victoria, Australia

J. DRÖSLER — Department of Psychology, University of Regensburg, Regensburg, Federal Republic Germany

D. H. FOSTER — Department of Communication, University of Keele, Keele, Staffordshire, England

C. D. FRITH — Division of Psychiatry, MRC Clinical Research Centre, Harrow, Middlesex, England

H. G. GEISSLER — Department of Psychology, Humboldt University, Berlin, German Democratic Republic

S. GROSSBERG — Department of Mathematics, Boston University, Boston, Massachusetts, U.S.A.

W. C. HOFFMAN — Department of Mathematical Science, Oakland University, Rochester, Michigan, U.S.A.

G. JOHANSSON — Department of Psychology, University of Uppsala, Uppsala, Sweden

B. JULESZ — Bell Laboratories, Murray Hill, New Jersey, U.S.A.

F. KLIX — Department of Psychology, Humboldt University, Berlin, German Democratic Republic

E. L. J. LEEUWENBERG — Department of Experimental Psychology, University of Nijmegen, Nijmegen, The Netherlands

H. LINDMAN — Department of Psychology, University of Melbourne, Parkville, Victoria, Australia

J. R. POMERANTZ — The John Hopkins University, Baltimore Maryland, U.S.A.

F. RESTLE

Department of Psychology, Indiana University, Bloomington, Indiana, U.S.A.

U. I. SCHEIDEREITER

Department of Psychology, Humboldt University, Berlin, German Democratic Republic

H. A. SIMON

Department of Psychology, Carnegie-Mellon University, Schenley Park, Pittsburgh, Pennsylvania, U.S.A.

A. S. WATSON

Department of Psychology, University of Stirling, Stirling, Scotland

Contents

General Introduction

In the area of psychology it is extremely difficult to think of a topic which is not somehow related to the problems of classification, concept formation and recognition. Even the study of issues concerned with human thought cannot bypass the question as to how invariants may possibly be established in the multitude of data. Such themes invariably take the kernel position in the study of perception. Perhaps no other subject has been approached with such a large variety of method. It is undoubtedly the lack of a convincing overall picture which has led to the great diversity of disciplines engaged in the study of perception. Of old, the process of abstraction has been studied in the context of *epistemology*. Especially from the ranks of philosophers and psychologists, scientists came forward in the early 20th century, directing attention to *'Gestalt' phenomena*. Over-simplified notions on human perception they swept aside; their own findings, however, were often not more penetrating than their motto, 'The whole is more than the sum of its parts'.

The emergence of *Selective Information theory* around 1950 has given rise to an impressive amount of research to establish its relevance for psychology. However, insufficient knowledge of 'perceptual alphabet' was the reason that the attempts were not as successful as had been expected. The latter disadvantage also applied to theories which in certain respects deal in a more complex way with the formation of concepts. Approaches of this type are: *learning theories*, *decision theories* and *cybernetics*. The disordered picture of the results of feedback theories, in which pre-existing knowledge plays a crucial part, compelled the researchers to express their ideas in terms of *network models*. Ideally, these models themselves should yield the relevant distinctive features leading to the classification of patterns. Unfortunately, however, until now no network model has been able to accomplish this task in a perceptually relevant manner. This statement, however, is not intended to refute the perceptual relevance of selective information theory or the idea that feedback and pre-existing knowledge play a role in perception.

As regards its contribution to the theory of perception, research in the field of *pattern recognition* may be regarded as having a more modest value, since the distinctive pattern features are built into the models at fore hand. This research is, indeed, chiefly aimed at the automatic classification of a very specific set of patterns. The need for wider and more flexible classes into which patterns may apparently be categorized, has led to the development of *figure grammars*. Uptill now, however, these also seem to be applicable only to a very specific set of patterns; in other words, this development may perhaps be important purely, for solving technical problems. Thus, it only seldom happens that there is no conflict between the starting-points of the figure grammar approach on the one hand and the findings in the psychology of perception on the other. Here again absolutely no refutation is implied of all the aspects of existing figure grammars or of pattern recognition models.

The growing conviction within the group of perception researchers that the human construction of a percept should once again be regarded as a conclusion which follows upon a process or reasoning has stimulated workers in the field of *Artificial Intelligence* (A. I.) to give expression to such construction of percepts in computer programs. Amongst other things, inventive '*scene-analysis*' programs have been worked out determining the three-dimensional positioning of objects from figures that are given in two dimensions. It remains unsatisfactory, however, that what could be established was at most a possible isomorphism between the input–output relation of the program and that of the perceptual process. Indeed, the multitude of interacting process elements in a program highly complicates the testing of the theoretical principles that are involved. In spite of the large amount of liberty taken and the latitude that is maintained in A.I. model construction, no simulation programmes of the perception process have yet been implemented which can summon up the Gestalt phenomena.

An area of research more amenable to testing—specifically with the aid of protocols—is that concerned with human thought processes ('*problem solving*'). This field of research, however, has yielded insights into perception which agree remarkably well with a series of theories from the field of perception research. The theories do not primarily deal with the perceptual process itself but rather with its outcomes. These *coding theories* are based on perceptual elements, the total number of which indicates the amount of structural information. These elements are not physical dimensions, which could e.g. be determined by means of data reduction techniques applied to relationship judgements between patterns; instead, they are specific relationships, which hierarchically build one upon the other. These relationships constitute the perceptual elements which correspond to structural aspects of the pattern code; in contrast, selective information theory is at most concerned with the metric or the quantitative values associated with each of the structural aspects. These coding theories, which show some resemblance to figure grammars, predict data from extrapolation experiments, complexity judgements, Gestalt phenomena, learning effects and context effects. These coding theories, in which the efficiency principle is of crucial importance are such that for overlearned sets of patterns they allow the deduction of the appropriate distinctive features as code elements.

Alongside the above-mentioned approach, there have recently been surprising developments on what might be seen as the more 'basic' perception *process*. Characteristic of the studies concerned is that the mathematical description of process aspects allows predictions on the interaction of many input data. This type of approach is indicated in the present volume under the heading: *theories on field effects*. These theories were already in existence at the very beginning of the 20th century; since that time they have hardly been affected by the above-mentioned movements thanks to the coherence of their concepts. Not only do these theories link up with each other on account of their mathematical nature but at the same time they exhibit points of connection with the coding theories mentioned above. Thus the manner in which a figure is scanned will determine the choice of interpretation ultimately given to the figure. Conversely, and probably of crucial importance to the status of these field theories is, amongst other things, the feedback from the final stage of the information assimilation process, as determined by means of the coding theories, to the first stages of the storage process. For example, the interpretation of a pattern can in the first instance determine the nature of the eye movements and then, in turn, these can influence the field effects of the sensory input.

The immediate occasion for coupling the two last-mentioned approaches was that between them a remarkable convergence of ideas was taking place in recent years. Once again, these two themes are:

(1) Analytical theories of field effects
(2) Coding theories of complex patterns

With regard to the latter theories, it may be noted that practically all their initiators appear in the present volume, although their contributions here deal chiefly with conclusions and implications of their coding theories.

The two classes of theories are in the first place characterized by the fact that while having perceptual relevance they also show the exactness of mathematical expression. It is unusual to find these qualities together. For the majority of the theories presented it can be said that they do not solely describe the results of specific experiments but that they offer explanations for them on a conceptual foundation. Because of these particular properties it is possible, in principle to arrive at either an assimilation of or a confrontation between the two classes of theories. The exploration of this possibility constitutes the chief aim of the present volume.

Pieces of research in the framework of the two themes of the present volume do not as yet give the impression of giving conflicting evidence. Possibly this may be due to the existing differences in method of approach. Studies on Theme 1 tend to be based more on phenomena ascertained by the peripheral sense-organs; whereas studies on Theme 2 sooner tend to concentrate on insights gained through introspective experiences. Connected to this distinction, there is another difference: research work on Theme 1 is in general more concerned with cause-to-effect (causal) relationships, whereas work on Theme 2 investigates effect-to-cause (final) relationships. Where the relevant data on brain-processes are lacking one must obviously resort to arguments like those of efficiency and optimalization if one is to describe relations between subjective experiences. This research leads to statements about rules that are concerned with the form of memory representation. These correspond to the final result of the perceptual process. The process itself is the object of study in Theme 1. Interestingly, the latter investigation, which in first instance may be more easily grasped in terms of analytical mathematics, can lead to findings that can be described in disjunctive terms. The latter terms offer possibilities for linking up with discrete mathematical expressions proper to the coding systems that arise from research work on Theme 2.

Thus it is possible for the coding rules not only to possess validity within— and appropriate to—the domain of subjective experience but also, to occupy a significant position outside that subjective domain.

Part I

Theories on Field Effects

Introduction

If we are to develop theories on the general structures of the human perceptual system we can naturally only do so by investigating it in relation to its surroundings. Such theories may be developed from two points of view.

The first viewpoint is that in which the perceiver is regarded as an element in a dynamic system. The perceiver needs to adapt himself to his environment in order, ultimately, to survive. The perceptual system, therefore, must be constructed in such a manner that it makes this adaptation possible. From the second point of view, it is not the adaptation of the perceiver that is put central, but his input–output behaviour. The theory in this case is built up in order to explain the behaviour. Naturally, theories developed on the basis of the first viewpoint must be able ultimately to explain the behaviour, and similarly the second class of theories must also be able to explain the adaptation phenomena. The two viewpoints may be typified as follows. In the first view, the theory on the perception system is deduced from the behaviour of the subject's surroundings and in the second, it is deduced from the behaviour of the subject himself.

Within the framework of a general theory on perception mechanisms, it is possible to construct models for specific phenomena. These may be tested. Of course the theory itself is not thereby tested. Certain explanations for a phenomenon are excluded from the framework of the general theory. The general theory therefore reduces the number of possible interpretations of a certain phenomenon and the phenomena are given a place within the framework.

Grossberg evolves a theory on the general structure of the perceptual system from the angle of adaptation philosophy. He visualizes the system as a network of centre-on, surround-off cells. The behaviour of the environment puts requirements on what type of network the system can be. Many different phenomena can thus be understood on the basis of but a few organizational principles. Pattern recognition, it is proposed, is feature detection by means of hierarchically ordered detectors.

Hoffman builds up his theory setting out from the perceiver's behaviour. He assumes that the perceiver receives information about his surroundings in a two-dimensional space. It is essential that the perceiver keeps giving the same reaction to some changing stimuli, i.e. that the perceiver remains aware of certain constancies such as shape or length. Hoffman uses a mathematical theory, Lie's theory of groups, which is able to indicate connections between operators that broadly transform a stimulus and local operators that effectuate an infinitely small transformation. The constancies can be expressed in these local operators.

In the sense of the Lie algebra, a complete group is made from these operators by adding new local operators. These predict new constancies. According to Hoffman, the brain contains representations of this group. Its elements are regarded as constancy processors. In the same way as the general operators are built up out of local operators, so the representations of the stimuli are built up by means of the constancy processors. Extension of the theory by making the local operators into contour tracing operators leads to the assumption that form recognition takes place by means of the structured sequence of short lengths of line. Surprisingly, this is the very concept on which Leeuwenberg's coding theories (see Part II) are based.

Foster proposes a theory which is also based on the perceiver's behaviour, though it describes a less extensive field. His theory deals with apparent motion. He gives an outline of a theory on apparent motion, setting out from the idea that perceived phenomena result from the minimalization of a quantity after the presentation of a stimulus. In specific models still to be determined an indication will naturally have to be made as to which quantity should be minimalized. This could, for instance, have some connection with the functions introduced by Buffart and Watson. Foster reports that his theory cannot fit in with a theory such as Hoffman's. The implication is that at least one of the two theories is false.

It is attractive to imagine visual space as metric space. This is certainly not obvious at first sight. As has been stated in the introduction, cognitive factors can affect visual space and in so doing disturb the metric character. However, one can accept this as such and yet attempt to find out whether in the absence of strong cognitive influence visual space may be regarded as metric space and if so what the metrics are. In order to determine experimentally whether there is cognitive influence on the nature of the space, subjects may be instructed in a manner such as could be expected to affect the possible metric character of the space. If one is able to demonstrate this influence and if one can manipulate it in a consistent fashion, then one can hope only that the space free of cognitive influences, is metric space.

If one regards visual space as metric space, one must investigate whether and to what extent objects in the physical space determine these metrics. The fact that there are stimuli that are perceived differently from their physical existence gives rise to considering visual space as non-Euclidean space. The most familiar non-Euclidean geometries are the Riemannian geometries[1]. Various theories on the nature of the visual space that are presented below (Blank, Caelli, Drösler, Watson) are in fact Riemannian geometries.

Blank discusses the geometry of the binocular visual space. He demonstrates that the visual space is not Euclidean but Riemannian. It follows from the fact that the space possesses in first order the Desarguesian property that it is a Riemannian space with a constant curvature. This is probably hyperbolic. There are subjects, however, who react in a Euclidean manner. According to

Blank, they have remembered the Euclidean interpretation of space.

Caelli et al. conclude from Hoffman's theory a model for the time-space (two dimensional) relation in the case of apparent motion. The basis of the model is the idea, that the signal propagation in the brain can not be faster than a velocity c. The space describing the relation is an elliptic space.

Drösler's theory is based on the perception of length, area and velocity in monocular, two-dimensional space. His treatment of the perception of these quantities as properties of a geometric space leads him to discard the well-known psychometric power laws. He offers a different explanation for these observations and arrives at the conclusion that the monocular visual space is a Riemannian space with a constant positive curvature, an elliptic space.

A concept in disagreement with Caelli's and Drösler's is Watson's concept. He emphatically states that the monocular visual time-space is Riemannian but does not possess a constant curvature. Although his theory deals only with monocular space, it can have consequences for perception in binocular space. Watson conceives of the Riemannian space as a deviation of Euclidean space by presuming that each brightness contrast in the space introduces a certain field, in principle perpendicular to this contrast.

This idea does not necessarily have to be seen as an ad hoc assumption, since Buffart in his paper on brightness perception has also introduced such fields (weighting coefficients). Possibly these are the same. According to Watson, the fields cause deviations from Euclidean space, so that each stimulus induces its own metrics in the visual space. On the basis of this, Watson makes predictions on the perception of visual illusions and aftereffects. There is, however, the possibility that his theory does not apply to illusions under special circumstances; a Poggendorf illusion, for instance, at a certain orientation is not an illusion.

Buffart presents a theory on contrast processing and brightness perception. According to him the visual system only reacts to luminance changes in a stimulus. He indicates how a stimulus is processed by the retina and how the outputs of the two retinas induce fields in the cortex. These fields form the basis of the brightness perception and the binocular interaction. The theory explains depth perception in random-dot stereograms, binocular rivalry, monocular brightness perception and brightness illusions. If the suggestion is correct that the fields introduced by Buffart and the fields proposed by Watson are identical, then the above mentioned problem of Watson's theory may be solved, for in that case eye movements can affect the Watson field and thus the metrics of space.

Note

(1) These are spaces in which the shortest distance between two points is not a straight line in the ordinary sense. Thus, for example, the shortest route from Sydney to Amsterdam goes over the surface of the earth, approximately via Calcutta. If one

were to ask someone who considered a line over the earth's surface as a straight line to prolong the Sydney to Calcutta line, he would arrive in North-West Europe. If one were to ask the same of somebody who measures in terms of Euclidean geometry, he will arrive somewhere in outer space.

Chapter 1

A Theory of Visual Coding, Memory, and Development

Stephen Grossberg*

1. Introduction

This paper reviews and extends some highlights of a psychophysiological theory of sensory processing and development. The theory is grouped into four stages. Each stage emerges as a solution to a basic environmental problem that organisms must solve in order to survive. This solution imposes certain statistical, geometrical, and dynamical constraints on all systems capable of solving the problem, notwithstanding the possible existence of many chemical devices to realize these constraints.

Stage one emerges from the following question: How are fluctuating patterns of data processed in cellular tissues that are besieged by noise and limited by a finite dynamic range? What keeps the patterns from either saturating or being hopelessly distorted by noise? One is led to study the collective properties of interacting excitatory and inhibitory populations undergoing mass action dynamics in feedforward and feedback anatomies. Otherwise expressed, these are nonrecurrent and recurrent on-centre off-surround networks undergoing shunting, or passive membrane, interactions. These structures suggest mechanisms for such phenomena as sensory adaptation, contrast enhancement, short term memory (STM), certain perceptual constancies (hue, brightness, lightness) and illusions (hysteresis, tilt after-effect, angle expansion, line neutralization), tuning by non-specific arousal, edge and velocity detection, masking, and periodic oscillations (both stable and unstable) in which variable frequencies, persistent phase leads and lags, or travelling waves exist.

Stage two emerges from the following question: How do persistently correlated presentations of two or more events yield an enduring reorganization of system dynamics? A familiar example of such a process is classical conditioning, wherein persistently presenting an animal with an indifferent cue,

* Supported in part by the Advanced Research Projects Agency of the Office of Naval Research (N00014-70-C-0350).

such as a ringing bell, before a familiar cue, such as food, enables the bell to elicit responses, such as salivation, which previously were under the control of the food but not the bell. More generally, the concept embraces a nonstationary prediction theory, or adaptive control theory, in which many examples of directed growth, chemical production, and substrate sensitization emerge as special cases. This theory suggests rules for long term memory (LTM) storage and retrieval that are proved to be universal in the following sense: these rules, if invented at a particular stage of evolution, could then be used in any later evolutionary specialization of anatomy or sensory preprocessing without biasing the mechanism's ability to learn arbitrarily complex patterns in arbitrarily many parallel channels at once. The theory describes a canonical order for computing vital operations such as STM and LTM temporal averaging; spatial averaging; pre-processing, filtering, addition, and correlation of signals—that are compatible with evolutionary specialization. The theory also suggests possible microscopic LTM mechanisms in special cases. In spite of the present experimental uncertainty about these microscopic variations, one can successfully study the commonly shared, surprising, and very powerful functional properties of this class of mechanisms. Indeed, certain experimentalists seem unaware that various of their favourite interpretations of present data have unworkable functional properties.

Stage three emerges from the following question: How do sensory codes reorganize themselves, or develop, in response to environmental pressures? This theory describes a canonical order for computing vital operations—such as STM data from Stage 1 with mechanisms from Stage 2 for reading this data into and out of LTM. One hereby sees how temporal sequences of sensory patterns can reorganize and generate fields of interacting feature detectors. Each feature detector is responsive to a prescribed convex set of patterns. In particular, if the detector responds to two particular patterns, then it also responds to average patterns derived from the two patterns, even if the average patterns have never been experienced. Using this property, hierarchically organized detectors can respond to complex gestalts of features Which features will be coded by a particular field of populations depends on positional gradients that exist in interfield connections before developmental coding takes place. These gradients embody a filtering process that determines a particular pattern of competition among the feature detectors in response to sensory patterns. Different gradients generate different patterns of competition. Detectors which compete successfully in response to a prescribed pattern have their activities stored in STM. This STM pattern is then read into LTM. Consequently the STM competition can be viewed as a competition for synaptic sites.

Stage 4 asks how the developing code can be stabilized in an arbitrary environment. One can prove that the mechanisms in Stage 3 can code arbitrary spatial patterns presented sequentially in time if the number of distinct spatial patterns is not too great compared to the number of classifying cells. In an arbitrary environment of patterns, no stable coding rule need exist. To stabilize the code, it is sufficient to use attentional mechanisms that describe how tentatively activated feature detectors can elicit feedback signals. These feedback signals represent an expectation, or template, with which the afferent test pattern is compared. If the expected and test patterns are too different—that is, an erroneous classification has occurred—then a nonspecific arousal, or alarm, system is triggered. The arousal suppresses the tentatively activated feature detectors and elicits a search routine which terminates when an appropriate population is activated. Several themes are important here. First, it is shown that not all sensory patterns need recode the network's feature detectors. Only patterns that generate a resonant state of activity can generate such a change. This resonant state expresses the intuitive idea that the system is attending to the pattern and has stored it in STM, whereupon it can induce LTM changes. In particular, mere passive presentation of patterns need not recode any feature detectors. Second, the idea that feedback signals representing a template, or expectation, can attenuate mismatched inputs or amplify matched inputs until a resonant state is generated seem to occur in many sensory systems, such as in olfactory coding at the prepyriform cortex of cats. Third, even if no feature detector uniquely classifies a sensory pattern, a resonant state need not be established unless the pattern of activity across feature detectors correctly classifies the pattern; that is, the code is context-dependent. Fourth, this mechanism is capable of universal recoding; namely, any set of arbitrary spatial patterns, as inputs, can be stably transformed, or recoded, into any set of arbitrary spatial patterns of equal size, as outputs. Finally, the attentional and search mechanisms imply other properties, some akin to negative afterimages and spatial frequency adaptation, that arise as manifestations of basic sensory designs. In particular, because the offset of an external cue can be used to trigger learned behaviour, one is led to postulate the existence of antagonistic pairs, or dipoles, of cortical populations. The one-cell in the pair is activated persistently by the presence of its cue, whereas the off-cell of the pair is activated transiently by offset of the cue. When such systems are modelled, it emerges that certain operations, such as rapid increments in a nonspecific arousal system (interpreted to be catecholaminergic) can reverse, or rebound, the relative activities in a dipole. Thus suppose that a mismatch occurs between afferent sensory data and the net feedback expectation released by tentatively activated feature detectors. Then nonspecific arousal rapidly increases among the feature detector populations, and selectively suppresses the most active on-cells by rebounding their off-cells. When this dipole structure is embedded into the generalization gradients of various fields of feature detectors, phenomena like negative afterimages and spatial frequency adaptation are found. Such phenomena therefore formally emerge as manifestations of basic constraints on the development, stabilization, and search for correct sensory codes. In particular, it is suggested that at least certain sensory critical periods are switched off by the gradual switching on of attentional feedback. If this feedback is interpreted, in particular, as signals from visual cortex to lateral geniculate nucleus (LGN), then differential attenuation or amplification of LGN activity by cortex would be expected given mismatch or match, respectively, of feedback expectations with afferent data.

Moreover, if the matching mechanism is realized by on-centre off-surround interactions (cf., Section 3), then the growth of LGN inhibitory connections should precede the end of the critical period in visual cortex. Finally, the catecholaminergic arousal system that is modulated by mismatch would also develop before the critical period ends, as would the dipole structure of the cortex. When this mechanism acts on the generalization gradients of various fields of feature detectors, phenomena like negative afterimages and spatial frequency adaptation are found.

Experiments and other theoretical efforts that are relevant to the theory are described in the papers [1]–[11]. Space limitations restrict the discussion below to a sketch of theoretical highlights.

2. Adaptation and Automatic Gain Control in On-centre Off-surround Networks

How do cellular systems accomplish the parallel processing of patterned data when they are subjected to noise and contain only finitely many sites (saturation)? Consider the general situation in which n populations of cells, or cell sites, v_i are given, $i = 1, 2, \ldots, n$, and each population is perturbed by a non-negative continuously varying input $I_i(t)$ through time. For example, $I_i(t)$ can count the frequency of unit signals that perturb v_i through time. Let v_i be activated by $I_i(t)$ and suppose that v_i's activity decays in the absence of input. In particular, let v_i contain B excitable sites of which $x_i(t)$ are excited and $B - x_i(t)$ are unexcited at time t. Suppose that $I_i(t)$ switches on unexcited sites by mass action. Also suppose that excited sites spontaneously become unexcited at some rate A. Then

$$\dot{x}_i = -Ax_i + (B - x_i)I_i, \tag{1}$$

where $0 \leq x_i \leq B$ and $i = 1, 2, \ldots, n$. Why is this system inadequate?

We will consider an example that has analogues in many biological situations. Let an observer inspect a collage of overlapping coloured patches. Let a white light illuminate the patches at various intensities. As the intensity of light varies, the amount of light of each wavelength that is reflected varies proportionally. Even if the light intensity varies over a large range, however, the colours in the collage look much the same. They are an invariant which is characterized by the *relative* amounts of light of each wavelength that are reflected. These relative amounts are *reflectances* that are characteristic of the coloured patches. In many situations, a relative index of activity that is distributed across many channels carries the information that characterizes a pattern. Hence we perturb (1) with inputs $I_i(t) = \theta_i I(t)$, where the θ_i are fixed relative intensities that characterize a pattern, and $I(t)$ is the total pattern intensity. Each choice of θ_i's such that $\theta_i \geq 0$ and $\sum_{k=1}^{n} \theta_k = 1$ (so that $I(t) = \sum_{k=1}^{n} I_k(t)$) characterizes a different pattern. How well does system (1) process the fixed ratios θ_i when the total activity $I(t)$ is parametrically set at different constant values?

The answer is 'badly'. Let (1) approach equilibrium in response to a fixed pattern $\theta = (\theta_1, \theta_2, \ldots, \theta_n)$ and a fixed total activity I. Then $\dot{x}_i = 0$ and (1) implies

$$x_i = \frac{B\theta_i I}{A + \theta_i I} \tag{2}$$

Now parametrically increase I as in the collage example. By (2), all x_i saturate at B. In other words, at high I values, all channels look 'white'. Now let I become small to avoid saturation. Then, especially if there is noise in the system, all channels look 'black'. The pattern θ is badly processed both at low and high I values.

The reason is clear. To compute the ratios $\theta_i = I_i(\sum_{k=1}^n I_k)^{-1}$, one needs input data from all channels at each population v_i; interactions are needed. In particular, writing $\theta_i = I_i(I_i + \sum_{k\neq i} I_k)^{-1}$, it is clear that increasing I_i increases θ_i ('excites' θ_i), whereas increasing any I_k, $k \neq i$, decreases θ_i ('inhibits' θ_i). When this intuition is translated into mass action dynamics, the simplest example is found of a type of system that occurs throughout the nervous system; namely, a feed-forward on-centre off-surround network undergoing shunting, or passive membrane dynamics. Thus let each I_i excite population v_i ('on-centre') and, inhibit all populations v_k, $k \neq i$ ('off-surround') by mass action (Figure 1). Then (1) is replaced by

$$\dot{x}_i = -Ax_i + (B - x_i)I_i - x_i \sum_{k\neq i} I_k. \tag{3}$$

Term $-x_i\sum_{k\neq i} I_k$ says that excited sites at v_i are turned off by inhibitory inputs from the off-surround of v_i. At equilibrium ($\dot{x}_i = 0$)

$$x_i = \theta_i \frac{BI}{A + I} \tag{4}$$

Several remarks about this formula are interesting. No matter how intense I becomes, x_i is proportional to θ_i. There is no saturation; each v_i has an infinite

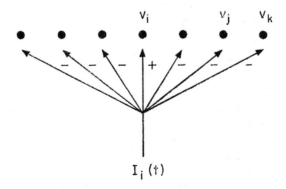

Figure 1. Nonrecurrent, or feedforward, on-centre off-surround network

dynamic range. In particular, even if v_i has only a small number B of excitable sites, automatic gain control by the off-surround of v_i gives v_i an infinitely adjustable dynamic scale. Moreover, the total activity

$$x = \sum_k x_k = \frac{BI}{A + I} \tag{5}$$

has an upper bound B that is independent of n and I; the total activity is *normalized*, or *adapts*. A retina in which similar data has been found is the mudpuppy retina [12], whose bipolar cell potentials receive signals from receptors (on-centre) and horizontal cells (off-surround). The bipolar cell potentials (cf., x_i in (4)) are sensitive to the ratio of on-centre to off-surround excitation (cf., θ_i in (4)), and obey a type of Weber-Fechner psychophysical law (cf., $BI(A + I)^{-1}$ in (4)). Moreover the bipolar potential, plotted as a function of the logarithm of its on-centre input (cf., $K = \ln I_j$), is shifted to the right when the off-surround input (cf., $L = \sum_{k \neq i} I_k$) is parametrically increased. This is also true of x_i in (4), since

$$x_i(K, L) = Be^K(A + e^K + L)^{-1} \tag{6}$$

and when L is changed from $L = L_1$ to $L = L_2$, $x_i(K + S, L_1) = x_i(K, L_2)$ for all $K \geq 0$ where the shift $S = \ln\left[(A + L_1)(A + L_2)^{-1}\right]$.

Also of interest is the fact that ratio processing in (4) still occurs after power law transformations. Thus, if I_i is a transduced receptor output in response to an external input J_i, where $I_i = J_i^P$, then (4) becomes

$$X_i = \lambda_i \frac{J^P}{A + J^P}$$

where λ_i is again constant. In Section 4, it is noted that a transduction law capable of noise suppression has the form $I_i = f(J_i)$, where $f(w)$ is a sigmoid, or S-shaped, function of w. In particular, $f(w)$ grows faster than linearly, e.g., $f(w) \cong w^2$, at small w values, before becoming approximately linear at intermediate w values, and then levelling off at large w values.

In vivo, the eye can adapt over an enormous dynamic range, but not an infinite one. Is not (4) too good to be physically true? System (3) is merely the simplest case of a mass action network perturbed by a feedforward on-centre off-surround anatomy. In (3), each v_i can inhibit all other v_k, $k \neq i$, with equal strength. More generally, consider

$$\dot{x}_i = -Ax_i + (B_i - x_i) \sum_{k=1}^{n} I_k C_{ki} - (x_i + D_i) \sum_{k=1}^{n} I_k E_{ki}, \tag{7}$$

$i = 1, 2, \ldots, n$. Here I_k can excite v_i if $C_{ki} > 0$ and inhibit v_i if $E_{ki} > 0$. Often C_{ki} decreases with distance more rapidly than does E_{ki}. Furthermore the inhibitory saturation point $(-D_i)$ is often negative, rather than 0, as in (4), with $D_i \ll B_i$. Equation (7) has the form of a passive membrane, or shunting, equation, with x_i replacing the mean voltage, the terms $-A_i x_i$, $(B_i - x_i)$ and $(x_i + D_i)$ representing voltage differences (with passive equilibrium scaled to zero), and the inputs driving conductance changes [14].

The properties of system (7) can vary substantially as its dynamical parameters A_i, B_i, D_i and anatomical parameters C_{jk} and E_{jk} are changed ([3], [4]). The activity pattern elicited by an input pattern can be broadened, exhibit spurious peak splits, outward peak shifts, curvature detection, variable contrast at variable background activity levels, suppression of uniform gradients, edge enhancement, and so on.

3. Suprathreshold Responses to Spatial Differences in Input Intensities

Below we note a mechanism to quench uniform input patterns and generate supraequilibrium responses only to spatial differences in the inputs across populations, in particular at the edges of a figure. The simplest case involves the system

$$\dot{x}_i = -Ax_i + (B - x_i)I_i - (x_i + C)\sum_{k \neq i} I_k \tag{8}$$

with $-C \leq x_i \leq B$. If $C > 0$, by contrast with (3), the equilibrium response $(\dot{x}_i = 0)$ to a pattern $I_i = \theta_i I$ is

$$x_i = \frac{(B + C)I}{A + I}\left(\theta_i - \frac{C}{B + C}\right). \tag{9}$$

If, for example, $B = (n - 1)C$, then $C/(B + C) = 1/n$. Now let the input pattern be uniform. Then all $\theta_i = 1/n$, so that no matter how intense I is, all $x_i = 0$. More generally, whenever $B \leq (n - 1)C$, the x_i's are suppressed even more vigorously by inhibition than when $B = (n - 1)C$. Consequently only values of $\theta_i > C/(B + C) > 1/n$ can generate a supraequilibrium response. Increasing C hereby contrast-enhances the network's response to input patterns. It has been suggested that this contrast-enhancement property can influence the size of certain visual illusions, such as tilt after-effect and angle expansion [4].

The quenching of uniform patterns is due to a competitive balance between a narrow on-centre I_i that interacts with a relatively large excitatory saturation point B, and a broad off-surround that interacts with a relatively small inhibitory saturation point $-C$. This conclusion generalizes to systems

$$\dot{x}_i = -Ax_i + (B - x_i)\sum_{k=1}^{n} I_k C_{ki} - (x_i + D)\sum_{k=1}^{n} E_{ki} \tag{10}$$

wherein inputs I_i can excite populations v_j near to v_i via the coefficients C_{ij} ('on-centre') and can inhibit populations v_j over a broad expanse of cells via the coefficients E_{ij} ('off-surround'). Since the equilibrium point of (10) is

$$x_i = \frac{I\sum_{k=1}^{n} \theta_k (BC_{ki} - DE_{ki})}{A + I\sum_{k=1}^{n} \theta_k (C_{ki} + E_{ki})} \tag{11}$$

a uniform pattern (all $\theta_i = 1/n$) is quenched (all $x_i \leq 0$) for any $I \geq 0$ whenever $B \sum_{k=1}^{n} C_{ki} \leq D \sum_{k=1}^{n} E_{ki}$, $i = 1, 2, \ldots, n$. In addition, suprathreshold increments in I, given a nonuniform pattern of θ_i's, can change the ratios $X_i = x_i (\sum_{k=1}^{n} x_k)^{-1}$ that characterize the network response. In the case of vision, these shifts can be used to discuss certain chromatic distortions at high luminances [11]. By changing the breadth of excitatory and inhibitory interactions across the network, one can alter the input patterns to which a population will respond. For example, let a vertical bar of light perturb the network. Suppose that the breadth of on-centre and off-surround interactions is less than that of the bar. Then cells near the centre of the bar will perceive a uniform field. Also cells far away from the bar will perceive a uniform field. Both types of cells will be incapable of generating suprathreshold responses. Only cells near the transition regions of light and dark will respond. Such a network detects the edges of the bar.

The above mechanism can also be used as a matching mechanism. To see this, we ask the following question: given a spatial pattern θ, how can a maximally mismatched pattern $\tilde{\theta}$ be generated? Intuitively, $\tilde{\theta}$ should be large where θ is small, and conversely. If both $\tilde{\theta}$ and θ are input patterns to the network, then their mismatched peaks and troughs will add to create an almost uniform net pattern, so that network activity is suppressed. By contrast, if $\tilde{\theta}$ is proportional to θ, then they will add to amplify network activity. The competitive balance between excitatory saturation point and on-centre coefficients vs. inhibitory saturation point and off-surround coefficients will determine how uniform the net pattern must be in order to suppress network activity. In particular, if the off-surround is too weak, then a mismatch will not suppress network output; cf., Section 1.

4. Contrast Enhancement and Short Term Memory

System (3) cannot store a pattern if the inputs are turned off, since then each x_i approaches zero at rate A. To store a pattern in STM, say in a field of cortical feature detectors [10], feedback signals are needed to keep the pattern active after inputs terminate [1]. These signals are distributed in an on-centre off-surround anatomy to prevent saturation. Then (3) is generalized to

$$\dot{x}_i = -Ax_i + (B - x_i)[f(x_i) + I_i] - x_i \left[\sum_{k \neq i} f(x_k) + J_i \right] \qquad (12)$$

$i = 1, 2, \ldots, n$. The function $f(w)$ is the mean signal generated by mean activity w. Term $(B - x_i)f(x_i)$ describes self-excitation of v_i's unexcited sites via the feedback signal $f(x_i)$. Term $-x_i \sum_{k \neq i} f(x_k)$ describes inhibition of v_i's excited sites by feedback signals $f(x_k)$ from all v_k, $k \neq i$. Term J_i is the total inhibitory input to v_i; e.g., $J_i = \sum_{k \neq i} I_k$ (Figure 2).

System (12) can either amplify or suppress noise too vigorously if $f(w)$ is improperly chosen. It has been proved [1] that a sigmoid (S-shaped) signal function $f(w)$ can suppress noise and other activities that fall below a prescribed

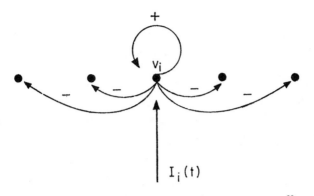

Figure 2. Recurrent, or feedback, on-centre off-surround network

quenching threshold. The pattern of activities that exceed the quenching threshold is contrast-enhanced, or sharpened, and thereupon stored indefinitely by the feedback signals (Figure 3). The total suprathreshold activity of (12) also adapts, and there can exist any number of stable equilibrium points of the total activity $x = \sum_{k=1}^{n} x_k$ as $t \to \infty$ if $f(w)$ is suitably chosen. See [2] for a review.

5. Nonspecific Arousal as a Parallel Tuning Device

Because a quenching threshold exists, variations in the level of non-specific arousal can act as a parallel tuning device across billions of feature detectors if the arousal level influences the efficacy of inputs on population activity. For example, suppose that inputs stream into the network from many sources and establish a complex pattern from which a choice of only the maximally excited population is desired. Simply lower the arousal level until only this population's activity exceeds the quenching threshold. By contrast, suppose that an unexpected event occurs and therefore that all recently presented cues should be stored in STM to help determine how to deal with the unexpected situation. It suffices for an unexpected event to trigger arousal and therefore amplify all activities above the quenching threshold. This property is needed to release unattended cues from overshadowing in response to unexpected events [10]. If the quenching threshold is pathologically low, then noise, arousal, or other non-cue inputs can be amplified and stored in STM, thereby creating a type of 'seizure' or 'hallucination' that can sometimes trigger travelling waves of activity across the field of cells ([1], [3]).

Generalizations of (12), such as the feedback analogue of (7), namely,

$$\dot{x}_i = -Ax_i + (B_i - x_i)\left[\sum_{k=1}^{n} f(x_k)C_{ki} + I_i\right]$$

$$-(x_i + D_i)\left[\sum_{k=1}^{n} g(x_k)E_{ki} + J_i\right], \tag{13}$$

16

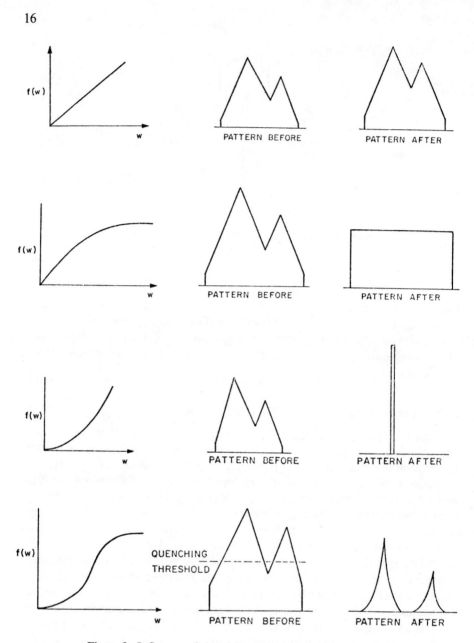

Figure 3. Influence of signal function $f(w)$ on STM storage

$i = 1, 2, \ldots, n$, have also been analysed ([3], [4]). They are capable of transforming the input pattern in various ways, such as generating hysteresis, splits, outward shifts, masking, and slow drifts in the spatial loci of maximal activity. Various of these properties have been invoked to explain psychological data. An illustration is cited below.

6. Masking and Line Neutralization

Two seemingly different phenomena will now be discussed as variations of a common theme. Consider the system

$$\dot{x}_i = -Ax_i + (B_i - x_i)\left[f(x_i) + I_i\right] - x_i\left[\sum_{k \neq i} f(x_k) + J_i\right] \qquad (14)$$

or equivalently

$$\dot{x}_i = -Ax_i + (B - x_i)\left[f(C_i x_i) + I_i\right] - x_i\left[\sum_{k \neq i} f(C_k x_k) + J_i\right]. \qquad (15)$$

In (14), different feature detectors v_i can have different numbers of sites B_i. Clearly *in vivo* not all features are coded by the same number of sites. Equivalently, in (15), all populations have the same number B of sites, but the signals from each population v_i can be amplified, or tuned, by a different scaling factor C_i. A combination of these effects can also be analysed. To fix ideas, imagine that the B_i are determined by development, and the C_i are controlled by slowly varying attentional inputs that can shunt the excitability of interactions across populations.

If a given pattern is presented to the field, which activities will be stored in STM? Denote all the populations with the same B_i as a *subfield*. It has been proved under weak hypotheses that only one subfield at a time can reverberate in STM [2]. All other population activities are totally quenched, or masked. Which subfield will be stored? Paper [2] proves that a complex tug-of-war can exist between development, attentional, and energetic factors such that the subfield which has the best balance of all these factors in a given time frame will be stored (Figure 4). In particular, a subfield with few sites can be stored if its features are heavily represented in the input display. Moreover, feature detectors can be totally silent in response to many inputs, yet can suddenly become active in response to a preferred input class. These detectors are available to the system, but do not create noise that would contaminate the processing of unrelated patterns.

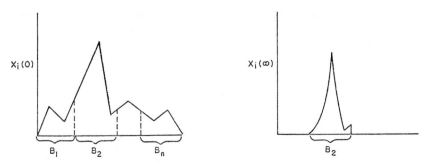

Figure 4. Suppression in STM of populations with more sites and/or signal amplification by a subfield with large initial activity

An analogous phenomenon occurs in system

$$\dot{x}_i = -Ax_i + (B_i - x_i)\left[\sum_{k=1}^{n} f(x_k)C_{ki} + I_i\right] - x_i\left[\sum_{k=1}^{n} f(x_k)D_{ki} + J_i\right] \quad (16)$$

wherein the excitatory coefficients C_{ki} and inhibitory coefficients D_{ki} both decrease as the distance $|i - k|$ between the populations v_i and v_k increases. Because of this, there exist nontrivial generalization gradients between the feature detectors of (16); that is, some detectors are more closely coupled to a given detector than others. Such a system is capable of partially contrast enhancing a pattern before storing it in STM, as in Figure 3. Suppose moreover that due to developmental biases, a certain population, say v_K, has more sites than nearby populations. Let $B_i = Be^{-E|K-i|^2}$ for definiteness. If an input is now presented to a population v_L near v_K, the locus of maximal STM activity will drift from v_L towards v_K. The drift rate will depend on how steep the slope of B_i is as a function of v_i between v_L and v_K. This 'normative' effect has been used to suggest an explanation of line neutralization [4].

A comparison of (14) and (16) shows that these systems differ only in the distribution of their excitatory and inhibitory coefficients. In particular, the neutralization effect can be viewed as a partial masking effect that is not stronger only because the lateral inhibitory interactions in (16) are not felt with equal strength across the entire field.

7. Slow Inhibition and Periodic Waves.

All the above systems make an approximation that is not always true *in vivo*. Namely, they assume that the inhibitory signals, such as $g(x_k)E_{ki}$ in (13), react to inputs as quickly as the excitatory signals $f(x_k)C_{ki}$. These inhibitory signals define the adapting level against which excitatory signals are evaluated. *In vivo* inhibitory signals often react slowly to create a stable baseline against which to evaluate more rapid excitatory fluctuations, as in retina [12] and hippocampus [15].

To discuss this situation, we consider inhibitory populations v_i^- that can be driven by excitatory populations v_i^+ and which can inhibit themselves and excitatory populations. When the v_i^- react slowly their activities $y_i(t)$ cannot be expressed in terms of the instantaneous excitatory activities $x_i(t)$ alone. Their averaging rates must be explicitly studied. Then (13) can be generalized to systems such as

$$\dot{x}_i = -Ax_i + (B - Cx_i)\left[\sum_{k=1}^{n} f(x_k)D_{ki} + I_i\right]$$
$$-(x_i + E)\left[\sum_{k=1}^{n} g(y_k)F_{ki} + J_i\right] \quad (17)$$

and

$$\dot{y}_i = -\hat{A}y_i + (\hat{B} - \hat{C}y_i)\left[\sum_{k=1}^{n} \hat{f}(x_k)\hat{D}_{ki} + \hat{I}_i\right] -$$

$$-(y_i + \hat{E}) \left[\sum_{k=1}^{n} \hat{g}(y_k)\hat{F}_{ki} + \hat{J}_i \right] , \tag{18}$$

which describe the interplay between excitatory activities, or activators, $x_i(t)$ and inhibitory activities or inhibitors, $y_i(t)$ via excitatory signals $f(x_i)$ and $\hat{f}(x_i)$, and inhibitory signals $g(y_i)$ and $\hat{g}(y_i)$, through time. Due to the lag in response of the y_i's to signals from the x_i's such systems are capable of generating sustained periodic waves of activity in response to various brief inputs [3].

A serious problem arises in these systems. Because the inhibitors y_i lag behind the excitors x_i that drive them, they can destroy the activity pattern that is stored by the x_i's. More precisely, slow inhibition readily destroys *order-preserving* oscillating patterns; namely, patterns for which a definite ordering $x_1 \leqq x_2(t) \leqq \cdots \leqq x_{n-1}(t) \leqq x_n(t)$ holds through time. In other words, the network cannot remember which populations should be most active.

8. A Dilemma: Order vs. Adaptation

A fundamental dilemma must now be solved: How can a system adapt without destroying the order that codes its pattern of activities? A possible solution is to choose a high inhibitory gain; namely, a fast rate of inhibitory response that approximately yields networks such as (13). In other words, it often happens that as the inhibitory gain is increased, the frequency of oscillations also increases, so that in the limit of an infinite inhibitory gain, a definite limiting pattern is established [3]. Consequently, fast oscillations can approximately preserve order, at least in a time interval of sufficiently short duration. How can order-preservation be achieved, however, given a slowly varying adaptational baseline, in a time interval of unlimited duration? A solution to this problem will now be described.

9. A Solution: Template Resonance

An order-preserving sustained oscillation can be generated if an input pattern $(I_1, I_2, \ldots, I_n)$ is kept on through time, even if no such oscillation exists when no input pattern is kept on [3]. This input pattern forms a template, or expectation, with which the system can 'resonate'. For example, suppose that a pattern of small template inputs is generated by another part of the network. Let a *proportional* pattern of test inputs be generated by an external source. If the total input pattern is sufficiently large, then an order-preserving oscillation can be generated and sustained. If the test input pattern does not (approximately) match the template pattern, then no sustained response is generated. This concept has been used to develop a model of the quenching by prepyriform cortex of unexpected scents [7].

What source keeps the template inputs active? The activity within some part of the network must be used to do this. If the cells that generate template inputs can also store an order-preserving pattern and have slowly varying inhibitors, then these cells must also receive template inputs. Reciprocal interactions between certain template sources are clearly needed to prevent an infinite regress. The *minimal* structure that enjoys the properties of order-preservation and slow adaptation is now apparent.

Let two network regions be given. Let each region be endowed with on-centre off-surround feedback signals that make adaptation and STM possible. Also let each region generate signals which act as a template for the other region, and let each region receive external inputs. Suppose that the external inputs to each region are briefly delivered and match the template signals that are thereby generated from the other region. By the above remarks, an order-preserving oscillation can be produced in each region, and can be sustained indefinitely. Several examples of such resonating structures have been suggested [7]. One is the resonance that occurs when feedforward sensory codes and feedback expectations are compatible, as in the matching example of Section 1. Such examples also show how templates can be learned; cf., Section 14. The examples include a hysteresis effect analogous to that experienced when two lines are slowly separated on their respective retinas, a search and lock mechanism for terminating eye motions when their respective images overlap, and a mechanism for reaching an action-oriented consensus when presently available cues (conditioned reinforcers) can satisfy momentary drive requirements (expressed through feedback via the contingent negative variation).

10. Suppression of Disordered States

Why is an order-preserving oscillation possible in response to a template? An answer is suggested by (9). The worst possible case illustrates the main idea. Let a template pattern be turned on and maintained. Suppose that the excitatory activities *could* reverse the ordering of the template pattern. Then the excitatory signals would also reverse this ordering. The *total* pattern of excitatory feedback signals plus template inputs would therefore be a sum of two patterns with opposite orderings. This total pattern would be close to a uniform pattern. In networks such as (9), one can control how close a pattern must be to a uniform pattern before it is suppressed, by a proper choice of B and C.

With this in mind, consider what happens when the excitatory activities that are elicited by the template pattern start to deviate from the template ordering. Then the total pattern of excitatory feedback signals plus template inputs becomes more uniform. The inhibitory signals produce this deviation in the excitatory activities by lagging behind the excitatory activities. The inhibitory signals also eliminate the difficulty by suppressing the excitatory activities until they can no longer generate large excitatory signals. For this to happen, it is essential that the inhibitory saturation point ($-C$ in (9)) be strictly smaller than the threshold for generating excitatory signals (at least 0 in (9)). The suppression of excitatory activities continues until the template inputs become relatively large compared to the suppressed excitatory feedback signals. The template inputs can thereupon reinstate their ordering in the excitatory activities. When the slowly varying inhibitory signals again begin to destroy this ordering, the process repeats itself.

11. Gain Control vs. Order in Patterned Oscillations

Because all of our networks undergo shunting interactions, certain deviations from order-preservation can be anticipated in particular cases, but do not destroy the coded STM message. For example, in the simplest system $\dot{x}_i = -Ax_i + (B - x_i)I_i$, $i = 1, 2, \ldots, n$, if all $x_i(0) = 0$ then

$$x_i(t) = \frac{BI_i}{A + I_i} \left[1 - e^{-(A+I_i)t}\right].$$

Both the asymptote and the reaction rate are increasing functions of input intensity. Hence there exists a tendency for the most intensely activated populations to phase lead less intensely activated population. If also self-inhibition of populations is sufficiently strong, then, in a given oscillatory cycle, the phase leading populations can also be inhibited before the phase lagging populations are inhibited, thereby momentarily destroying order-preservation. This deviation does not, however, prevent the most intensely active populations from coding the most important features, since phase lead is coupled to total activity.

Apart from phase leads, all the populations can still oscillate with a common frequency, as occurs in the olfactory cortex during its resonant activity [16]. A deeper issue is the following: How well can a field of populations be decomposed by afferent signals into subsets, or channels, each with its own overall frequency of oscillation, and with persistent phase leads and lags among the oscillating populations of each subset? Since these channels define the functional units of the network, an analysis of how they depend on external input patterns and internal network design (e.g., interfield positional gradients and intra-field competitive geometry) should be very useful to the understanding of cortical coding.

12. Long Term Memory

The derivation and basic neural properties of this mechanism are reviewed in [9], and applied to such non-neural examples as syncytium formation during sea urchin gastrulation in [8]. One derives equations for the STM traces x_i of cells v_i and for the LTM traces z_{jk} along the directed pathways e_{jk} from v_j to v_k. These equations have the form

$$\dot{x}_i = A_i x_i + \sum_{k=1}^{n} B_{ki} z_{ki} + C_i(t) \tag{19}$$

$$\dot{z}_{jk} = D_{jk} z_{jk} + E_{jk} x_k, \tag{20}$$

$i, j, k = 1, 2, \ldots, n$. Term A_i is the STM decay rate, terms B_{jk} and E_{jk} are signals from v_j to v_k, $C_i(t)$ is an input, and D_{jk} is the LTM decay rate. The terms A_i, B_{jk}, D_{jk} and E_{jk} can depend on the system's STM and LTM in a complicated way without interfering with pattern learning. Signal B_{jk} sometimes differs from E_{jk} because E_{jk} expresses the influence on the LTM trace z_{jk} at the synaptic knobs from v_j to v_k, whereas B_{jk} expresses the net influence of v_j on the postsynaptic cells v_k after the signal passes through the knobs.

For present purposes, three main properties are needed. In (19), each signal B_{ki} is gated by z_{ki} on its way from v_k to v_i. All such gated signals are added at v_i before they influence the STM trace x_i. In (20), each LTM trace z_{jk} is a time average (with averaging rate D_{jk}) of the product of the signal from v_j to v_k with the STM trace at v_k. These properties are needed to build a system capable of self-organizing its codes, or of returning its feature detectors through experience.

13. Development of Feature Detectors

When the above STM and LTM mechanisms are joined together, fields of feature detectors can be reorganized through experience in response to temporal sequences of spatial patterns ([5]–[7]). The basic idea is illustrated in Figure 5. A network region V_1 (e.g., 'lateral geniculate') sends signals to region V_2 (e.g., 'visual cortex') via trainable pathways. Region V_1 is capable of normal-

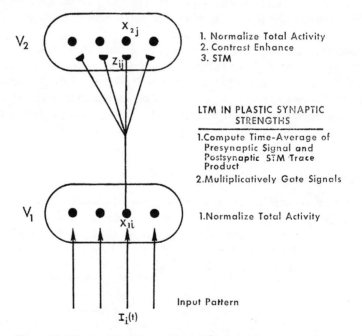

Figure 5. Minimal feedforward model of developmental tuning using STM and LTM mechanisms

izing its total activity (within its functional subregions). Region V_2 can normalize its total activity, contrast enhancement the V_1-to-V_2 signals, and store the contrast-enhanced patterns in STM. The STM pattern thereupon feeds back to cause slow changes in the LTM traces of the V_1-to-V_2 pathways. These LTM changes are the basis for reclassification by V_2 of spatial patterns at V_1. Feedback between STM and LTM continues during input presentations until a dynamic equilibrium is established. Because V_2 normalizes its patterns, it can be used as a source of inputs to a region V_3, and so on. One can therefore build a hierarchy of self-organizing feature detectors in which higher-order feature detectors can code complex gestalts of features.

The above concept of two regions, each with prescribed functional properties, joined by signals that have a filtering capability, is a special case of a theory of neural coding that is described in [6]. This theory includes some suggestions about amacrine cell functioning, where amacrine cell and ganglion cell analogues appear in the V_2 region of an appropriate example.

The simplest example of the above developmental model is sketched below. Let patterns $I_i(t) = \theta_i I(t)$ be normalized at V_1. Let the normalized STM activity of the ith population v_{1i} be θ_i for simplicity. By (19), the simplest total signal from V_1 to the jth population v_{2j} in V_2 is

$$S_j = \sum_{k=1}^{n} \theta_k z_{kj}. \tag{21}$$

Each population v_{2j} receives such a signal. The input pattern $(S_1, S_2, \ldots, S_m)$ of V_1-to-V_2 signals is then contrast-enhanced, normalized, and stored in STM by V_2. Consider the simplest case in which V_2 chooses for storage the population that gets the largest signal. Suppose v_{21} is the population; that is,

$$S_1(0) > \max\{\epsilon, S_k(0) : k \neq 1\}, \tag{22}$$

where ϵ represents the quenching threshold. Then $x_{21}(t) = 1$ and $x_{2k}(t) = 0$, $k \neq 1$. Inequality (22) has an informative geometrical meaning. Let $\theta = (\theta_1, \theta_2, \ldots, \theta_n)$ and $z_j = (z_{1j}, z_{2j}, \ldots, z_{nj})$. Then (21) becomes

$$S_j = \theta \cdot z_j; \tag{23}$$

that is, S_j is the inner (or dot) product of the n-dimensional vectors θ and z_j. Given any n-vector $\xi = (\xi_1, \xi_n)$, define the Euclidean length $|\xi| = \sqrt{\sum_{k=1}^{n} \xi_k^2}$. Then (23) can be rewritten as

$$S_j = |\theta||z_j| \cos(\theta, z_j) \tag{24}$$

where $\cos(\theta, z_j)$ is the cosine of the angle between θ and z_j. In other words, S_j projects θ on z_j, and multiplies the projection $|\theta| \cos(\theta, z_j)$ by $|z_j|$. Thus if all vectors $|z_k|$ have fixed length, $k = 1, 2, \ldots, m$, then S_1 is maximal if θ is more parallel to z_1 than to any z_k, $k \neq 1$. Speaking geometrically, (22) says that V_2 chooses the population that gets the maximal population in response to θ. Note that *all* the values $z_{jk}(0)$ determine which population(s) in V_2 will reverberate in STM (interfield gradient!).

Next the STM reverberation feeds back to LTM. Consider the following simple version of (20):

$$\dot{z}_{jk} = (-z_{jk} + \theta_j) x_{2k}. \tag{25}$$

Given this law, it is easily proved that successive presentation of θ makes z_1 become parallel to θ, normalizes the length $|z_1|$ of z_1, and maximizes $S_1 = \theta \cdot z_1$ over all vectors z_1 such that $|z_1| \leq |\theta|$. In other words, presenting θ tunes v_1 to maximally respond to θ. Even in this simplest example, each v_{2j} responds to a convex set $P_j = \{\theta : \theta \cdot z_j > \max(\epsilon, \theta \cdot z_k : k \neq j)\}$ of input patterns at V_1, where ϵ stands for the quenching threshold (Section 4). Thus, if v_{2j} responds to two given patterns, it also responds to any average pattern derived from the two, even if the average pattern has never before been experienced. The size of P_j depends on the choice of all interfield positional gradients z_j, which help to determine, along with the competitive interactions within V_1 and V_2, which features V_2 will try to code. Given this property, what will a field V_3 code if it receives patterned signals from V_2? A population in V_3 will code convex sets of spatial patterns across V_2. Each population in V_2 is a feature detector, so a spatial pattern across V_2 is a global construct that describes how much of each feature is in the input pattern delivered to V_1. A convex set of spatial patterns across V_2 describes the tolerated changes in each feature's activity that are compatible with unchanged coding at V_3. Cells in V_3 can hereby generate stable responses as the input patterns to V_1 undergo significant global transformations. When feedback between fields V_i and V_{i+1}, $i \geq 1$, can occur the patterns of resonant activity across the fields can uniquely classify a given input pattern at V_1, even if no feature detector in any field individually classifies this input pattern.

When many patterns $\theta^{(r)}$, $r = 1, 2, \ldots, R$, can perturb V_1 in some temporal sequence, V_2 can sometimes classify them into convex sets of patterns that reliably excite the same feature detectors through time. A precise condition for stable coding is found in [6]. Given arbitrarily many patterns and a fixed number of cells in V_2, this is not generally true.

14. Resonance and Search

The paper [7] shows how to stabilize the code in a general environment. This paper, along with [6], indicates that a purely chemically defined critical period for developmental tuning can have unpleasant coding properties. By contrast, the gradual switching-in of attentional mechanisms, perhaps in parallel with a chemical critical period mechanism, can stabilize the code in an arbitrary environment with no adverse effects.

Paper [7] suggests that after a population in V_2 is activated by a pattern θ at V_1, it can send a pattern θ^* of learned feedback signals to V_1. If the patterns θ and θ^* at V_1 do not match, then output from (a channel parallel to) V_1 is attenuated, thereby releasing a nonspecific arousal system that perturbs V_2. Because V_2's cells are now organized into antagonistic pairs of on-cells and off-cells, or 'dipoles' (Figure 6), the incorrectly activated population in V_2 is actively inhibited. Simultaneously, the arousal induces a search for an appropriate population. This search continues until some population in V_2 can resonate with V_1.

Keeping the incorrectly activated populations inhibited requires the use of a slowly varying process. This process has been interpreted to be a chemical transmitter system, suggested to be catecholaminergic, that gates nonspecific arousal on its way to V_2. This idea originally arose in a neural theory of reinforcement (see [10] for a review and references) wherein cell dipoles regulate net incentive motivation through time. This theory formally explains many paradoxical phenomena about reinforcement; for example, how an amphetamine can calm an agitated syndrome that is really a form of underaroused emotional depression, even though it would not have this effect on overaroused emotional depression.

15. Concluding Remarks

The last example focuses on an important aspect of this work; namely, that a few functional principles, derived as solutions to familiar but pervasive environmental problems to which a surviving organism must adapt, and rigorously explicated to facilitate an understanding of their nontrivial collective properties, can unify and extend our understanding of psychophysiological pheno-

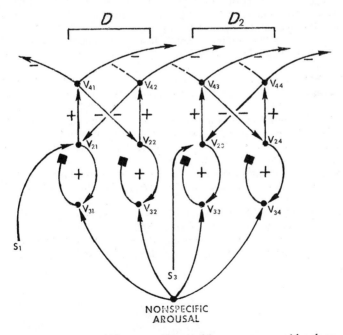

Figure 6. Nonspecific arousal is gated (square synapses) by slow transmitter accumulation-depletion in on-centre off-surround networks that join on-cells to on-cells and off-cells to off-cells

mena by a remarkable degree. If nothing else, this procedure confronts us with unexpected and nontrivial consequences of our present beliefs, and provides a rigorous and transparent conceptual superstructure with whose aid new concepts can be more effectively fashioned.

References

1. Grossberg, S. Contour enhancement, short term memory, and constancies in reverberating neural networks. *Stud. Appl. Math.*, **52**, 213 (1973).
2. Grossberg, S., Levine, D. S. Some developmental and attentional biases in the contrast enhancement and short term memory of recurrent neural networks. *J. Theor. Biol.*, **53**, 341 (1975).
3. Ellias, S. A., Grossberg, S. Pattern formation, contrast control, and oscillations in the short term memory of shunting on-centre off-surround networks. *Biol. Cybernetics*, **20**, 69 (1975).
4. Levine, D. S., Grossberg, S. Visual illusions in neural networks: line neutralization, tilt aftereffect, and angle expansion. *J. Theoret. Biol.*, **61**, 477 (1976).
5. Grossberg, S. On the development of feature detectors in the visual cortex with applications to learning and reaction-diffusion systems. *Biol. Cybernetics*, **21**, 145 (1976).
6. Grossberg, S. Adaptive pattern classification and universal recoding, I: parallel development and coding of neural feature detectors. *Biol. Cybernetics*, **23;** 121 (1976).
7. Grossberg, S. Adaptive pattern classification and universal recoding, II: feedback, expectation, olfaction, illusions, *Biol. Cybernetics*, **23**, 187 (1976).
8. Grossberg, S. Communication, memory and development. In: Rosen, R. and Snell, F. (eds.): Progress in Theoretical Biology. New York: Academic Press, 1977.
9. Grossberg, S. Classical and instrumental learning by neural networks. In: Rosen, R. and Snell, F. (eds.): *Progress in Theoretical Biology*, p. 51. New York: Academic Press, 1974.
10. Grossberg, S. A neural model of attention, reinforcement, and discrimination learning. In: Pfeiffer, C. (Ed.): *International Review of Neurobiology*, **18**, 263 (1975).
11. Grossberg, S. Neural expectation: cerebellar and retinal analogs of cells fired by learnable or unlearned pattern classes. *Kybernetik*, **10**, 49 (1972).
12. Werblin, F. S. Adaptation in a vertebrate retina: intracellular recording in Necturus. *J. of Neurophysiol.*, **34**, 228 (1971).
13. Cornsweet, T. N. *Visual Perception*, New York: Academic Press (1970).
14. Hodgkin, A. L. *The Conduction of the Nervous Impulse*. Springfield, Ill.: C. C. Thomas (1964).
15. Eccles, J. C. In Kimble, G. A. (Ed.): *Anatomy of Memory*, p. 57. Palo Alto, Calif.: Science and Behavior Books, Inc., 1965.
16. Emery, J. D., Freeman, W. J. Pattern analysis of cortical evoked potential parameters during attention changes. *Physiol. Beh.*, **4**, 69 (1969).

Chapter 2

The Lie Transformation Group Approach to Visual Neuropsychology

William C. Hoffman

Abstract. The following five postulates are taken as characterizing visual neuropsychology: (1) the Figure–Ground Relation; (2) the cortical vector-fields found by Hubel and Wiesel and others; (3) the visual constancies; (4) visual form memory as invariant perception of forms; and (5) the Neuron Doctrine, i.e. the neuron is the fundamental structural, functional, and trophic unit of the CNS.

The visual field of view is the inside of a surface and is projected as such on the retina. Hence it is a manifold in the topological sense. Upon this visual manifold we perceive certain visual forms. The latter are characterized by certain Lie derivatives (usually prolonged) that 'drag the flow' along the contours that appear in the Figure–Ground Relation. The basic path-curves (those of the 'feature detectors') are the orbits of the Special Linear Group (shape constancy), the dilation group (size constancy), the Lorentz group (motion constancy), and the rotation group in plane-time. Each of these constancy–transformation group correspondences is treated in detail in terms of the Lie derivatives involved. The necessity for closure in the sense of Lie's Second Fundamental Theorem requires the presence of certain new constancies and also predicts the developmental sequence of infant vision in proper observed order.

The constancies are characterized by certain invariances, which in turn correspond to invariant orbits of the corresponding Lie transformation groups. These orbits appear to be embodied in the basic morphology of the pyramidal and stellate cells of the visual cortex. Given the known cytoarchitecture of the visual cortex this correspondence permits the following of an afferent volley through the visual cortex from the termination of the optic tract in layers IV and III to the plexiform layer and the so-called motor cortex in layers IV, V, and VI in a way characteristic of known visual processing and the relative invariants of the Lie transformation groups involved.

The dissection of the visual manifold into simply connected submanifolds (sub-forms) is discussed and related to eye-scanning movements, vectorfields along the contours of the Figure–Ground Relation, and the action of one-parameter Lie transformation groups over simply connected domains.

The experimental data in support of allocation of basic form vision, i.e. the orbits of the constancies, to the visual cortex primarily and higher form vision to the psychovisual cortex (Areas 18 and 19) are reviewed. How higher visual form perception then results via prolongation of the basic Lie derivatives, as embodied in neuron morphology, is dicussed and shown to be consistent with the electrohistological results of Hubel and Wiesel. The properties of contact structures with respect to their defining vectorfields and covectorfields are briefly reviewed and the relation to higher visual forms and texture and gradient in the visual image discussed. It is further shown that such contact structures are consistent with modern cognitive theory in that only the basic Lie derivatives of the constancies are 'stored', everything else being constructed anew each time by flows along their prolongations upon the particular visual manifold being viewed.

I. Introduction

The great preponderance of research on form perception has been directed toward the psychophysics of the phenomenon, i.e. the nature of, and laws governing, the parameters of form perception. Here we emphasize the other side of the phenomenon: how the forms themselves are processed and recognized by the visual system. The bases of our considerations are five in number: (1) the Figure–Ground Relation, which establishes the presence of visual contours that bound visual forms; (2) the directionally sensitive cortical columns found by Hubel and Wiesel and others; (3) the visual constancies: shape constancy, size constancy, etc.; (4) the Neuron Doctrine that the neuron is the fundamental structural, functional, and trophic unit of the CNS; and (5) the unification of the several sensory modalities of the perceptual system into a consistent body-image.

Item (2) in the above list is the basis for the so-called concept of 'feature detectors'. The latter have been regarded as cortical embodiments of diffraction gratings, autocorrelators, holograms, digital computers, harmonic analysers, and the like by investigators whose knowledge of the total context of brain function should have made them at least wary of such analogies. Here we assert only the one thing that we are sure of, namely, that neuronal functions take place by flows along neuronal processes, in ways that are delimited and controlled by synaptic junctions. In this context, Hubel and Wiesel's cortical microcolumns simply mark the presence of a cortical vectorfield, i.e. a collection of points (the so-called retinotopic mapping) together with the associated local directions.

A vectorfield is a tangent space, neonatally to $\mathbb{R}^3 \times \mathbf{T}$, and later on to the organized visual manifold $\mathfrak{M}$, or its planar projection onto the observer's frontal plane

$$\overline{\mathfrak{M}} = \text{proj}_{(x,y)}\mathfrak{M}. \tag{1}$$

Here y is the S's vertical, and x denotes distance along the horizontal axis through his egocentre parallel to the horizon. $\mathfrak{M}$ is a manifold in the technical, mathematical sense. No one has X-ray vision (though we *can hear* through obstacles), with the consequence that what we see is the inside of a big 'bowl', convoluted and offering the capability of depth perception, but nonetheless a surface imbedded in $\mathbb{R}^3$.

The planar projection $\overline{\mathfrak{M}}$ of the field of view is thus like what one perceives while viewing a landscape painting (see also Fig. 81 of Gibson (1950)). Using $\overline{\mathfrak{M}}$ in the subsequent analysis rather than $\mathfrak{M}$ itself simplifies the mathematics dramatically without any real loss of generality. The metric tensor of the visual manifold is a subjective, individual entity that is essential only to the determination of the psychophysical parameters involved. In any case the laboratory configuration for perceptual experiments frequently either already is a frontal plane display parallel to $\overline{\mathfrak{M}}$ or can be made so.

Upon $\mathfrak{M}$, and hence $\overline{\mathfrak{M}}$, all the contours that constitute the Figure–Ground Relation are emblazoned. These bounding contours are what constitute the forms that we see, though not their intensity (brightness), texture, or colour. Texture turns out to be a non-contact structure, intensity is related to frequency of discharge and can, like loudness in the auditory case, be formulated as a non-uniform translation Lie group, and colour involves motion and rotation processing in two opposite orientations. (The same pyramidal neuron, but two counterrotating flows.) Here our main concern is with form perception, and we limit attention to that.

We have said that Hubel and Wiesel's directionally sensitive cortical elements constitute a cortical vectorfield, i.e. $T\mathfrak{M}$, where T denotes the tangent functor that takes a given manifold into the collection of all tangent spaces upon it. By the same token, the Figure–Ground Relation on $\mathfrak{M}$ is the dual, in the mathematical sense, to $T\mathfrak{M}$. In other words, the Figure–Ground Relation evidences the presence of a covectorfield, a so called contangent bundle $T^*\mathfrak{M}$ (Abraham and Marsden, 1967). Mathematically then, Hubel and Wiesel's cortical vectorfield is equivalent, by duality, to the figure–ground relation and vice versa.

By this duality we are well on our way then to understanding how the visual system of the cortex perceives forms, i.e. as direction-field elements strung head to tail (Figure 1). But there is more to it than that. The essential feature is imparted by the presence of the visual constancies: shape constancy, size constancy, object constancy (or form memory), and certain new constancies that are predicted by the requirement for closure (holonomy) of our mathematical theory. These constitute the first phase of visual processing. That is, the 'feature detectors' discovered to date, and certain hyperbolic ones not yet found experimentally but which must be present from psychological necessity, are constancy processors. If one places an electrode or chemical stimulus upon the exposed visual cortex, sparks, 'stars', bars, whirling spirals, etc. are evoked. These are

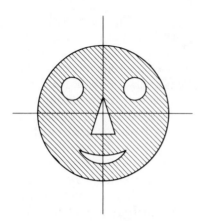

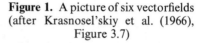

Figure 1. A picture of six vectorfields
(after Krasnosel'skiy et al. (1966),
Figure 3.7)

exactly the orbits of the transformation groups involved in the constancies (see Table 1). It is eminently reasonable that the perceptual distortions imposed by our geometrico-physical world should first be removed in processing for the recognition of visual forms. Otherwise, in Von Fiandt's phrase (1966), our perceptions would always appear to be rubbery, perpetually deforming objects. The memory economy of having an archetypal single form is indicated by what happens if one places the same electrode upon the exposed psychovisual cortex (areas 18 and 19). What is then evoked are higher visual forms, such as those we see, though without any apparent size or location, as if the object were hovering in space (Pitts and Mc Culloch, 1947). This latter aspect strongly suggests that size and shape constancy had been imposed by earlier visual 'Preprocessing'. Much the same conclusion follows from Smythies (1956) 'bright phase' evoked images, which had the character of the basic geometric forms of the constancy orbits, and the subsequent 'dark phase' evoked images involving higher visual forms.

The upshot then is that the so called visual cortex (area 17) and the psychovisual cortex (areas 18 and 19) comprise a hierarchy of visual processing, the earliest level, the primary termination of the optic radiation in area 17, being that of the constancies. The neurons in area 17 have the correct morphology and cytoarchitecture (layer location) to be 'infinitesimal generators' of the constancies. According to axiom (4) above, the neuron is thus a 'local' microscopic element whose flows and interactions with other neurons generate $\mathfrak{M}$ at the 'global', psychological scale. Characteristic of each neuron's action is its morphology and connectivity. Thus, in mathematical terms, a neuron constitutes a 'local phase portrait', in the sense of the qualitative theory of differential equations. The nature of the particular neuron morpology involved in the local phase portrait follows from the correspondence between characteristic differential equation (Pfaffian system) and Lie derivative. The constancies, corresponding as they do to invariant orbits, are generated by the action of certain Lie derivatives, each of which 'drags the flow' along the constancy orbits (invariant path-curves). Recognition then takes place 'by exception', i.e. by cancellation rather than activation. The non-specific recruiting response precedes very slightly the specific afferent, which acts to essentially cancel the former (Li, Cullen, and Jasper, 1956a,b). When one is asleep or under the influence of an anaesthetic, the specific afferent stimuli still bombard the perceptual system, but one is unconscious of them owing to the lack of an input from the arousal system. Only when the nonspecific blackboard is cancelled by the specific chalk mark are we aware of the form involved.

Well and good for the basic forms of the constancies, but how can one proceed from these basic forms (Table 1) to the higher forms characteristic of everyday perception? The answer is provided by the process of prolongation of Lie derivatives, which generates higher and higher differential invariants. Neuropsychologically, this process is embodied in the growth and proliferation of the neuronal processes. In particular, in the visual system its presence is evident in the functioning of certain of Hubel and Wiesel's complex and hypercomplex cells (Hoffman, 1970). We note that the prolonged Lie derivative acts on the so called canonical variables (ibid) generated by flows through the neurons of the visual cortex to generate higher visual forms on whatever visual manifold it is that is momentarily being viewed. The exact nature of these prolongations, and hence the higher differential invariants involved, will vary with the manifold (Guggenheimer, 1963, sec. 7–2), (Hoffman, ibid), so that, once again, the removal of geometrico-physical distortion by preprocessing by the constancies is vital to essentially consistent reproduction, and hence recognition, of higher visual forms. But in keeping with what is known from modern information-processing psychology, the actual higher form, though readily recognizable, will differ very slightly from one occasion to the next.

Table 1. Correspondences between the visual constancies and certain Lie transformation groups on $\mathbb{R}^2 \times \mathbf{T}$

Perceptual invariance	Lie transformation group	Orbits
Shape Constancy	*Unimodular Group* SL($\mathbb{R}$, 3)	
Location in the field of view	Horizontal translations	
(Form memory)	Vertical translations	
	Time translations	
Orientation	Rotations, SO$_2$	
Afferent binocular vision	Pseudo-Euclidean Rotations	
(Efferent binocular function)	Pseudo-Euclidean Rotations in plane-time: $\mathbb{R}^2 \times \mathbf{T}$ (Invariant: xyt)	
Size constancy	*Dilation group (Homotheties)*	
Motion-invariant perception	*Lorentz group of order 2*	
Cyclopean, egocentered perception	Group of rotations, SO$_3$, in Plane-time: $\mathbb{R}^2 \times \mathbf{T}$	

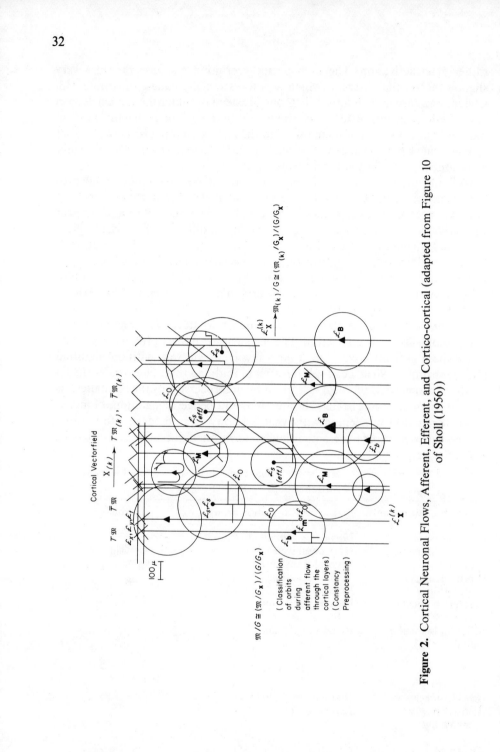

Figure 2. Cortical Neuronal Flows, Afferent, Efferent, and Cortico-cortical (adapted from Figure 10 of Sholl (1956))

Again in accord with modern cognitive neuropsychology, only the basic constancy processors are stored, all other perceptions being generated anew each time by the prolongation process. Of this, and how it relates to neuron morphology and cytoarchitecture, we shall have more to say later.

We now pass to a more detailed study of the visual constancies, their action and neuropsychological correlates, and their relation to the parameter groups involved, but at this point sum up in the following diagram from Sholl (1956) modified to show the apparent neuro-anatomical counterparts of our mathematical model (see Figure 2).

II. The Visual Constancies as Invariants of Certain L.T.G.'s
   (Lie Transformation Groups)

The neonatal child comes equipped with his full complement of perikarya at birth, apart from a small number of 'microneurons' (Altman, 1967) that develop postnally by mitosis. Some thousands of neurons die daily during our lifetime but what does grow and proliferate all during life and keep pace with the growth of memory and learning are the neuronal arborescences. Neuronal processes continually grow, branch, and form additional connections all during our conscious life. In our view, this is what engrams memory and learning.

Initially the neonate's neurons are so called neuroblasts, unipolar or bipolar, with little development above layer IV of the visual cortex. As such, they have every appearance of being cortical embodiments of the following twelve infinitesimal generators of $GL(\mathbf{R}^3)$ (Campbell, 1966, p. 386):

$$\left(\partial_x = \frac{\partial}{\partial x}, \partial_y = \frac{\partial}{\partial y}, \partial_t = \frac{\partial}{\partial t}\right), \ x(\partial_x, \partial_y, \partial_t), y(\partial_x, \partial_y, \partial_t), t(\partial_x, \partial_y, \partial_t). \quad (2)$$

Here x and y are rectangular coordinates in $\overline{\mathfrak{M}} \subset \mathbf{R}^2 \times \mathbf{T}$, as above and $t \in \mathbf{T}$ is subjective time.

As shown elsewhere (Hoffman, 1966a, 1967), this set of Lie derivatives acting upon 'plane-time' ($\overline{\mathfrak{M}} = \text{proj} \, \mathfrak{M} \subset \mathbf{R}^2 \times \mathbf{T}$) generates efferent binocular function at once as a result of the necessity for 'closure' of the Lie algebra. The primacy of motion detection, both psychologically (Tauber and Koffler, 1966) and neurophysiologically (Hubel and Wiesel, 1963) leads to the adjunction of the Lorentz group of order 2 governing the invariants of movement perception, after which afferent binocular function and egocentred movement perception quickly follow, again as consequences of the mathematical theory. To these are now adjoined, in the normal course of development, size constancy (4 years) and rotation constancy (6–11 years), the latter completing the requirements for shape constancy. This progression is in accord with the several Piagetian stages involved (Hoffman, 1976).

The Lie derivatives in (2) can thus be combined with equal weights, as in Table 2, in which case they correspond to the constancies, or they can be combined as linear combinations with differing weights, as for example

$$\kappa_1(-y\partial_x) + \kappa_2(x\partial_y), \quad (3)$$

Table 2. Visual constancies versus the corresponding Lie transformation groups

Perceptual invariance	Lie transformation group	Lie derivative
Shape constancy	Affine (Unimodular) group SL(3)	
Location in the field of view	Horizontal & vertical translations	$\pounds_x = \partial_x, \quad \pounds_y = \partial_y$
(Form memory)	Time shifts	$\pounds_t = \partial_t$
Orientation	Rotation group SO_2	$\pounds_0 = -y\partial_x + x\partial_y$
Afferent binocular perception	Pseudo-Euclidean (hyperbolic) rotations	$\pounds_b = y\partial_x + x\partial_y$
(Efferent binocular perception)	Pseudo-Euclidean rotations in plane-time	$\pounds_B = x\partial_x - y\partial_y$ $\pounds_{B1} = t\partial_t - x\partial_x$ $\pounds_{B2} = t\partial_t - y\partial_y$
Size constancy	Dilation group	$\pounds_s = x\partial_x + y\partial_y$ $\pounds_{s1} = x\partial_x + t\partial_t$ $\pounds_{s2} = y\partial_y + t\partial_t$
Motion invariance	Lorentz group of order 2	$\pounds_m = -\pounds_0$ $\pounds_{m1} = \tau\partial_x + x\partial_\tau$ $\pounds_{m2} = \tau\partial_y + y\partial_\tau$
(*Cyclopean* or *egocentred*, *perception*)	Rotation groups SO_3 in plane-time	$\pounds_M = \pounds_m = -\pounds_0$ $\pounds_{M1} = x\partial_\tau - \tau\partial_x$ $\pounds_{M2} = y\partial_\tau - \tau\partial_y$

x = horizontal distance from the perceptual centre in whatever frame of reference is applicable under the transformation; y = corresponding vertical distance; $= c't$,
t = time measured in cortical (neuropsychological) units, c' = maximum flow velocity of cortical signals propagated by neuronal processes.

which generates ellipses as orbits rather that the circular orbits of the group of $\pounds_0 = -y\partial_x + x\partial_y$. With such additional parameters as in (3) teleceptor and proprioceptor inputs can selectively influence neuron structure. A round pattern viewed obliquely would thus excite only those neuronal processes that correspond to the appropriate values of κ_1 and κ_2. Subsequent processing for the constancies would be such as to make the values of κ_1 and κ_2 equal. (Think of the classical example of the round plate upon the dinner table, whose projection on the retina is ellipitical.) Presumably this is how the constancies are detected and processed out during the flow of an afferent volley through the visual cortex. Binocular convergence and conjugate eye deviation are involved in an essential way in the determination of the parameters κ_1 and κ_2, and hence shape constancy, though not size constancy.

The 'constancies' are invariances of visual perception under the distortions of our geometrico-physical environment. The latter, being geometric in nature, can be regarded as transformation groups, and in fact as Lie transformation groups (or Lie modules (Nelson, 1967) since Lie derivatives are basic to the present argument involving the local structure of the Neuron Doctrine).

A Lie transformation group consists simultaneously of a continuous group and a manifold (like $\mathfrak{M}$ or $\overline{\mathfrak{M}}$) upon which the local structures are mutually consistent. Symbolically, one writes

$$G \times M \xrightarrow{\tau} M \tag{4}$$

meaning that the group action τ, which depends upon $g \in G$, acts upon $u \in M$ to give $'u \in M$. The group G is the so-called parameter group of the transformation group. Written out in coordinate form for the case of $\mathfrak{M}$ and an r-fold parameter group, (4) would read

$$'x = f_1(x, y; a_1, a_2, \ldots, a_r), \quad 'y = f_2(x, y; a_1, a_2, \ldots, a_r),$$
$$\mathbf{a} = (a_1, \ldots, a_r) \in G \tag{5}$$

In vectorial form, (5) would read

$$'\mathbf{x} = \mathbf{f}(\mathbf{x}; \mathbf{a}), \quad \mathbf{x} = (x, y) \in \overline{\mathfrak{M}}, \quad \mathbf{a} \in G. \tag{6}$$

Let us now consider an example of how such a transformation group behaves, remembering that our main interest lies with perceptual invariances under geometrically imposed transformations of our visual field of view. One of the most illuminating transformations seems to be rotation, 'Orientation' in Table 2, corresponding to the group SO_2. Under such rotations, the form which is invariant is that of a circle.

The rotation of an object with coordinates x, y through an angle φ is expressed by the following special case of the transformation equations (5):

$$'x = x \cos \varphi - y \sin \varphi, \quad 'y = x \sin \varphi + y \cos \varphi,$$

or in vector-matrix notation,

$$'\mathbf{x} = \begin{pmatrix} x \\ y \end{pmatrix} = \begin{pmatrix} \cos \varphi & -\sin \varphi \\ \sin \varphi & \cos \varphi \end{pmatrix} \begin{pmatrix} x \\ y \end{pmatrix} = \begin{pmatrix} f_1(x, y; \varphi) \\ f_2(x, y; \varphi) \end{pmatrix}. \tag{7}$$

Suppose now that we calculate $'x^2 + 'y^2$ from (7). One obtains

$$'x^2 + 'y^2 = x^2 + y^2 = c^2 = \text{const.}, \tag{8}$$

which is again the equation of a circle. This is exactly what is meant by an invariant under the transformation (7), namely, a geometric object which remains unchanged under that transformation. Such invariant curves are called *orbits*, or *trajectories*, or 'path-curves' of the transformation.

The foregoing has been a rotation of the entire x, y-plane through a finite 'global' angle φ. Important for our purposes is the infinitesimal transformation, which produces a 'small' or 'local' rotation through the infinitesimal angle $\delta \varphi$. Since

$$\cos(\delta \varphi) = 1 - \frac{(\delta \varphi)^2}{2!} + \ldots = 1 + o(\delta \varphi)$$

$$\sin(\delta \varphi) = \delta \varphi - \frac{(\delta \varphi)^3}{3!} + \ldots = \delta \varphi + o(\delta \varphi),$$

the finite transformation equations (7) become

$$\begin{pmatrix} 'x \\ 'y \end{pmatrix} = \begin{pmatrix} 1 - \delta\varphi \\ \delta\varphi & 1 \end{pmatrix} \begin{pmatrix} x \\ y \end{pmatrix} + o(\delta\varphi) = \begin{pmatrix} x - y\delta\varphi \\ x\delta\varphi + y \end{pmatrix} + o(\delta\varphi),$$

or

$$\delta\mathbf{x} = \begin{pmatrix} \delta x \\ \delta y \end{pmatrix} = \begin{pmatrix} 'x - x \\ 'y - y \end{pmatrix} = \begin{pmatrix} -y \\ x \end{pmatrix} \delta\varphi + o(\delta\varphi). \qquad (9)$$

This is the so-called *infinitesimal transformation* of the transformation group. For a compact, simply-connected manifold, the burden of Lie's First Fundamental Theorem (Hamermesh, 1962) is that the finite, 'global' transformation, such as that of (7), can be generated by repeated applications of the infinitesimal transformation.

It is worthy of note that such infinitesimal transformations are, without exception, locally linear. That is, the manifold variables (x, y) and the parameter variable $\delta\varphi$ are separated and occur as factors rather than as inextricably intertwined, usually in badly nonlinear fashion, as in (7) and (5) or (6).

The coefficient vector of $\delta\varphi$ in (9) can also be written as $(-y, x)^{\text{tr.}} = \begin{pmatrix} -y \\ x \end{pmatrix}$, or simply $(-y, x)$. Here $-y$ and x constitute the components of a vectorfield $\mathbf{X}$ that is always directed tangentially to the circle(s) (8):

$$\mathbf{X} = (-y, x). \qquad (10)$$

It is this vectorfield that generates the circular flow of the transformation. The Lie derivative 'drags the flow', in the manner of a dynamical system, along the orbits of the transformation.

The vectorfield of the infinitesimal transformation can be determined as above, by expanding in Taylor series and linearization, or by differentiating the finite transformation equations with respect to the parameter(s) and evaluating the resultant partial derivatives at the identity. Each such expression will constitute a component of the vectorfield(s) involved. Thus, for the above example of the rotation group we calculate, from (7),

$$\frac{\partial f_1}{\partial \varphi} = -x \sin \varphi - y \cos \varphi, \quad \frac{\partial f_2}{\partial \varphi} = x \cos \varphi - y \sin \varphi,$$

and evaluate these derivatives at the value $\varphi = 0$ (which constitutes the identity for the group of rotations) to obtain

$$\left. \frac{\partial f_1}{\partial \varphi} \right|_{\varphi=0} = -y, \quad \left. \frac{\partial f_2}{\partial \varphi} \right|_{\varphi=0} = x, \qquad (11)$$

the same as in (10). The general r-parameter case is somewhat more complicated, owing to the presence of a matrix $(\partial f_i / \partial a_p)$ rather than a single vector (see (Eisenhart, 1961)), but here we shall only be concerned with such one-parameter subgroups of the plane as those above.

Finally the Lie derivative, which 'drags the flow' along the orbit (Guggenheimer, 1963), and which characterizes the particular Lie transformation group and the Lie module acting, will be considered. A basis for the tangent space to $\mathfrak{M}$ at (x, y) is $(\partial_x, \partial_y) = \nabla$. For ordinary functions the Lie derivative $\pounds_X$ is the inner product of the vectorfield X and this basis:

$$\pounds_X = \langle X, \nabla \rangle = \sum_{i=1}^{2} X_i \partial_{x_i} = X_1(x, y)\partial_x + X_2(x, y)\partial_y. \tag{12}$$

As such, the Lie derivative is a directional derivative in the direction of the vectorfield $X = (X_1(x, y), X_2(x, y))$. For the rotation group SO_2, X is $(-y, x)$ and we have, as the Lie derivative for the group of rotations,

$$\pounds_0 = \pounds_{(-y,x)} = -y\partial_x + x\partial_y. \tag{13}$$

The Lie derivative (13) acts as the 'infinitesimal generator' of SO_2 in the following sense. The *exponential map*, defined in general as

$$\exp(a\pounds_X), \tag{14}$$

permits one to traverse orbits of the group of $\pounds_X$ globally rather than locally as for $\pounds_X$ itself. Equation (14) is to be thought of in an operational sense, i.e.

$$\exp(a\pounds_X) = 1 + \sum_{n=1}^{\infty} \frac{a^n}{n!}\pounds_X^n, \tag{15}$$

where $\pounds_X^n$ is defined recursively:

$$\pounds_X^n = \pounds_X(\pounds_X^{n-1}), \ (n = 1, 2, \ldots), \quad \pounds_X^0 = 1. \tag{16}$$

We thus have a power series in the operator $\pounds_X$, which when applied to (x, y) leads to the finite transformation equations and when applied to a function of x and y, $f(x, y)$, transforms it to $f('x, 'y)$.

In the case of SO_2, the rotation group of the plane, we have

$$\begin{aligned}
'x = \exp(\varphi\pounds_0)x &= 1 - \varphi y - \frac{\varphi^2}{2!}x + \frac{\varphi^3}{3!}y + \frac{\varphi^4}{4!}x - \frac{\varphi^5}{5!}y + \cdots \\
&= \left(1 - \frac{\varphi^2}{2!} + \frac{\varphi^4}{4!} + \cdots\right)x - \left(\varphi - \frac{\varphi^3}{3!} + \cdots\right)y \\
&= x \cos\varphi - y \sin\varphi.
\end{aligned}$$

$$\begin{aligned}
'y = \exp(\varphi\pounds_0)y &= 1 + \varphi x - \frac{\varphi^2}{2!}y - \frac{\varphi^3}{3!}x + \frac{\varphi^4}{4!}y + \frac{\varphi^5}{5!}x + \cdots \\
&= \left(1 - \frac{\varphi^2}{2!} + \frac{\varphi^4}{4!} - \cdots\right)y + \left(\varphi - \frac{\varphi^3}{3!} + \frac{\varphi^5}{5!} - \cdots\right)x \\
&= x \sin\varphi + y \cos\varphi.
\end{aligned}$$

These equations are the same as the finite transformation equations (7).

The action of a Lie derivative on a function that is an *absolute invariant* under the action of the L.T.G. is to annul it. From (15), for a function $u(x, y)$,

$$u('x, 'y) = \exp(a\pounds_X)u(x, y) = u(x, y) + a\pounds_X u + \frac{a^2}{2!}\pounds_X^2 u + \cdots$$

If u is an invariant under the action of the group of $\pounds_X$, then $u('x, 'y) = u(x, y)$ for all (x, y) and $('x, 'y)$, i.e., for all a, and

$$a\pounds_X u + \frac{a^2}{2!}\pounds_X^2 u + \cdots = 0.$$

Since a is arbitrary, the only way for the above expression to vanish is to have

$$\pounds_X u(x, y) = 0, \tag{17}$$

and expression (17) is what characterizes an *absolute invariant*.

For example, in the case of the rotation group we know that the absolute invariants are circles. This fact is reflected by their annulment under the action of the Lie derivative $\pounds_0$ of SO_2:

$$\pounds_0(x^2 + y^2 - c^2) = -2xy + 2xy = 0. \tag{18}$$

A *relative invariant* is one that belongs to the same family, the individual members of the family simply being shifted into some other member of the family under the action of the transformation group. For example, the family $y = cx$ of radial lines through the origin does not change under the action of the rotation group even though any particular line is rotated into a different one. Applying $\pounds_0$ to $y/x = c$ yields

$$(-y\partial_x + x\partial_y)(y/x) = -y\left(-\frac{y}{x^2}\right) + x\cdot\frac{1}{x} = 1 + (y/x)^2, \tag{19}$$

which is again a function of the original curve y/x. This behaviour characterizes relative invariance. If $F(x, y) = c_1$ and $F('x, 'y) = c_2$ are only different members of the same family of curves, and one curve goes into another under the transformation group of $\pounds_X$, then

$$F('x, 'y) - F(x, y) = \sum_{n=1}^{\infty} \frac{a^n}{n!}\pounds_X^n F(x, y) = c_2 - c_1 = \text{const.}$$

It follows that $\pounds_X F = c = \text{const.}$ for every member of the transformed family, and so for the original family, since the families are one and the same. Thus, as in the above example,

$$\pounds_X F = f(F), \tag{20}$$

where f is some point function of c that indexes the family of curves $F = \text{const.}$

Both absolute and relative invariants will prove important for our purposes. In the case of an absolute invariant, we have 'perception by exception' in the sense that the form is recognized by its being annulled by the action of the appropriate Lie derivative. For a relative invariant, on the other hand, the form is processed and simply handed on in a recognizable fashion to be an absolute invariant at some subsequent stage in the chain of visual processing.

Shape Constancy

Shape constancy refers to the psychological tendency for the shape of an object to be perceived in its actual form, even though it may be viewed obliquely, so that the image cast upon the retina is an oblique projection of the actual shape of the object. The psychophysical parameter governing shape constancy is the angle of obliquity γ. The latter can be resolved into a rotational component (φ) and an elevation angle component (ϵ). As we shall shortly see, this resolution is also the natural one in terms of the Lie subgroups comprising shape constancy. Thus shape constancy (obliquity invariance) can be resolved into rationally invariant perception and slant-invariant perception.

We now proceed to an analysis of the subgroups of the affine group, SL_2, that generates shape constancy. The infinitesimal generators of the non-time-varying portion of this group are, for $\mathbf{R}^2$,

$$\partial_x, \quad \partial_y, \quad y\partial_x, \quad x\partial_y, \quad x\partial_x - y\partial_y. \tag{21}$$

The finite transformations corresponding to (21) comprise the family of area-preserving parallel projections, which are especially appropriate to shape constancy in that our perception of an object's intrinsic shape is essentially unaffected by its obliquity with respect to our line of sight. The standard example in psychology texts is that of the dinner plate upon the table, which we see as round even though its projection upon one's retina is elliptical in shape.

Parallel projection leaves invariant the type of conic section. That is, under parallel projection a given kind of conic goes again into one of the same kind. This conic-preserving property of parallel projection is essential to shape constancy. It would not do to have the circular dinner plate suddenly jump into a hyperbolic or parabolic shape, as would be possible, for instance, if it were the full projective group that was involved.

In cortical processing (or rather, preprocessing) embodying the constancies, shape constancy and size constancy appear to be imposed separately, as indicated by their differing developmental rates and maturation times. Area is apparently first preserved in the cortical visual processing, then the dilations and contractions that express size constancy next. It is interesting to note in this connection that both shape constancy and Piaget's conservation of area become instilled in the developing child at about age six, and indeed most of Piaget's types of conservation can be related to the corresponding constancies (Hoffman, 1976) in terms of the particular age of maturation involved.

A brief consideration of the Lie derivatives (21) together with their temporal counterparts

$$\partial_t, \quad t\partial_t - x\partial_x, \quad t\partial_t - y\partial_y, \tag{22}$$

shows that shape constancy can be subdivided naturally into several subconstancies, namely, those indicated in Table 2 above. We next take up each of these subconstancies in turn.

Sh. (1) Location in $\overline{\mathfrak{M}}$ as Invariance Under the Group of Translations

The first two subgroups of SL_2, defined by the Lie derivatives

$$\pounds_x = \pounds_{(1,0)} = \partial_x, \quad \pounds_y = \pounds_{(0,1)} = \partial_y, \tag{23}$$

generate the horizontal and vertical translation groups of the plane, respectively. The exponential maps for $\pounds_x$ and $\pounds_y$ applied respectively to the coordinate pair (x, y) yield the following finite transformation equations:

Horizontal transl^n group: $(x, y) \xrightarrow{\text{exp}} ('x = x + a, 'y = y)$. $\qquad$ (24)

Vertical transl^n group: $\quad (x, y) \xrightarrow{\text{exp}} ('x = x, 'y = y + a)$. $\qquad$ (25)

Thus, as the parameter a varies from $-\infty$ to $+\infty$ in (24) and (25), the action of $\pounds_x$ traces out a family of horizontal straight lines; similarly, the orbits of $\pounds_y$ are vertical straight lines. The same result is obtained by solving the Pfaffian systems

$$\frac{dx}{1} = \frac{dy}{0} \quad \text{and} \quad \frac{dx}{0} = \frac{dy}{1}, \tag{26}$$

which correspond to $\pounds_x f(x, y) = 0$ and $\pounds_y f(x, y) = 0$, respectively. Solution of the first of equations (26) yields $y = $ const., which is the equation of a horizontal straight line, while solution of the second gives $x = $ const., a vertical straight line, as before.

As will be seen below in Sec. III, the requirement of closure of the set of Lie derivatives in the sense of Lie's Second Fundamental Theorem necessitates $\pounds_x$ and $\pounds_y$ being multiplied by c', the peak velocity of nerve signal propagation in the cortex, whenever the perception of movement is involved. The effect is to impart to the translation operators, in the moving stimulus case, the dimension of reciprocal time, i.e. subjective distance *per unit of subjective time*. This apparently is an instance of Pitts and McCulloch's (1947) principle of exchangeability of time and space.

It is worthy of note that there exists a well formed neuroanatomical substrate for translational invariance. As Sutherland and Young have found in lower animals and Colonnier (1964) in higher, there exists a rectangular grid of nerve fibres in the visual cortex. In the case of higher animals this rectangular grid is situated in the plexiform layer and becomes criss-crossed during development by a feltwork of finer oblique fibres as well.

Sh. (2) Form Memory as Invariance of Form Perception under
Time Translations

Recognition-type memory, at least in its simple, ikonic form, is simply another name for the invariance of a particular form perception under time changes. It may thus be expressed as invariance under the group of time translations, whose Lie derivative is

$$\pounds_t = \partial_t. \tag{27}$$

Whenever motion-invariant perception is involved, (27) must be replaced, if the requirements of Lie's Second Fundamental Theorem are to be met, by

$$\pm \pounds_t/c', \tag{28}$$

and we again have an apparent instance of Pitts and McCulloch's principle of exchangeability of time and space.

Although the statement that recognition-type memory constitutes invariant perception under time changes may impress the reader as a truism, it apparently constitutes a novel interpretation of form memory, forced on us (trivially) by the mathematical theory. It does not appear, moreover, to be found in such terms anywhere in the extant psychological literature.

Lie groups have discrete subgroups. Time can thus flow either continuously or in discrete 'ticks' for the time-invariant perceptions governed by $\pounds_t$. The exchangeability of time and space, mentioned above, presumably provides the basis for whatever timing rhythm may be present, for in the brain only the hippocampus displays any sort of even approximately regular rhythm. But some sort of 'neurophysiological clock' could perhaps be organized out of the spontaneously discharging neurons found by Jung (1961) on the basis of Slutsky's theorem (Slutsky, 1937) to the effect that a moving average of perfectly random events will display eventually regular periodic oscillations.

Sh. (3) Orientation Constancy as Invariance under the Group SO_2 of Rotations of the Plane

As Krech and Crutchfield (1958) put it,

> 'Mr. Anyman is perceived as Mr. Anyman with his characteristic body proportions whether he is seen lying down, standing upright, or balancing on his head.'

Our perceptions of form are thus invariant, to within reasonable limits, under tilts of either the observer or the observed object out of the vertical reference direction. The nature of shape constancy thus also requires the presence of the Lie derivative of the group SO_2:

$$\pounds_0 = \pounds_{(-y, x)} = -y\partial_x + x\partial_y. \tag{13}$$

In general an object's tilt involves not only rotation in the frontal plane through an angle φ but also an obliquity angle θ measured from the sagittal plane. This is evident from the well known formula for the cosine of the angle of obliquity γ between two points whose spherical coordinates are (θ_1, ϕ_1) and (θ_2, ϕ_2), respectively:

$$\cos \gamma = \cos \theta_1 \cos \theta_2 + \sin \theta_1 \sin \theta_2 \cos (\phi_2 - \phi_1).$$

The ϕ displacement is subsumed by a rotation, the θ displacement by a 'co-

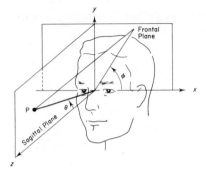

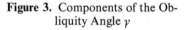

Figure 3. Components of the Obliquity Angle γ

latitude angle' away from the sagittal axis Oz: (Figure 3). The latter will turn out to be closely related to the Hillebrand hyperbolas, the hyperbolic orbits of binocular vision, considered in the next Section.

The psychophysical parameter governing rotation constancy is the angle of rotation, referred to some standard subjective orientation such as the observer's vertical. Here, for mathematical convenience in our coordinate representations, we choose the subject's horizontal, which is perpendicular to his vertical. The angle of rotation will not in general be a full 360° (Hake, 1966) but will cover some appreciable sector. The orbits, exponential map, etc. of the group of $\mathfrak{L}_0$ were found in equations (7)–(13) above. Here the only additional thing to note is that the orbits also follow from the correspondence between Lie derivative and characteristic equations (Pfaffian system)

$$\mathfrak{L}_X = X_1 \partial_x + X_2 \partial_y \qquad \frac{\mathrm{d}x}{X_1(x, y)} = \frac{\mathrm{d}y}{X_2(x, y)} = \frac{\mathrm{d}a}{1}, \tag{29}$$

which has already been invoked in (26). For $\mathfrak{L}_0$, the characteristic equations are

$$\frac{\mathrm{d}x}{-y} = \frac{\mathrm{d}y}{x}, \tag{30}$$

which can be immediately integrated to give the family of circular orbits (8).

The neuronal structures that have the proper morphology (i.e. are topological equivalents of families of circles) and location (cytoarchitecture) to be neuroanatomical correlates of $\mathfrak{L}_0$ are the pyramidal neurons with recurrent collaterals (Sholl, 1956) and the pericellular nests, essentially of spheroidal character, that terminate the optic radiation about the stellate cells of layer III of the visual cortex and certain pyramidal cells of the visual cortex (Lorenté de No, 1949). It is worthy of note that such terminations can only influence these cortical neurons transsynaptically, thus avoiding the dilemma that the orbits (8) of $\mathfrak{L}_0$ are not structurally stable. This property is vitally important in any biological system.

Before proceeding further we make a short mathematical side trip onto the topic of canonical variables. The form of a Lie derivative can be simplified dramatically by the use of the latter. The use of such *canonical variables* enables us to reduce the infinitesimal transformation to *canonical form*, in which the group acts simply by translation in the canonical variable. This is apparently what the visual cortex does during its processing of an afferent volley. That is, it establishes the basic invariants, which become the canonical coordinates for subsequent visual processing including the differential invariants basic to higher form perception.

Mathematically speaking, canonical coordinates are obtained via a particular change of variables, so we first of all consider what effect a change of variables

$$\xi = \xi(x,y), \quad \eta = \eta(x,y) \tag{31}$$

has on the vectorfield defining the Lie derivatives. Let (12) denote the Lie derivative in its original form and $\hat{\pounds}_{\Xi}$ its form in the new coordinates

$$\hat{\pounds}_{\Xi} = \hat{\pounds}_{(\Xi_1,\Xi_2)} = \Xi_1(\xi,\eta)\partial_\xi + \Xi_2(\xi,\eta)\partial_\eta. \tag{32}$$

The change of variables (31) yields the new vectorfield components of $\hat{\pounds}_{\Xi}$ by the following 'chain-rule' calculation (with $(x_1, x_2) = (x,y)$):

$$\Xi_{kp}('\xi, '\eta) = \left.\frac{\partial'\xi_k}{\partial a_p}\right|_{a=a_0} = \sum_{i=1}^{2} \frac{\partial'\xi_k}{\partial'x_i}\frac{\partial'x_i}{\partial a_p}\bigg|_{a=a_0} = \sum_{1}^{2} X_{ip}('x, 'y)\frac{\partial'\xi_k}{\partial'x_i}, (k = 1, 2) \tag{33}$$

or, dropping the primes,

$$\Xi_1(\xi,\eta) = \pounds_x\xi, \quad \Xi_2(\xi,\eta) = \pounds_x\eta. \tag{34}$$

Hence

$$\hat{\pounds}_{\Xi} = (\pounds_x\xi)\,\partial_\xi + (\pounds_x\eta)\partial_\eta, \tag{35}$$

where $\pounds_x\xi$ and $\pounds_x\eta$ must be expressed in terms of the new ξ, η-coordinates by means of the change of variables formula (31).

Canonical coordinates may be found from the above change-of-variables formula by the following procedure. Of all possible new vectorfield components $\Xi_1(\xi, \eta)$ and $\Xi_2(\xi, \eta)$, one utilizes that change of variables which makes all Ξ_k, $(k = 1, 2)$, but one vanish. The non-vanishing Ξ_k will be set equal to 1. Equation (34) thus yields, for example,

$$\Xi_1 = \pounds_x\xi = 0, \quad \Xi_2 = \pounds_x\eta = 1. \tag{36}$$

The ξ and η that result in this way are said to be canonical variables, and $\hat{\pounds}_{\Xi}$ reduces to

$$\hat{\pounds}_{\Xi} = \partial_\eta. \tag{37}$$

Equation (37) is the Lie derivative of translations in the canonical variable η, and the group action has been reduced, by the change to canonical variables, to that of *translations*. The latter are much simpler ordinarily than the group action represented by the original Lie derivative

$$\pounds_X = X_1(x, y)\partial_x + X_2(x, y)\partial_y.$$

As an example we apply the above formalism to the Lie derivative $\pounds_0 = \pounds_{(-y,x)}$. The new coordinates (ξ, η) will be given as the solution of the pair of Lagrange partial differential equations

$$\pounds_0 \xi = -y\partial_x \xi + x\partial_y \xi = 0, \quad \pounds_0 \eta = -y\partial_x \eta + x\partial_y \eta = 1.$$

The corresponding characteristic equations are then

$$\frac{dx}{-y} = \frac{dy}{x} = \frac{d\xi}{0}, \frac{dx}{-y} = \frac{dy}{x} = \frac{d\eta}{1}.$$

From the first of these we obtain the invariant $u = x^2 + y^2 = $ const., which, when utilized in the second, yields, by composition,

$$\frac{x\,dy - y\,dx}{x^2 + y^2} = d\eta$$

or

$$\eta = \arctan \frac{y}{x} = \varphi, \tag{38}$$

the usual polar angle of rectangular polar coordinates.

The Lie derivative $\pounds_0$ of equation (13) can thus be reduced to the Lie derivative

$$\hat{\pounds}_0 = \partial_\varphi, \tag{39}$$

of translations in the angular direction (i.e., along the circumference of the circular orbits). This is of course geometrically obvious, but as we shall see, it, together with the canonical form for the Lie derivative of size constancy, have some rather deep neuropsychological consequences.

Sh. (4) Binocular Perception, Afferent and Efferent

The final component of shape constancy involves the invariances of binocular perception, both afferent and efferent. (The latter refers to such things as conjugate eye deviation, binocular convergence, etc.) The effect of binocular distortion on viewing has been known since the ancient Greeks, who always carefully built a slight curvature into their columns to make them appear straight. In more modern times binocular visual space has been extensively investigated by Luneburg (1947, 1948, 1950), Blank (1953, 1957), and others (Zajaczkowska, 1956a, 1956b; Shipley, 1957a, 1957b; Gunther, 1961a, 1961b; Kienle, 1963).

Invariance under the action of efferent binocularity appears to be especially important, for it is the first constancy to be developed neonatally, and all the other constancies are eventually processed by it, according to the neuroanatomical indications. The reason is not far to seek: Those higher animals that possess a high degree of binocular fusion also have greater depth perception and visual acuity. On the other hand, those animals that lack any significant degree of binocular fusion achieve depth perception by accomodation and impression of parallactic movement. The continual nodding motions of birds, rabbits, and other prey-type creatures illustrates the point, as does also the tossing of the horse's head when he is startled. The resultant vertical displacement of the eyes generates a motion parallax that provides a counterpart of the interocular distance of the binocular animal.

On the other hand, as the Helmholtz circumhoropter and Blumenfeld alley experiments indicate, binocular fusion inevitably introduces distortion into the visual field. If visual perception is to cooperate in a coherent whole with the other sensory modalities and our body image, then the brain must possess some type of intrinsic structure for correcting this distortion and converting our binocular vision into Cyclopean, egocentered visual perception. This transformation worked by the brain is a mapping from Luneburg's binocular visual space (Luneburg, op cit; Blank, op cit) to egocentered, Cyclopean perceptual space and back again for the oculomotor adjustments necessary for binocular convergence and conjugate eye deviation.

This group of transformations is also expressed by certain subgroups of SL(2) and SL(3). One is SO_2 above. Another, appropriate to afferent binocular perception is the group of

$$\pounds_b = \pounds_{(y,x)} = y\partial_x + x\partial_y. \tag{40}$$

The orbits of $\pounds_b$ may be found in the usual way either by flows determined from the characteristic equations

$$\frac{dx}{y} = \frac{dy}{x} \implies -x\,dx + y\,dy = 0 \implies -x^2 + y^2 = \text{const.},$$

or by the exponential map

$$\sum_0^\infty \frac{t^n}{n!} \pounds_b^n x = x\,\text{ch}\,t + y\,\text{sh}\,t = {}'x, \qquad \sum_0^\infty \frac{t^n}{n!} \pounds_b^n y = x\,\text{sh}\,t + y\,\text{ch}\,t = {}'y,$$

whence, as before

$$-'x^2 + 'y^2 = -x^2 + y^2 = \text{const.}$$

The orbits are rectangular hyperbolas, which constitute the orbit family for the group of pseudo-Euclidean rotations (Greub, 1963; Klein, 1960).

We shall not treat in any great detail the reasoning that leads to the geometry of binocular visual space, since that is discussed elsewhere in this symposium volume (Blank, 1978). We simply adduce *Luneburg's Principle*, restated from Blank (1958):

> *The process of visual perception is such as to transform the Hillebrand hyperbolas into polar rays emanating from the egocenter and the Vieth-Müller circles into egocentered in the 'plane of regard'* (the plane through the two eyes and the observed point).

This last term is made clear by Figures 4 and 5. Figure 6, taken from Luneburg (1947), shows a few actual Hillebrand hyperbolas and Vieth-Müller circles as they would appear in the plane of regard. The parameter of the former is the *bipolar latitude* ψ, of the latter, the *bipolar parallax* γ.

In the parallel projection onto the x, y-plane that we are considering, i.e. $\overline{\mathfrak{M}} = \text{proj } \mathfrak{M}$, the Hillebrand hyperbolas and Vieth-Müller circles in the plane of regard become, for the physical space, projected hyperbolas and ellipses,

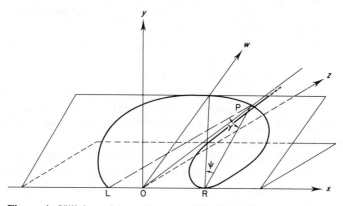

Figure 4. Hillebrand hyperbolas and Vieth-Müller circles in the plane of regard (the xw-plane)

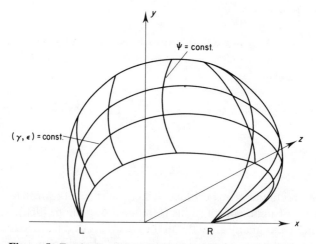

Figure 5. Equivalent Vieth-Müller torus. The curves $\psi =$ const. are meridians; the curves $\epsilon =$ const., circles of constant bipolar latitude

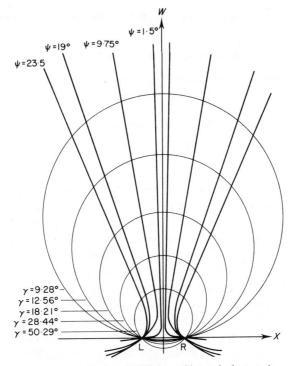

Figure 6. Actual plot of Hillebrand hyperbolas $- w^2 + x^2 + 2xw \cot 2\psi = 1$ for a range of ψ-values, together with a family of actual Vieth-Müller circles. Note that the Hillerbrand hyperbolas essentially coincide with their linear asymptotes for distances large with respect to the interocular distance

while for the subjective space, the projections are rays through the egocentre and egocentred ellipses. By well known properties of the affine infinitesimal transformation (Kowalewski, 1931, Chap. 5), the above families of curves are 'affinely equivalent' respectively to circles and hyperbolas in physical space, but, for the associated subjective frame of reference, to circles and an egocentred star of rays. Shape constancy, by definition, acts to undo this projection transformation, or 'affine equivalence'.

The relations between the Lie derivatives governing the respective invariances in projected physical and subjective space are then

Projected Binocular (Physical) Space		*Projected Subjective Space*	
Hillebrand hyperbolas:[1]	$\mathbf{\pounds}_{\natural} = \tilde{y}\partial_{\tilde{x}} + \tilde{x}\partial_{\tilde{y}}$	$\mathbf{\pounds}_{s} = x\partial_{x} + y\partial_{y}$	(41a,b)
Vieth-Müller circles:	$\mathbf{\pounds}_{\gamma} = -(y - \cot \gamma)\partial_{x} + x\partial_{y}$	$\mathbf{\pounds}_{0} = -y\partial_{x} + x\partial_{y}.$	(42a,b)

The coordinates $\tilde{x}$, $\tilde{y}$ in which $\mathbf{\pounds}_{\natural}$ is expressed are the x, y-coordinates rotated through an angle of $\psi + \frac{1}{4}\pi$.[1] The Lie derivative $\pounds_b$, when expressed in terms of $\pounds_b$ and $\pounds_B$, reads as follows

$$\pounds_b = -(\sin 2\psi \, \pounds_b + \cos 2\psi \, \pounds_B),\tag{43}$$

where $\pounds_b$ is defined as in (40), and $\pounds_B$ is given by

$$\pounds_B = x\partial_x - y\partial_y.\tag{44}$$

We note that in terms of afferent-efferent progression, (43) is equivalent to

$$\pounds_B = -\tan 2\psi \, \pounds_b - \sec 2\psi \, \pounds_b.\tag{43'}$$

Technically speaking, it is the Lie derivative $\pounds_b$ that governs the hyperbolic in-variants of afferent binocular perception. However, for consistency with our projected visual field coordinates, x and y, the above resolution has been made into afferent binocular perception governed by $\pounds_b$ and what we have earlier identified (Hoffman, 1966), on the basis of the associated neuroanatomical structure and function, as efferent binocular function $\pounds_B$. And if the rotated coordinates $\tilde{x}$ and $\tilde{y}$ have been established in earlier cortical processing by $\pounds_0$, as would be possible according to the known cortical cytoarchitecture, then $\pounds_b$ would govern afferent binocular function *in these coordinates*. A comparison of the orbits of $\pounds_b$ (Figure 6) with pyramidal neuron morphology (Sholl, 1956, Plate 4) suggests that this may in fact be the case. But in any case, $\pounds_b$ and $\pounds_B$ act, according to (43), along some given hyperbola $\psi = $ const. Both these Lie deri-vatives are referred to the egocentre, thus enabling one to maintain consistency between body image and the oculomotor and other sensory modalities.

The role of $\pounds_0$ in orientation constancy has already been considered, but in (41b) we have a new Lie derivative whose orbits are rays (straight lines) emanat-ing from the observer's egocentre, as required by Luneburg's subjective visual space. This Lie derivative is known to govern the group of dilations (homo-theties). Since dilations and contractions now enter, the perception of perspec-tive effects becomes possible, and the affine transformation need no longer be area-preserving. Once the transformation group characterizing shape con-stancy has been augmented by the dilation group, then central as well as parallel projection will be possible. However, unlike the case for the full projective group, this augmentation may be achieved without compromising shape con-stancy.

The occurrence of $\pounds_s$ among the Lie derivatives governing the Cyclopean, egocentred stage of visual processing indicates the close connection between shape constancy and size constancy. The former, in its mature egocentred form, cannot be achieved without first developing size constancy, which is in accord with the known developmental sequence of these faculties.

The parameters for shape constancy thus appear to be ψ, ϵ, and γ. For size constancy, the parameters would be, on the basis of the principle of orthogonal control, γ and eye accomodation, i.e. curvature of the lens. We now proceed to a detailed analysis of size constancy.

Size Constancy

The *group of dilations* (homotheties, magnifications, similarities) of the plane has the matrix representation

$$'\binom{x}{y} = \begin{pmatrix} a & 0 \\ 0 & a \end{pmatrix} \binom{x}{y} = \begin{pmatrix} e^b & 0 \\ 0 & e^b \end{pmatrix} \binom{x}{y}. \tag{45}$$

The matrix transformation (45) generates uniform dilations of the x, y-plane, with $b = \ln a, (-\infty \le b \le \infty)$, as parameter. The Lie derivative of the group follows in the usual way, either from the equivalent of (11) or from the approximation $e^{\delta b} = 1 + \delta b + o(\delta b)$, as

$$\pounds_s = \pounds_{(x,y)} = x\partial_x + y\partial_y. \tag{46}$$

As we saw above, the group of $\pounds_s$ arises naturally in the transition from <u>binocular visual space to subjective Cyclopean space</u>. The neurons that have the proper morphology to be cortical counterparts of $\pounds_s$ are the stellate cells, largely concentrated in layer III of the visual cortex (Sholl, 1956), (Hoffman, 1968). Here they are associated trans-synaptically with the pericellular nests of terminal arborescences of afferent axons that terminate in layers IV and III (Sholl, 1956, Figure 12) and the recurrent collateral axons of Sholl's P4 type neurons (Sholl, 1956) in the ways required by the correspondences (41) and (42). The orbits of $\pounds_s$ follow in the usual way from the characteristic equation associated with (46):

$$\frac{dx}{x} = \frac{dy}{y} \Longrightarrow \ln x = \ln y + \text{const.} \Longrightarrow y/x = \text{const.} \tag{47}$$

The last expression is the equation of a family of radial lines emanating from the origin. We note that this family of straight lines is orthogonal to the families of circles constituting the orbits of $\pounds_0$, $\pounds_m$, and $\pounds_M$. The principle of orthogonal control asserts in this context that the extent of rotations is limited by some pair of the orthogonal rays and the range of a given expansion or contraction is governed by some pair of concentric arcs of circles.

The canonical coordinate for $\pounds_s$ is found in the usual way to be $\lambda = \ln r$. Thus

$$\pounds_s = r\partial_r = \partial_\lambda. \tag{48}$$

Size constancy also applies to time varying situations. Hence we adjoin the two corresponding Lie derivatives

$$\pounds_{s1} = x\partial_x + t\partial_t, \quad \pounds_{s2} = y\partial_y + t\partial_t. \tag{49}$$

The Perception of Movement. The Lorentz Group

There are two things, it seems, calculated to bring out the beast in people. One is how the brain works. The other is the theory of relativity. Here we bravely bring up the two together, since relativistic considerations are inevitably involved in the perception of movement. As with binocular perception, this topic is being treated in detail in another paper (Caelli, 1978), and here we do no more than outline the essentials.

In the case of moving stimuli, the traversal of the visual manifold by the moving object has to be referred to the observer's egocentre (if we are to be able to reach out and catch the ball). There are thus two different frames of reference *in the perceptual system* that are involved: a fixed one at the egocentre (the 'fixed observer' in SRT ('Special Relativity Theory') parlance) and one moving with the object (the 'moving frame' of SRT). Between these two frames of reference, one moving and one stationary, a signal—a volley of nerve impulses— propagates. This is a *signal function* in the sense of SRT (Schutz, 1973). And now we come to the essential point. Just as in a physical system, wherein the signal velocity (that of light) is finite, so too do cortical nerve impulses propagate with a finite velocity. Burns (Glees, 1961, p. 403) has found that the electrical response at the surface of an isolated block of cortex spreads outward at a rate of about 2 m/sec, which value is in accord with the known conduction velocity along fine axons and along apical dendrites during antidromic conduction (Ochs, 1965, p. 456). No matter how the propagation of the cortical signal may take place, whether by axonal discharge, graded electrotonic conduction along the dendritic arborescence, or whatever (Estable, 1961), all experimental evidence points to a *finite* velocity of nerve signal propagation. Hence the perception of movement cannot be Galilean, i.e., accomplished simply by linear transformation between the fixed and moving frames. If causality—the temporal order of events—is to be preserved during motion, then it is the Lorentz transformation that must apply (Zeeman, 1964). Causality is a vital requirement in evolution: an animal will not survive if its perception of the environment is at variance with the latter.

In analogy to the fixed and moving frames of physical space, for which the signal propagation velocity is $c = 3 \times 10^5$ km/sec, there exist fixed and moving frames, with respective origins O and O', upon the projected visual manifold $\mathfrak{M}$. The origin O' moves with respect to O with relative velocity v'. The velocity of signal propagation c' is the peak velocity of the cortical nerve impulse. The coordinates of a point on $\mathfrak{M}$ in the O-frame will be denoted by x, y, z, t. The same point referred to the O'-frame will have coordinates x', y', z', t'.

If the temporal order of events is preserved in both frames, the respective arc lengths must be equal (Rindler, 1960):

$$ds^2 = ds'^2,$$

where

$$ds^2 = (ds)^2 = (c' \, dt)^2 - (dx)^2 - (dy)^2 - (dz)^2,$$
$$ds'^2 = (ds')^2 = (c' \, dt')^2 - (dx')^2 - (dy')^2 - (dz')^2$$

This invariance of the local metric has the further consequence that the time and space variables transform according to the Lorentz transformation, which in its general vectorial form reads (Stephenson and Kilmister, 1958)

$$\mathbf{r}' = \gamma'(\mathbf{r}^* - \mathbf{v}'t), \quad t' = \gamma'(t - \frac{\mathbf{v}' \cdot \mathbf{r}}{c'^2}), \tag{50}$$

where

$$\mathbf{r}^* = \gamma'\mathbf{r} - \frac{(1 - \gamma')(\mathbf{v}' \cdot \mathbf{r})\mathbf{v}}{\gamma'v'^2} \tag{51}$$

and γ' is the Lorentz factor

$$\gamma' = 1/\sqrt{1 - (v'/c')^2}. \tag{52}$$

The Lorentz transformation has the desirable properties that

1° The form of the transformation from one frame to another is symmetric, i.e. the same when inverted, the obvious changes being made in velocity sense.
2° Finite points remain finite under the transformation.
3° The law of addition of velocities under the transformation is such that the peak velocity c' of signal propagation is an invariant.

There is also the Fitzgerald contraction: a moving length l_0 will appear to the stationary observer as foreshortened in the direction of motion

$$l = l_0 \sqrt{1 - (v'/c')^2}. \tag{53}$$

(This aspect of the perception of movement will be discussed by Dr. Caelli.) The clock paradox also applies: a clock moving with respect to an observer appears to be slow compared to his own clock. One is tempted to conjecture that this sort of time delay lies at the base of many motional aftereffects, wherein a transverse sort of form is seen following cessation of the moving stimulus itself.

If a phenomenon is invariant under the Lorentz transformation *and* under translations and rotations *and* time translations, then it will be invariant between *any* two coordinate systems in uniform motion relative to one another (Rindler, 1969). The general transformation between two such frames in general motion with respect to each other consists, first of all, of a spatial rotation and translation to make the x-axis of the O-frame coincide with the direction of motion of O'; then a time translation to ensure that the two origins O and O' coincided initially; third, a Lorentz transformation in the 'standard configuration' of parallel translation of the frames; and finally, another pair of the first two kinds of transformations to eventually arrive at the coordinates of the primed system. This over-all combination of linear transformations built around the Lorentz transformation (50) is called the *general Lorentz transformation* or *Poincare transformation*.

The infinitesimal generators of the general Lorentz group are (Hamermesh, 1962, p. 308):

$$\pounds_1 = z\partial_y - y\partial_z, \quad \pounds_2 = x\partial_z - z\partial_x, \quad \pounds_3 = y\partial_x - x\partial_y,$$
$$\pounds_4 = \tau\partial_x + x\partial_\tau, \quad \pounds_5 = \tau\partial_y + y\partial_\tau, \quad \pounds_6 = \tau\partial_z + z\partial_\tau, \quad \tau = c't. \quad (54)$$

We note before going on that any effect whose speed is finite and invariant in homogeneous space could be used just as well to derive the Lorentz transformation. For instance—to drive home the point—the signal function could consist of the projection of cannon balls. But only *one* such transformation can hold for arbitrary inertial systems, viz., that for the peak velocity of signal propagation c'.

In the case at hand, signals propagate along neuronal processes, in each of which there may be a slightly different maximal velocity of impulse propagation (c'_k for the kth neuron). Let $\pounds_{jk}$ be the jth Lie derivative in (54) but with τ replaced by $\tau_k = c'_k t$, ($k = 1, \ldots, N$). Then $\pounds_{jk}$ is a so-called fibre derivative (Boothby, 1975) which acts to annul the space-time metric along a tubular neighborhood:

$$\tau_k^2 - x^2 - y^2 - z^2. \quad (55)$$

In other words, the group of $\pounds_{jk}$ is invariant along the orbit (55). Letting k run, we have a *mixed L.T.G.* (Eisenhart, 1961, p. 58). The *universal covering group* (Hamermesh, 1962) of this L.T.G. will then define, strictly speaking, a Lorentz transformation applicable in the present instance. Although c' in (54) would then be $\max_k c'_k$, the group of (54) can be used without any essential loss of generality. The difference will be of the order of $c'^2 - c'^2_k$, and the latter will be small for a homogeneous group of nerve fibres.

The metric

$$s^2 = \tau^2 - x^2 - y^2 - z^2$$

defines Minkowski space, over which the Lie derivatives (54) act invariantly. Here we concern ourselves with the projection of Minkowski space onto $\mathfrak{M} = \text{proj} \, \mathfrak{M}$, i.e. the x, y, t-space of 'plane-time'. This projection follows simply by setting $z = 0$ in (56) and the projected Lie group action by taking $z = 0$ in (54). This yields the three-dimensional 'Lorentz group' (Hamermesh, 1962), whose Lie derivatives are

$$\pounds_m = -\pounds_0 = y\partial_x - x\partial_y, \quad \pounds_{m1} = \pounds_{(\tau,x)} = \tau\partial_x + x\partial_\tau,$$
$$\pounds_{m2} = \pounds_{(\tau,y)} = \tau\partial_y + y\partial_\tau. \quad (57)$$

We denote these vectorially by $\pounds_m = (\pounds_m, \pounds_{m1}, \pounds_{m2})$ for convenience in writing. These Lie derivatives leave invariant the plane-time metric

$$s^2 = \tau^2 - x^2 - y^2. \quad (58)$$

The orbit space is now a hyperboloid of one sheet asymptotic to the 'null cone' in plane-time. The horizontal cross-sections are circles, just as for $\pounds_0$, but now oriented positively clockwise rather than counter-clockwise. The hyperboloids (58) are 'time-like' or 'space-like' according as s is real or imaginary.

The Lie subalgebra of (57) has the multiplication table

$$[\mathfrak{L}_m, \mathfrak{L}_{m1}] = -\mathfrak{L}_{m2}, \quad [\mathfrak{L}_m, \mathfrak{L}_{m2}] = \mathfrak{L}_{m1}, \quad [\mathfrak{L}_{m1}, \mathfrak{L}_{m2}] = \mathfrak{L}_m. \tag{59}$$

It is worthy of note that the derived Lie algebra consisting of (59) and the bracket products of the translation operators $\mathfrak{L}_x, \mathfrak{L}_y, \mathfrak{L}_t$ is closed in its own right. This corresponds to the case of animals with little or no binocular fusion. Space must seem to have a hyperbolic nature to these creatures when moving stimuli are involved.

If one calculates the local phase portrait of $\mathfrak{L}_m$ from the associated characteristic equation

$$\frac{\mathrm{d}x}{y} = \frac{\mathrm{d}y}{-x},$$

the local phase portrait turns out to be a family of circles, positively oriented clockwise. The cortical counterpart is presumably either the pericellular nests surrounding the pyramidal cells or else Sholl's P_3 or P_4 type neurons, those with recurrent collaterals.

III. The Lie Algebra $\mathfrak{B}$ Associated with the Constancies

Recall that it was Lie's fundamentally new idea in the study of transformation groups to investigate not the global (or 'finite') behaviour of the T.G. but rather its action over a neighbourhood of the identity, i.e. a so-called Lie group germ. This approach led immediately to the idea of *infinitesimal transformation*, which Weyl (1925) later reformulated in abstract terms as the *Lie algebra* of the T.G. Let it be emphasized that we are here discussing the Lie algebra of a set of vectorfields on a manifold (Boothby, 1975), *not an abstract Lie algebra*. Confusion between the two concepts has apparently led some critics astray (Regnier).

The L.T.G. action may thus be regarded in two ways, either as taking place through a single, finite displacement or as a succession of infinitesimal transformations along certain distinguished paths, the orbits of the T.G. In the second version the action may be regarded as generating a 'flow' connecting initial and terminal points of the transformation. The transformation is thus generated by Lie derivatives that 'drag the flow' along the orbits of the T.G.

Lie's First Fundamental Theorem is based on Lie's Fundamental Partial Differential Equation (*hereafter*, P.D.E.). The latter asserts in effect that the possibly badly nonlinear transformation equations (5) and (6), in which the manifold variable $\mathbf{x}$ and the parameter group variable $\mathbf{a}$ are inextricably intertwined, can be replaced, locally, by a simple multiplication of the manifold vectorfield by the parameter-group vectorfield. Then the First Fundamental Theorem says that if Lie's Fundamental P.D.E. is satisfied, the solution will define a L.T.G. We then have the following important theorem (Cohen, 1931, Appendix):

Every (compact) L.T.G. that involves r essential parameters $a_1, \ldots, a_r$ is generated by r linearly independent Lie derivatives $\mathfrak{L}_{x_1}, \mathfrak{L}_{x_1}, \ldots, \mathfrak{L}_{x_1}$ in terms of *which every Lie derivative of the L.T.G. can be expressed as a linear combination with constant coefficients*

$$\pounds_X = \sum_{\rho=1}^{r} \kappa_\rho \pounds_{X_\rho}, \quad \kappa_\rho = \text{const.} \tag{60}$$

Moreover, for arbitrary choices of the constants $\kappa_1, \ldots, \kappa_r$, the infinitesimal transformation corresponding to (60) belongs to the L.T.G.

In other words, the set of Lie derivatives $\pounds_{X_1}, \ldots, \pounds_{X_r}$ is a basis for the algebra of Lie derivatives of the L.T.G., and equation (60) defines vectorspace. To make this vectorspace into an algebra as well, a product operation is needed. This is provided by the *Lie product*, or *bracket*,

$$[\pounds_{X_\rho}, \pounds_{X_\sigma}] = \pounds_{X_\rho}(\pounds_{X_\sigma}) - \pounds_{X_\sigma}(\pounds_{X_\rho}). \tag{61}$$

Before proceeding to a discussion of its significance, however, we note the implications of (60) for modern cognitive psychology. First of all, theorem (60) asserts that an r-parameter group can be reduced locally to a one-parameter L.T.G. along an orbit. Thus an orbit in parameter group space must be established before such a 'feed forward' can be made. Secondly, and most important for modern cognitive theory, however, it asserts that the κ_ρ may be selected by the subject's decision procedure ('selective attention'), dropping some forms out, emphasizing others, or even singling one particular one out upon which to concentrate. In that case all κ_ρ will be set equal to zero but the one corresponding to form of dominant interest.

The Lie derivatives $\pounds_{X_1}, \ldots, \pounds_{X_r}$ will define a Lie algebra provided the associated set of bracket products (61) are 'closed' in the sense that

$$[\pounds_{X_\rho}, \pounds_{X_\sigma}] = \sum_{\mu=1}^{r} c_{\rho\sigma}^{\mu} \pounds_{X_\mu}, \quad c_{\rho\sigma}^{\mu} = \text{const.} \tag{62}$$

In other words, the family of Lie products is constrained to lie on a linear manifold spanned by the $\pounds_{X_1}, \ldots, \pounds_{X_r}$.

Expression (62) is at the heart of Lie's Second Fundamental Theorem. The latter asserts that if there exists a family of vectorfields satisfying (62), then there will also exist a family of vectorfields $\{A_\rho\}$ for the parameter group that satisfy (up to isomorphism) the corresponding closure condition:

$$[A_\alpha, A_\beta] = \sum_{\gamma=1}^{r} c_{\alpha\beta}^{\gamma} A_\gamma,$$

(Bourbaki, 1972, p. 295), in which case Lie's Fundamental P.D.E. is integrable, and we do in fact have a L.T.G. The conditions for existence of the L.T.G. are completed by Lie's Third Fundamental Theorem: The latter asserts that the family of vectorfields $\{X_\rho\}$ will exist whenever the structure constants $c_{\rho\sigma}^{\mu}$ satisfy the antisymmetry condition $c_{\rho\sigma}^{\mu} = -c_{\sigma\rho}^{\mu}$ and the Jacobi identity:

$$\sum_{\mu}\{c_{\rho\sigma}^{\mu}c_{\mu\lambda}^{\nu} + c_{\sigma\lambda}^{\mu}c_{\mu\rho}^{\nu} + c_{\lambda\rho}^{\mu}c_{\mu\sigma}^{\nu}\} = 0, \ (\nu = 1, \ldots, r). \tag{63}$$

That (63) is an integrability condition for the L.T.G. is well known (Cohn, 1957). Conditions (62) and (63) thus permit the possibility of forming Gestalten from the local orbits of the $\pounds_{X_\rho}$'s. The importance of the relation (62) is difficult to overemphasize. It is the keystone of the Lie theory and, as indicated above in connection with the visual Gestalt, has profound consequences for perceptual psychology. For instance, the requirement of closure of the algebra of Lie derivatives in the sense of (62) leads to the theoretical prediction of certain new constancies, which have been subsequently verified. It also yields the developmental sequence of infant vision in its known normative form (Hoffman, 1966). The theoretically predicted constancies are those shown in parentheses in Tables 1 and 2.

We take this opportunity to present an updated table of the Lie products involved in $\mathfrak{B}$, the Lie algebra of mature visual perception. The only differences between the table of $\mathfrak{B}$ in (Hoffman, 1966) and Table 3 are that in the motional Lie derivatives $\pounds_m = (\pounds_m, \pounds_{m1}, \pounds_{m2})$ and $\pounds_M = (\pounds_M, \pounds_{M1}, \pounds_{M2})$, the variable t has been replaced by $\tau = c't$, and the time varying components $\pounds_{s1}$ and $\pounds_{s2}$ of size constancy have been added.

IV. Neuron Morphology and Cytoarchitectural Flows

By the term *cytoarchitectural flow* we mean something neurophysiological rather than neuroanatomical. The cytoarchitecture does not flow, at least over the short term; what does happen is that an afferent volley does flow through the depths of the cortex via neurons of particular morphology that occur in specific locations among the cortical layers (Sholl, 1956).

Neuron morphology is of two basically different types, pyramidal and stellate. The pyramidal type has a predominantly cylindrical character, while the stellate type is mainly radially symmetric in form (Colonnier, 1964). These forms are such as to suggest the orbits of hyperbolic flows and sources and sinks, respectively (Hirsch and Smale, 1974). However, we believe there is more to it than that, and have advanced the idea elsewhere (Hoffman, 1968, 1971) that the pyramidal and stellate neurons have morphologies characteristic of 'feature detectors' for the constancies. That is, any given neuron is actually a cortical counterpart of the *local phase portrait* (Hirsch and Smale, ibid; Hochstadt, 1965) that corresponds to the Lie derivative of one of the subgroups considered above. The neuron thus achieves its function by flows along its structure, the morphology of the latter being itself characteristic of the function of that neuron. By the neuron's connectivity it achieves, by integration with its fellows, the generation of an over-all Gestalt. That is—provided of course, that that connectivity embodies the Lie product in such a way as to make the process holonomic, or involutive (Nelson, 1967). In addition, the neuron grows its morphology under the impact of the long term memory process to embody more and more complicated memories, starting from the simple neonatal form of the neuroblast. This point will be discussed further in connection with differential invariants and prolongation of Lie derivatives in Sec. V below.

Table 3. Multiplication table for the Lie algebra $\mathfrak{B}$ of mature visual perception

$[\pounds_p, \pounds_\sigma]$	$\pounds_x$	$\pounds_y$	$\pounds_t$	$\pounds_B$	$\pounds_{B1}$	$\pounds_{B2}$	$\pounds_m$	$\pounds_{m1}$	$\pounds_{m2}$	$\pounds_M$	$\pounds_{M1}$	$\pounds_{M2}$	$\pounds_b$	$\pounds_s$	$\pounds_{s1}$	$\pounds_{s2}$	$\pounds_0$
$\pounds_x$	0	0	0	$\pounds_x$	$-\pounds_x$	0	$-\pounds_y$	$\pounds_\tau$	0	$-\pounds_y$	$\pounds_\tau$	0	$\pounds_y$	$\pounds_x$	$\pounds_x$	0	$\pounds_y$
$\pounds_y$	0	0	0	$-\pounds_y$	0	$-\pounds_y$	$\pounds_x$	0	$\pounds_\tau$	$\pounds_x$	0	$\pounds_\tau$	$\pounds_x$	$\pounds_y$	0	$\pounds_y$	$-\pounds_x$
$\pounds_t$	0	0	0	0	$\pounds_t$	$\pounds_t$	0	$c'\pounds_x$	$c'\pounds_y$	0	$-c'\pounds_x$	$-c'\pounds_y$	0	0	$\pounds_t$	$\pounds_t$	0
$\pounds_B$	$-\pounds_x$	$\pounds_y$	0	0	0	0	$-2\pounds_b$	$\pounds_{M1}$	$-\pounds_{M2}$	$-2\pounds_b$	$\pounds_{m1}$	$-\pounds_{m2}$	$-2\pounds_m$	0	0	0	$2\pounds_b$
$\pounds_{B1}$	$\pounds_x$	0	$-\pounds_t$	0	0	0	$\pounds_b$	$-2\pounds_{M1}$	$-\pounds_{M2}$	$\pounds_b$	$-2\pounds_{m1}$	$-\pounds_{m2}$	$\pounds_M$	0	0	0	$-\pounds_b$
$\pounds_{B2}$	0	$\pounds_y$	$-\pounds_t$	0	0	0	$-\pounds_b$	$-\pounds_{M1}$	$-2\pounds_{M2}$	$-\pounds_b$	$-\pounds_{m1}$	$-2\pounds_{m2}$	$-\pounds_M$	0	0	0	$\pounds_b$
$\pounds_m$	$\pounds_y$	$-\pounds_x$	0	$2\pounds_b$	$-\pounds_b$	$\pounds_b$	0	$\pounds_{m2}$	$-\pounds_{m1}$	0	$\pounds_{M2}$	$-\pounds_{M1}$	$-2\pounds_B$	0	$\pounds_b$	$-\pounds_b$	0
$\pounds_{m1}$	$-\pounds_\tau$	0	$-c\pounds_x$	$-\pounds_{M1}$	$2\pounds_{M1}$	$\pounds_{M1}$	$-\pounds_{m2}$	0	$-\pounds_m$	$-\pounds_{m2}$	$2\pounds_{B1}$	$-\pounds_b$	$-\pounds_{M2}$	$-\pounds_{M1}$	0	$\pounds_{M1}$	$\pounds_{m2}$
$\pounds_{m2}$	0	$-\pounds_\tau$	$-c\pounds_y$	$\pounds_{M2}$	$\pounds_{M2}$	$2\pounds_{M2}$	$\pounds_{m1}$	$\pounds_m$	0	$\pounds_{m1}$	$-\pounds_b$	$2\pounds_{B2}$	$-\pounds_{M1}$	$-\pounds_{M2}$	$\pounds_{M2}$	0	$-\pounds_{m1}$
$\pounds_M$	$\pounds_y$	$-\pounds_x$	0	$2\pounds_b$	$-\pounds_b$	$\pounds_b$	0	$\pounds_{m2}$	$-\pounds_{m1}$	0	$\pounds_{M2}$	$-\pounds_{M1}$	$-2\pounds_B$	0	$\pounds_b$	$-\pounds_b$	0

$\pounds_{M1}$	$-\pounds_\tau$	0	$c'\pounds_x$	$-\pounds_{m1}$	$2\pounds_{m1}$	$2\pounds_{m1}$	$\pounds_{m1}$	$-\pounds_{M2}$	$-2\pounds_{B1}$	$\pounds_b$	$-\pounds_{M2}$	0	$\pounds_M$	$-\pounds_{m2}$	$-\pounds_{m1}$	0	$\pounds_{m1}$	$\pounds_{M2}$
$\pounds_{M2}$	0	$-\pounds_\tau$	$c'\pounds_y$	$\pounds_{m2}$	$\pounds_{m2}$	$2\pounds_{m2}$	$2\pounds_{m2}$	$\pounds_{M1}$	$\pounds_b$	$-2\pounds_{B2}$	$\pounds_{M1}$	$-\pounds_M$	0	$-\pounds_{M1}$	$-\pounds_{m2}$	0	0	$-\pounds_{M1}$
$\pounds_b$	$-\pounds_y$	$-\pounds_x$	0	$2\pounds_m$	$\pounds_M$	$\pounds_M$	$\pounds_M$	$2\pounds_B$	$\pounds_{M1}$	$\pounds_{M2}$	$2\pounds_B$	$\pounds_{m2}$	$\pounds_{m1}$	0	0	$\pounds_m$	$-\pounds_m$	$-2\pounds_B$
$\pounds_s$	$-\pounds_x$	$-\pounds_y$	0	0	0	0	0	0	$\pounds_{M2}$	$\pounds_{M1}$	0	$\pounds_{m1}$	$\pounds_{m2}$	0	0	0	0	0
$\pounds_{s1}$	0	$-\pounds_x$	$-\pounds_t$	0	0	0	0	$-\pounds_b$	$-\pounds_{M2}$	0	$-\pounds_b$	0	$-\pounds_{m2}$	$-\pounds_m$	0	0	0	$\pounds_b$
$\pounds_{s2}$	$-\pounds_y$	0	$-\pounds_t$	0	0	0	0	$\pounds_b$	0	$-\pounds_{M1}$	$\pounds_b$	$-\pounds_{m1}$	0	$\pounds_m$	0	0	0	$-\pounds_b$
$\pounds_0$	$\pounds_x$	$-\pounds_y$	0	$-2\pounds_b$	$-\pounds_b$	$-\pounds_b$	$-\pounds_b$	0	$-\pounds_{m2}$	$-\pounds_{m1}$	0	$\pounds_{M1}$	$2\pounds_b$	$\pounds_m$	0	$-\pounds_b$	$\pounds_b$	0

$\tau = c't$

$$\pounds_x = \frac{\partial}{\partial x}, \quad \pounds_y = \frac{\partial}{\partial y}, \quad \pounds_t = \frac{\partial}{\partial t}, \quad \pounds_\tau = \frac{\partial}{\partial \tau}; \quad \left(\partial_{\text{variable}} = \frac{\partial}{\partial(\text{variable})} \right).$$

$$\pounds_B = x\partial_x - y\partial_y, \quad \pounds_{B1} = t\partial_t - x\partial_x, \quad \pounds_{B2} = t\partial_t - y\partial_y;$$

$$\pounds_m = y\partial_x - x\partial_y = \pounds_M = -\pounds_0, \quad \pounds_{m1} = \tau\partial_x + x\partial_\tau, \quad \pounds_{m2} = \tau\partial_y + y\partial_\tau;$$

$$\pounds_M = \pounds_m = -\pounds_0, \quad \pounds_{M1} = x\partial_\tau - \tau\partial_x, \quad \pounds_{M2} = y\partial_\tau - \tau\partial_y;$$

$$\pounds_b = y\partial_x + x\partial_y, \quad \pounds_0 = -y\partial_x + x\partial_y, \quad \pounds_{s1} = x\partial_x + t\partial_t, \quad \pounds_{s2} = y\partial_y + t\partial_t.$$

That the neuron is the cortical counterpart of the local phase portrait of the dynamical system associated with a Lie group germ has been treated elsewhere at length (Hoffman, 1968), and here we shall do no more than attempt to unify the approach somewhat further with the ideas broached in (Hoffman, 1971) for registration of proprioceptor inputs. Subsequently we will trace the course of an afferent volley through the depths of the cortex, discussing the sequence of Lie derivatives (and thus Lie subgroups) that acts upon the position and time information presented to the visual cortex by the optic radiation. This last will be largely conditioned by the requirement that neuronal processing must be such as to induce at each stage some relative invariant of the groups of the Lie derivatives in $\mathfrak{B}$. In its full generality—just any invariant—this can lead to a great multiplicity of possible Lie derivative sequences, and hence neuronal interactions. In the interest of brevity we will limit the treatment here to those sequences that preserve the same relative invariant throughout.

A Possible Means for Incorporating Psychophysical Parameter Inputs Into Neuron Morphology

We first take up, then, the following possible means for incorporating parameter group inputs into neuronal structure and function. The approach is based on formula (60) and (Hoffman, 1971). Suppose a certain neuron embodies, in some portion of its morphology, some Lie derivative of $\mathfrak{B}$:

$$\mathfrak{L}_{(1)} = X_1(x, y, t)\partial_\xi + X_2(x, y, t)\partial_\eta, \tag{64}$$

where ξ and η denote any two of the three variables x, y, t (or τ). Expression (64) applies to a one-parameter Lie (sub)group in plane-time. Consider now a corresponding 2-parameter (sub)group:

$$\mathfrak{L}_{(2)} = \kappa_1 X_1 \partial_\xi + \kappa_2 X_2 \partial_\eta, \tag{65}$$

where κ_1 and κ_2 might correspond respectively to the relative infinitesimal contributions of visual azimuth and elevation angle, say. Any other pair of psychophysical parameters would do as well.

If we form the bracket product of $\mathfrak{L}_{(1)}$ and $\mathfrak{L}_{(2)}$, we obtain

$$[\mathfrak{L}_{(1)}, \mathfrak{L}_{(2)}] = (\kappa_2 - \kappa_1)[X_1\partial_\xi, X_2\partial_\eta] = (\kappa_2 - \kappa_1)(X_1\partial_\xi X_2\partial_\eta - X_2\partial_\eta X_1\partial_\xi), \tag{66}$$

which vanishes, thus implying the interchangeability of $\mathfrak{L}_{(1)}$ and $\mathfrak{L}_{(2)}$, whenever $\kappa_2 = \kappa_1$. We propose this as a *possible* means for incorporating proprioceptor inputs into neuronal structure. That is, interactions ('circulating neuronal activity' or interneurons) take place either within the same neuron or between neurons of appropriate morphology that tend toward interchangeability $([\mathfrak{L}_{(1)}, \mathfrak{L}_{(2)}] = 0)$. When interchangeability has been established, then $\kappa_1 = \kappa_2$. This yields a reference value for κ_1 from which the original difference value of

κ_2 can be determined as

$$\kappa_2 = \kappa_1 + (\kappa_2 - \kappa_1),$$

simply by selection among the neuron's processes and synaptic junctions. We thus have a sort of combinatorial selection principle among neuronal processes that adjusts any given stimulus pattern in such a way as to compare local parameter values. If several Lie derivatives are involved, as with $\pounds_m$, $\pounds_M$, and $\pounds_B$, for instance, then several such parameter differences would be adjusted to zero by selection among neuronal processes of appropriate parameterization, and several pairs of parameters corresponding to proprioceptor inputs would be determined thereby.

We hasten to add that such a means of incorporating parameter-group inputs seems to be *possible*, based on formula (60) and what little is known of the details of neuronal interconnectivity and real-time function. But it is, at this stage, only a theoretical prediction, available as a null hypothesis but untested experimentally. It does point up the importance of microelectrode studies of several adjacent neurons *simultaneously* that would provide us with a real-time picture of lateral inhibition and facilitation as well as the lateral and 'vertical' flows through the cortex.

The Course of an Afferent Volley Through the Visual Cortex

We have elsewhere (Hoffman, 1968) argued that, based on the appropriate neuronal morphology, $\pounds_x$ and $\pounds_y$ must reside in the plexiform layer; $\pounds_s$ is represented by stellate cells; and $\pounds_b$, $\pounds_B$, and some aspects of $\pounds_m$ are represented morphologically by pyramidal neurons.

Now an afferent form stimulus will in general be rather more complicated than a constancy orbit (or orbits). But when one of the latter is presented, it must be processed in such a way as to either recognize it at the outset or else preserve it as a relative invariant pending its recognition by annulment, i.e. as an absolute invariant, at some later stage of cortical processing. These considerations (and some tedious but routine calculations) yield Table 4.

A brief examination of Table 4 makes it clear why most primary visual afferents terminate in layers III and IV (Sholl, 1956, Figure 12). $\pounds_s$ is common to nearly all the relative invariant sequences, and layer III consists predominantly of stellate cells (Sholl, op cit). The other initial members of a sequence, such as $\pounds_0$, $\pounds_m$, $\pounds_b$, consist of Lie derivatives whose morphological counterparts would be either pericellular nests or pyramidal neurons, with or without recurrent collaterals (Hoffman, 1968). (In assessing morphological counterparts it is essential not to overlook the fact that the cortex is subject to considerable folding (Sholl, op cit; Hoffman, 1971).) The concentration of type P4 neurons at the top of layer IV (Sholl, op cit), just below the mass of stellate cells in layer III, suggest interactions between $\pounds_s$ and $\pounds_0$ or $\pounds_s$ and $\pounds_m$. This possibility is supported also by the table of Lie products (Table 3), in which the corresponding brackets vanish, so that the associated Lie subgroups are abelian.

Table 4. Relative invariants corresponding to absolute invariants and their associated Lie Derivatives

(1) Constancy	(2) Absolute invariants	(3) Lie derivatives & sequences giving (2) as relative invariant	(4) Lie derivative(s) for which (2) is an absolute invariant	
Shape constancy				
Location				
Horizontal	(y, t) = const.	$\pounds_s; \pounds_y, \pounds_t; \pounds_B$	$\pounds_x$	→ 0
Vertical	(x, t) = const.	$\pounds_s; \pounds_x, \pounds_t; \pounds_B$	$\pounds_y$	→ 0
Temporal	(x, y) = const.	$\pounds_s; \pounds_x, \pounds_y; \pounds_B$	$\pounds_t$	→ 0
Orientation	$x^2 + y^2$ = const.	$\pounds_s$	$\pounds_0, \pounds_m, \pounds_M$	→ 0
Afferent binocularity	$x^2 - y^2$ = const.	$\pounds_s; \pounds_B$	$\pounds_b$	→ 0
Efferent binocularity	xyt = const.	$\pounds_s; \pounds_x, \pounds_y; \pounds_t$	$\pounds_B$	→ 0
Size constancy	y/x = const.	$\pounds_0, \pounds_m; \pounds_b; \pounds_{s1}, \pounds_{s2}; \pounds_M; \pounds_B; \pounds_t$	$\pounds_s$	→ 0
	t/x = const.	$\pounds_{m1}; \pounds_s, \pounds_{s2}; \pounds_{M1}; \pounds_B; \pounds_y$	$\pounds_{s1}$	→ 0
	t/y = const.	$\pounds_{m2}; \pounds_s, \pounds_{s1}; \pounds_{M2}; \pounds_B; \pounds_x$	$\pounds_{s2}$	→ 0
Invariant movement perception	$\tau^2 - x^2 - y^2$ = const.	$\pounds_s; \pounds_B$	$\pounds_m$ (also $\pounds_0$)	→ 0
Cyclopean (Ego-centred) perception	$x^2 + y^2 + \tau^2$ = const.	$\pounds_s$	$\pounds_M$ (also $\pounds_0, \pounds_m$)	→ 0

Many other sequences of cortical neuron interactions are possible besides those of Table 4 if one simply requires that the sequence of neuronal processing lead through *some* chain of relative invariants to *some* absolute invariant, not necessarily the one first presented as a stimulus pattern. However, an adequate discussion of all these possibilities would be so lengthy as to require a paper in its own right.

It is also worthy of note in Table 4 that $\pounds_s$ precedes, in nearly all instances, one or more of $\pounds_x$, $\pounds_y$, or $\pounds_t$ in the afferent phase. ($\pounds_M$ and $\pounds_B$ are regarded as marking the commencement of the efferent phase.) Sholl (op cit, p. 14) has the following to say concerning the cytoarchitecture of the plexiform layer:

(The plexiform layer) 'is packed with two kinds of fibres. There are large numbers of very fine axons running from considerable distances parallel to the surface. Many of these are the axons of stellate cells situated deeper in the cortex whose axons run outwards and then, turning at right angles, run parallel to the pial surface. The other fibres are relatively stouter and are the terminations of the apical dendrites of pyramidal cells situated at all depths of the cortex.'

This configuration is consistent with Colonnier's rectangular grid of nerve fibers in the plexiform layer, crisscrossed by a feltwork of finer fibres (Colonnier,

1964), as well as the phylogenetic configuration in lower animals (Young, 1965).

The well nigh universal progression from $\mathfrak{L}_s$ to $\mathfrak{L}_x$, $\mathfrak{L}_y$, $\mathfrak{L}_t$ may also constitute an explanation of Stryker and Sherk's (1975) anomalous findings with respect to a visual field enriched in rectilinear contours. The microelectrode was advanced through the depths of the cortex in their experiments, rather than being held within the plexiform layer. Inevitably then their observations would represent a blend of the radially symmetric response of the stellate cells of $\mathfrak{L}_s$ and the rectilinear response of $\mathfrak{L}_x$ and $\mathfrak{L}_y$, which act along the rectangular grid of orbits $(x, y) = $ const.

V. Higher Form Vision, Prolonged Lie Derivatives, and Symplectic Manifolds

We come now to the final aspect of our model of visual perception and in effect close the loop by returning to the introductory discussion of the manifolds $\mathfrak{M}$, $\overline{\mathfrak{M}}$, and the mathematical expression of transformation group (4).

We have seen that neonatally the General Linear Group $GL(\mathbb{R}^3 \times T)$ provides a basis for visual perception, as in equation (2). It is known (Boothby, 1975) that $GL(\mathbb{R}^n)$ is a basis for the *tangent bundle*[2] to $\mathbb{R}^n$, i.e.

$$GL(\mathbb{R}^n) \cong T\mathbb{R}^n.$$

However, we are interested in the perception of visual contours, not perinatal vectorfields, so we need something more than (67), viz., a visual form in the sense of the following arbitrary function of $(x, y) \in \mathfrak{M}$ and the first m derivatives of y with respect to x:

$$F(x, y, y', \ldots, y^{(m)}) = \text{const.} \tag{68}$$

We have now replaced y as an independent variable in the plane with the function $y(x)$, which actually defines a contour in $\overline{\mathfrak{M}}$, and its several derivatives. We are then on $\overline{T\mathfrak{M}}$ rather than $T\mathbb{R}^2$. Since contours are involved, so too are differential forms, and hence the mathematical dual of $\overline{T\mathfrak{M}}$, the so-called cotangent bundle,[2] $\overline{T\mathfrak{M}}$.

The importance of the transition from y to $y(x)$ is difficult to exaggerate in terms of the psychology involved. Once the perceptual system has established a contour to follow along, feed-forward phenomena become possible, and even such things as continuity ('good continuation') in the visual Gestalt follow. It is essentially the difference between passive and active visuomotor experience. Active determination of a contour $y(x)$, having finer and finer degrees of precision $y^{(k)}(x)$, $(k = 1, 2, \ldots, m)$, enables one to learn whatever form may be involved better and more quickly.

The way this process comes about neuropsychologically is once again through the action of the Lie derivative $\mathfrak{L}_X$, which 'drags the flow' along the contour to which X is bound as tangent vectorfield. But there has to be something more to yield a polygonal arc—beyond the 'limit of visual acuity'—approximation to a smooth contour in the physical world. This is provided by the prolonged Lie derivative

$$\mathbf{£}_X^{(m)} = \mathbf{£}_X + \sum_{k=1}^{m} X_{(k)}(x,y,y', \ldots , y^{(k)}) \, \partial_y(k),$$ (69)

which generates so-called contact transformations on $\overline{\mathfrak{M}}$ (Hoffman, 1970). What this means is that the successive tangent vectors to a given contour line up head-to-tail in such a way as to make a polygonal arc approximation to that contour. When they do not, the vectorfield on $\mathfrak{M}$ generates texture and gradient, rather than form, in the visual image. This corresponds to a higher order tangent bundle $\overline{T\mathfrak{M}}_{(k)}$ and cotangent bundle $\overline{T\mathfrak{M}}_{(k)}$, as well as the extended T. G.

$$G \times \mathfrak{M}_{(k)} \rightarrow \mathfrak{M}_{(k)}.$$

The Lie derivative itself leads to absolute or relative invariants, as we have seen above in equations (17) and (20). The kth order differential invariant is similarly given by annulment of a function by $\mathbf{£}_X^{(k)}$:

$$\mathbf{£}^{(k)} u_k(x, y, y', \ldots, y^{(k)}) = 0 \Longleftrightarrow u_k \text{ is a } k\text{th } order \ differential \ invariant.$$ (70)

When in place of a function we have a differential form

$$\mathbf{£}^{(k)} \quad (dy^{(k-1)} - y^{(k)} \, dx) \quad = 0, (k = 1, 2, \ldots, m)$$ (71)

then this constitutes a distinguished 1-form associated with the manifold $\overline{\mathfrak{M}}$ (or some submanifold of it), and we have a *contact transformation*. The coefficients $X_{(k)}$ in (69) can readily be determined from the fact that d and $\mathbf{£}_X^{(k)}$ commute.

But if the absolute invariant is known, as in processing for the constancies, and the first differential invariant as well, then all else follows practically automatically. In place of the representation (68) for an arbitrary mth order form, we may write (Hoffman, 1970)

$$\frac{d^{m-1}u_1}{du^{m-1}} = G_m\left(u, u_1, \frac{du_1}{du}, \ldots, \frac{d^{m-2}u_1}{du^{m-2}}\right),$$ (72)

so that the perception of forms with arbitrary degrees of complexity is possible in terms of derivatives of $(m-1)$st order involving only the first differential invariant and the absolute invariant. Lateral inhibition is really only another name for the taking of first differences, so that a progressive network of such lateral inhibitions would provide a cortical counterpart of (72).

It was argued in (Hoffman, 1970) that this is how the visual and pshcyovisual cortex actually generate basic and higher perceptions, i.e. as absolute and differential invariants satisfying (17) and (70), respectively. The complex and hypercomplex response fields found in areas 18 and 19 by Hubel and Wiesel appear to be neuroanatomical correlates of higher differential invariants that are generated in the way indicated by (72). From this point of view, the so-called 'feature detectors' in the visual cortex are actually constancy detectors, or better, constancy processors. Evoked visual contours from area 17 are just the orbits of the constancies. On the other hand, evoked visual forms in the psychovisual cortex constitute higher forms, but lacking any definite size or location in space, suggesting that the redundancy inherent in the many ways of presenting a form stimulus has been removed at an earlier stage by constancy deprocessing.

There is one aspect of the progression from absolute to differential invariant in the visual cortex-psychovisual cortex flow that we did not touch upon in the earlier paper (Hoffman, 1970), and we take the opportunity to discuss that matter.

If an absolute invariant is presented as a stimulus, it must be processed as a relative invariant rather than be annulled if it is to be passed on to the psychovisual cortex in such a way as to be processed as a first, or higher order, differential invariant. We now demonstrate that this is in fact possible for the simple case involving u and u_1 only. In that event the form (68) presented as a stimulus may be written as

$$F(u(x, y), u_1(x, y, y')) = 0, \tag{73}$$

where u and u_1 are the absolute and first differential invariant, respectively, of the group of $\pounds_X$. The form (73) will be acted upon by the cortical counterpart of $\pounds_X$ somewhere in the visual cortex to yield

$$\pounds_X F = (X_1 \partial_x + X_2 \partial_y) F(u, u_1) = \frac{\partial F}{\partial u} \pounds_X u + \frac{\partial F}{\partial u_1} \pounds_X u_1$$

$$= \frac{\partial F}{\partial u_1} \pounds_X u_1(x, y, y'). \tag{74}$$

The right hand side of (74) will not vanish in general, and hence F will not be an absolute invariant of the group of $\pounds_X$. But is F then a relative invariant of the group under prolongation, i.e. the group of $\pounds_X^{(1)}$? If so, it will, as indicated by (70), be annulled by the action of $\pounds_X^{(1)}$. To show that this is actually what happens, let u_1 be a canonical variable, i.e.,

$$\pounds_X u = 0, \qquad \pounds_X u_1 = 1, \qquad \pounds_X^{(1)} u_1 = 0, \tag{75}$$

from which it follows, since $\pounds_X = \pounds_X^{(1)} - X_{(1)} \partial_{y'}$, that

$$\pounds_X = \pounds = \partial_{u_1} = -X_{(1)} \partial_{y'}.$$

Then from (74) and the second of (75),

$$\pounds_X^{(1)} \pounds_X F = \pounds^{(1)} \pounds F = \pounds^{(1)} \Phi(u, u_1), \tag{76}$$

where

$$\frac{\partial F}{\partial u_1} = \Phi(u, u_1).$$

64

It then follows from (76) that

$$\mathfrak{L}^{(1)}\Phi = \frac{\partial \Phi}{\partial u}\mathfrak{L}u + \frac{\partial \Phi}{\partial u_1}\mathfrak{L}^{(1)}u_1 = 0. \tag{77}$$

It follows from the definitions and equation (77) that the original form stimulus $F(u, u_1)$ is a relative invariant of the group of $\mathfrak{L}_X$ and, in turn, an absolute invariant of the prolonged L.T.G. The form F will therefore be recognized by annulment at this later stage of visual processing. The kth order case will be more complicated but proceed in essentially the same fashion.

Prolongation of the Lie derivative to obtain higher invariants, and so a higher form, is not an intrinsic operation. Though $\mathfrak{L}_X$ remains the same throughout, $\mathfrak{L}_X^{(k)}$ may change depending upon the visual manifold at hand (Guggenheimer, 1963). This is strongly suggestive of modern cognitive psychology, according to which only the basic 'information processors' are permanently stored, all else being generated anew each time that some appropriate stimulus is presented. Thus the form will be recognized all right, but it will differ slightly each time from what it was before.

The manifold upon which the prolonged Lie derivative acts to induce contact transformations is a so-called symplectic manifold (Abraham and Marsden, 1967). Such manifolds are intimately connected with the simplicial category, which plays a fundamental role in Piagetian and Bruner psychology, in particular the Concrete Operations Period of Piaget's developmental sequence (Hoffman, 1976).

Notes

(1) As noted, the coordinates $\tilde{x}$ and $\tilde{y}$ are obtained from the x, y-coordinates by rotation through an angle of $\phi + \pi/4$. The equation of the Hillebrand hyperbolas $x^2 - w^2 - 2xw \cot 2\phi = 1$ is thus reduced to canonical form $(\tilde{x}^2 - \tilde{w}^2)/(\sin 2\phi/\cos 4\phi) = 1$, or with $z = 0$, so that $w = y$, to $(\tilde{x}^2 - \tilde{y}^2)/(\sin 2\phi/\cos 4\phi) = 1$, over $\mathfrak{M}$. The projected form of the Hillebrand hyperbolas is an invariant under the group of (41a).
(2) A tangent bundle to a space S is the collection of all tangent spaces to S. Similarly, a cotangent bundle to S is the union of all cotangent spaces to S. The two kinds of bundles are dual to one another.

References

Abraham, R. L. and J. Marsden (1967). *Foundations of Mechanics*, Addison-Wesley, Reading, Mass.
Altman, J. (1967). Postnatal growth and differentiation of the mammalian brain, with implications for a morphological theory of memory, in *The Neurosciences*, G. C. Quarton et al. (eds.), Rockfeller Univ. Press, N.Y., pp. 723–743.
Blank, A. (1953). The Luneburg Theory of Binocular Visual Space, *J. Opt. Soc. Am.*, **43**, 717–727.
Blank, A. (1957). The Geometry of Vision I, II, *British J. Physiol. Optics* (N.S.), **14**, 154–169; 222–235.
Blank, A. (1958). Analysis of Experiments in Binocular Space Perception, *J. Opt. Soc. Am.*, **48**, 911–925.

Blank, A. (1978). (this volume).

Boothby, W. H. (1975). *An Intro. to Differentiable Manifolds and Riemannian Geometry*, Academic Press, N.Y.

Bourbaki, N. (1972). *Éléments de mathématique. Groupes et algebres de Lie*, Chaps. 2 & 3, Hermann, Paris.

Caelli, T. M. (1978). (this volume).

Campbell, J. E. (1903). *Intro. Treatise on Lie's Theory of Finite Cont. Transformation Groups*, Clarendon Press, Oxford.

Cohen, A. (1931). *An Introduction to the Lie Theory of One-Parameter Groups*, Hafner, N.Y.

Cohn, P. M. (1957). *Lie groups*, Cambridge U. Press, Cambridge.

Colonnier, M. (1964). The Tangential Organization of the Visual Cortex, *J. Anatomy (London)*, **98**, 327–344.

Eisenhart, L. P. (1961). *Continuous Groups of Transformations*, Dover, N.Y.

Estable, C. (1961). Considerations on the histological bases of neuro-physiology, in *Brain Mechanisms and Learning*, A. Fessard et al. (eds.), Blackwell, Oxford, pp. 309–334.

Geldard, F. A. (1972). *The Human Senses*, Wiley, N.Y., 2nd edn.

Gibson, J. J. (1950). *The Perception of the Visual World*, Houghton Mifflin, Boston.

Glees, P. (1961). *Experimental Neurology*, Clarendon Press, Oxford.

Greub, W. (1963). *Linear Algebra*, Springer-Verlag, Berlin, 2nd ed.

Guggenheimer, H. W. (1963). *Differential Geometry*, McGraw-Hill, N.Y.

Gunther, N. (1961a). Attempted Establishment of an Exact Theory of Visual Space (in German), *Optik*, **18**, 3–21.

Gunther, N. (1961b). New Knowledge on the Extent of the Visual Space, *Optik*, **18**, 569–570.

Hake, H. W. (1966). Form Discrimination and the Invariance of Form, in *Pattern Recognition*, L. Uhr (ed.), Wiley, N.Y. Pp. 142–173.

Hamermesh, M. (1962). *Group Theory and its Application to Physical Problems*, Addison-Wesley, Reading, Mass. Chap. 8.

Hirsch, M. W. and S. Smale (1974). *Differential Equations, Dynamical Systems, and Linear Algebra*, Academic Press, N.Y.

Hochstadt, H. (1964). *Differential Equations: A Modern Approach*, Holt, Rinehart & Winston, N.Y.

Hoffman, W. C. (1966). The Lie algebra of visual perception, *J. Math. Psychol.*, **3**, 65–98. Errata, *ibid.*, **4** (1967), 348–349.

Hoffman, W. C. (1967). *The Differential Topology of Form Perception*, unpublished monograph.

Hoffman, W. C. (1968). The Neuron as a Lie Group Germ and a Lie Product, *Quart. Applied Math.*, **25**, 423–440.

Hoffman, W. C. (1970). Higher Visual Perception as Prolongation of the Basic Lie Transformation Group, *Math. Biosciences*, **6**, 437–471.

Hoffman, W. C. (1971). Memory Grows, *Kybernetik*, **8**, 151–157.

Hoffman, W. C. (1976). A Mathematical Framework for Piagetian Psychology, preprint.

Hubel, D. H. and T. H. Wiesel (1963). Shape and arrangement of columns in cat's striate cortex, *J. Physiol.*, **165**, 559–568.

Jeannerod, M. et al. (1968). Deplacements et fixations du regard dans l'exploration libre d'une scene visuelle, *Vision Res.*, **8**, 81.

Jung, R. (1961). Neuronal Integration in the Visual Cortex and its Significance for Visual Information, in *Sensory Communication*, W. A. Rosenblith (ed.), M.I.T. Press, Cambridge, Mass. Pp. 627–674.

Kienle, G. (1963). Geometrische Axiome, nicht-euklidische Abbildungsmodelle und Sehraum, *Optik*, **20**, 353–372.

Klein, F. (1960). *Vorlesungen uber nicht-euklidische Geometrie*, Chelsea, Bronx, N.Y.

Kowalewski, G. (1931). *Vorlesungen uber allgemeine naturliche Geometrie und Liesche Transformationsgruppen*, Walter de Gruyter Co., Berlin.

Krasnosel'skiy, M. A., A. I. Perov, A. I. Povolotskiy, and P. P. Zabreiko (1966). *Plane Vector Fields*, Acad. Press, N.Y.

Krech, D. and R. S. Crutchfield (1958). *Elements of Psychology*, Knopf, N.Y.

Li, Ch.-L., C. Cullen, and H. H. Jasper (1956a). Laminar Microelectrode Studies of Specific Somatosensory Cortical Potentials, *J. Neurophysiol.*, **19**, 111–130.

Li, Ch.-L., C. Cullen and H. H. Jasper (1956b). Laminar Microelectrode Analysis of Cortical Unspecific Recruiting Responses and Spontaneous Rhythms, *J. Neurophysiol.*, **19**, 131–143.

Lorente de No, R. (1949). Chapter XV of *Physiology of the Nervous System*, by J. F. Fulton, Oxford U. Press, N.Y.

Luneburg, R. K. (1947). *Mathematical Analysis of Binocular Vision*, Princeton Univ. Press, Princeton.

Luneberg, R. (1948). Metric Methods in Binocular Visual Perception, in *Courant Anniv. Volume*, K. O. Friedrichs et al. (eds.), Interscience, N.Y. Pp. 215–240.

Luneburg, R. K. (1950). The Metric of Binocular Visual Space, *J. Opt. Soc. Am.* **40**, 627–642.

Nelson, E. (1967). *Tensor Analysis*, Princeton U. Press, Princeton.

Noton, D. and L. Stark (1971). Scanpaths in Eye Movements during Pattern Perception, *Science*, **171**, 308–311.

Ochs, S. (1965). *Elements of Neurophysiology*, Wiley, N.Y.

Pitts, W. and W. S. McCulloch (1947). How we know universals. The perception of auditory and visual forms, *Bull. Math. Biophysics*, **9**, 127–147.

Regnier, A. Recherches sur le verbalisme. Les algebres de Lie de la perception visuelle, preprint.

Rindler, W. (1960). *Special Relativity*, Oliver & Boyd, Edinburgh.

Rindler, W. (1969). *Essential Relativity*, Van Nostrand-Reinhold, N.Y.

Schutz, J. W. (1973). *Foundations of Special Relativity: Kinematic Axioms for Minkowski Space-Time*, Springer-Verlag, N.Y.

Shipley, T. (1957). Convergence Function in Binocular Visual Space. I. A Note on Theory, *J. Opt. Soc. Am.*, **47**, 795–803.

Sholl, D. A. (1956). *The Organization of the Cerebral Cortex*, Hafner, N.Y.

Slutsky, E. (1937). The Summation of Random Causes as the Source of Cyclic Processes, *Econometrica*, **5**, 105–146.

Smythies, J. R. (1959a,b). The Stroboscopic Patterns. I. The Dark Phase. II. The Phenomenology of the Bright-Phase and After-Images, *British J. Psychol.*, **50**, 106–116; 305–324.

Stephenson, G. and C. W. Kilmister (1958). *Special Relativity for Physicists*, Longman, Green, London.

Stryker, M. P. and H. Sherk. Modification of Cortical Orientation of Selectivity in the Cat by Restricted Visual Experience: A Reexamination, *Science*, **190**, 904–905.

Tauber, E. S. and S. Koffler (1966). Optomotor Response in Human Infants to Apparent Motion: Evidence of Innateness, *Science*, **152**, 382–383.

Von Fieandt, K. (1966). *The World of Perception*, Dorsey Press, Homewood, Ill.

Weyl, H. (1925). Theorie der Darstellung kontinuierlicher halb-einfacher Gruppen durch lineare Transformationen. I, II, III, *Werke*. Vol. 2, pp. 543–647.

Young, J. Z. (1965). Two memory stores in one brain, *Endeavour*, **24**, 13–20.

Zajaczkowska, A. (1956a). Experimental Determination of Luneburg's Constants σ and K, *Quart. J. Exp. Psychol.*, **8**, 66–78.

Zajaczkowska, A. (1956b). Experimental Test of Luneburg's Theory. Horopter and Alley Experiments, *J. Opt. Soc. Am.*, **46**, 514–527.

Zeeman, E. C. (1964). Causality implies the Lorentz group, *J. Math. Physics*, **5**, 490–493.

Chapter 3

Visual Apparent Motion and the Calculus of Variations

David H. Foster

Abstract. The rapid sequential presentation of two distinct objects in the human visual field induces, under suitable conditions, the illusion of a single object undergoing a smooth continuous transformation from the first to the second form. It is suggested that in generating this illusion the visual system operates according to variational principles and chooses those impleting motions which, in some suitable space, have minimum energy. Implications of this hypothesis are discussed in relation both to experimental data on apparent motion and to the general problem of visual pattern recognition.

1. Introduction

An illusion of movement occurs when two suitably shaped and suitably timed, spatially resolvable flashes of light are presented in sequence to the eye (Exner, 1875; Wertheimer, 1912). When this apparent motion is visually indistinguishable from the perception of a real object undergoing movement, the illusion is called *optimal motion* or *beta* motion (Wertheimer, 1912; Kenkel, 1913; Kolers, 1972). A common demonstration of beta motion is given by cinematography and certain flashing neon displays. The illusion has particular importance in that it evidences an active figure-construction process by the visual system; for, as Kolers (1972, p. 18) has emphasized, the phenomenon does not involve a simple perceptual replication of one of the stimulus figures across the intervening space, but the generation of an illusory object that smoothly and continuously changes in both position *and form* to fit with the disparate stimuli.

Two of the classical theories of apparent movement are the excitation theory of Wertheimer (1912) and Köhler (1923), and the figural theory of Linke and Hillebrand (see Neff, 1936). In the excitation theory, the separate stimulation of regions of the retina is assumed to give rise to a spread of activity in the neural substrate which coincides with that occurring in real motion (Motokawa, 1970,

Chapter 10); in the figural theory, it is supposed that motion is inferred by the system because of the disparity in the locations and form of the two stimuli which are perceived as being different representations of the same object. Neither theory adequately fits all the experimental data (Kolers, 1972, Chapter 11). In particular, the excitation theory is incompatible with the 'motion-in-depth' effects obtainable with some stimulus pairs (Neuhaus, 1930; Kolers and Pomerantz, 1971), and in its vector form due to Brown and Voth (1937), the excitation theory gives false predictions for the direction of motion which can be induced between certain single and multiple stimuli (Kolers, 1972, Chapter 4); on the other hand, the figural theory fails to explain why motion is more likely to be seen between patterns which are close together and 'different' than between patterns which are further apart and the same (Kolers and Pomerantz, 1971; Navon, 1976).

A composite model which accounts for several apparent movement phenomena, including the case of motion seen between 'different' patterns, has been described by Kolers (1972, Chapter 7). The model has two separate channels, one for motion and space generation and one for pattern generation, linked to each other by a correlator unit. Navon (1976) has suggested an alternative unified scheme, which involves a difference in processing time for shape and location determination. These models are, however, essentially organizational, and not of the form that enables, for example, the path of the motion between two given patterns to be predicted.

It is suggested in the present study that the distinction between object position and form that occurs in the above theories is, at least technically, unnecessary, and there are, as will be seen, advantages in treating the two variables on the same basis. Thus given an object A say, and some transformed version $\tau(A)$ of A, if the transformation $\tau = \tau_1$ comes from the group of translations of the plane, then the disparity may be viewed as one in location (Figure 1(a)), whereas if $\tau = \tau_2$ comes from the group of linear transformations of the plane, then the disparity may be viewed as one in shape (Figure 1(b)). But, if both the groups are embedded in a larger group, say the group of affine motions of the plane, then as mappings preserving linear structure, τ_1 and τ_2 have exactly the same status. The question of the disparity in A and $\tau(A)$ in Figure 1(a) and (b) may then be decided in terms of some suitable distance measure on the affine group. Specifying the distances of the transformations τ_1 and τ_2 from the iden-

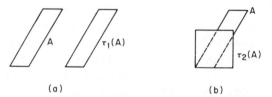

(a)   (b)

Figure 1. Stimulus pairs A, $\tau(A)$ for (a) $\tau = \tau_1$ a rigid motion and (b) $\tau = \tau_2$ a linear transformation

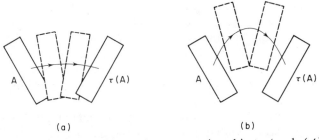

Figure 2. Two possible motions connecting objects A and $\tau(A)$

tity transformation does not, in fact, fix the motion completely. For example, in Figure 2 a bar-shaped object A and transform $\tau(A)$ are shown with hypothetical beta motions following in (a) a shallow curve and in (b) a sharp curve. Which, if either of the motions is actually selected by the visual system ought, in accordance with Maupertuis, to correspond to the 'shortest' or 'least-energetic' of the possible paths in perceptual space. In general, the problem of finding those curves for which some appropriate energy function achieves a minimum value among all curves having the same end-points is dealt with by the calculus of variations (see, for example, Gelfand and Fomin, 1963; Milnor, 1963). In the present case, these curves are in the manifold formed by all the local transformations which can be applied to A. Depending on the model chosen, there is a naturally associated energy function, which, for a given transformation τ, gives rise to at least one energy-minimizing time-parameterized family of transformations, connecting the identity to τ. This family of transformations is usually unique.

In what follows, two schemes for apparent motion are described. The first is oriented towards the excitation theory and the second towards the figural theory. Both make use of variational principles and both can be adjusted to fit most of the experimental data on the existence or otherwise of motion between various objects. It is in their predictions of the shape of the motion, however, that the models are found to differ. These predictions are compared with the corresponding data, and their significance discussed in relation to the general problem of visual pattern recognition.

2. Notation and Definitions

For simplicity we deal with the monocular situation, though there is little difficulty in extending the discussion to the binocular case. Let R denote the real line. Consider a fixed 2-dimensional plane R^2, perpendicular to the visual axis, and let R^2 be endowed with a fixed mapping C of R^2 into R, the *background field*, which assigns to each point in R^2, unless otherwise indicated, some specified luminance $C(x) \geqq 0$ (white-light stimuli, say). A visual *object* or *pattern A* on R^2 is (at least) a mapping of a non-empty subset U_A of R^2 into R such that $A(x) \geqq 0$ is the luminance of the object at the point $x \in U_A$. Neither background C nor objects A need be continuous functions and the *domain* U_A of A, which can coincide with R^2, need not be an open set. Depending upon the occasion, we may assign to an object a certain mathematical structure, for example, the metric structure arising from the standard metric structure on R^2, or the topological structure arising from the standard topological structure on R^2. Note that there is no loss in generality in using R^2 as background, instead of some fixed sphere centred at the eye, since we shall be concerned only with local properties of the visual field.

Let U be a subset of R^2. The action of an injective mapping $\tau: U \to R^2$, taking U into R^2, on an object A with domain $U_A = U$ is defined by:

$$(\tau(A))(p) = A(\tau^{-1}(p)) \quad \text{for all } p \in \tau(U).$$

The transformed object associates with each point p in its domain the luminance at its preimage $\tau^{-1}(p)$. The mapping τ and its inverse $\tau^{-1}: \tau(U) \to U$ will frequently be assumed differentiable (i.e. τ is a *diffeomorphism* into R^2). The class of a function, vector field, etc. and its domain of definition will always be understood to be such that everything is well-defined.

We now formulate the definition of beta motion in terms of the above quantities. It is convenient, though not strictly necessary, to consider beta motion as if it actually occurs on the plane R^2. Provided all sets and mappings defined on R^2 are understood to be specified only to within visual indistinguishability (Zeeman, 1962; Zadeh, 1965), the subjective illusory motion may certainly be replaced by an equivalent objective real motion. Accordingly, if F denotes the set of all objects on R^2, then given the sequential presentation to the visual system of some object A and transform $\tau(A)$ of A, beta motion between A and $\tau(A)$ is the generation by the visual system of a smooth time-parametrized curve ω in F joining these two objects. It is a smooth curve in the sense that we consider it arising from the action of a (differentiable) 1-parameter family of transformations $\phi: [0, 1] \times U_A \to R^2$, satisfying $\phi(0, p) = p$ and $\phi_1(p) = \tau(p)$ for all $p \in U_A$. The mapping $p \to \phi_t(p) = \phi(t, p)$ is a diffeomorphism of U_A onto $\phi_t(U_A)$. We use γ to denote the mapping $t \to \phi_t$, of $[0, 1]$ into the space of all diffeomorphisms of U_A into R^2. The curve ω in F (see Figure 3) may thus be written

$$\omega: t \in [0, 1] \to (\gamma(t))(A) \in F.$$

Usually A is referred to as the *initial object* and $\tau(A)$ as the *final object*. The

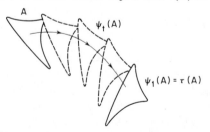

Figure 3. Action of a 1-parameter family of local transformations ϕ_t taking object A into transform $\tau(A)$

symbol τ will always be reserved for the corresponding transformation. Note that the above definition automatically includes the 'plastic deformation' motion described by Kolers and Pomerantz (1971). By hypothesis, the curve ω or γ is chosen such that for some *Lagrangian L*, the *action* $S(\gamma)$ of γ, defined by

$$S(\gamma) = \int_0^1 L(\gamma(t), \gamma'(t))\, dt, \tag{1}$$

where $\gamma'(t)$ is the tangent vector to the curve γ at the point $\gamma(t)$, is minimized within the class of all paths joining $\gamma(0)$ to $\gamma(1)$. The integral $S(\gamma)$ is sometimes called the *energy* (Milnor, 1963).

3. A Figural Theory with Scalar Potential

As was pointed out in the introduction, the excitation theory of apparent motion due to Wertheimer and Köhler and its subsequent modifications have been shown to be inconsistent with certain experimental results. For example, the vector model has been shown by Kolers (1972, Chapter 5) to be false in that with the display of Figure 4(a), a vector addition of forces induced by the stimuli in perceptual space gives the motion of Figure 4(b), whereas it is the split motion of Figure 4(c) that is actually observed.

Nevertheless, with the introduction of a figural component into the excitation scheme, it is possible to account for many of the otherwise anomalous findings by Kolers (1972) and Navon (1976) concerning motion between multiple stimuli, and also for the data obtained by Foster (1975b) concerning the form of the path shapes. The scheme is as follows.

Suppose that there is in perceptual space an interaction between initial object A and final object $\tau(A)$ in such a way that a vector field $F: R^2 \to R^2$ is created in the vicinity of the two objects, and that this vector field arises in the same way as in electrostatics, that is,

$$F(r) = \int_{U_A} \frac{(r-p)}{|r-p|^3}\, ds(p) - \int_{\tau(u_A)} \frac{(r-q)}{|r-q|^3}\, ds(q),$$

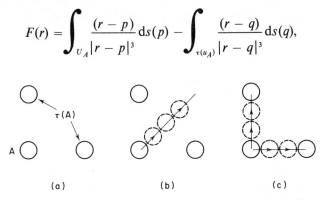

$$(a) \qquad\qquad (b) \qquad\qquad (c)$$

Figure 4. (a) Patterns used in test of vector model (Kolers, 1972, Chapter 5), (b) predicted motion, (c) experimentally observed motion

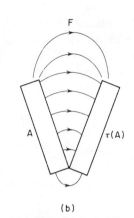

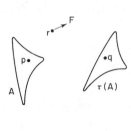

(a)   (b)

Figure 5. (a) Vector field F at r due to stimulus elements at
p and q. (b) Field F due to two bar-shaped objects

where $p \in U_A$, $q \in \tau(U_A)$ (see Figure 5(a)) and ds is the usual surface measure
on R^2. In the case that A is bar-shaped and τ is drawn from the group $E(2)$ of
rigid motions of the plane, F has the form shown in Figure 5(b).

Associated with the vector field F there is a scalar potential function V for
which $F = -\text{grad } V$. We suppose in accordance with the figural theory that the
visual system introduces an illusory object in motion to reconcile the separate
occurrence of A and $\tau(A)$. We further suppose that this illusory object is constrained to transform in such a way that it minimizes the action integral (1) for
the Langrangian L of the form $T - V$, where T is the 'kinetic energy' assigned by
the visual system to the object. It is the imposition of a figure-rationalizing constraint on the natural motion determined by the vector field that makes possible
the satisfactory description of, for example, the split motion referred to earlier.
The term T is obtained in the following way (Marsden et al. 1972). Let D denote
the space of all diffeomorphisms of the domain U_A of A into R^2. Let $\rho \in D$ and
let tangent vectors X, $Y \in T_\rho D$, the tangent space to D at ρ. For each point ρ
in U_A, $X(p)$ and $Y(p)$ are in the tangent space to R^2 at $\rho(p)$. An inner product
$(,)\rho$ on $T_\rho D$ may be defined thus:

$$(X, Y)_\rho = \int_{U_A} \langle X(p), Y(p) \rangle \, ds(p),$$

where $\langle,\rangle$ is the usual inner product on R^2. For a smooth curve $\gamma : [0, 1] \to D$, T
is then defined at time t by

$$T(t) = \tfrac{1}{2}(\gamma'(t), \gamma'(t))_{\gamma(t)}.$$

For the particular case of the bar-shaped objects of Figure 5(b), D may be
replaced by $E(2)$, and the predicted action-minimizing motion $(\gamma(t))(A)$, $t \in$
$[0, 1]$, is then found to be approximately circular. This motion is similar to,
though not precisely the same as, the observed motion (Foster, 1975b) shown in
Figure 6(a).

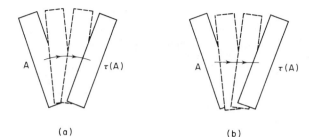

Figure 6. (a) Approximate motion between two bar-shaped objects predicted by scalar potential model. (b) Motion predicted by model with scalar potential component removed

The existence of the vector field is an essential requirement for the path to be curved. If the field is omitted, and the action-minimizing curves γ determined for $L = T$, the resulting motion is found (Foster, 1975b) to correspond to that of a free body, as in Figure 6(b).

The situation when the final object B is not the result of application to the object A of $\tau \in E(2)$, but of $\tau \in E(3)$, the group of rigid motions of R^3, necessarily requires some motion out of the plane R^2. Figure 7 shows the vector field for a pair of bar-shaped objects. (The field is similar to that in Figure 5(b).) If the action-minimizing curve γ is to remain within $E(3)$ for the configuration of Figure 7, the departure of $(\gamma(t))(A)$ from the plane must be minimal. In particular, the motion cannot take the form shown in Figure 8, i.e. a full semicircular rotation in depth. A semicircular motion is, however, obtained experimentally. Thus although motion in R^3 is not incompatible with the scalar potential model described here, the paths are not always of the right form.

A significant property of all the observed motions is that they appear to arise as the actions of segments of 1-parameter groups that is $\gamma(s)\gamma(t) = \gamma(s + t)$ for $s, t, s + t \in [0, 1]$. In the next section we simplify the model by dropping the scalar potential and changing the kinetic energy term in such a way that the local 1-parameter groups are precisely the paths which locally minimize action.

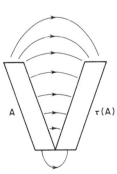

Figure 7. Vector fields for a pair of bar-shaped objects

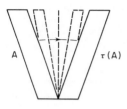

Figure 8. 'Motion-in-depth' between two bar-shaped objects. Top of illusory object appears to move through full semicircle, bottom remains fixed

4. A Pure Figural Theory

Consider again an arbitrary initial object A and final object B, and suppose that $B = \tau(A)$ for some local diffeomorphism of A such that τ may be embedded in a flow, that is, that $\tau = \psi_\tau$ for some local l-parameter group of local transformations $\psi: [0, 1] \times U \to R^2$; in fact such that $\tau = \psi_1$. (Although the collection of such embeddable τ may not be dense in the C^r manifold of all diffeomorphisms having the domain U, this is unlikely to be an important restriction in practice.)

We may then associate with τ a vector field X^ψ, namely the vector field on R^2 Induced by the local l-parameter group ψ_t thus:

$$X^\psi(p) = \frac{\mathrm{d}\psi_t(u)}{\mathrm{d}t} = (\gamma'(t))(u),$$

where $p = \psi_t(u)$ (see Figure 9).

Since every vector field gives rise to a flow, attention may be concentrated on the set of vector fields. So that motions in depth may be included, we shall, in fact, consider the set X of all vector fields defined on some suitably large (compact) subset M of R^3 containing the region of visual interest. The space X is then a Hilbert space with inner product

$$(X, Y) = \int_M \langle X(p), Y(p) \rangle \mathrm{d}v(p).$$

The natural Lagrangian is then given by

$$L(X, Z(X)) = (Z(X), Z(X)),$$

where $Z(X)$ is the value of the vector field Z on X at the point $X \in X$. Then paths $c: [0, 1] \to X$ that minimize the action between fixed end-points $c(0) = 0$ and

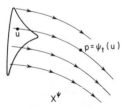

Figure 9. Action of local l-parameter group of local transformations ψ_t

$$c(1) = X,$$

$$\int_0^1 L(c(t), c'(t))dt,$$

are precisely the rays in $\mathcal{X}$ emanating from the origin, i.e., the curves c for which

$$c(t) = tX, \quad t \in [0, 1].$$

We now return to consideration of the original collection of embeddable diffeomorphisms. The curve tX, $t \in [0, 1]$, defines a 1-parameter family of embeddable transformations ϕ_t, $t \in [0, 1]$ by

$$\phi_t = \psi_1^{tX},$$

where ψ_1^{tX} is the local diffeomorphism defined by the flow of tX at time 1. But,

$$\psi_1^{tX} = \psi_t^{X}$$

i.e. the local diffeomorphism defined by the flow of X at time t. Note that ψ_1^0 is the identity. The curve tX, $t \in [0, 1]$, thus corresponds to a local 1-parameter group connecting the identity to the diffeomorphism ψ_1^X.

Thus, as with the scheme of the preceding section, if the visual system resolves the disparity between patterns A and $\tau(A)$ by generating beta motion, and if it chooses those motions which minimize the above action integral, then it will effect a local 1-parameter group of local transformations. In the case that the metric structure is preserved throughout the motion, this model then predicts, correctly, the motions illustrated in Figures 6(a) and 8.

For beta motion in which the final object $B = \tau(A)$ is not a rigid transform of the initial object A, but for which τ is embeddable in a flow, the predicted action-minimizing motion is still of the form of a local 1-parameter group. Thus, in Figure 10, the curve should, and, experimentally, is observed to, go smoothly into the straight line. Other examples are easy to construct.

In the remainder of this study we shall be concerned solely with this pure figural model.

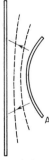

Figure 10. Motion between two objects A, $\tau(A)$, when τ is not a rigid transformation

A

$B = \tau(A)$

5. Rigid Motion vs. Plastic Deformation

There is an inbuilt ill-definedness in the model which is a consequence of specifying not the pair of objects A, B inducing the beta motion, but their relationship $\tau : A \rightarrow \tau(A) = B$. The ambiguity arises in that in general there exists more than one diffeomorphism τ for which as subsets of the plane $\tau(A) = B$. Suppose τ_1 and τ_2 are two such transformations, i.e. $\tau_1(A) = \tau_2(A) = B$, with corresponding action-minimizing curves γ_1 and γ_2. Which of the motions is actually effected depends on the nature of the transformations τ_1 and τ_2 and on the relative actions or lengths of their associated paths γ_1 and γ_2. When τ_1 and τ_2 preserve the same structures (for example, the metric structure), then the motion should certainly correspond to the γ_i which has the smaller action. When τ_1 and τ_2 do not preserve the same structures, the outcome may depend on the precise form of the object A, and not just on the transformation τ. Kolers and Pomerantz (1971) have described two kinds of motion obtainable with the type of objects shown in Figure 11. Subjects reported seeing either a rigid 'motion-in-depth' or a 'plastic deformation', with the latter more probable at shorter interstimulus intervals. The 'motion-in-depth' presumably arises from the identification $\tau : A \rightarrow \tau(A) = B$, with $\tau \in E(3)$, and the 'plastic deformation' from the identification $\tau : A \rightarrow \tau(A) = B$, with $\tau \in A(2)$, the group of affine motions of the plane. The action integral associated with the 'plastic deformation' is smaller than that associated with the 'motion-in-depth'.

6. Motion Between Dissimilar Patterns

The analysis up to now has been concerned with beta motion between objects A and B for which $B = \tau(A)$, where τ is a local transformation embeddable in a differentiable flow, i.e. B is at least a smooth transform of A. But good beta motion is in fact obtainable between objects A and $\tau(A)$ where τ is only a homeomorphism, that is, τ preserves the connectivity of curves in A but not necessarily their smoothness. Figure 12(a) shows such a pair, where for suitable timings, the circle expands smoothly into the square (Kolers and Pomerantz, 1971).

By applying the analysis described at the end of Sec. 4 piece-by-piece, i.e.,

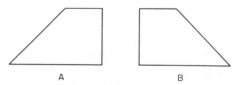

A   B

Figure 11. Patterns which yield either a rigid 'motion-in-depth' or a 'plastic deformation' (Kolers and Pomerantz, 1971; Kolers, 1972, Chapt. 6)

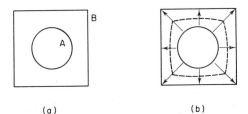

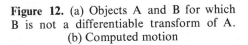

(a)   (b)

Figure 12. (a) Objects A and B for which
B is not a differentiable transform of A.
(b) Computed motion

taking 1-parameter families like those of Figure 10 and suitably 'glueing' them together, we get the continuous (but not differentiable) flow shown in Figure 12(b). Note that although the mappings ψ_t are only homeomorphisms, the actual motion $t \to \psi_t(p)$ remains differentiable, i.e. smooth.

An alternative to this 'glueing' together of piecewise-smooth flows is the 'replacement' of the homeomorphism τ by an embeddable diffeomorphism τ' and the effecting of a single smooth flow in the usual way. Provided τ' is close to τ, so, in terms of indistinguishability, $|\tau(x) - \tau'(x)| < \epsilon$, for all x in U_A, where ϵ is a measure of visual acuity, this substitution should be acceptable. When, however, there is no embeddable diffeomorphism close to the mapping τ relating A to B, then two possibilities arise: first, beta motion does not occur; second, beta motion does occur, but between A and the transform $\tau'(A)$ which is closest to B and for which τ' is embeddable. The second possibility is actually seen (Kolers, 1972, Chapter 4) in that subjects, when presented with patterns in the form of, for example, a hollow arrow and square, sometimes report 'a perception of plastic deformation in the course of the movement and sudden replacement at the terminus' (Kolers and Pomerantz, 1971).

What is meant by one pattern B being close to another pattern A has not been made precise for the general case. One measure might be

$$d(A, B) = \sup_{q \in B} \inf_{p \in A} |p - q|,$$

which simply records the greatest departure from overlap. This leads us to consider the following situation. Suppose patterns A and B are such that there exists

(1) an embeddable diffeomorphism τ such that $\tau(A) = B$ and such that the magnitude $\|X\| = (X, X)^{\frac{1}{2}}$ of the associated vector field $X(\psi_1^X = \tau)$ is large;

(2) an embeddable diffeomorphism τ' such that $d(B, \tau'(A))$ is small and such that the magnitude $\|X'\| = (X', X')^{\frac{1}{2}}$ of the associated vector field $X'(\psi_t^{X'} = \tau')$ is small.

In terms of actions, or distances, a motion from A to $\tau'(A)$ with subsequent replacement by B should then be the preferred solution. An example of such preferred motion has been described by Navon (1976). The patterns were letters formed into circles as shown in Figure 13.

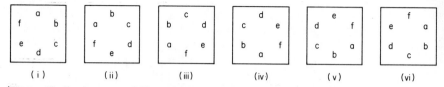

Figure 13. Irrelevance of 'figural identity' on motion. When arrays are presented in cyclic order, anticlockwise circular motion is only occasionally observed. The elements a, b, c, d, e, f can be either familiar or unfamiliar symbols (Navon, 1976)

The arrays were presented to the eye in cyclic order (i), (ii), ..., (vi), (i), (ii), ... Of the two most likely apparent motion effects, namely (a) the elements revolving in an anticlockwise direction, and (b) the elements changing shape but staying in the same location, the 'stationary' interpretation was the most frequently observed.

7. Relationship of Apparent Movement to Form Perception

The principal objection to a figural theory of apparent movement is that motion is frequently obtainable between patterns which are not in the common sense the 'same', for example, circles and squares, and letters of the alphabet. Nevertheless, the observations by Sigman and Rock (1974) and by Corbin (1942), Rock and Ebenholtz (1962), and Attneave and Block (1973) indicate that there is necessarily some kind of intelligent rationalization involved in the production of apparent movement, and it is the perceived relationship of the stimuli, not the retinal distribution of their luminances, which is of importance.

Part of the problem centres on what is meant by the 'sameness' of patterns (Kolers, 1972, Chapter 4). Strictly, two objects A and B can only be the same if they define the same subsets of R^2, i.e., $A = B$. An equivalence $\sim$ of the form '$A \sim B$ if $B = \sigma(A)$ for some transformation σ belonging to the group of rigid motions $E(2)$' may be argued to be no different in form from an equivalence $\sim$ of the form '$A \sim B$ if $B = \sigma(A)$ for some transformation σ belonging to the group of homeomorphisms of the plane'. The first equivalence defines 'sameness' with respect to metric structure and the second with respect to topological structure. It is certainly possible, for some structures S and transformations σ to decide visually whether objects A and B can be associated as $\sigma : A \to \sigma(A) = B$, for σ preserving S, although not all transformations preserving S may be thus distinguished. For example, when S is the usual topological structure on R^2, one can recognize the difference in connectivity between an intact and broken circle, but not between the maze-like patterns cited by Julesz (1975).

The above considerations may be shown (Foster, 1975a) to lead to the notion that there is an underlying structure S_0 associated with the visual perception and identification of objects, and a set $\Gamma_{S_0}^*$ of transformations σ_0 which preserve S_0 and which can be visually effected. Visual recognition with respect to some arbitrarily fixed structure S may then be interpreted as being determined by what transformations preserving S also belong to $\Gamma_{S_0}^*$.

The figural resolution that is achieved in proper beta motion (when $B = \tau(A)$, $\tau = \psi_1$, see Sec. 6) and the incomplete figural resolution that occurs in 'motion-with-replacement' (when $B \neq \psi_1(A)$) are then both manifestations of this underlying identification, in which A is recognized as B with respect to S_0 and motion is induced to resolve the separate occurrences. Although in the case of apparent movement this underlying structure is weak (i.e., there exist many bijective mappings preserving it), it is not trivial (i.e., not all bijective mappings preserve it). Thus, Kolers (1972, Chapter 7) reports that the patterns of the form shown in Figure 14 usually give rise to a flicker effect when alternately presented, and 'motion-with-replacement' is only occasionally obtained. Navon (1976) has also shown that although the letters of Figure 13 are equivalent to one another (Sec. 6), this equivalence does not extend to a larger diamond-shaped figure, for when the latter is substituted for one of the letters in the array, circular motion is seen.

8. Conclusion

Of the two models for apparent movement that have been described here, it is the pure figural one that accounts best for the available experimental data. In this model each transformation τ is associated with a vector field X for which the flow ψ_t^X, $t \in [0, 1]$, is such that $\psi_1^X = \tau$. The curve γ describing the motion between an object A and transform $\tau(A)$ is then associated with the evolution of the time-varying vector field tX. It is significant that the motion defined by γ corresponds with the flow generated in the ordinary way by a *time-invariant* vector field, *namely* X. This does not mean, however, that the assumption of variational principles could have been replaced by the assumption of the constancy of vector fields or the stationarity of flow, since there would then be no natural way to compare stationary flows that intersect or to relate the length of flows to the distance between patterns.

Although much use has been made here of the connection between vector fields and families of transformations, it should be emphasized that there are certain technical difficulties in expressing the approach within a Lie algebra–Lie group framework (Hoffman, 1966, 1968, 1970, 1978). The group of diffeomorphisms of a manifold does not generally admit an ordinary Lie group

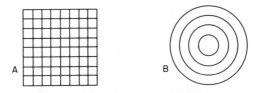

Figure 14. Displays that usually give rise to flicker instead of motion (Kolers, 1972, Chapt. 7)

structure and the exponential mapping may not cover a neighbourhood of the identity (see, for example, Ebin and Marsden, 1970).

In the pure figural model described in this study, there is no explicit mention of the time-dependence of apparent movement on interstimulus interval. For the model with scalar potential, time-dependence enters naturally in the setting-up of the vector field. For the pure figural model there are two possibilities. If the motion were generated at a constant rate, then clearly, the interstimulus interval would have to be chosen so that it is compatible with the impletion. Although consistent with the data of the 'motion-in-depth' vs. 'plastic deformation' experiments, Kolers (1972, Chapter 3) has shown that in other cases the 'velocity' of the flow increases linearly with pattern separation. An alternative explanation has been suggested by Sigman and Rock (1974). They argue that a motion rationalization scheme would not be expected to operate when the objects appeared simultaneously or when the delay between the two was so great that some stimulation in the intervening region would be expected to be detected in the real motion situation (Kaufman, et al., 1971). The dynamics are thus a consequence of the cognitive process.

If, as has been advocated here, apparent movement is intimately related to pattern perception, then, at least in the case of proper beta motion, the analysis of the forms of the paths effected may provide a method for the investigation of the mechanisms subserving visual recognition (Foster, 1972, 1973). It has been proposed (Kahneman, 1967) that apparent movement is connected with meta-contrast, a shape-sensitive visual masking phenomenon (Alpern, 1952; Kolers, 1968; Kahneman, 1968). Although both phenomena can involve interactions between different photoreceptor systems (Foster and Idris, 1974; Foster, 1976) evidence relating to the space and time dependence of each (Kolers, 1972, Chapter 8) indicates that this is unlikely.

Acknowledgement

I thank Professor Paul A. Kolers and Pergamon Press Ltd. for permission to reproduce in modified form figures from *Aspects of Motion Perception* (1972).

References

Alpern, M. (1952). Metacontrast: Historical Introduction. *American Journal of Optometry and Archives of American Academy of Optometry*, **29**, 631–646.

Attneave, F. and Block, G. (1973). Apparent movement in tridimensional space. *Perception and Psychophysics*, **13**, 301–307.

Brown, J. F. and Voth, A. C. (1937). The path of seen movement as a function of the vector-field. *American Journal of Psychology*, **49**, 543–563.

Corbin, H. H. (1942). The perception of grouping and apparent movement in visual depth. *Archives of Psychology*, No. 273.

Ebin, D. G. and Marsden, J. (1970). Groups of diffeomorphisms and the motion of an incompressible fluid. *Annals of Mathematics*, **92**, 102–163.

Exner, S. (1875). Ueber das Sehen von Bewegungen und die Theorie des zusammengesetzen Auges. *Sitzungsberichte Akademie Wissenschaft Wien*, **72**, 156–190.

Foster, D. H. (1972). A method for the investigation of those transformations under which the visual recognition of a given object is variant. I. The theory. *Kybernetik*, **11**, 217–223.

Foster, D. H. (1973). A hypothesis connecting visual pattern recognition and apparent motion. *Kybernetik*, **13**, 151–154.

Foster, D. H. (1975a). An approach to the analysis of the underlying structure of visual space using a generalized notion of visual pattern recognition. *Biological Cybernetics*, **17**, 77–79.

Foster, D. H. (1975b). Visual apparent motion and some preferred paths in the rotation group SO(3). *Biological Cybernetics*, **18**, 81–89.

Foster, D. H. (1976). Rod-cone interaction in the after-flash effect. *Vision Research*, **16**, 393–396.

Foster, D. H. and Idris, I. I. M. (1974). Spatio-temporal interaction between visual colour mechanisms. *Vision Research*, **14**, 35–39.

Gelfand, I. and Fomin, S. (1963). *Calculus of Variations*, Prentice Hall, Englewood Cliffs, N.J.

Hoffman, W. C. (1966). The lie algebra of visual perception. *Journal of Mathematical Psychology*, **3**, 65–98.

Hoffman, W. C. (1968). The neuron as a lie group germ and a lie product. *Quarterly of Applied Mathematics*, **25**, 423–440.

Hoffman, W. C. (1970). Higher visual perception as prolongation of the basic lie transformation group. *Mathematical Biosciences*, **6**, 437–471.

Hoffman, W. C. (1978). The lie transformation group approach to visual neuropsychology. (This volume).

Julesz, B. (1975). Experiments in the visual perception of texture. *Scientific American*, **232**(4), 34–43.

Kahneman, D. (1967). An onset-onset law for one case of apparent motion and metacontrast. *Perception and Psychophysics*, **2**, 577–584.

Kahneman, D. (1968). Method, findings, and theory in studies of visual masking. *Psychological Bulletin*, **70**, 404–425.

Kaufman, L., Cyrulnik, I., Kaplowitz, J., Melnick, G., Stoff, D. (1970). The complementarity of apparent and real motion, *Psychologische Forschung*, **34**, 343–348.

Kenkel, F. (1913). Untersuchungen über den Zusammenhang zwischen Erscheinungsgröße und Erscheinungsbewegung bei einigen sogenannten optischen Täuschungen. *Z. Psychol.*, **67**, 358–449.

Köhler, W. (1923). Zur Theorie der stroboskopischen Bewegung. *Psychologische Forschung*, **3**, 397–406.

Kolers, P. A. (1968). Some psychological aspects of pattern recognition. In P. A. Kolers and M. Eden (eds.), *Recognizing Patterns*. Cambridge, Massachusetts: M.I.T. Press.

Kolers, P. A. (1972). *Aspects of motion perception*. Oxford: Pergamon Press.

Kolers, P. A. and Pomerantz, J. R. (1971). Figural change in apparent motion. *Journal of Experimental Psychology*, **87**, 99–108.

Marsden, J., Ebin, D., and Fischer, A. (1972). Diffeomorphism Groups, Hydrodynamics and relativity. *Proceedings of the Thirteenth Biennial Seminar of the Canadian Mathematical Congress* (Vol. 1), pp. 135–280.

Milnor, J. (1963). Morse theory, *Annals of mathematics studies No. 51* Princeton, New Jersey, Princeton University Press.

Navon, D. (1976). Irrelevance of figural identity for resolving ambiguities in apparent motion. *Journal of Experimental Psychology: Human Perception and Performance*, **2**, 130–138.

Neff, W. S. (1936). A critical investigation of the visual apprehension of movement. *American Journal of Psychology*, **48**, 1–42.

Neuhaus, W. (1930). Experimentelle Untersuchung der Scheinbewegung. *Archiv für die gesamte Psychologie*, **75**, 315–458.

Rock, I. and Ebenholtz, S. (1962). Stroboscopic movement based on change of phenomenal rather than retinal location. *The American Journal of Psychology*, **75**, 193–207.

Sigman, E. and Rock, I. (1974). Stroboscopic movement based on perceptual intelligence. *Perception*, **3**, 9–28.

Wertheimer, M. (1912). Experimentelle Studien über das Sehen von Bewegung. *Zeitschrift für Psychologie*, **61**, 161–265.

Zadeh, L. A. (1965). Fuzzy sets. *Information and Control*, **8**, 338–353.

Zeeman, E. C. (1962). The topology of the brain and visual perception. In: *The topology of 3-manifolds and related topics*. New Jersey: Prentice-Hall.

Chapter 4

Metric Geometry in Human Binocular Perception: Theory and Fact

Albert A. Blank

Abstract. Empirical evidence suggests that the simplest formal representation of binocular perceptual space involves an egocentric or polar reference frame. The relation between the physical stimulus frame and the egocentric perceptual frame proves to be multivalent, its character being determined almost wholly by the disparities between the retinal images, not by proprioception with respect to the attitude of the eyes. The metric geometry of binocular perceptual space is definitely not Euclidean. Each observer seems to have a characteristic metric which has negative curvature for most if not all observers. Within the bounds of experimental error, it appears that the curvature is essentially constant for well-spaced points. Thus the metric is that of the well-known hyperbolic geometry of Lobachevsky and Bolyai. Experiments both supporting and conflicting with the theory are treated.

The conspicuous outward sign of human ability to perceive space in full three-dimensionality is a two-eyed forward looking visual system. The disparities in the two-dimensional retinal images, through some internal processing, yield information about the third dimension, which is called *depth*. This paper does not speculate about the mechanism of depth perception. It constructs a formal system that will give a way of constructing a chart of the three-dimensional space of binocular vision, visual space, by mapping it into the physical space of stimuli.

1. Visual and Physical Reference Frames

The experimental base for the theory isolates the factor of binocularity. The observer's head is fixed to avoid motion parallax. Because the region of distinct binocular vision is severely restricted in fixed gaze, the more natural scanning mode of observation is used; the observer is asked to actively survey the entire presented configuration in making settings. At best the stimuli are composed of a number of low intensity lights in a totally dark surround. The lights are adjusted to equal sensory brightness and made as small as possible to approximate geometrically ideal points. In this way the well-known monocular depth cues of size, overlay and relative brightness are largely avoided.

If precise information about the attitude of the eyes in the head were available to the observer, the optical system could be used as a rangefinder and a veridical perception of space could be obtained, each point being localized when fixated at the intersection of the two lines of sight. In the kind of reduced experimental environment we treat, the accurate judgement of physical distance is notoriously unreliable (cf. Helmholtz, 1925 pp. 312 ff.) and there is a great deal of other evidence that the visual system does not operate like a rangefinder. Binocular perception of space is far from veridical. Nonetheless, it is convenient to introduce angular coordinates associated with the lines of sight.

Following Luneburg (1947), we introduce cartesian coordinates xyz in physical space as follows: For the head in normal erect position the y-axis is taken as the transverse line through the rotation centres of the eyes oriented positively toward the left. The origin is taken midway between the rotation centres. The z-axis is directed vertically upward and the x-axis, sagitally forward. The unit of length is taken as half the distance between the ocular centres; thus the left eye is centred at $L = (0, 1, 0)$, the right, at $R = (0, -1, 0)$.

For a point $P = (x, y, z), x > 0$, we introduce angular coordinates α, β, θ which define the directions of the lines of sight when the eyes fixate P. The angle θ is the angle of elevation of the plane PLR with respect to the horizontal xy-plane; α and β measure azimuth of the left and right lines of sight LP and RP with respect to the sagittal vertical planes through the corresponding eyes, see Figure 1.

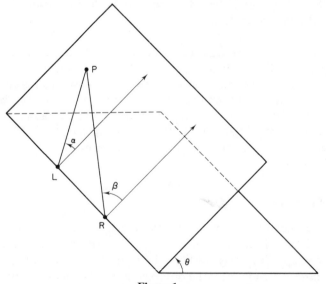

Figure 1

We shall be concerned mainly with the horizontal plane $\theta = 0$ which has been studied more thoroughly than the full space.

It is convenient to replace the monocular azimuth angles α and β by the bipolar coordinates γ and ϕ where $\gamma = \beta - \alpha$, the *convergence* of the eyes, is the angle between the lines of sight and $\phi = \frac{1}{2}(\alpha + \beta)$, the *bipolar azimuth*, is the mean of the monocular azimuths. The locus of constant convergence passing through the point P in the plane $\theta = $ constant is the circle through the points $\dot{L}$, R and P, the so-called *Vieth-Müller circle* (see Figure 2).

If A is the forward point where the median plane meets the circle, the bipolar azimuth ϕ is the angle subtended by the minor arc PA. The locus of constant ϕ in the plane $\theta = $ constant is a rectangular hyperbola, passing through the left eye for $\phi > 0$, the right eye for $\phi < 0$, and degenerating to the median line $y = 0$ for $\phi = 0$.

Luneburg (1947), p. 21 seems to have been the first to note that an observer perceives an array of points lying on a Vieth-Müller circle in the horizontal plane as a circle, not on the periphery, as the physical reality would indicate, but with his self at the centre. The locus of points $\phi = $ constant is also assigned a sensory role by Luneburg, that of a perceived line of constant direction from the observer; also see Helmholtz (1925), p. 258. In 3-space, Luneburg took the bipolar coordinates γ, ϕ, θ of the physical bipolar frame as polar coordinates in the visual perceptual frame. Specifically, he assumed that if r is a measure of perceived distance from the observer then r depends on γ alone, that perceived elevation ϑ is essentially the same as physical elevation θ, and that perceived

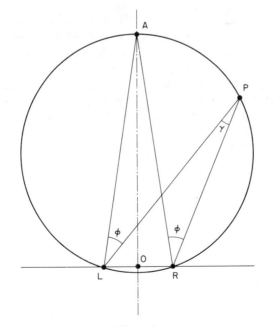

Figure 2

azimuth φ referred to the median plane is essentially the same as physical azimuth ϕ. Quantitative experimental evidence on this postulate will be treated later. For the time being let us accept it as a first approximation.

2. Iseikonic Transformations

There is a significant complication that must be incorporated into the relation between the visual polar and physical bipolar frames. It should not be assumed a priori that distinct physical configurations, each perceived in isolation, are perceptually distinct. Over much of the physical field of view the observer is not particularly aware of the attitude of his eyes unless they are straining in an extreme position. Proprioception with respect to the attitude of the eyes is not likely to be a significant factor in space perception over most of the visual field.

In Blank (1957), p. 2, I work from the hypothesis that the retinal images almost entirely are the carriers of spatial information. Assuming the possibility of creating the same retinal images in different physical ways, this means that the observer will see those different physical configurations in the same way. We may test this by showing an observer the two halves of a stereogram in both normal view and rotated about vertical axes through the corresponding eyes, Figure 3. (It is assumed that these are separate viewings and the rotation is not carried out in the observer's view.) If the rotations are not so large as to cause strain, the observer usually detects no difference in the two views except, possibly, for a change of direction. Even this change does not occur if the rotations are equal and opposite.

This simple hypothesis provides an elegant explanation of the classical three-thread experiment of Helmholtz. We describe a version of that experiment with minimal cues: Let three points of light be placed in an observer's horizontal plane. Let one point be movable along the sagittal ray ($x > 0$) and the other two be fixed symmetrically about the median at the points $(y_0, \pm \phi_0)$. The movable central light is adjusted at the instruction of the observer to yield the perception of straight alignment between the fixed points. Empirically there is a position of the fixed lights, dependent upon ϕ_0, at which visual straightness actually coin-

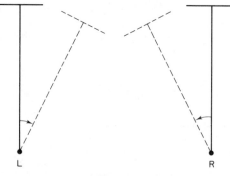

Figure 3

cides with perceptual straightness. For fixed lights nearer the observer at, say, (γ'_0, ϕ_0) with $\gamma'_0 > \gamma_0$, a perceptually straight array will be physically concave toward the observer. How is this explained by the hypothesis?

Let $P = (\gamma, 0)$ be the setting of the movable light in the condition of coincidence between physical and visual straightness, Figure 4. The fixed points are denoted by $P_+ = (\gamma_0, \phi_0)$ and $P_- = (\gamma_0, -\phi_0)$. The retinal images for each eye are defined only by the differences in monocular azimuth angle for that eye.[1] With $P = (\alpha, \beta)$ as a reference point, where $\alpha = -\gamma/2$ and $\beta = \gamma/2$, we note that the retinal images for the left eye are determined by the differences $\alpha_+ - \alpha = \phi_0$ and $\alpha_- - \alpha = -\phi_0$. These differences are not affected if the entire fan of lines of sight to the three points from the left eye is rotated rigidly about a vertical line through L. Similarly, a rigid rotation of the corresponding fan for R leaves the differences in angle unchanged. If we rotate the two fans nasally by the angular magnitude λ, we substract λ from all values of the left monocular azimuth and add it to those of the right monocular azimuth. This amounts to adding the positive constant 2λ to all values of the convergence angle and leaving the bipolar azimuth unchanged. Now the intersections of the corresponding lines of sight in the two fans fall closer to the observer and no longer lie on a physically straight line. In fact, the array of intersections has become concave toward the observer, as in Figure 5. According to our hypothesis, an array of lights placed

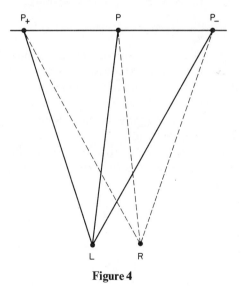

Figure 4

---

[1] This is a good approximation only if the dimensions of the eye are small relative to the distances of the points from the eye. Otherwise there are parallax effects in scanning vision because of the separation between anterior and posterior nodal points and the centre of rotation. At larger distances from the eye the retinal image is essentially a rigid picture which does not change as the eye moves. Under our hypothesis, space perception with fixed head for configurations outside the proximal field essentially derives from scanning by the retina of these rigid images.

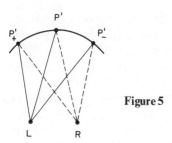

Figure 5

at these intersections should yield the perception of straightness. Similarly, equal temporal rotations of the eyes should yield perceptually straight arrays which are convex toward the observer. This is qualitatively identical with Helmholtz's observations.

In Blank (1958b), p. 923f. I have analysed data from Zajaczkowska's trials of this experiment in relation to the hypothesis. Except in the proximal region, where the geometrical optics of the eye becomes a factor, there is substantial numerical agreement with the predictions by the hypothesis.

Luneburg (1947), p. 17ff. introduced a class of *iseikonic* transformations of the full three-dimensional space, the particular transformation

$$\begin{cases} \gamma' = \gamma + \tau \qquad (\tau \text{ constant}) \\ \phi' = \phi \\ \theta' = \theta \end{cases} \tag{1}$$

being a special case. This last transformation, according to Luneburg (1947), was used by A. Ames to construct binocular distorted rooms intended to have the same perceptual effect as a given rectangular room, Ittelson (1952), p. 50ff. If the intended result were fully achieved, this would generalize to three-dimensional space the method by which we explained how to construct transverse perceptually straight lines from a given transversal.

In actual observation, the binocular distorted rooms are perceptually nearly equivalent. When each room is observed from its prepared vantage point, it appears almost identical with the others in size, shape, and position relative to the observer. Close observation of the interior ($\tau > 0$) and exterior ($\tau < 0$) rooms do reveal slight curvature of the lines on the floor and the edges where ceiling, walls, and floor meet. Luneburg (1947), p. 91ff. attributed this near identity of the rooms and the slight discrepancies among them to a most interesting cause: the iseikonic transformations over a considerable region of the visual field are close approximations to isometries of the observer's visual space. The particular transformation (1) should, in fact, approximate a perceptual translation toward or away from the observer. Unfortunately for this hypothesis of Luneburg, such a translation would change the perceived relative position of the room to the observer, and no such change is found.

In Ittelson (1952) the binocular distorted rooms are described as binocularly equivalent to the true rectangular room in the sense that binocular disparities are preserved in the transformation and the rooms are monocularly equivalent in the sense that the images on both retinas are congruent to the corresponding ones formed by the rectangular room. The transformation (1) preserves binocular disparities but the rooms are *not* monocularly equivalent, see Blank (1957), p. 22. This lack of equivalence can be detected through slight curvatures in the floor lines of the stereograms in Ittelson (1952), p. 52. In fact, it is impossible to construct a room which is monocularly equivalent for both eyes to a given room: for any physical point but those in the horizontal and median planes, nasal or temporal rotation of the retinal images, as by rotation of the halves of a stereogram, will change the elevations of the lines of sight unequally; there can be no physical point at the intersection of the new lines of sight. We conclude that for no two physical solids is exact monocular equivalence for both eyes simultaneously possible.

In Blank (1957), it is conjectured that the transformation (1) is essentially correct, perhaps with some modification of the parameter γ (see section 4). The question is really not settled empirically for the full three-dimensional space, but its basic validity for the horizontal plane under a variety of experimental conditions has been established, see Blank (1958) and Hardy (1953). The empirical work of Foley (1967), largely supports the same conclusion and detects the usual departures from the simple law in the proximal region.

3. Modifications of the Bipolar Reference Frame

The bipolar reference frame is a good first approximation to a visual polar frame. For precise numerical calculation it is necessary to determine the physical reference curves of the visual polar frame more exactly by experiment. In Hardy (1953), pp. 36 ff., it is noted that an actual circle of apparent equidistance from the observer is somewhat flatter than a Vieth-Müller circle, the deviation decreasing as distance from the observer increases, but the data are unpublished. Foley (1966) has confirmed the effect for 10 observers.[2] The differences between observers are marked. An example of an approximate data fit for observer G.R. (unpublished data of Hardy, Rand and Rittler) gives the equation of the visual egocentric circle passing through the point $\gamma = \gamma_0, \phi = 0$ as

$$\gamma = \gamma_0(1 - 0{\cdot}19\phi^2) \tag{2}$$

for $0{\cdot}03 < \gamma_0 < 0{\cdot}11$ and $-0{\cdot}39 < \phi < 0{\cdot}39$ (angles measured in radians). It is emphasized that other observers will yield different results. In particular, for asymmetric observers, odd powers of ϕ must appear. In any case, the locus $\gamma =$ const. is not precisely an egocentred circle.

Foley (1965) has determined further that visual and bipolar azimuth cannot be equated but are linearly related:

$$\varphi = 1{\cdot}1\phi \qquad (|\phi| \leq 56°). \tag{3}$$

[2] A number of these observers exhibit considerable skewing such as aniseikonia could produce.

For the purposes of the general formal theory which follows, the specific physical reference curves corresponding to the visual polar frame of the observer matter only for the purpose of specific calculation. The essence of the theory is unaffected by differences in the reference curves.

4. The Metric of Visual Space

Luneburg (1948), pp. 224–230 and Blank (1958a) have attempted to define the visual geometry by metric methods. In the last paper, particularly, an effort is made to base the concept of visual space on the simplest possible behaviours. Without going deeply into axiomatic foundations of metric geometry here (see Blank 1958a, 1959 and Busemann 1955 for details), I simply note that the possibility of treating visual space as a metric geometry rests upon two postulated properties of a human observer:

1. He is able to interpolate and visually align between any two given points other points, ad lib., without affecting the perceived geometrical relations among points already present:
2. He is able to order distances; that is, given any two pairs of points (P_1, Q_1) and (P_2, Q_2) in the visual field he can compare the separation between the points of one pair with that of the other and determine whether the first is visually greater than the second.

It is specifically excluded that line segments may be freely extended without altering visual geometrical relations among points already present.

Among the metric geometries, the ones most familiar to mathematicians are Riemannian, those for which the differential metric is representable by a positive definite quadratic form. Of these, the simplest geometries are those of constant Gaussian curvature: Euclidean of zero cruvature, hyperbolic (Lobachevski and Bolyai) of constant negative curvature, elliptic (Riemann) of constant positive curvature. Luneburg (1947, 1948) noted that these three are the only possible geometries for visual space provided that the space admits the complete group of isometries generated by rotation, reflection and translation. As experimental evidence for this, Luneburg adduces the Ames binocular distorted rooms. This is at best fragmentary support for such a strong hypothesis.

In 1958a, I reach the same end by a less precipitate route than Luneburg, one more easily susceptible to experimental verification. The hypothesis that visual space is Riemannian is separated from and made antecedent to the hypothesis that the space has constant curvature.

Given the regularity of visual space (a first order differentiability condition suffices), it is possible to verify the Riemannian property by testing symmetry of perpendiculars. To describe such a test, we first frame some preliminary definitions. Let (P_1P_2) be an open line segment and Q_1 any point not on the line P_1P_2. If there is a point Q on (P_1P_2) nearest to Q_1, it is called the *foot* of Q_1 on (P_1P_2). If there exists a point Q_2 aligned with Q_1Q on the opposite side of Q from Q_1 and if Q is the foot on $(P_1 P_2)$ of all points on $[Q_1 Q_2]$, then the segment $[Q_1 Q_2]$ is called *perpendicular* to $[P_1 P_2]$. Symmetry of perpendiculars exists if perpendicularity of $[Q_1 Q_2]$ to $[P_1 P_2]$ implies perpendicularity of $[P_1 P_2]$ to $[Q_1 Q_2]$.

Symmetry of perpendiculars is easy to test by the following method. Let P_1 and Q_1 be the far points in a configuration of five points, P_1, P_2, Q_1, Q_2, Q extending over a sizeable part of the visual field, Figure 6. Keep P_1, P_2 and Q_1 fixed. Ask the observer for the position of point Q on $(P_1 P_2)$ nearest to Q_1. Then ask him for the position of Q_2, displaced as little as possible from the original placement of Q_2, that is aligned with $Q_1 Q$. Allow him to change his mind about the setting of Q if he wishes. Give the observer a rest and note the position $\overline{Q_1}$ of Q. Now ask the observer for the position $\overline{Q_2}$ of Q on $P_1 P_2$ nearest to Q_2. Rest the observer while noting the position $\overline{Q_2}$.

Next displace both Q and P_2 and ask the observer for the position $\overline{P_1}$ of Q on $(Q_1 Q_2)$ nearest to P_1. Rest the observer and note position $\overline{P_1}$. Then have him align P_2 with $P_1 Q$ using as small a displacement as possible. Determine position $\overline{P_2}$ on $(Q_1 Q_2)$ perceived nearest to Q_2. If the four settings of Q coincide within experimental scatter, symmetry of perpendiculars is supported.[3]

To the best of my knowledge the foregoing experiment has not been performed.

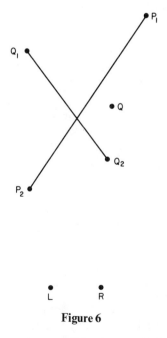

Figure 6

[3] The details of this proposed experiment involve extending certain segments. This is not generally acceptable. Specifically, extension of segments in a direction away from the observer is not admissible, as we shall see. There is, as yet, no reason to forbid extension toward the observer as in this experiment.

The following qualitative check on the Riemannian property was made by me. One easily constructs small apparent squares in the visual field; that is, arrays of four points perceived as vertices of convex quadrilaterals having equal sides which meet perpendicularly. If such squares can be constructed in arbitrary localizations and orientations in visual space, the Riemannian property would be established. The trouble with such qualitative observation is that it is open to suggestion; the observer has little doubt of his ability to construct squares of any size. Yet, in fact, unless the geometry is Euclidean, it is impossible to construct large squares in arbitrary position. Riemannian geometries can be defined by this locally Euclidean character; that is, their infinitesimal elements are Euclidean. For such geometries construction of squares 'in the small' is therefore always possible. However, if a Riemannian geometry is not Euclidean, its Gaussian curvature is not identically zero and the possibility of constructing squares of arbitrary size in general position fails in regions large enough for the curvature to be detectable.

The Desarguesian property involves the existence of planes. A plane is a surface which contains the entire line joining any two of its points. In Euclidean three-space, there exists one and only one plane containing any three non-collinear points. This is the Desarguesian property, and it is held by only two other Riemannian geometries, those of constant negative and positive curvature, the hyperbolic and elliptic geometries.

In Blank (1958a), the Desarguesian property is given a form easily susceptible to experimental test:

Let P_1, P_2, P_3 be any triple of noncollinear points. Let Q_1 be any interior point of the segment $(P_2 P_3)$—the midpoint will do—and Q_3, any point of $(P_1 P_2)$. The segments $(P_1 Q_1)$ and $(P_2 Q_2)$ have a unique intersection point X.

It is essential to test the Desarguesian property with a triangle $P_1 P_2 P_3$ extending over a very large part of the visual field. This, for the reason that constant curvature may be a good first approximation over extended regions of visual space. Departures from constant curvature would not be found if the test configuration did not span even larger regions.

Foley (1964a, 1964b) carried out the indicated experiment and reported that departures from the Desarguesian property were generally small, and for most observers, probably within the limits of discriminability. For the other observers we leave open the possibility that there are measureable, if not great, departures from constant curvature.

5. The Curvature of Visual Space

At this point we have reached the joining of two formal structures. The first, at the interface between visual space and physical space, is concerned with the coordination of the two spaces through the transformations (1) and through the definition of the egocentric reference curves by relations like (2) and (3). The second structure is the intrinsic metric geometry of visual space, postulated to be one of the three classical geometries of constant curvature. If there is a unified description of purely binocular perception, by combining these structures, we now have the means through well-defined measurements to obtain it.

It might seem necessary to decide first which of the three classical geometries describes visual space before attempting its metric description. Actually, measurements that yield values of the visual psychometric also yield the sign of the curvature of the space—and vice versa—see Hardy (1953), pp. 20 ff. and Blank (1961). Nonetheless, it is desirable to be able to adduce evidence for the sign of the curvature independent of evaluations of the psychometric and hence of any predetermined coordination between visual and physical space. We cite two such experiments.

The now classical experiment of Blumenfeld (1913) was used by Luneburg first to characterize the sign of the curvature. In the observer's horizontal plane, Blumenfeld placed two lights Q_0^+ and Q_0^- fixed symmetrically on the left and right sides, respectively, of the x-axis. At each of various stations nearer to the observer, he placed a pair of lights, Q_i^+ and Q_i^- ($i = 1, 2, 3, \ldots$), one on either side of the median, these being movable transversely to the left and right. The movable pairs were set in curvilinear arrays extending toward the observer by two different criteria defining what we shall call the Equidistance Alley and the Parallel Alley. For the Equidistance Alley the pair Q_i^+, Q_i^- was set at positions E_i^+, E_i^-, respectively, so that the span from E_i^+ to E_i^- was perceptually symmetrically disposed across the median line and equal to the span between the fixed points Q_0^+ and Q_0^-. For the Parallel Alley the pair was set at positions P_i^+, P_i^- so that the two arrays $Q_0^+, P_1^+, P_2^+, P_3^+, \ldots$, and $Q_0^-, P_1^-, P_2^-, P_3^-, \ldots$ extended toward the observer symmetrically on the right and left of the median and appear as straight, parallel lines. For most observers, the alleys were set as in Figure 7, with the Parallel Alley falling inside the Equidistance Alley. That the two alleys are not the same is striking evidence that visual space is not Euclidean.

The criterion of equidistance has an unambiguous meaning in a Riemannian geometry, but the concept of parallelism requires interpretation in all but Euclidean geometry. To some observers, the concept seems to mean something else than to others; some find it ambiguous and do not give stable responses, see Hardy (1951). Blumenfeld found that some of his observers were better able to accept and utilize the instruction to set the sides of the Parallel Alley as perpendiculars to a transverse line. But which transverse line? Luneburg postulated that the Parallel Alley is perpendicular to the sensory transverse axis through the egocentre, the left side being perpendicular to the ray $\varphi = \pi/2$, the right, to the ray $\varphi = -\pi/2$. If this is correct, visual space has negative curvature (the opposite would be true if the alley were perpendicular to the transversal joining Q_0^+ and Q_0^-). Fortunately, tests of the experienced observers G.R. and M.C.R. of Hardy (1951, 1953) verified that for them, at least, perpendicularity to the lateral axis coincided with the vaguely defined concept of parallelism they had employed earlier.

In order to avoid all questions of ambiguous interpretation I used an entirely different method of deciding the sign of the curvature, (1961). In Euclidean

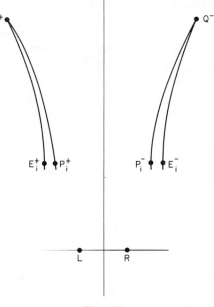

Figure 7

geometry, the segment joining the midpoints of two of the sides of a triangle has half the length of the third side, in hyperbolic geometry, the segment has less than half the length; in elliptic geometry, it has more than half. Six out of the seven observers tested showed the negative curvature of hyperbolic geometry by this criterion. The seventh remembered the Euclidean theorem and evidently employed it as a criterion. Other experimental investigators, see Hardy (1951), have also encountered observers who bring preconceptions into the laboratory and such observers account for much of the variability between observers. On the whole, it seems likely that binocular visual space is hyperbolic for all normal observers.

In the following, we shall assume that visual space is hyperbolic. It shall be realized that if there are any observers for which visual space is truly elliptic, or Euclidean, this will be made immediately evident in the course of evaluating their visual psychometrics and the appropriate related formalism should then be used; see Hardy (1953).

6. The Psychometric of Visual Space

The goal now is to describe the visual geometry of any given binocular stimulus. For lack of sufficient experimental evidence about the full three-dimensional space, we restrict ourselves to the horizontal plane. We take an egocentric visual frame with polar coordinates r(radius) and φ(azimuth). We assume that the physical reference curves of the visual polar frame are known and given in the form.[4]

$$r = F(\gamma, \phi) = \text{constant}$$
$$\varphi = G(\gamma, \phi) = \text{constant}. \tag{4}$$

The intrinsic metric of visual space describes the visual separation s between any pair of points $(r_1, \varphi_1), (r_2, \varphi_2)$. It can easily be found in polar coordinates for each of the three classical geometries from the appropriate form of the law of cosines. In hyperbolic geometry, omitting an arbitrary factor corresponding to free choice of a unit of length, we obtain

$$\cosh s = \cosh r_1 \cosh r_2 - \sinh r_1 \sinh r_2 \cos(\varphi_2 - \varphi_1). \tag{5}$$

If we insert the values of r and φ given in terms of the physical parameters γ, ϕ, we obtain the *visual psychometric*

$$\cosh s = \cosh F(\gamma_1, \phi_1) \cosh F(\gamma_2, \phi_2)$$
$$- \sinh F(\gamma_1, \phi_1) \sinh F(\gamma_2, \phi_2) \cos[G(\gamma_2, \phi_2) - G(\gamma_1, \phi_1)]. \tag{6}$$

The importance of the psychometric is that it contains complete geometrical information about binocular perception in the horizontal plane. For observer G.R. for whom F and G are given by (2) and (3) in the form

$$\begin{cases} F(\gamma, \phi) = \dfrac{\gamma}{1 - 0{\cdot}19\phi^2} \\ G(\gamma, \phi) = 1{\cdot}1\phi \end{cases} \tag{7}$$

The description of visual space is presumably complete.

Tacitly, in the discussion leading to (6), we have assumed that there is a unitary geometric structure to binocular visual space within which the perception of all binocular stimuli are organized. In other words, the underlying metric of visual space does not change with the stimulus. This unitary structure should then be characterized by the intrinsic metric (5). No such assumption is being made in (4). The iseikonic transformation (1) permits us to change, by addition of a constant all values of γ in a given stimulus configuration to produce a quite different configuration which yields the same perception as the original one. Thus, the depence on γ of the physical to visual coordination (4) and, hence, that of the psychometric (6) vary from stimulus to stimulus. We are left with the problem of finding a systematic rule for this variation.

For experimental purposes it is not necessary to write down *a priori* the rules for systematic variation of (4) with the stimulus. We can use (4) for measurement within any given stimulus configuration and map out the perceptual counterpart of that configuration in visual space. Having done that for a variety

---

[4] If the observer has bilateral symmetry, F will be an even function in ϕ and, G an odd function in ϕ. In general, slight asymmetries occur. Observers having aniseikonia or other anisometropic peculiarities may show conspicuous departures from this rule. See Blank (1957), p. 169.

of configurations, we may infer what the systematic rule should be. This, in fact, is what actually happened historically; see Blank (1958b), p. 924b.

Concerning the coordination (4), it is important to note explicitly the tacit assumption that the physical reference curves for the visual polar frame are the same for all stimuli. Some support for this assumption may be found in a demonstration of Luneburg (1947), but detailed quantitative evidence has yet to be obtained.

It is convenient to introduce coordinates in the horizontal plane that are invariant under the iseikonic transformation (1). It will be recalled that we are dealing with configurations consisting only of finitely many light points (γ_i, ϕ_i), $i = 1, 2, \ldots, n$. Take

$$\hat{\gamma} = \min \gamma_i \tag{8a}$$

and set

$$\Gamma_i = \gamma_i - \hat{\gamma}. \tag{8b}$$

In the iseikonic transformation (1), both γ_i and γ will be altered by adding the same constant; consequently, Γ_i will not be changed. It is important to realize that the iseikonic transformations yield binocular equivalence in the distal region but are only approximately correct at near. In the far region (except for asymmetric observers) the dependence of r on ϕ is weak. Furthermore $\varphi = 1 \cdot 1\phi$ seems to hold generally, Foley (1965). The quantity φ exhibits little dependence on γ. For binocularly equivalent configurations, therefore, we may replace (4) by the simpler relations

$$r = f(\Gamma)$$

$$\varphi = 1 \cdot 1\phi \tag{9}$$

Thus to a fair approximation, we have reduced the problem of determining the psychometric (6) for binocularly equivalent configurations to the evaluation of a single function of one variable, the function f in (9). We must also hope to find regularities that will permit us to describe how the functions f differ for stimuli that are not equivalent.

In Hardy (1955) and Blank (1953, 1958b, 1961), I have given methods for evaluating $f(\Gamma)$ by hyperbolic trigonometry. In those papers, the second equation of (9), for want of more refined knowledge, was taken as $\varphi = \phi$. To date, the only comprehensive empirical studies of the form of f that I know are those of observers M.C.R. and G.R. at the Knapp Laboratories, Hardy (1953). What I say next is based only on this limited and approximate evidence.

The function f as determined by a variety of independent experiments, unconnected by iseikonic transformation, is actually independent of the particular stimulus. It is a convex decreasing function of Γ. The function f is a personal characteristic of the observer and varies greatly from observer to observer.

One of the consequences of the invariance of f is strikingly unexpected: there is a maximal hyperbolic distance $\omega = f(0)$ from the observer in visual space, and this distance is attained in any stimulus by the point at minimum convergence, $\gamma = \hat{\gamma}$. In other words, there is a kind of backdrop in visual space and every stimulus configuration rests against this backdrop. An interesting way to demonstrate the presence of this backdrop is to use the capacity for divergent fusion as follows. With the help of polaroids, Hardy (1953), p. 65 f., or a septum, two points on a transverse line $x =$ const. can be presented, each to the ipsilateral eye, to be fused binocularly. If the distance between the two points is less than the intercentral separation of the eyes, fusion yields an impression equivalent to that obtained by presenting for binocular view a single light at the intersection of the lines of sight. If the monocular targets are separated so that the lines of sight are parallel or even diverge, fusion is maintained and a single light perceived even though no equivalent single binocular target exists. On a clear moonless night, we present such a double target in convergent view so that it is seen as a single light against the background of the star-studded sky. For this purpose it is desirable to make the light definitely perceptually brighter than the stars. Now we separate the target lights gradually. The perceived light appears to recede until at the position of parallel view it seems to rest among the stars in the dome of the sky. Further separation, into the realm of divergence, does not make the light recede further. Instead, as the target lights separate in divergence, the perceived light remains fixed and the dome of the sky appears to shrink toward the observer until divergence can be pushed no longer, at which point the stars seem to be clustered on a tight little ball immediately over the bridge of his nose.

The demonstration with the starry sky is easily explained by the invariance of $f(\Gamma)$. Before the target light entered the divergent realm, the stars were visually the most distant objects in the stimulus and rested on the hyperbolic backdrop at intrinsic distance $\omega = f(0)$. As the target light entered into divergence, it became the visually farthest point in the field of view, came to apparent rest at intrinsic distance ω, while the stars having gradually increasing Γ, hence diminishing values of f, appeared to come nearer to the observer.[5]

7. Further Reflections

In constructing this formal approach to binocular space perception, I have attempted to isolate hypotheses in a rather general framework for which there are only two basic requirements:

1. That an experimentally reproducible determination of the physical reference curves of the visual polar frame be attainable:

---

[5] C. J. Campbell and I induced L. H. Hardy to offer us a free dinner if we could show him something that appeared farther than the stars. We then showed Hardy this demonstration. He refused us the dinner on the ground that the target never looked more remote than the stars did originally.

2. That there exist a unitary intrinsic geometry in which binocular space perceptions are organized.

All the rest is detail filled in by analysis, measurement, qualitative observation and conjecture. For the existence of a valid theory only the two basic requirements are essential. The details can be modified as the phenomena warrant. Such a general framework guides us to pointed questions and to experiments designed to furnish such details without being so restrictive that each turn of the experimental evidence is likely to undermine the whole structure and force us to tear all down and build entirely anew.

Despite the apparent completeness of the theory, there is an abundance of questions left to be resolved; the field is far from closed. Let us consider some of the open problems.

(a) The Approximation Problems

As I indicated in several places, there is no complete quantitative determination of the psychometric (6) for any observer, even in the horizontal plane. For the Knapp Laboratory observers G.R. and M.C.R. there is what appears to be a good first approximation, Hardy (1953), pp. 60 ff. For these observers, it may even be possible to recover enough information from the Knapp Laboratory data to make higher order corrections. Thus, for G.R. we can refine the equations of the physical reference curves by using (2) and (3) over a large part of the visual field. For other observers, the data are not comprehensive enough. Clearly, we are not yet able to predict whether corrections like (2) and (3) for observer G.R. will prove useful. Yet we can seek straws in the wind.

Let us suppose that the physical-visual coordination (4) always gives flatter representations of egocentric circles than the Vieth-Muller Circles $\gamma = $ const. Let γ^* be the convergence angle of that point where the representation of the egocentric circle through (γ, ϕ) crosses the x-axis. Observer G.R., for example, has

$$\gamma^* = \gamma/(1 - 0.19\phi^2)$$

but the relation varies greatly among observers. Let us suppose that the correct form of the transformation (1) for the horizontal plane is

$$\gamma^{*\prime} = \gamma^* + \tau$$
$$\phi' = \phi$$
$$\theta' = \theta = 0.$$

We have already remarked that difficulties arise in the proximal region when we attempt to account for the results of the Helmholtz three-thread experiments. The difficulty is exhibited by an examination of the quantity

$$\frac{\gamma_1 - \gamma_0}{1 - \cos\phi_0} \tag{10}$$

where $(\gamma_0, \pm\phi_0)$ are the coordinates of the fixed lights and $(\gamma_1, 0)$ those of the movable central light. The quantity (10) should be nearly constant, but Zajacz-kowska's observers (1955) predominantly show an increase in the values of this quantity in the near region; see Blank (1957), p. 924, Table III. However, if we replace γ by γ^* in (10), the difference $\gamma_1^* - \gamma_0^*$ will decrease at an increasing rate as γ_0^* increases toward the proximal region. Thus there will be a compensation in the right direction.[6] Of course, without determining the correct form of (2) for each of these observers we have no way to tell whether this compensation is adequate or perhaps even excessive.

It is interesting, too, to examine another experiment of Zajaczkowska (1956). In this, she repeats the Blumenfeld Alleys for three conditions: long narrow 'classic' alleys extending toward the observer from points 420 cm forward of the observer and 4° to the left and right, 'Intermediate' alleys (300 cm forward and about 6° left and right), and 'broad' alleys (139 cm forward and about 12° left and right). If the values of $\omega = f(0)$ are calculated by the methods of Hardy (1953), her observers' broad alleys generally show markedly lower values of ω than the classic alleys; see Blank (1958b), p. 919, Table 2. The theory says, of course, that ω is constant. Suppose, however, that in (9) we replace Γ by $\Gamma^* = \gamma^* - \hat{\gamma}^*$, where $\hat{\gamma}^* = \min \gamma^*$, in accordance with our revision of the iseikonic transformations. Would this compensate and equalize the values of ω? Unfortunately, the form of $F(\gamma, \phi)$ in (4) is not known for Zajacz-kowska's observers, and the observers G.R. and M.C.R. for whom $F(\gamma, \phi)$ can be found did not execute the broad alleys experiment. So there is no direct test. Still we know that the corrected distance function $f^*(\Gamma^*)$ is close to the already calculated function $f(\Gamma)$ for G.R. since the correction (2) has little effect for the small values of ϕ associated with the classic alleys (from which $f(\Gamma)$ was calculated). We can use $f^*(\Gamma^*)$ to predict G.R.'s setting of the broad alleys. Then we can calculate what the values of the uncorrected $f(\Gamma)$ would be for this setting and see if the calculated value $\omega = f(0)$ is actually markedly lower for the broad than the classic alleys. Doing this, we find $\omega = \cdot89$ for the broad alleys as compared with $\omega = 1\cdot48$ for the classic alleys. This is consistent with the kind of result the uncorrected theory gave for Zajaczkowska's observers.

All this discussion about 'what might happen if . . .' is arrant speculation. Yet it raises issues that warrant investigation and, so, is useful I hope.

(b) Extended Application of the Theory

There are large relatively unexplored domains. The problem of establishing and testing the psychometric of visual space has been attacked only in the horizontal plane. The full three-dimensional space has received little experimental attention.

Most important the incorporation of motion into a complete space-time system has yet to be undertaken. There are intriguing hints of effects akin to the

---

[6] There will also be some compensation in Zajaczkowska's data through use of (3) to replace ϕ_0 by $1\cdot1\phi_0$, but this is a relatively minor adjustment.

Lorentz contraction of special relativity to be found in visual space time; Blank (1957), p. 234. There are observations (unpublished) that suggest localized curvature of space-time in the neighbourhood of light points, this is somewhat suggestive of aspects of general relativity.

Certainly much remains to be thought about and experimented upon.

(c) Conflict with the Theory

Now I want to raise another and more serious issue. Foley (1972) describes the experiment depicted schematically in Figure 8. A light A is fixed in the visual field. The observer is aksed to set a light B so that line OB from the observer to B is apparently perpendicular to the line from A to B and also to make the spans AB and OB equally long. Next, the observer is asked to set C so that CO is perpendicular and equal to BO in length. The triangles ABO and BOC are isosceles right triangles with equal legs. If the visual space is Riemannian of constant curvature, the triangles must be congruent and the hypotenuses AO and CB must be equal. Yet for Foley's 'large configuration' 79% of 24 observers judged BC to be longer than OA and, for his 'small configuration, 87%. What are we to make of this? It certainly seems that some hypothesis must have failed us. Could the experiment extend into a region large enough to make a nonconstant curvature detectable? Could the space be non Riemannian (Foley thinks so)? Is it conceivable that the concept of a unitary visual space is at fault? Is it necessary to find a criterion for distinguishing stimuli the theory can handle from those it cannot and to develop a patchwork quilt of theories covering different domains of perception? Or, though it seems unlikely, is it possible that there is some element of suggestion in the instructions or in the configuration itself that induces the observer's response? Is the result an artifact of the experimental technique?[7]

These are questions I can only leave with you. I am unable to find or even guess at answers without returning to the darkness of the optics laboratory and renewing the cycle of speculation, testing, and analysis.

Permit me to close with a quotation from Dirac (1954) that I have used before when writing about another apparent contradiction in the development of the theory of visual space that finally got resolved in an unforeseen and simple way: 'The moral of the story is that one should have faith in a theory that is beautiful. If the theory fails to agree with experiment, its basic principles may still be correct and the discrepancy may be due merely to some detail that will get cleared up in the future.'

---

[7] For example, the technique developed at the Knapp Laboratory, largely under the guidance of Gertrude Rand, would not involve asking the observer to verbalize the result of an experiment. Thus, in this case, the observer would not be asked whether BC appears longer than OA but asked to reveal that judgement by an action. For example, after the final position of C was set, the observer might be required to set a light X on BC so that BX would be equal to OA.

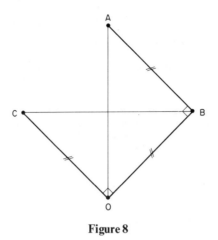

Figure 8

References

Blank, A. A. (1953). The Luneburg theory of binocular visual space, *J. Opt. Soc. Am.*, **43**, no. 9, 717–727.

Blank, A. A. (1957). The Geometry of Vision, *Brit. J. Physiol. Optics*, **14**, 154–169, 222–235.

Blank, A. A. (1958a). Axiomatics of binocular vision, *J. Opt. Soc. Am.*, **48**, no. 5, 328–334.

Blank, A. A. (1958b). Analysis of Experiments in Binocular Space Perception, *J. Opt. Soc. Am.*, **48**, no. 12, 911–925.

Blank, A. A. (1959). The Luneburg theory of binocular space perception. In *Psychology—A Study of a Science* McGraw-Hill, New York, N.Y.

Blank, A. A. (1961). Curvature of Binocular Visual Space, *J. Opt. Soc. Am.*, **51**, no. 3, 335–339.

Blumenfeld, W. (1913). Untersuchungen über die scheinbare Grösse in Sehraume, *Z. Psychol. u. Physiol. d. Sinnesorg.*, **65**, no. 1, 241.

Busemann, H. (1955). *The Geometry of Geodesics* Academic Press, New York, N.Y.

Dirac, P. A. M. (1954). Letter. *Sci. Monthly*, **79**, no. 4.

Foley, J. M. (1964a). Desarguesian property in visual space, *J. Opt. Soc. Am.*, **54**, no. 5, 684–692.

Foley, J. M. (1964b). Visual space: a test of the constant curvature hypothesis, *Psychon. Sci.*, **1**, 9–10.

Foley, J. M. (1965), Visual space. A scale of perceived relative direction, *Proc. Am. Psych. Assn.*, pp. 49–50.

Foley, J. M. (1966). Locus of Perceived Equidistance as a function of viewing distance, *J. Opt. Soc. Am.*, **56**, no. 6, 822–827.

Foley, J. M. (1967). Binocular Disparity and Perceived Relative Distance, *Vision Res.*, **7**, 655–670.

Foley, J. M. (1972). The size-distance relation and intrinsic geometry of visual space, *Vision Res.*, **12**, pp. 323–332.

Hardy, Rand and Rittler, (1951). Investigation of visual space, the Blumenfeld Alleys, *Arch. Ophthal.*, **45**, p. 53.

Hardy, Rand, Rittler and Blank, Boeder, (1953). *The Geometry of Binocular Space Perception.* Knapp Memorial Laboratories, Institute of Ophtalmology, Columbia University College of Physicians and Surgeons, New York, N.Y.

Helmholtz, H. L. F. (1925). *Physiological Optics* (trans.), vol. 3, Opt. Soc. Am., Rochester, N.Y.

Ittelson, W. H. (1952). *The Ames Demonstrations in Perception* Princeton Univ. Press, Princeton, N.J.

Luneburg, R. K. (1947). *Mathematical Analysis of Binocular Vision*, Princeton Univ. Press, Princeton, N.J.

Luneburg, R. K. (1948). Metric methods in binocular visual perception, in *Studies and Essays*, Courant Anniversary Volume Interscience, New York, N.Y.

Zajaczkowska, A., (1955). *An Experimental Study of Luneburg's Theory of Visual Perception*, Doctoral dissertation, University of London.

Zajaczkowska, A., (1956). *J. Opt. Soc. Am.*, **46**, p. 514.

Chapter 5

Apparent Motion: Self-excited Oscillations Induced by Retarded Neuronal Flows

Terry Caelli, William C. Hoffman and Harold Lindman

Abstract. There is sufficient evidence to indicate that the perception of real and apparent movement is not governed by linear (Galilean) velocity formulations. It is contended that the geometric structure of perceived apparent movement is elliptic Riemannian space and that the motion is induced by self-excitatory neurophysiological counterparts of retarded actions. An equation is developed which explains past data and predicts the existence of apparent movement. Experimental results support the model, relate the parameters to real movement parameters and examine a new distance illusion due to ϕ-movement.

It is known that when two light sources of specific luminance and form are presented sequentially to the visual system, apparent motion can be perceived between them. Under definite spatio-temporal conditions this motion is seen to be smooth and continuous (beta or optimal; Kolers, 1972) and is independent of whether the display is periodic (repetitive; Tyler, 1973) or simply occurs between the two lights once.

However, to date no formal model for the phenomena has been developed which adequately relates the spatial and temporal constraints of the display to the mechanisms within the visual system which generate the perception of the motion (Kolers, 1972). For example, Kolers (1972, Chapter 11) partitions past theories of apparent motion into four kinds: epiphenomenal, equivalence, figural and excitation theories. A typical, rather vague level of explanation is seen in the last theory where apparent motion is contended to arise from:

> separately stimulated retinal loci generate regions of excitation in corresponding areas of cortex which, when properly timed, interact with each other electrically. (Kolers, 1972, p. 180).

This particular model may well describe the general processes involved but it does not precisely predict the spatiotemporal constraints which induce even the simplest form of beta motion. Even more recent approaches to apparent motion suffer from this lack of quantification. For example, Foster (1975) contends that beta motion occurs between two visual forms if and only if they are equivalent under an affine transformation of three-dimensional Euclidean space. Again, this may well be true but it is not sufficient to predict the parametric values of time and distance which determine the motion.

The aim of this paper is to develop a model for the simplest form of apparent motion (beta motion between two light sources) which will determine the spatio-temporal domain of the effect, and which is based on known processes within the visual system.

The Model

Of fundamental importance to any model for apparent motion is a definition of the type of motion involved. Kolers (1972) clearly demonstrates that apparent motion, related to the stimulus space, does not obey the linear (Galilean) formulation of motion since a finite apparent motion can be observed when the interstimulus interval (ISI) is zero. That is, it is impossible, under the linear formulation (velocity = distance/time) to travel a finite distance in zero time.

In a companion paper (Caelli, Hoffman and Lindman, 1976) we have considered the phenomena of real motion perception. There we have shown that, owing to the finite value of cortical signal propagation, phenomena analogous to the Special Theory of Relativity occur in the afferent phase of processing real motion by the human visual system. Here we extend the model to the efferent phase of motion processing and find again that the upper limit for the velocity of cortical signal propagation plays a key role.

Put simply, phi phenomena are induced, in the present view, when the visual system becomes unable to process the motion stimulus as fast as it is presented. The finite value of nerve signal propagation velocity along the processes of the cortical neurons results in a retardation—a lag behind—of the efferent phase with respect to the afferent volleys in the visual system. The two phases are thus, no longer essentially simultaneous in real (cortical) time, with the result that self-excited oscillations are generated.

The latter comes about as follows. We have shown elsewhere (Caelli, Hoffman and Lindman, 1976; Hoffman, 1966) that afferent motion processing is governed by the Lie derivatives of the Lorentz group. The efferent phase is governed by the Lie derivatives of egocentred rotational motion, L_M:

$$L_M = y\frac{\partial}{\partial x} - x\frac{\partial}{\partial y}, \quad L_{M1} = x\frac{\partial}{\partial \tau} - \tau\frac{\partial}{\partial x}, \quad L_{M2} = y\frac{\partial}{\partial \tau} - \tau\frac{\partial}{\partial y} \quad (1)$$

Consider the second of these, which governs time varying (τ) motion of a horizontal (x) system, such as the basic phi motion configuration of two alternately flashing lights. (We note, however, that a similar vertical configuration could be treated in exactly the same fashion using L_{M2}, and an oblique configuration by a linear combination of L_{M_1} and L_{M_2}). We then proceed in the standard way to determine the trajectories of the L_{M_1}-motion. Form the corresponding Pfaffian system (Hoffman, 1966):

$$\frac{\mathrm{d}x}{-\tau} = \frac{\mathrm{d}\tau}{x} = \frac{\mathrm{d}a}{1} \tag{2}$$

where a is a psychophysical parameter for the efferent processing of motion. Equation (2) can also be written as the system:

$$\frac{\mathrm{d}x}{\mathrm{d}a} = -\tau, \frac{\mathrm{d}\tau}{\mathrm{d}a} = x \tag{3}$$

From equation (3) we immediately have the differential equation for simple harmonic motion:

$$\frac{\mathrm{d}^2 x(a)}{\mathrm{d}a^2} + x(a) = 0 \tag{4}$$

We now postulate, in accordance with the proposed afferent-efferent lag, that the argument of $\mathrm{d}^2 x/\mathrm{d}a^2$ is not 'a' but 'a retarded'; that is, $a - h$. Consequently, equation (4) takes the form:

$$\frac{\mathrm{d}^2 x(a - h)}{\mathrm{d}a^2} + x(a) = 0 \tag{5}$$

This retarded form (equation 5) of simple harmonic motion (equation 4) corresponds to a system for self-excited retarded oscillations (Minorsky, 1962) which is equivalent to the perturbed equation for harmonic motion.

$$\frac{\mathrm{d}^2 x(a)}{\mathrm{d}a^2} + x(a) = h\frac{\mathrm{d}^3 x(a)}{\mathrm{d}a^3} - \frac{h^2}{2!}\frac{\mathrm{d}^4 x(a)}{\mathrm{d}a^4} + \ldots -(-1)^n\frac{h^n}{n!}\frac{\mathrm{d}^{n+2} x(a)}{\mathrm{d}a^{n+2}} + \ldots \tag{6}$$

The right hand side of equation (6) acts to generate the self-excited oscillations. The left hand side governs the basic, unperturbed phase portrait of the oscillation. We now proceed to a qualitative study of this phase portrait in the (x, τ) plane, or phase plane (Figure 1(a)).

We consider, to a first approximation without any essential loss of generality concerning the oscillatory behaviour, the homogeneous version of equation (6). This is the equation of simple harmonic motion and its trajectories are topologically equivalent to those of the complete self-excited oscillation determined by equation (6). We thus consider the equation of simple harmonic motion (4) whose trajectories are:

$$x^2 + \tau^2 = K^2 \quad \text{or} \quad x^2 + c^{*2}t^2 = K^2, \tag{7}$$

where c^* corresponds to the limiting neural propagation rate of the afferent-efferent volleys (Caelli, Hoffman and Lindman, 1976).

Equation (7) gives rise to the concentric circles in the phase plane (Figure

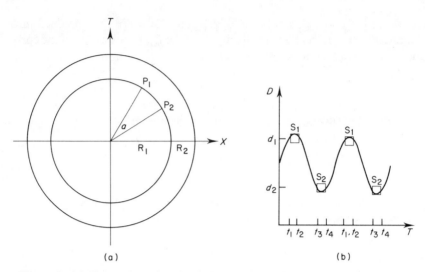

Figure 1. (a) Phase plane for simple harmonic oscillators (T corresponds to time and X to distance) (b) Stimulus configuration for apparent motion: (S_1, S_2), and induced sinnsoidal motion over distance (D) with respect to time (T)

1(a)), where R_1 and R_2 correspond to different K values. For apparent motion t corresponds to the onset-to-onset interval (exposure time (e) plus the inter-stimulus interval (i)) determining the temporal phase of the oscillation. The parameter K corresponds to the maximum distance (visual angle) over which beta motion will occur, which is equivalent to the maximum temporal range ($\tau = c^*t$) for the motion (Figure 1(a)).

According to the present model the parameter c^*, which determines the afferent-efferent lag resulting in the oscillations, is related to the maximum neural propagation rate. However, in the stimulus domain, this value would seem appropriately measured by the maximum velocity of perceived real movement (Kaufman et al., 1971). Consequently it is intended that:

$$d^2 + c^{*2}(e + i - \bar{i})^2 = K^2 \tag{8}$$

predicts the spatio-temporal bounds on apparent beta motion where d is the separation distance of the lights, c^* is the observer's maximum velocity of perceived movement, $e + i$ corresponds to the onset-to-onset interval, and $\bar{i}$ is the interstimulus interval which corresponds to the induction of apparent motion at distance $d = K$.

For beta (optimal) motion, observers report perceiving smooth and continuous motion between the two sources (Kolers, 1972). As a first approximation, the present model predicts this motion to be sinusoidal (Figure 1(b)) and to exist within the circular region described by equation (8) (Figure 1(a)). This region corresponds to velocites greater than c^* and thus accords to Kaufman's (1971) conjecture.

Possibly the most extensive parametric data on beta motion is that of Neuhaus (1930). These data are shown in Figure 2. It can be seen as distance increases the band width for the occurrence of apparent motion (between the two dots) decreases. Least square solutions for K and c^* in (8) are:

$$c^* = \left(\frac{\sum_i d_i^2 \sum_i t_i^2 - n\sum_i d_i^2 t_i^2}{n\sum_i t_i^4 - (\sum_i t_i^2)^2} \right)^{\frac{1}{2}} \tag{9}$$

and

$$K = \frac{\sum_i d_i^2 + c^{*2} \sum_i t_i^2}{n} \tag{10}$$

where $t_i = (i_i - \bar{i} + e)$ and $\bar{i}$ corresponds to the maximum distance which will induce beta motion, for a given e value.

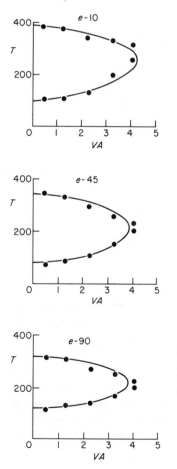

Figure 2. Neuhaus' (1930) data for beta motion over three exposure times (10, 45, 90 msecs) and predicted oscillation elliptical domains. (VA: visual angle in degrees, T: onset-to-onset interval in msecs)

When applied to the Neuhaus data (Figure 2) equations (9) and (10) resulted in c^* values of 29, 31 and 39 degrees per second for e values of 10, 45, and 90, respectively. Similarly, K values of $4 \cdot 11°$, $3 \cdot 82°$ and $3 \cdot 80°$ were found for the 10, 45, and 90 mseconds exposures. These values were plotted for (8) and the best fitting ellipses are shown in Figure 2. The apparent consistencies between the Neuhaus (1930) data and (8) support the oscillation model and the elliptical nature of the space-time involved, even though the former is only a first order approximation to the full oscillation equation (6). However, the relatively low values for c^* indicate need for direct estimations of c^* before the model can be fully tested. This range of c^* values has been observed by others (20–40°/second; Kaufman et al., 1971) but larger values (around 50°/second) have been found (De Silva, 1929).

The aim of the following experiments was to demonstrate that once c^* was determined, the spatio-temporal domain for beta motion could be directly predicted and that the best fitting value of K corresponds to the maximum separation distance for which beta motion will occur.

Another prediction of this model is that perceived time and distance of beta motion is distorted according to the elliptical relationship between time and distance (7). Wertheimer (1912) noted that when four lights forming a square were sequentially illuminated to induce apparent motion, a circular motion inside the Euclidean positions of the lights was observed.

Such a result can be explained in terms of the elliptic space-time of beta motion. If $d(x, y)$ represents the Euclidean distance between the two lights then the corresponding elliptical distance $(S(x, y))$ is:

$$S(x, y) = d(x, y) \cdot \frac{\theta}{\sin \theta} \tag{11}$$

where the angle subtended by the arc (X, Y), at the centre, is 2θ. Consequently, given two lights with appropriate spatiotemporal conditions to induce beta motion, then the observer, when asked to judge distance will assume the elliptic distance is Euclidean and thus underestimate the distance between the lights in accord with (8). A third experiment was also run to investigate this further illusory character of beta motion.

Finally Kolers (1972) and Foster (1972) generally report that beta motion, particularly between two light sources, adopts a linear motion (direct Euclidean path). If the elliptical structure of beta motion is valid then such linear motions could only occur when the distance between spatio-temporal points is small. In opposition to this linear motion, it is predicted that as distance increases the path of this simple beta motion should be curved, either rotatory or of a pendulum action. Although pendulum-type motion has already been observed by others (Hall, Earle and Crookes, 1952) the curvature of the perceived motion path has not been measured or explained, in terms of a general model for the induction of apparent motion.

Experiment 1. The Measurement of c*

Method

Subjects

Four undergraduate students at Melbourne University were employed as Subjects. Each S was tested on the Bausch and Lomb Ortho-Rater and results indicated normal binocular vision. Subjects also reported that they had no problems with their vision.

Stimulus and Apparatus

The stimulus consisted of a dot moving across a Hewlett-Packard oscilloscope with P15 phosphor. The dot subtended a visual angle of 10' of arc and an illuminance of 3·14 foot Lamberts, and the horizontal path of motion subtended a visual angle of 7° to the observer. The motion was induced by means of a positive ramp function generated from a Wavetek function generator (Model 111). The dot remained stationary for 50% of a cycle, then moved continuously across the screen for the 7° amplitude. Consequently increasing the frequency increased the velocity of the dot.

The benefit of this technique for generating motion is that when the motion becomes too fast to perceive, the S can still observe the flicker rate of the cycle. That is, the 'sheet of light' appears to flicker.[1]

Procedure

These experiments were carried out over a 10-day period. The first four days consisted of one hour training sessions per S, while the latter six days constituted the experimental sessions. Both training and experimental sessions had the following format. Subjects were seated, in a semi-illuminated experimental room, one metre from the oscilloscope. They were given five minutes adaptation to the environment and then shown two ascending and two descending series of velocities. In the ascending series they were asked to detect when the moving dot (initially clear, then blurred) lost its motion and the display appeared to a 'flickering sheet of light' without any real motion. In the descending series they were asked to detect when the flickering source gave away to the perception of a dot moving continuously across the screen, and to specify its path of motion (to the right or left).

Subjects were instructed to rest their heads on a chin rest and to fixate on the stationary dot position at all times. These two ascending and two descending

[1] Some confusion in the literature has evolved concerning the definition of c^*. While De Silva (1929) defined it as that velocity where a light source appeared as a stationary 'sheet of light', Pollock (1953) defined it as that value above which Subjects could not tell direction of motion.

series were repeated each day and the starting position of each run was randomized.

Results

The mean velocity for each ascending and descending series was tabulated for each day over each Subject. Grand means and standard deviations were then calculated over the six sessions for each Subject (Table 1). These values for the maximum velocity of perceived movement (c^*) are consistent with past findings (Kolers, 1972) on the first three Ss, being around 50°/second. However the fourth $S(JQ)$ consistently reported much higher values for c^* (Table 1), ranging around 97°/second.

Experiment 2: Spatio-Temporal Domain of Beta Motion.

Having determined c^* for each S, the aim of this experiment was to investigate the predicted elliptic function (5) for beta motion.

Method

Stimulus and Apparatus

A computer program was written to display two point sources of light on a Hewlett-Packard oscilloscope (CRT) with P15 phosphor. Each dot subtended a visual angle of 10′ of arc to the observer (seated one metre from the scope) and had an illuminance of 3·14 Foot Lamberts. The experimenter could change (increment or decrement) the exposure times, interstimulus intervals (between dots 1 and 2, then 2 and 1) and distance between dots by a series of switches in the experimental room. The parameters of the program were set such that, for a given dot separation distance, dot exposure time, the interstimulus intervals (ISI's) could not be increased or decreased faster than 10 mseconds per 2 seconds.

Table 1. c^* values for the four experimental subjects over six ascending and descending series (degrees/second)

	Subject			
	DH	CB	SL	JQ
Mean	50·28	58·46	60·31	97·44
Standard Deviation	1·79	2·43	2·54	2·34

Procedure

Subjects were seated at a distance of one metre from the CRT. A stimulus run consisted of one of 6 dot separation distances (1, 2, 3, 4, 5 and 6° of visual angle) and the exposure time (10, 45 or 90 mseconds). The S was instructed that he/she would see either two flashing dots or one dot moving smoothly and continuously back and forth across the scope.

Each run consisted of one ascending and one descending series on the ISI's (which were always symmetric). For the ascending series the ISI's were set at 0, then increased at the rate of 10 msecond for 2 seconds until S reported continuous oscillating motion. At this stage the current ISI was printed out on a teletype and then the series continued until the S reported a loss of ϕ-motion; that is, the occurrence of partial or no motion. This value was also obtained. The ISI's were then increased a random amount, and the descending series commenced.

In the descending series the ISI's were decreased until S reported the occurrence of beta motion and then the disappearance of the motion. These ISI values were listed on the teletype and the ISI's were reset to zero in readiness for the next run at a different visual angle. The S was presented with the six visual angles in random and then given a 10-minute rest. He/she was then run again over these ascending and descending series. On each day a new exposure time was employed. Consequently over a three-day period each S received two ascending and two descending series on each visual angle for three different exposure times. Each run over the six angles took about twenty minutes, thus making the daily testing period of fifty minutes.

Previous to the test days in the Ss were trained for a week in discriminating between no motion, partial motion and beta (smooth and continuous) motion. During these sessions the same ascending and descending series were employed, except that Ss were instructed to respond when the class of motion changed. In both trial and test conditions Ss were always asked to fixate on the centre of the screen and to place their chins on the chin rest in front of the scope.

Experiment 3: Distance Illusion Due to Beta Motion

Stimulus and Apparatus

Four pale green light emitting diodes (LEDs) with fast decay rates (equivalent to P15 phosphor) were used as the experimental stimuli. They were positioned on two bars straddling two retort stands such that the two on the bottom bar were 5 cms below the two on the top. The two top LEDs were coupled to four timers such that they would be alternatively displayed to induce beta motion. The bottom two LEDs were left on permanently. Subjects were seated a distance of one metre from the stands with his/her chin on a chin rest.

Procedure

The experimental conditions for beta motion between the upper two LEDs were determined for 10, 45 and 90 mseconds exposures on each LED and two visual angles (2°, 4°). For each of these six conditions the *S* was to judge the distance between the upper two lights by reporting when the bottom two lights appeared to be the same distance apart as the upper two. This task was performed when beta motion was not present (NB, Table 3) and when beta motion (B, Table 3) was induced.

For each of the six spatio-temporal conditions and for the NB and B states, the *S* was given three adjustment runs. Each run commenced by the experimenter randomly positioning the two lower lights along the bar. The *S* was to instruct the experimenter to move each lower light towards or away from the centre of the bar until he perceived the distances as being equal.

Results

Figure 3 gives the mean ISI values (plus the relevant exposure time to constitute an onset-to-onset measure, τ) for the ascending and descending series corresponding to the band width limits for beta motion.

The convergence of the temporal limits, over distance, replicates Neuhaus' data (1930, Figure 2). A similar method of limits was employed in both experiments, so that these data should also be representative of the phenomena.

The c^* values observed for each Subject were used in (7) to estimate the *K* values (Figure 3). This spatial limit for beta motion was found to be around 7° of visual angle and supports the inability of Subjects to perceive beta motion around and above this value. The appropriate oscillation (ϕ-surface) ellipsoids were then plotted from the measured c^* and estimated *k* values (Figure 3) and would seem to reflect the observed limits for each subject.

In order to test this apparent agreement between (7) and the observed data a regression analysis was performed. By equating $k^2 - d^2$ in (7) with the predictor, and c^{*2} (τ^2) in (7) with the observed scores, Pearson product moment correlations were found to be 0·94*, 0·72*, 0·65* and 0·93* for each of Subjects DM, CB, SL and JQ respectively (*$p < 0.01$, Figure 3). These results indicate a strong linear relationship between the terms in (7) and consequently support the oscillation equation for beta motion.

Frequences of perceived motion paths were tabulated over the three exposure times for each visual angle. Subjects SL and JQ reported no linear motion while the remaining *S*s reported increasing rotatory or pendulum motion as the visual angle increased (Table 2). Since Subject SL only reported rotatory motion her data was not included in Table 2.

Finally, reports of perceived distance were averaged over each condition and exposure time (Table 3) and these results indicate a perceived contraction effect due to the induction of beta motion.

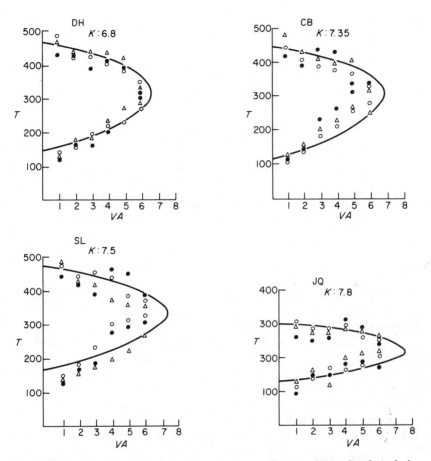

Figure 3. Observed limits of beta motion over distance (*VA*: visual angle in degrees) for three exposure times (*e*: △-10, ○-45, ●-90 msecs) over each subject (*T*: onset-to-onset interval). Ellipsoids correspond to predicted limits of beta motion

Table 2. Percentage reports of Linear (L), Pendulum (P) and Rotary (R) motion over distance for each Subject

		DH				CB				JQ		
		L	P + R	P	R	L	P + R	P	R	P + R	P	R
Distance	1	54	46	17	29	92	8	8	0	100	38	62
	2	50	50	13	37	38	62	46	16	100	25	75
	3	46	54	17	37	13	87	71	16	100	46	54
	4	33	67	46	21	4	96	54	42	100	63	37
	5	26	74	26	48	15	85	20	65	100	75	25
	6	20	80	30	50	10	90	5	85	100	71	29

Table 3. Perceived distances between lights in beta and non-beta motion conditions over each Subject ($2° = 3·5$ cms, $4° = 7·0$ cms)

Subject

	d	DH 2°	DH 4°	CB 2°	CB 4°	SL 2°	SL 4°	JQ 2°	JQ 4°
B: beta	$\bar{x}$	2·83	6·05	3·07	6·32	3·11	6·66	2·78	6·21
	σ_x	0·20	0·37	0·28	0·33	0·17	0·17	0·12	0·30
NB: non-beta	$\bar{x}$	3·47	7·03	3·59	7·07	3·56	7·09	3·56	7·03
	σ_x	0·37	0·22	0·44	0·20	0·16	0·26	0·07	0·23
	B/NB	0·82	0·86	0·86	0·89	0·87	0·93	0·78	0·88

Discussion

The distortion of perceived distance, observed band widths of onset-to-onset interval over distance, and the critical value of c^* all seem to support the hypothesis that beta motion is induced by self-excited oscillations within the visual system. The differences between the estimated c^* values from Neuhaus' (1930) data and the observed c^* values in this experiment (Table 1) are explained by the differences between the display sources. In Neuhaus' (1930) experiment normal lights were employed with very slow decay. However in the present experiment P15 phosphors were employed with very fast decays, thus eradicating possible incorrect estimations of exposure times and the possibility of both lights interfering with each other. Such overlapping sources would tend to considerably slow down c^* and consequently increase the band width of beta motion (Figures 2, 3).

This consistency between temporal limits and c^* is seen when the first three Ss results (DM, CB, SL) are compared with the last (JQ) (Figure 3). Subject JQ reported a very high c^* and also gave a very narrow band width for beta motion in comparison to the first three Subjects.

One of the major problems with conceiving of apparent motion as linear motion is that the motion would have to induced before the onset of the second source. If this were not the case and the motion was linear, then it would have to occur after the onset-to-onset interval (Kolers, 1972). Consequently the light sources must not be the sole determinants of the induction of beta motion in the visual system. Such motions must exist as active transformations and the specific configurations of time and distance must trigger their activity in the perceived geometric space of the stimulus elements.

As mentioned above such oscillations may be induced by 'retarded actions' (Minorsky, 1962). That is, where there exists a system which has the capacity to induce oscillatory motion, then such motion will be spontaneously generated by the introduction of a retardation (phase plane lag, Figure 1) either in the temporal or spatial domains (Minorsky, 1962).

In the case of apparent motion this phase lag is specifically determined by spatio-temporal conditions in accord with equation (7). The temporal domain (Figure 3, equation (7)) is limited by c^*, (the maximum velocity of perceived movement). Thus c^* would seem to be a direct index of some limiting neural propagation rate or the 'vertical component' (Kolers, 1972) in motion perception. Secondly, the resultant lateral retardation between stimulus elements would then seem to occur in Kolers' (1972) 'horizontal component' (involving balances between excitatory and inhibitory states of neighbouring cortical cells in order to induce motion).

This model more closely fits the excitation theories (Kolers, 1972, p. 180) than any other. However, it not only predicts precise functional relationships between the spatio-temporal parameters (equation 7), but also submits the proposition that such motions are constructed as oscillations induced by the retardation between afferent and efferent processes. This phase lag, or retardation, is a determining factor in the distance illusion (Table 3) and would seem to be a constant of about 2 radians in the phase plane ($\sin \theta/\theta \cong 0.86$, Table 3; Figure 1).

From equations (1) and (8) the smooth geometric orbits of beta motion thus follow naturally as a result of egocentred movement constancy, the efferent phase of motion constancy (Hoffman, 1966; Caelli, Hoffman and Lindman, 1976).

Such relations have been further quantified in this experiment and many other confirmations of this elliptical structure of beta motion have been observed. For example, when two segments (both collinear with each other) are displayed in place of two dots, the smooth beta motion assumes the path of one line rotating in depth, one into the other as seen by the observer. Such depth and rotational effects are generated by the oscillatory motion in a spherical space.

Other effects can be predicted from this model. For example, as distance appears to contract, time should appear to dilate (from (8)) in order to preserve the curvature of the elliptical path of motion. Secondly, this formulation for beta motion indicates that the visual system (laterally) processes time and distance in equivalent ways. That is, a specific value of $(e + i)$ is equivalent to a given distance or visual angle (equation (8)) under the relation $c^*(e + i) = \tau$.

Whereas Foster (1972, 1975) formulates beta motion in terms of the affine transformations in Euclidean space, this oscillation model represents apparent motion as the outcome of the rotation group action (1) by visual processing corresponding to certain constancies. Finally, the model contends that the perception of beta motion comes about as an efferent stage of visual processing whenever 'phase lags' are introduced by retarded (delayed) actions initiated by specific spatio-temporal configurations of the stimulus elements.

116

References

Caelli, T. M., Hoffman, W. C. and Lindman, H. Subjective special relativity effects in real motion perception. In J. A. Keats and W. Wallace (Eds.) *Geometric and algebraic models for Behavior.* Tunra Press: University of Newcastle (In Press).

De Silva, H. R. An analysis of the visual perception of movement. *British Journal of Psychology*, 1929, **19**, 268–305.

Foster, D. H. A method for the investigation of those transformations under which the visual recognition of a given object is invariant. *Kybernetiek*, 1972, **11**, 223–229.

Foster, D. H. Visual apparent motion of some preferred paths in the rotation group SO(3). *Biological Cybernetics*, 1975, **18**, 81–89.

Hall, K. R., Earle, A. E. and Crookes, T. G. A pendulum phenomenon in the visual perception of apparent movement. *Quarterly Journal of Experimental Psychology,* 1952, **4**, 3, 109–120.

Hoffman, W. C. The Lie Algebra of visual perception. *Journal of Mathematical Psychology*, 1966, **3**, 65–98, *Errata*, ibid, 1967, **4**, 348–349.

Kaufman, L., Cyrulnik, K., Kaplowitz, J., Melnick, G. and Stoff, D. The complementarity of apparent and real motion. *Psycho. Forsch.*, 1971, **34**, 343–348.

Kolers, P. A. *Aspects of motion perception.* New York: Pergamon Press, 1972.

Minorsky, N. *Nonlinear oscillations.* Princeton: Van Nostrand, 1962.

Neuhaus, W. Experimentelle Untersuchung der Scheinbewegung. *Archiv für die gesamte Psychologie*, 1930, **75**, 315–458.

Pollock, W. T. The visibility of a target as a function of its speed of movement. *Journal of Experimental Psychology*, 1953, **45**, 434–449.

Tyler, C. W. Temporal characteristics in apparent movement Omega movement vs. Phi movement. *Quarterly Journal of Experimental Psychology*, 1973, **25**, 182–192.

Wertheimer, M. Experimentelle Studien uber das Sehen von Bewegung. *Zeitschrift fur Psychologie*, 1912, **61**, 161–265. Translated in part in T. Shipley (Ed.) *Classics in Psychology.* New York: Philosophical Library, 1961.

Chapter 6

Alternatives to the Power Law; Psychophysics of Visual Extent Reconsidered*

Jan Drösler

Abstract. The logarithmic and power laws for visual length and area do not inform us about the geometry of the visual field.

The present paper collects—beginning with Helmholtz—empirical information pertaining to the metric of monocular space perception. Conflicting evidence is thus raised, supporting *two* of the Riemannian geometries.

A reconciling hypothesis is formulated and tested in a number of experiments. Results support the contention that neither the logarithmic nor the power law of visual extent are appropriate representations.

Field effects are consistently described by a new (complex) pyschophysical function of a complex argument.

Psychophysics of visual extent should enable us to calculate perceived area from perceived length. This is not the case. In his review Krantz (1972) reports perceived length to grow very nearly proportional to physical length. Judgements of apparent area seems to be dependent of physical area by a power law. If subjects are not outrightly induced to judge squared length, the power law exponent is less than one. If apparent size were predictable from apparent length, both should show similar psychophysical functions, say identical power law exponents.

Perceived velocity should be predictable from perceived length given the stimulus dynamics. Again contemporary psychophysics leaves us at a loss: another power law is given in the literature (Mashhour, 1964), bearing no conceptual relationship to the first two, the exponent being considered a purely empirical matter.

* This work was supported in part by grant Dr 58/3 from Deutsche Forschungsgemeinschaft.

118

1. Perception of Area

1.1 The Geometry of Monocular Space Perception

The following discussion will be confined to the relation between perceived length and perceived area at first. Traditional psychophysical reasoning in this connection can be faulty in one of two aspects—or both: First of all the power law may be inappropriate here, its log-log distortion might obscure deviations of data from the curve. On the other hand, the implied procedure of calculating seen area from seen length might be wrong. In Psychology we should have been accustomed for a long time to using other procedures apart from simple squaring, the Euclidian algorithm.

The question for the geometry applicable to the case seems to be the fundamental one. A pilot experiment was devoted to the problem, following a line of reasoning which Blank (1961) introduced into the study of binocular space perception. The subject views a triangle ABC monocularly in a perimeter apparatus. Sides AB and AC each subtending 67 degrees of visual angle. After suitable dark adaptation, fixating A, the subject has to halve AB and then AC by guiding a pinpoint light E (later F) movable by the experimeter (see Figure 1).

In the second part of the experiment, lights ABC and F were displayed. The subjects' task is to guide the experimeters variable light G, so that the distance GF appears in the same orientation as BC but of half its length.

If monocular visual geometry were Euclidian, point G should coincide with E as determined in the first part of the experiment. This did not occur. Point G fell about two thirds short of distance FE.

There was no interference of measurements for point F and for point E, making statistical analysis superfluous: in the triangle of Figure 1, line FE appears longer to all three subjects than Euclidian geometry will take into account.

If the analysis remains confined to the Riemannian geometries, where free movability is given, i.e. movement does not alter the form of an object, the result of this pilot experiment can be interpreted as supporting a hypo-

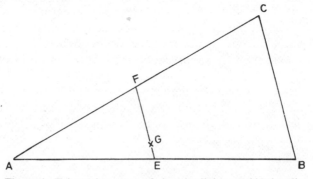

Figure 1. Triangular array of pinpoint lights used in the pilot experiment. S fixates point A. Point G is movable by E

thesis of a geometry of constant positive Gaussian curvature for *monocular* visual space perception. This would be just opposite to what Luneburg (1947) found for *binocular* visual space perception, which was constant negative curvature.

The hypothesis of a Riemannian geometry of constant positive curvature is supported by the psychophysical function reported for apparent area. A power law exponent of less than one for the dependence of perceived area upon physical area means, that apparent area grows slower than the square of apparent length. This is characteristic for the dependence of area upon length in a geometry of constant positive curvature, spherical geometry in the two-dimensional case.

Under these circumstances, the question of whether the power law can serve as a suitable psychophysical function has to be put up for test more rigorously.

1.2 Dependence of Perceived Area on Perceived Length

The major asset of the power law, as pointed out by Luce and Galanter (1963) is its being the solution to the functional equation

$$\frac{\phi(s)}{\phi(t)} = \frac{\phi(s')}{\phi(t')}$$

with $s/t = s'/t'$.

Thus, by any psychophysical power law $\phi(s)$, subjective ratios are preserved in different realms of the stimulus continuum.

For perceived length, this would mean unlimited size constancy. Now, as is well known, size constancy breaks down as soon as the stimulus is 'too far' away. In great distance, a cow is likely to be mistaken for a dog. The power law, moreover, does not take care of the fact, that our monocular visual field is bounded. Given a certain distance of stimulus presentation, discrimination becomes impossible as soon as the visual field is filled by the stimulus area. For the present discussion, an alternative psychophysical function for visual extent is being sought.

A function, which does not suffer from these limitations is

$$A(\psi) = 2\pi R^2 (1 - \cos \psi) \qquad (1)$$

with

$\pi: = 3 \cdot 14 \ldots$
$R: =$ the radius of curvature of monocular visual space, with $R > 0$, and
$\psi: =$ perceived visual angle

$A(\psi)$ would represent the perceived area of a circle of perceived radius ψ. The formula represents the algorithm for computing a circular area on the surface of a sphere, a two dimensional manifold of constant positive curvature.

2. Perception of Length

2.1 A Proposed Psychophysical Function for Visual Angle

Usage of formula (1) presupposes knowledge of parameter R and, above all, the psychophysical function $\psi(\alpha)$, giving the dependence of the subjective visual angle ψ as a function of the angle α by which the stimulus radius is subtended. These relationships are represented in Figure 2 which, for simplicity, can be taken for an analogue of an optical system although no anatomical arguments are implied here.

In Figure 2 s stands for the stimulus extension, ψ for the perceived length on the curved visual field. The point C represents the 'optical centre' of the psychophysical system. Its distance from the visual surface is f, the 'focal length'. The point 0 denotes the origin of the spherical visual surface of radius R.

Figure 2 can be used to derive, how the length of arc ψ, perceived magnitude, depends on the physical visual angle α. By elementary trigonometry we get

$$\psi(\alpha) = \alpha - \sin^{-1}\left(\frac{(R-f)}{R}\ \sin\alpha\right) \qquad (2)$$

with

α: = angular stimulus extension
f: = focal length of the psychophysical system.

This expression will be considered as a proposed psychophysical function for visual angle $(-\pi/2 < \alpha < \pi/2)$ the graph of which is shown in Figure 3.

Even for constant Gaussian curvature $1/R^2$ of the monocular visual field,

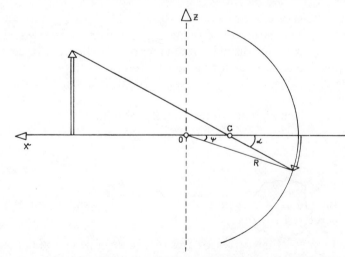

Figure 2. Section of the proposed psychophysical system. The stimulus (on the left) is mapped into a curved visual field (right). Response magnitude is given by the angle ψ

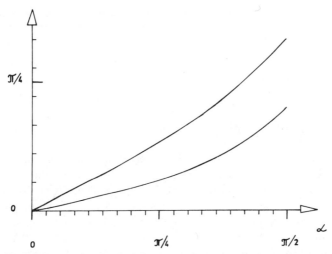

Figure 3. Psychophysical function for perceived visual angle $\psi(\alpha)$. Different focal lengths f lead to different functional relationships, so that equal angular stimulus extension, α, does *not* bring about equal perceived visual angles $\psi(\alpha)$ Parameter values $R = 1$, $f = 0.5$ (upper curve), $f = 0.2$ (lower curve)

different focal lengths, f, will produce different perceived angular extensions for equal stimulus angle α.

Since the 'optical' properties of the psychophysical system are unknown, f represents a parameter to be estimated. The radius of the Gaussian curvature R stands for a second unknown parameter.

An analysis of Figure 2 leads, after some elementary trigonometry, to the result

$$\cos \psi = \frac{(R - f)}{R} \sin^2 \alpha + \cos \alpha \left[1 - \frac{(R - f)^2}{R^2} \sin^2 \alpha\right]^{\frac{1}{2}}. \qquad (3)$$

For ease of computation, stimulus distance from the optical centre C of the system will be taken to be f. This in effect includes an unknown scale factor into stimulus magnitude s without bringing about any complications since an unknown scale factor is immanent in response magnitude anyhow.

Then

$$\text{tg } \alpha = s/f$$

Substituting yields

$$1 - \cos \psi = f\{s^2 - [Rs^2 + f^4]^{\frac{1}{2}} + Rf\}/R[s^2 + f^2]$$

The function $1 - \cos \psi$, which carries the stimulus dependent variation in the psychophysical function (1) for perceived area of a circular stimulus is thus shown to be a hyperbola in s^2. It runs through the origin and, with growing stimulus radius approaches an asymptote of f/R. Its most notable property is its convex shape. Approximation of this path by a power law will therefore lead to an exponent of less than one in accordance with the literature (cf. Krantz, 1972).

Table 1. Estimated parameters from experiment on perceived area of circular discs

Subject Nr.	Radius of Gaussian curvature	Focal length	Scale factor
1	28·3	6·52	50·0
2	28·9	7·11	50·0
3	43·8	20·7	50·0

Parameter Estimation. To estimate the parameters R and f an experiment was run to asses perceived area of circles as a function of stimulus radius. Nine different wooden discs, ranging in radius equally spaced from 10 cm to 30 cm were presented in random order five times each. Disc number 5 of 20 cm radius was shown to the subject at the beginning and arbitrarily assigned the size of 10. Three subjects viewed the discs monocularly from a distance of 60 cm. They were instructed to judge apparent area rather than diameter. The standard was available for the subject if called for between trials.

Parameters were estimated using Chandler's (1968) iterative procedure. Results are given in Table 1.

The third parameter for each subject represents a scale factor, which adjusts the arbitrary units of the subjects' responses to those of stimulus size. The psychophysical relationship between stimulus diameter and perceived area of circular discs is given in Figure 4 for one subject.

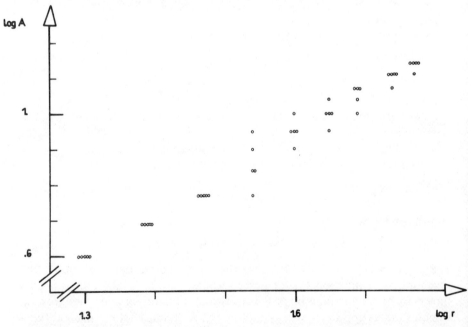

Figure 4. Dependence of perceived area A on stimulus radius, both axes in log scale

2.2 The Perception of Straightness

A worthwhile subject to discuss is the influence of the visual field's geometry upon apparent curvature of lines. On the surface of a sphere great circles are well known to represent geodesic lines, the shortest connection between any two points on the surface. In the visual field curves of $\varphi = $ const. are such great circles as are the lines of constant longitude on the globe. Let us calculate the shape of curves in the stimulus field, which project on the curves of $\varphi = $ const. in the visual field, if the monocular visual system operates in the manner proposed here.

The problem is to calculate the intersection of the stimulus field $x = $ const. with the cone, determined by the focus $F(f, 0, 0)$ as its apex and a circle $\varphi = $ const. Since apex as well as the defining circle's centre are located on the x-axis, any circle on the surface of the cone will be described by

$$(x - x_0)^2 + y^2 + z^2 = R_0^2$$

where x_0 is the location of its centre and R_0 is its radius. Since all these circles are to subtend an angle of φ with the x-axis

$$y/(x - x_0) = \operatorname{tg}\varphi$$

will hold. The radius R_0 will grow according to

$$\frac{R}{R_0} = \frac{R - f}{R - f - x_0}$$

Here R is the visual field's radius of Gaussian curvature and f is its focal length as defined before. If the last two relations are substituted, one gets

$$\left(\frac{(R - f)^2}{\sin^2 \varphi} - \frac{R^2}{\operatorname{tg}^2 \varphi}\right)y^2 - \frac{2R^2 (R - f - x)}{\operatorname{tg}\varphi}y + (R - f)^2 z^2 = R^2 (R - f - x)^2$$

For any stimulus plane with fixed x this formula represents a hyperbola in the normal orientation, provided $\varphi = $ const. and

$$\frac{(R - f)^2}{\sin^2 \varphi} - \frac{R^2}{\operatorname{tg}^2\varphi} < 0$$

This will be the case, if $R^2 > (R - f)^2$, as long as the focal length f is smaller than the radius of curvature R.

This means that a line in the stimulus field will have to be more or less convex towards the fixation point, in order to be perceived as the shortest connection between any two points on it, i.e. 'straight'.

The effect of the psychophysical function (2) is shown in Figure 5.

Here a configuration was generated, which will be perceived as a rectangular checkerboard by a psychophysical system with parameters $R = 1 \cdot 0$ and $f = 0 \cdot 38$. (The discontinuities in the lines are due to the method of generating the figure on a computer display.)

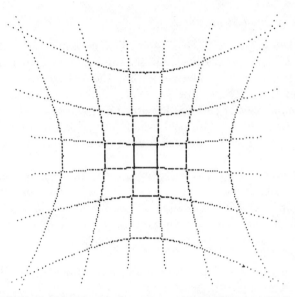

Figure 5. Stimulus configuration, which will be perceived as a rectangular checkerboard by a psychophysical system with parameters $R = 1.0$ and $f = .38$ at viewing distance $2f$

Empirically, this corresponds to what Helmholtz (1896) reports: stimulus points have to be arranged along a line curved convexly towards the fixation point to be perceived on a straight line in peripheral vision. Helmholtz's theoretical approach, however, is different from the one persued here. Helmholtz is holding eye movement responsible for the phenomenon. Anatomical suspension of the eye ball, he argues, does not allow independent rotations about its three axes. Two of these rotations invariably bring about a certain amount of rotation about the third axis, the magnitude of which can be calculated by Listing's law:

$$-\operatorname{tg}\frac{\gamma}{2} = \operatorname{tg}\frac{\alpha}{2}\operatorname{tg}\frac{\beta}{2}$$

with α, β, γ the respective angles of ocular rotation. Starting from this relationship, Helmholtz calculates a distorted checkerboard stimulus pattern, which is perceived as rectangular, if the subject fixates the various stimulus regions.

The present development is not concerned with eye movement. As a matter of fact, Helmholtz does not answer the question, as to why his distorted checkerboard is seen straight even if the subject does not alter the line of sight.

Before this question is discussed further, let us test, whether a visual system like the one proposed here, can under fixation see a normal checkerboard straight at times. The answer is positive. If $R - f$ becomes zero in formula (4) the expression greatly simplifies:

$$y = x \operatorname{tg} \varphi$$

or

$$y = \text{const.}\Big|_{x \text{ and } \varphi}$$

This means, that straight lines will be perceived as such if the focal length coincides with the radius of Gaussian curvature.

A similar result is reached if the radius of curvature grows beyond bounds, and the visual field becomes flat. For equation (4) this means again

$$\lim_{R \to \infty} y = x \operatorname{tg} \varphi$$

if we first shift the origin of x to the systems' focus. An analogue to a 'flat visual field' is standard photography.

2.3 The Resulting Psychophysical Function for Length

Formula (1) describes a rather special case of visual psychophysics, monocular perception of circular areas, centrally fixated. The general psychophysical function is of interest, therefore, which maps any point of the stimulus plane into a point of the (monocular) visual field. For this discussion the coordinate system of Figure 2 has to be enlargened to three dimensions. The 'optical' axis will mark the x coordinate, with the z coordinate pointing upwards a right handed system fixes the y coordinate pointing into the page as in Figure 2.

As was demonstrated in the preceding paragraph, straight lines through the origin of the y-z stimulus plane will be perceived as straight. Polar coordinates are convenient, therefore, to describe the psychophysical relationship. If the stimulus radius is r and its argument β, whereas perceived radius is ϕ with argument γ we get

$$\gamma = \beta$$

and

$$\phi(r) = \operatorname{tg}^{-1}\frac{r}{f} - \sin^{-1}\left\{ \frac{R-f}{R} r (f^2 + r^2)^{-\frac{1}{2}} \right\}$$

as the resulting psychophysical function, provided, we keep stimulus distance fixed at f units from the optical centre C.

3. Distortions in the Visual Field

3.1 Applications to the Perception of Human Faces

To pursue the effects of positive constant curvature of our visual geometry, checkerboards are not suited too well. Because of permanently shifting fixation 'straightness' of lines apparently becomes an attribute of lines which operates somewhat independently of present visual impression. Any line tested by shifting fixation to be straight can be relied on to remain straight under normal stimulus conditions. An analysis was carried out, therefore, with stimulus material devoid of any straight line.

Human faces comprise just that kind of stimulus manifold. Two cartoonists, Szewczuk (1955) and Köhler (1975), were taken as 'subjects'. Photographs of 50 public personalities' faces served as the stimuli.

In a first analysis, parameters of Gaussian curvature and focal length according to the model (1) were estimated, using Chandler's, 1968, iterative procedure. For this purpose some 30 identifiable point-pairs in each photograph as well as in the corresponding cartoon were measured as to their y and z coordinates, using a Cartesian system with origin halfway between the pupils of the eyes, the connection of which defined the y-axis.

A scale factor was also estimated to secure a common unit of length in both photograph and cartoon. Thus inter-pupil distance of the photograph was fixed as 0·2 units of length.

The results for the 50 photograph-cartoon pairs divide the material into two different classes as in Table 2.

The larger group of 41 cases shows a focal length of equal size as the radius of Gaussian curvature. These cartoons are of photographic character. Their radius of Gaussian curvature is relatively large, had the faces contained straight lines, they would have been drawn straight.

This is not so for the rest of nine cases. Here the radius of Gaussian curvature is smaller, its mean value being of about half the size of the first group. The more important relationship appears for focal length. Its mean value is about half of that for radius of Gaussian curvature. The cartoons are grossly distorted with respect to the corresponding photographs.

A sequence of illustrations can perhaps demonstrate this result. Figure 6 represents an artist's impression (Szewczuk, 1955) of a persons face. The following illustration (Figure 7) should render surprise concerning the fact that the cartoon (Figure 6) can be taken as a 'picture' of the person or can at all be recognized. The rectified version, which was copied on transparent paper from a photograph, reveals by comparison, how much distortion the cartoon contains. The process of transforming a photograph into a line drawing does not concern us here.[1]

Table 2. Parameters estimated from comparison of cartoons and photographs of human faces

No. of cases	Gaussian curvature		focal length	
	mean	s.d.	mean	s.d.
51	3·73	·629	3·73	·001
9	2·08	·547	1·05	·263

[1] In an earlier paper (Drösler, 1975) it was shown to be a process of redundancy reduction followed by a stage of irrelevance reduction. If photographic density at point x of a photograph is $S(x)$, contour formation can be represented by a binary coding of $|\nabla S|$, with

$$\nabla S = \text{grad } S = \frac{\partial S(x)}{\partial x}$$

127

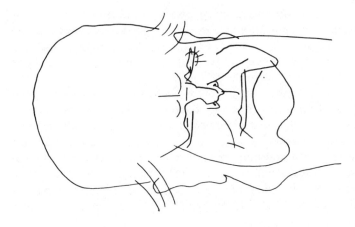

Figure 8. Computer generated distortion of Figure 7, using the psychophysical function proposed here, with $R = \cdot96, f = \cdot22$

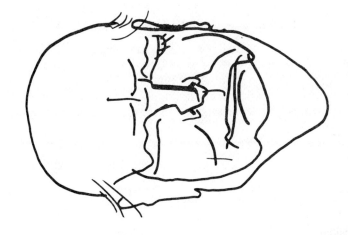

Figure 7. The same face as in Figure 6, rectified using a photograph of the persons face

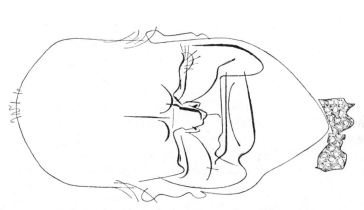

Figure 6. Artistic cartoon of a human face by Szewczuk (1955)

Major distortion of this amount occurs in about 20% of the analysed drawings. There appears to be no difference in this proportion between the two artists.

The rectified Figure 7 was coded and read into a computer. A program was written which operated inversely to the psychophysical function (2). This is the same program, which generated the distorted checkerboard of Figure 5, that will be perceived as straight under certain conditions. The result is Figure 8, a drawing, which is distorted in a highly similar way as the artist's cartoon.

Peculiar about these findings is the fact, that it is the distorted picture, which appears to be more typical and more recognizable. Moreover, a variation of viewing conditions for the cartoon do not noticeable effect its visual properties. Thus the parameter of focal length apparently does not represent a physiological or optical property of the visual system. It could well be a characteristic of the central processor.

4. Perception of Velocity

4.1 The Resulting Psychophysical Function for Velocity

This section is concerned with visual perception of moving targets. The range of velocities considered is restricted to slow motion of less than ·25 radians of visual angle per second. The psychophysical function is usually taken to be a power law. This appears surprising because the psychophysical functions for length and for the perception of time intervals in the region of interest here are linear (Stevens, 1957).

Differentiating (2) with respect to time leads to a psychophysical function for visual angular velocity

$$\frac{d\psi}{dt} = \frac{d\alpha}{dt} - \left[1 - \frac{(R-f)^2}{R^2}\sin^2\alpha\right]^{-\frac{1}{2}}\frac{(R-f)}{R}\cos\alpha\,\frac{d\alpha}{dt} \qquad (5)$$

which is, for constant α, a linear function of stimulus velocity $d\alpha/dt$. On the other hand, there are experimental data from Mashhour (1964) who estimates a power function exponent of ·8 for his set of data.

A critical evaluation of the customary experimental procedure shows that the power law is strongly invalidated by a characteristic experimental error: Subjects usually view the stimuli passing by a window of constant width and at different speeds. This arrangement does not take into account the different states of adaptation to velocity which are brought about by the various stimulus durations. A re-examination of Mashhour's data, e.g. leads to a psychophysical function for velocity which is empirically strictly linear, as will be shown.

Critical evaluation of experiments on velocity perception rests on the principal argument to be developed in this section: Perceived motion in psychophysical experiments cannot be viewed as constant even if the physical stimulus velocity does not change during the experiment. The perceived velocity undergoes change over time even though the stimulus velocity remains constant. It is therefore necessary to choose a model for motion perception which incorporates these conditions. This requirement is met by systems theory which is applicable to the study of relationships between time dependent signals.

4.2 Adaptation to Velocity

A transformation g is being sought which transforms a stimulus process $r(t)$ into a perceptual process $s(t)$. Here $r(t)$ is the time dependent stimulus velocity and $s(t)$ is the perceived velocity which can also change with time.

$$s(t) = g[r(t)]. \tag{6}$$

The transformation g is postulated to be a linear transformation

$$g[r_1(t) + r_2(t)] = g[r_1(t)] + g[r_2(t)] \tag{7}$$
$$g[cr(t)] = cg[r(t)].$$

If the system is considered to be at rest at the beginning of each experimental trial with the stimulation starting marking the onset of the trial, it can be shown, that these restrictions lead to a functional dependence between the stimulus process and the perceptual process (c.f. any textbook on systems theory, e.g. Kuo, 1962, p. 175).

$$s(t) = \int_0^t h(\tau)\, r(t - \tau)\mathrm{d}\tau. \tag{8}$$

Here τ is a variable of integration denoting 'age' of the specific stimulus. A stimulus $r(t - \tau)$ is one which was given τ units of time ago. The integral can be viewed as a kind of moving average, its terms are the preceding stimuli, which have been weighted by a variable $h(\tau)$. This weighting function is a characteristic of the system under study.

Empirical validation of the model is carried out by calculating the function h from the known functions r and s. These variables are connected in (8) by a convolution integral. The function $h(\tau)$ can be tested for invariance by using other input-output pairs.

With a linear system the characteristic weighting function $h(\tau)$ can be calculated as soon as a stimulus process and the corresponding time dependent perceptual process has been established experimentally. In the usual experiment the stimulus process consists of a step function $u(t)$ of varing amplitude and duration. Mashhour has recorded his subjects' responses in detail so that they can be re-evaluated. Figure 8 shows the data replotted. Their time dependence differs from that of the stimulus: A description of the psychophysical data calls for superimposing a decreasing exponential function upon the step function.

Equation (8) is not directly solvable for $h(\tau)$ by elementary methods. Laplace-transforms, however, greatly simplify the necessary computations.

$$\{f(t)\} = \int^{\infty} f(t)\, e^{-tp}\, dt \quad t \geq 0$$

are functions of a new (complex) variable p. This transformation maps the operation of convolution into an algebraic product:

$$\{s(t)\} = \{h(t)\} \cdot \{r(t)\}. \tag{10}$$

The brackets area reminder of the fact that transforms are multiplied rather than the functions themselves.

After multiplication and re-transforming if necessary by use of available transform tables, a solution for $h(t)$ can be found.

A stimulus course well-defined over time is given in experiments which have the subject view a moving spot target on a screen. The simplest case uses a moving spot of uniform direction and constant velocity. Here $r(t) = v = u(t)$ with $v(t)$ the stimulus velocity at time t and $u(t) = \text{const. } t > 0$. Perceptual process $s(t)$ can be constructed from Mashhour's (1964) raw data (p. 162). His data are plotted in Figure 9. To test for linearity of the psychophysical function, they have been transformed to a single stimulus speed ($v_1 = 19$ minutes of arc per second) arithmetically.

Figure 9 shows a process of adaptation which comes to rest at a certain level of subjective velocity which is different from zero.

Calculating the system characteristic $h(\tau)$ using formula (10) asks for a mathematical expression for the curve in this figure. This curve will be described by

$$s(t) = a + (1 - a)\exp(-bt) \quad t \geq 0$$

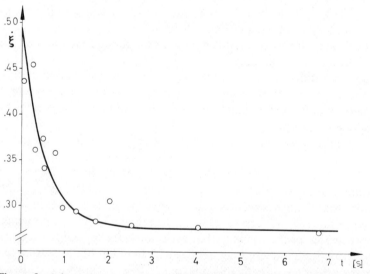

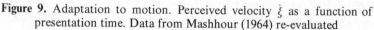

Figure 9. Adaptation to motion. Perceived velocity ξ as a function of presentation time. Data from Mashhour (1964) re-evaluated

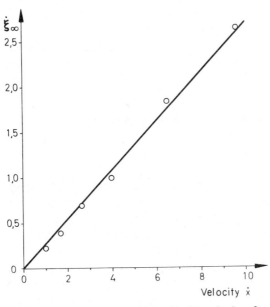

Figure 10. Psychophysical function for velocity after suitable adaptation. Data from Mashour, 1964, re-evaluated

Using transformation (5) this special pair $r(t)$, $s(t)$ yields for $h(\tau)$

$$\{h(t)\} = \frac{\{a + (1 - a)\exp(-bt)\}}{\{u(t)\}} = \{a\delta(t) - (1 - a)\,b\exp(-bt)\} \qquad (11)$$

In this expression $\delta(t)$ denotes the Dirac-impulse. The system function $h(t)$ weights all stimuli coming in 'now' (at time $t = $ zero) impulsively with positive weight a. Furthermore, all past stimuli are weighted negatively with a weighting factor decreasing exponentially with time.

4.3 Applications to Various 'Illusory' Phenomena of Motion Perception

A number of phenomena reported in the literature can serve as applications of (11), testing the proposed psychophysical function at the same time.

(a) Negative after-effect in the visual perception of velocity. If the uniform motion of a stimulus spot is stopped instantly the subjects report seeing a motion in the opposite direction for some time. The effect can be produced rather easily if a number of points moving radially towards a centre are stopped suddenly. An experiment of this kind is conducted by stopping a spiral rotating around its centre. Using an Archimedian spiral $r = a\psi$ uniform physical motion in radial direction for all points results. Depending on the direction of rotation the points move towards the centre or away from it. A problem like this can be

treated like one of unidimensional motion. The time course of the stimulus is given by a stepwise increase of stimulus velocity from zero to a constant value $u(t)$ at the beginning of the experiment. The end of the presentation is marked by an equally stepwise decrease of stimulus process as $r(t)$ together with the newly computed $h(\tau)$ into (10) permits calculation of the expected time dependent course of perception:

$$\{s(t)\} = \{\delta(t) - (1 - a)b \exp(-bt)\} \{u(t) - u(t - t_1)\}$$
$$= \{a + (1 - a) \exp(-bt) - [a + (1 - a) \exp(-b(t - t_1))]$$
$$u(t - t_1)\}.$$

This calculation shows that at the onset of stimulation a similar time course of perception as shown in Figure 11 is expected. The subjects should report an exponentially decreasing impression of velocity until adaptation at the constant level $s(t) = a$ takes place. If stimulus velocity suddenly drops to zero at time t_1 a different time course of perception is superimposed. It is numerically equal to the first one but different in algebraic sign. This leads to a departure of the reported impression of velocity into the negative half plane. With continuing time an adaptation at level $s(t) = -a$ comes about. This level superimposed upon the already prevailing one leads to $s(t) = 0$.

This means that after stopping a moving stimulus spot a negative after-effect of velocity for some amount of time is to be expected. These predictions are not contradicted by empirical data which have been gathered long ago by Wolgemuth (1911) and Hunter (1914): Our system characteristic $h(t)$ predicts the well known after-effects in visual motion perception.

(b) Rubin's wheel. It is possible to generate reported paths of perceived motion which differ marked from the stimulus path by suitable choice of a path

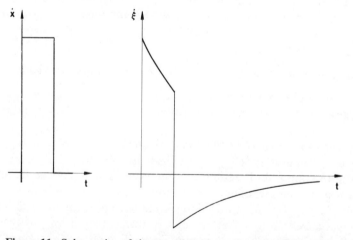

Figure 11. Schematics of the negative after-effect of motion perception. Stimulus course on the left, perceptual intensity on the right

for stimulus motion. Effects of this kind are conventionally labeled 'illusions' even though it is well-known that there is no need for a special label like this. The ever present properties of the perceptual system just show up more distinctly than usual.

An example is given by the cycloid path of motion which is followed by any point at the periphery of a rolling wheel (Rubin, 1921). The time dependent path of a point P defines a two-dimensional stimulus process $r(t)$. This can be split up into a horizontal component $r_x = u(t) + \sin t$ and a vertical component $r_y = \cos t$. By separating these components the expected perceptual process $s(t)$ can be calculated unidimensionally for each of them. The components of velocity in both directions are given by the first derivatives

$$v_x = u(t) + \cos t$$

$$v_y = -\sin t.$$

$$\{s_x(t)\} = \{\delta(t) - (1 - a)b \exp(-bt)\} \{u(t) + \cos t\} \qquad (12)$$

$$= a + (1 - a) \exp(-bt) - \frac{(1 - a)^2}{1 + b^2} \exp(-bt)$$

$$+ \sqrt{A^2 + B^2} \sin(t - \theta)\}$$

$$\{s_y(t)\} = \{\delta(t) - (1 - a)b \exp(-bt)\} \{-\sin t\} \qquad (13)$$

$$= \left\{ \frac{(1 - a)b^2}{1 + b^2} \exp(-bt) + \sqrt{A^2 + B^2} \cos(t - \theta) \right\}$$

with $A = 1 + (1 - a)b^2/(1 + b^2)$,

$$\theta = \operatorname{arc} \cos B/\sqrt{A^2 + B^2}, \quad B = (1 - a)b/(1 + b^2).$$

Formulas (12) and (13) show that the expected time course of perception can be characterized in the following manner: Periodic stimulus components elicit periodic components in the perceptual process $\left[\sqrt{A^2 + B^2} \sin(t + \theta)\right]$ and $\left[\sqrt{A^2 + B^2} \cos(t + \theta)\right]$.

Specifically circular stimulus motion should result in an impression of circularity. Still the subjective course of motion $s(t)$ differs markedly from the stimulus path $r(t)$. The non-periodic term of the horizontal stimulus component produces adaptation in the subject. Therefore the subjects should report a slower progress of the wheel compared to strict rolling. The cycloid stimulus path should elicit the impression of a prolate cycloid. This difference can be described qualitatively by noting that in places where the cycloid shows peaks (pointing downwards) the prolate cycloid shows loops (Figure 12).

In experiments these loops have been recorded by Rubin (1921) and others. The model again does not contradict the experimental data.

(c) Scheffler's 'illusion' of motion. Scheffler (1962) demonstrated another. 'illusion' of motion in which discrepancies between the stimulus path and the

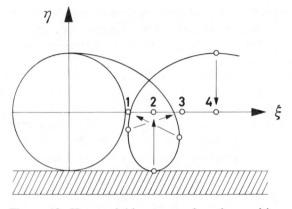

Figure 12. Hypocycloid perceptual path, resulting from a cycloid stimulus path. Points 1 to 4 are calculated perceived positions of the wheels centre, which on account of adaptation to motion appears to move progressively slower

time course of reported motion arise. The experiment uses the following stimulus arrangement: A spot moves within physical uv-coordinates in v-direction with constant velocity. The uv-plane is marked by a distinct texture. Now the uv-frame as a whole is moved in terms of new physical xy-coordinates. The origin of the uv-system moves in the x-direction with constant velocity and in the y-direction also with constant velocity. Scheffler's 'illusion' of motion comes about as soon as the y-component of motion of the uv-system is numerically set equal to the velocity of the stimulus spot in this uv-system. In this case the stimulus components of motion in the y-direction cancel. Still the subjects report a component of perceived motion in the y-direction in addition of that of the x-direction.

Scheffler's data provide a lead concerning the magnitude of the adaptation level in visual perception of motion. The illusion is brought about by the fact that even though two stimulus components of motion cancel, the resultant of the corresponding perceived components does not necessarily vanish. Under the proposed psychophysical system this can only be the case if the adaptation level is different for stimulus motion in the two coordinate systems being used here. Their only difference lies in their texture. From the direction of the reported motion which is approximately 45° from the vertical the influence of different textures on the size of the adaptation level can be estimated.

(d) The Hess phenomenon. Metzger (1932) reports an experiment which is attributed to Hess. The apparatus consists of a screen which has cut-outs in two places (Figure 13). A marker is being run behind this screen from left to right so that the upper portion remains invisible at the beginning. When the upper portion of the marker comes into view in the shorter cut-out subjects report a lagging of this portion behind the lower portion which has been visible from the

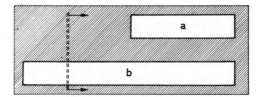

Figure 13. Apparatus for producing the Hess phenomenon (Metzger, 1932). A pointer moves behind the screen from left to right, reaching cutout *b* first, later cutout *a*. Ss report a lagging of the marker in cut-out *a*

beginning. The lag vanishes after a short time and both parts of the marker are reported to be moving in line. These data do not contradict the model presented here. The subjects' localization of moving target can be predicted from the equations by integrating the predicted velocities. The results are in line with the Hess phenomenon.

5. Summary and Conclusions

This investigation sets out in noting a deplorable defect in visual psychophysics: Perceived length, area and velocity are regarded by many authors as depending on stimulus extent, r, by a power function $\phi(r) = \gamma r^\beta$, with γ and β parameters to be estimated empirically. Psychophysics is not able, however, to predict perceived area from perceived length or any other response magnitude from one of the rest. The power law exponents empirically just do not match the proper way.

A different psychophysical function is, therefore, developed here which displays the desired properties. It is, in effect, a linear function of stimulus extension. The main portion of this report is, therefore, devoted to the explanation of how the multitude of perceptual distortions can occur under a linear psychophysical law for visual extent. Discussion is limited to monocular perception.

An experiment on perceived area of circular discs was performed. Results show, in accordance with the literature, that perceived area increases at a smaller rate than the square of the stimulus radius. Contrary to other investigators, this is not taken as an indication of a power law. The conclusion is drawn, instead, that visual geometry is Riemannian with constant positive Gaussian curvature. A two parameter model for the dependence of perceived area $A(\psi)$ of circular discs on perceived length ψ of their radius is thus rather obvious:

$$A(\psi) = 2\pi R^2(1 - \cos \psi)$$

with

$A:$ = perceived area
$\pi:$ = 3·14 . . .
$1/R^2:$ = Gaussian curvature of monocular visual geometry
$\psi:$ = perceived visual angle

This is just the formula for calculating the area of a circle on the surface of a sphere, which is representative of a surface of constant positive Gaussian curvature. What is less obvious, turns out to be the psychophysical function $\psi(\alpha)$ for the visual angle:

$$\psi(\alpha) = \alpha - \sin^{-1}\left[\frac{(R - f)}{R}\sin \alpha\right]$$

with

α: = angular stimulus extension

f: = focal length of the psychophysical system.

If the focal length of the psychophysical system equals the radius of Gaussian curvature, R, perceived visual angle will be equal to its physical counterpart. If, however, focal length is smaller, perceived visual angle will be smaller than α.

It is the departure from proportionality between physical and perceived visual angle which helps account for the distortions in vision. Helmholtz (1896) noted, that in order to be perceived as a straight line, the stimulus has to be a hyperbola, curved convexly towards the fixation point. This is exactly what the present psychophysical function predicts, including the limiting case of straight lines being perceived as such if they pass through the point of fixation.

A major point in this development is the notion, that while R is a personal constant of the observer, this is not the case for f, the focal length. Its numerical value depends on the frontal distance of the stimulus plane from the observer. Thus, physically identical stimuli are perceived grossly different if viewed at different distances. Speaking in the language of geometry, diminishing the stimulus distance will not produce the perception of pure motion but of motion as well as a change of form. This can be demonstrated by the use of stimulus material devoid of simple cues for distortion, such as human faces.

Differentiating our psychophysical function leads, for constant visual angle α, again to a linear psychophysical function for velocity:

$$\frac{d\psi}{dt} = \frac{d\alpha}{dt} - (1 - k^2 \sin^2\alpha)^{-\frac{1}{2}} k \cos \alpha \frac{d\alpha}{dt}$$

with

$$k = (R - f)/R.$$

In contrast, the literature again reports a power law with exponent markedly different from one. This contradiction can be resolved by taking adaptation to velocity into account. If experimental data are evaluated for perceived velocity after a constant time interval of presentation, the empirical psychophysical function is linear, provided the time interval is of suitable length to secure adaptation at all stimulus velocities.

In conclusion it is noted that certain distortions in the visual field with respect to stimulus form are not the effect of different and complicated psychophysical functions but are simple reflections of a specific non-Euclidian geometry of monocular visual space.

References

Blank, A. A., Curvature of Binocular Visual Space. An Experiment. *J. Opt. Soc. Am.* **51**, 335–339, 1961.

Chandler, J. P., *Parameter estimation program STEPIT*. Bloomington, Ind.: Indiana University (Quantum Chemistry Program Exchange), 1968.

Drösler, J., *A Mathematical Model for the Perception of Motion*. Paper read at the 2nd European Mathematical Group meeting at Nijmegen, Holland, Nov. 4, 1971.

Drösler, J., Die Erzeugung von Konturen im visuellen Wahrnehmungsfeld. p. 383–386 in W. H. Tack (ed.): *Bericht über den 29. Kongreß der Deutschen Gesellschaft für Psychologie in Salzburg 1974*, Vol. 1, Göttingen: Hogrefe, 1975.

Helmholtz, H. von, *Handbuch der physiologischen Optik* (2nd edn.) Vol. 1, Hamburg: Voss, 1896.

Hunter, W. S., The after-effect of visual motion. *Psychol. Rev.* **21**, 245–277, 1914.

Köhler, H. E., *Gezeichnete Zeitgenossen*. Frankfurt: Societäts-Verlag, 1975.

Krantz, D. H. Visual Scaling. Chapt. 26 in Jameson, Dorothea & Hurvich L. M. (eds.): *Visual Psychophysics*. Berlin: Springer, 1972.

Kuo, F. F., *Network analysis and synthesis* (2nd edn.). New York: Wiley, 1966.

Luce, R. D. and Galanter, E., Psychophysical Scaling, Chapt. 5 in: Luce, R. D., R. R. Bush and E. Galanter (eds.), *Handbook of Mathematical Psychology*, New York: Wiley, 1963.

Luneburg, R. K., *Mathematical Analysis of Binocular Vision*. Princeton, N.J., Princeton University Press, 1947.

Metzger, W., Versuch einer gemeinsamen Theorie der Phänomene Fröhlich und Hatzelhoffs und Kritik ihrer Verfahren zur Messung der Empfindungszeit. *Psychol. Forsch.*, **16**, 1932.

Mashhour, M., *Psychophysical relations in the perception of velocity*. Stockholm: Almquist and Wiksell, 1964.

Rubin, E. *Visuell wahrgenommene Figuren*. Kopenhagen: Gyldendalska, 1921.

Scheffler, P., Paper read at the Institut für Psychologie, Marburg University, 1962.

Stevens, S. S., On the psychophysical law. *Psychol. Rev.*, **64**, 153–181, 1957.

Szewczuk, M., *Stars und Sterne*. Hamburg: Rowohlt, 1955.

Wolgemuth, A., On the after-effect of seen movement. *Brit. J. Psychol. Monogr. Suppl.*, *Nr.* **1**, 1–117, 1911.

Chapter 7

A Riemann Geometric Explanation of the Visual Illusions and Figural After-effects

A. Watson

Abstract. Since the terms 'geometric illusion' and 'figural after-effect' are used so widely it would be as well if we clarify their use in this essay, and make clear the area it is envisaged that the present formulation should be capable of encompassing. Therefore for our purposes the geometric illusions and figural after-effects are to be considered as arising from a subject making an implicit judgement as to whether a curve can be extended to some particular point or not, or whether two shapes look the same in two different contexts, or whether a line is longer or shorter in several different contexts. In this paper a tentative attempt is made to explain the illusions of this type by assuming that 'visual space' is non-Euclidean and that the departure from Euclidean geometry is the result of the interaction between the elements within the 'visual space'. (Formally the interaction is represented by a 'field force'.) If the 'space', that the brain constructs from the information received by the eyes, is non-Euclidean and dependent on context, then it is not surprising that the subjective geometric judgements made under the influence of varying contexts, are at variance (and therefore illusory) with the physical Euclidean measurements (which do not depend on context).

1. Introduction

Von Békèsy in his book *Sensory Inhibition* has attempted to show that lateral inhibition may be able to account for some of the visual illusions. Ganz (1964, 1966) has proposed that the figural after-effects are, in part, the result of lateral inhibition by the inducing field after-image on the test field, and he has remarked that the visual illusions can be explained if it is assumed that the lateral inhibition effect acts simultaneously as well as successively. Robinson (1968) also has attempted to use the lateral inhibition hypothesis to explain the illusions, but according to him, the mechanism cannot account for the true illusions, e.g. Müller-Lyer and Ponzo illusions. Many other critics have pointed out also that the retina, the supposed locus of the inhibition mechanism is not an important determinant of the illusions, for the retina can be bypassed as in the case of the Julesz random dot stereoptsis patterns, and in the case of apparent contour illusions (Gregory 1971, 1972), yet the illusions still arise.

In order to avoid the difficulties incurred by any physiologically based theory, Eriksson (1970) advocates an approach to a theory from a non-reductionist point of view. In this spirit he has attempted to explain the illusions. He assumes that the lines in the visual field have an influence on one another, and this influence can be represented by a repulsive and attractive field of force. Whilst his ideas have some appeal, he is unfortunately ambiguous as to the conditions under which one is to use the two opposing fields of force (Robinson 1972). Also any fixed visual angle force field explanation, it must be pointed out, cannot be correct if the illusions occur over a large range of visual angles, as they undoubtedly do.

In this paper we will adopt the same standpoint as Eriksson, and propose a 'force field' theory which is logically independent of any physiological process, but which nonetheless has some properties (assumptions) that can be related to basic physiological facts. We will first informally introduce the basic concepts and assumptions (Section 2.1), and then develop these ideas in a more formal mathematical manner in Section 2.2. We will then apply the theory in Section 3 to a variety of illusions and investigate the ordinal agreement between the theory and experimental data. In Section 4 the assumptions necessary to explain the figural after-effects will be presented and in Section 5 they will be applied to some well known situations. In Sections 6 and 7 we will present data to show that exact numerical predictions can be made and that the theory is parsimonious.

2.1 Preamble

In the discussion of visual phenomena one question appears to have been neglected, or presumed answered, in the literature and that is 'What kind of space is visual space?' Before the question can be answered, it must be decided first of all how knowledge can be acquired about any space, whether it be visual or physical space. As far as physicists are concerned, physical space is just as abstract as all the other concepts of physics (see the introduction to A. S. Eddington's *The Mathematical Theory of Relativity*). One arrives at the nature of physical space by performing a particular sequence of operations and summarizing the results in terms of numbers, for physicists feel that the nature of physical space needs to be discovered experimentally and is not given *a priori*. (It was found that physical space is non-Euclidean). If it is accepted that the nature of any particular space is a matter to be settled by observation, then the question 'What kind of space is visual space'? must be decided in a manner similar to the way physicists answer the same question about physical space. One must define operations and then ask subjects to perform the operations under different conditions and then analyse the results. The operations need not involve the use of numbers. However, the operations decided upon must require the subject to use, in making a response, only what he sees and the instructions must not involve the previously learned properties and concepts of Euclidean geometry. It is pointless presenting geometric figures to a subject and asking him what he sees. The subject will undoubtedly construe the question as requiring him to identify the presented figures as belonging to one of the categories of geometric shapes, and this obviously prejudges the matter.

It has been found by geometricians that direction and length are two of the most important properties of a space (but these are not the only properties of space). Hence for our purpose we can decide to use visual judgements of direction and visual judgments of equality of length. The judgements are to be determined by the usual psychophysical methods. From these judgements the underlying nature of visual space can be constructed.

With the above considerations in mind, let us examine some simple visual arrays and deduce the nature of visual space. Possibly the simplest visual array which could be presented to a subject is the intersection of two straight lines. Undoubtedly any subject would recognize the presented figure as being that of two intersecting straight lines. However, if the subject is required to say at what angle the lines intersect, then the difference between physical Euclidean space (physical space is Euclidean to a very good approximation) and visual space will be revealed immediately, for the acute angle is usually overestimated (Helmholtz 1867, trans. 1962). Again, if a triangle is presented to a subject, he will say that it looks like three mutually intersecting straight lines, but if the triangle is 'exploded' and each angle is presented separately with no clue that the angles are part of a triangle, then the sum of the perceived angles will not add up to 180°. Thus one is faced with a contradiction in that, if the triangle is composed of three mutually intersecting straight lines in a Euclidean visual space, then the angles must add up to 180°, or, if the sum of the perceived angles is greater than 180°, then the lines joining the vertices of the triangle cannot be straight. The contradiction disappears if it is assumed that visual space is non-Euclidean. Further, consider the figure presented in Figure 1. A subject asked to report what he sees, will say he sees a triangle behind a square, but if you direct his attention to the 'line' AB, for example, he will say that DB does not look the continuation of AB, i.e. the subject reports seeing a triangle which does not have straight sides! Subjects can recognize geometric representations without necessarily 'seeing' them as geometric figures in a Euclidean space. Hence it appears that when a subject is asked to make judgements on the basis of the presented visual information rather than merely identify geometric figures, then it is revealed immediately that visual space is non-Euclidean.

The visual illusions can be considered to be the result of a subject making an implicit judgement as to whether a curve can be extended to some particular

142

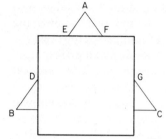

Figure 1. Square with a 'triangle' behind

point or not, or whether two shapes look the same in two different contexts, or whether a line is longer or shorter in several different contexts. Thus they too constitute evidence for the conclusion that visual space is different from physical Euclidean space, for the results of the visual 'measurements' do not correspond with the physical Euclidean measurements.

Now let us consider an idealized experiment. Suppose a subject is asked to look at two equal black lines projected onto a white screen. He will agree that the two lines are of equal length. Now suppose that, as the subject is looking at the lines, arrow-heads are projected onto the ends of one of the two lines such that the subject now sees the familiar Müller-Lyer figure. The subject now will say that the original lines do not appear to be equal in length. The only change that has occurred is the addition of the arrow-heads and this has altered the perceived length of one of the lines. Since the line has not altered its length physically, then one is forced to the conclusion that either the line has been 'contracted' with respect to visual space (assuming this to be Euclidean), or that visual space has been deformed with respect to physical space.

There are, in general, two different ways a 'force field' can be represented. One way is to assume that the lines in the visual field are displaced by mutual interaction, and that the visual space remains unchanged by the presence of the lines. The alternative way is to assume that the lines and curves affect the basic geometry of the visual space such that the distance between the lines is altered. The first method of representing the 'force field' assumes that the visual space is Euclidean whilst the second method presumes that the geometry is variable and non-Euclidean in agreement with the arguments made earlier.

Previous theories, e.g. Eriksson's invariably have made the first assumption and have not been successful. Thus we are left with the second alternative which is that visual space is non-Euclidean and its geometry is dependent upon the lines and curves in the visual field. The main advantage of making this second assumption accrue from the possibility of having two sorts of 'deformation'; one, the familiar displacement effects, and the second, the possibility of curvature of the space. Given this flexibility inherent in the approach it should be possible to construct a theory which, by a suitable combination of the two effects, can account for the diverse phenomena subsumed under the heading of geometric illusions.

If it is agreed that the seeming interaction between the lines and shapes on an otherwise homogeneous surface can be represented by means of a 'force field', then the hypothesis must reflect to some extent the fact that the interaction occurs within the nervous tissue. In the visual system the nerve fibres tend to run in parallel from the retina to the cortex. However, at each cell station there is a plexus of nerves perpendicular to the parallel fibre system, and it has been shown (Creutzfeldt (1961)) that these sheets are, in the main, inhibitory and provide a means of interaction within the visual system. (Hence the illusions can still arise even though the retina is bypassed, for it is not the only place in the visual system where lateral inhibition can occur.).

If the visual system is excited by a stable distribution of light, then the mutually interacting nerves must come to some equilibrium. But what is this equilibrium? Consider the analogy with a chain hung between two points. Here the system consists of mutually interacting elements which, if left undisturbed, will adopt a particular equilibrium shape no matter how large the links are, or what tension is applied at the end points, or how far apart the two suspension points are. The shape can be described in terms of two factors; the first represents the magnitude of the dip, the second represents the distance between the suspension points. Hence, if the analogy has any validity, then we can hazard a guess at the 'force field' necessary to explain the interaction within the visual system. In the non-reductionist framework we will assume that the 'force field' is dependent upon two factors; the first being a function of the intensity differences (corresponding to the magnitude of the dip), the second being a function of the spatial distribution of intensity such that the apparent 'range of effect' alters from one configuration to another (so that the 'shape' of the 'force field' remains invariant).

Clearly when the stable distribution is removed then the visual system must return to equilibrium, and this return must take a finite time. During the recovery period, the figural after-effects are observed. The physiological processes involved in this return to equilibrium are far from being understood. However, a few observations have been made which give some indication as to the probable course of events.

The first observation is the familiar recovery of nerves after excitation. During the recovery period the nerves tend to fire less than usual, and hence it has been suggested that the 'negative after-image' is the psychological counterpart of this recovery process. If it is assumed that the pairwise interaction takes place at a much faster pace than the rate of recovery, then we would expect the 'force field' to be negative with respect to the simultaneous illusion, and to slowly disappear. Again, there is evidence to show that the above account is an over-simplification. Nerves which have been strongly excited do not recover in a simple manner, but paradoxically, during the recovery period, start firing strongly. It can be speculated that this paradoxical firing is associated with the phenomenon known as 'positive after-image'. Hence we speculate that during the 'positive after-image' phase the 'force field' should be the same as for the simultaneous illusion.

We have suggested that the 'force field' is dependent upon the brightness of the figures. Indeed, given the occurrence of brightness contrast effects it could be inferred that the distance between the bright patches should be affected as well since both aspects of vision are dependent in some manner on the firing rates of nerves. According to Cornsweet (1970) brightness contrast can be explained in terms of the mutual inhibition of 'on' centres. But, in addition to the interaction between 'on' centres, there also may be a similar interaction between the 'off' centres i.e. 'darkness' contrast effects. Tentatively, we make the assumption that if the outline figure is bright with respect to the background, then the 'force field' is due to the interaction between the 'on' centres, and if the outline figure is dark with respect to the background then the 'force field' is due to the interaction between the 'off' centres. In either case the effect can be represented mathematically by taking the modulus of the intensity differences.

Not only can it be argued that the nerves in the visual system interact but also it can be argued that all parts of the system must be involved all the time in the perception of space (Walker 1973). In which case, it might be expected that despite changes in the visual input, the angular width of perceived space will remain invariant, in that no more or fewer nerves are involved in the process. From the non-reductionist point of view, in order to reflect this supposed invariance we will make the assumption in the present theory that if an expansion occurs in part of the visual space then a contraction must occur elsewhere to compensate.

Hence, with the above considerations in mind, the present theory assumes that visual space is non-Euclidean, and that the departure from Euclidean geometry is the result of the interaction between the elements with the visual field. Formally, the interaction is represented by a context dependent 'force field' having the properties outlined above. If the space which the brain constructs from the information received by the eyes, is non-Euclidean and dependent upon context, then it is not surprising that the subjective judgements made under the influence of varying context, are at variance with the physical Euclidean measurements (which do not depend on context.)

2.2 The Mathematical Theory

Since in the majority of cases the illusions are presented using lines on a flat surface, the formulation of the theory will be tailored to meet this restriction.

Assumption 1.1. The subject, when presented with a surface on which there are lines and curves, sees that surface as a 2-dimensional surface.

The perceived 2-dimensional surface will be referred to as 'visual space', and here the concept is used as a theoretical intermediary between the physical stimulus and the subject's verbal responses, and enables predictions to be made about the latter from a knowledge of the former.

Assumption 1.2. The lines and curves on the physical surface produce a small departure from the natural geometry of 'visual space', which is assumed to be Euclidean in the absence of any lines.

Assumption 1.3. The 'visual spaces' are all Riemann spaces.

One way of representing the geometry of a Riemann space is in terms of a metric equation. The most general metric equation for a 2-dimensional space can be written as,

$$\mathrm{d}s^2 = g_{11}\mathrm{d}x^1\mathrm{d}x^1 + g_{12}\mathrm{d}x^1\mathrm{d}x^2 + g_{22}\mathrm{d}x^2\mathrm{d}x^2 \tag{1}$$

where $\mathrm{d}s$ is the distance between neighbouring points with coordinates x^i and $x^i + \mathrm{d}x^i$, and g_{ij} is a covariant tensor of the second rank, whose components (g_{11}, g_{12}, and g_{22}) are functions of the coordinates x^i and is known as the 'fundamental tensor' of the Riemann space. The quadratic differential form $g_{ij}\mathrm{d}x^i\mathrm{d}x^j$ ($i, j = 1, 2$; with the usual summation convention) is called the metric, and is also the square of the 'line element' $\mathrm{d}s$, which has the property that it remains invariant from one coordinate system to another. For our purposes s (and its increment) will be interpreted as perceived distance, and x^1 and x^2 (and their corresponding increments) will be interpreted as physical distance as measured on the presented surface. Given a knowledge of the metric tensor then if, on the basis of the physical measurements of x^i, s is predicted to have the same numerical value in two different contexts, then further it is predicted that a subject will say that the two distances appear equal in length.

In the case of a surface with no lines on it, we have assumed that the geometry of the perceived surface is Euclidean, and the metric equation is

$$\mathrm{d}s^2 = (\mathrm{d}x^1)^2 + (\mathrm{d}x^2)^2 \tag{2}$$

This is the familiar Pythagoras theorem of Euclidean geometry.

Assumption 2.1. When lines are present on the surface, then the geometry of the visual space becomes non-Euclidean, and the metric equation becomes,

$$\mathrm{d}s^2 = (1 + h_1)(\mathrm{d}x^1)^2 + (1 + h_2)(\mathrm{d}x^2)^2 \tag{3}$$

Here, h_1 and h_2 are small (numerically) functions of the coordinates, the form of the functions being determined by the distribution of lines. They represent the deformation or 'field force' produced by the lines. What-ever form h_1 and h_2 take they must satisfy 4 conditions. (1) The deformation produced by any array must be finite on any of the lines. (This ensures that the figures do not rupture.) (2) The departure from Euclidean geometry should be a decreasing function of the distance from any line. (This will ensure that the effect at large distances can be neglected.) (3) The functions must be even valued, otherwise a change in sign of the coordinates would change the sign of any effect. (4) The range of effect must be dependent upon the size of the figures. With these 4 restrictions in mind the following assumptions will be made.

Assumption 2.2. h_1 and h_2 represent the 'force field' and are given by the following equations,

$$h_1 = \frac{\partial^2}{\partial x^2} f_1 \qquad h_2 = \frac{\partial^2}{\partial y^2} f_2$$

$$f_1 = \iint |A| me^{-(x-u)^2/am^2} e^{-(y-v)^2/am^2} \, du dv$$

$$f_2 = \iint |A| ne^{-(x-u)^2/an^2} e^{-(y-v)^2/an^2} \, du dv$$

(4)

(For notational convenience we have changed the coordinates, $x = x^1$, and $y = x^2$.) (u, v) is the position of a small area $du dv$ of intensity A above the background, a is a constant, and m and n are scale factors in the x and y directions respectively. The integration extends over all the lines and curves, and determines the size of the effect at (x, y).

Assumption 3. The distance across the 'visual space' remains constant.

Consequently, if an expansion occurs in one place, a corresponding contraction must occur also.

In order to produce a simple analytic formula, two further subsiduary assumptions will be made. These assumptions are made for mathematical convenience only and are not mundane to the theory.

Assumption 4. The units of length in the vertical and horizontal directions are the same.

Assumption 5. All the 'constants' (intensity, range, etc.) are independent of position and orientation in the visual field.

Obviously these two assumptions are unlikely to be met in reality, but they do reduce the mathematical complexity of the equations. Further, it is a moot point as to the degree to which the illusions vary with position and orientation under the conditions assumed by the theory. (i.e. A flat homogeneously illuminated screen with no perceivable edges, viewed centrally and with no gross movement of the eyes.)

Given that h_1 and h_2 have been found for a particular configuration then the natural geometry of the perceived surface is known and we can proceed to examine particular aspects of the geometry.

A large percentage of the illusions are associated with length and straightness. Both these aspects are contained in the concept of a geodesic. A geodesic can be defined in at least two different ways: (1) In terms of the shortest distance between two points, and clearly this aspect can be used to examine 'distance' illusions. (2) In terms of straightness, for it is the curve along which a unit vector can be parallelly propogated (i.e. The unit vectors which define direction can be joined continuously end to end such that the resultant curve preserves the same orientation along its complete path). This second aspect of a geodesic can be used to examine the apparent 'bending' illusions. When the two different ideas are expressed mathematically it is found that they lead to the same equations

$$\frac{d^2 x^k}{ds^2} + \begin{Bmatrix} k \\ ij \end{Bmatrix} \frac{dx^i}{ds}\frac{dx^j}{ds} = 0 \quad (i, j, k = 1, 2) \tag{5}$$

$$\begin{Bmatrix} k \\ ij \end{Bmatrix} = \frac{1}{2} g^{km} \left[\frac{\partial g_{im}}{\partial x^j} + \frac{\partial g_{jm}}{\partial x^i} - \frac{\partial g_{ij}}{\partial x^m} \right] \tag{6}$$

$$g^{km} g_{ij} = \delta_{ki} \delta_{mj}$$

Since the above equation is in terms of the fundamental tensor g_{ij} which can be found for each figure then, after the above differential equations have been solved, either distance or direction can be investigated. It is not necessary to make any further assumptions as to the judgements of distance and direction for these geometric ideas are contained in the concept of a geodesic. Indeed, given the assumption that the visual space is Riemann space then we are compelled by logic to use equation (5) to define a geodesic and hence distance and direction.

3. Visual Illusions

3.1 Poggendorff Illusion

This illusion consist of two parallel lines intersected by a broken diagonal line which does not appear to be collinear. Let the two parallel lines lie vertically on a homogeneous surface which is at 90° to the line of sight of the subject. Let the two vertical lines have a high contrast ratio and be a distance $2b$ apart, and let the diagonal line have a low contrast ratio. In addition, let the vertical lines be long, and the diagonal line be short. Under these conditions it is reasonable to suppose that the effect of the diagonal line will be negligible compared to the vertical lines. Suppose the subject is asked to fixate at the point of intersection (taken to be the origin) of the diagonal line and one of the vertical lines (considered to lie along the y axis). The problem is now to predict where the subject will judge that the diagonal line, if extended, would cut the second vertical line.

It will be assumed that the subject will behave as if he were taking the diagonal line as defining the initial gradient of a geodesic and extending that geodesic until it crosses the second vertical line. (i.e. Judgements of direction are made according to the intrinsic properties of visual space.)

Let the intensity of the vertical lines be A/unit area, and let their width be $2w$. Then from equation (4), after performing the integration, h_1 and h_2 can be found,

$$h_1 = 2\frac{C}{a} \left[\left(\frac{2x^2}{ab^2} - 1\right) e^{-x^2/ab^2} - \left(1 - \frac{2(2b - x)^2}{ab^2}\right) e^{-(2b - x)^2/ab^2} \right] \tag{7}$$

where $C = 2wA\sqrt{a\pi}$, and we have assumed that the range factor m is equal to b. Since there is no variation in the y direction, $h_2 = 0$. Therefore the metric for the space is

$$ds^2 = (1 + h_1)dx^2 + dy^2 \tag{8}$$

We must now determine the equation of the geodesic which is the extension of the diagonal line, given that the gradient of the diagonal line is k, and that it passes through the origin. From equations (8), and (6) we find that equation (5) becomes in this case

$$\frac{d^2x}{ds^2} + \frac{d}{dx}\log(1 + h_1)^{\frac{1}{2}}\frac{dx^2}{ds} = 0$$

$$\frac{d^2y}{ds^2} = 0$$

Solving these equations we find that,

$$\frac{dx}{ds}(1 + h_1)^{\frac{1}{2}} = r, \quad \frac{dy}{ds} = t$$

By assumption 2.1

$$(1 + h_1)^{\frac{1}{2}} \cong (1 + \tfrac{1}{2}h_1)$$

$$\therefore x + \tfrac{1}{2}\int h_1 dx = rs + p, \quad y = ts + q$$

But $y = 0$, when $s = 0$, therefore $q = 0$.

In a zero order perturbation C can be set equal to zero and therefore

$$\frac{dy}{dx} = k = \frac{t}{r},$$

and without any loss of generality we can set $t = 1$.

$$\therefore y = s$$

and

$$\frac{y}{k} + p = x + \frac{C}{a} \left[-xe^{-x^2/ab^2} + (2b - x)e^{-(2b-x)^2/ab^2} \right]$$

But when $y = 0$, $x = 0$, and therefore

$$p = 2b\frac{C}{a}e^{-4/a}$$

Thus the equation of the geodesic is

$$y = kx + k\frac{C}{a}\left[(2b - x)e^{-(2b-x)^2/ab^2} - xe^{-x^2/ab^2} - 2be^{-4/a}\right] \tag{9}$$

Thus if we set $x = 2b$, in the above equation then we can predict that a subject will judge that the diagonal line cuts the second vertical line below the point at which the physical line cuts it. This is the normal illusion, and the extent of the illusion is given by

$$y = -4bk\frac{C}{a}e^{-4/a} \tag{10}$$

i.e. The illusion is proportional to the width of the vertical lines, proportional to the gradient of the diagonal line, and proportional to the relative brightness of the vertical lines. The first two predictions have been confirmed by Weintraub and Krantz (1971). Figure 2 is a graph of the size of the illusion against the $\log_{10}$ of the relative brightness of the vertical lines. Clearly the prediction is confirmed, at least for the subject used in the experiment. Figure 3 shows the agreement between some empirical data and equation (9) for one subject with a fixed

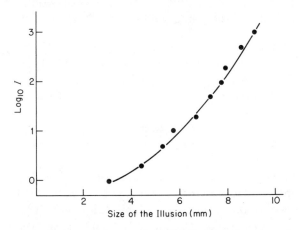

Figure 2. Size of Poggendorff illusion as a function of line brightness. Width between the vertical lines 11 cm, breadth of vertical lines 3 mm, gradient of the diagonal 0·9, and distance of subject's eye from screen, 46 cm

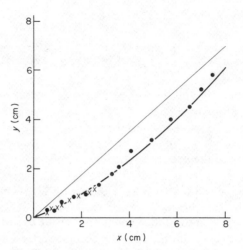

Figure 3. Apparent position of the extension of the diagonal line between the verticals of the Poggendorff illusion. The full curve represents the theoretical predictions based upon equation (9) with $k = 0.89$, $b = 4$ cm, $C/a = 0.67$, $a = 1.7$. The straight line is the Euclidean extension of the diagonal line

stimulus display. The points were generated by asking the subject to position a point such that it looks to lie on the extension of the diagonal line. (The dashed line is the physical projection of the diagonal line.) The parameters, $a = 1.7$, and $C/a = 0.67$ were chosen (see Section 7) to give the best fit.

At this junction it might be worthwhile to derive an approximate formula for the perceived size of an acute angle. If the separation, $2b$, between the vertical lines is made very large (and eventually infinite), then equation (9) becomes

$$y = k \left[x + \frac{C}{a} x \left[\left(\frac{8}{a} - 1 \right) e^{-4/a} - 1 \right] \right] \qquad (11)$$

If θ is the angle between the diagonal and the vertical line, then the perceived angle θ' is given by

$$\tan \theta' = \tan \theta \left[1 + \frac{C}{a} \left[\left(\frac{8}{a} - 1 \right) e^{-4/a} - 1 \right] \right]^{-1} \qquad (11a)$$

Empirically, a has been found to vary from 1.6 to 1.9, and C to vary from 0.1 to 1.5, and therefore it is predicted that $\theta' > \theta$ i.e. acute angles should appear larger than the physical angle. If the vertical line is semi-infinited and ends at the intersection, then the value of C is reduced, and the size of the effect will be smaller but nonetheless in the same direction. Also, in the case where two equal acute angles which have different contrast ratios are presented to a subject, it is predicted that the brighter one will be said to look larger.

3.2 Enclosure Illusion

This illusion is obviously a special case of the Müller-Lyer illusion in which the inter 'fin' angle is 180°. (i.e. The illusion consists of two vertical lines with a joining horizontal line.)

As in the Poggendorff illusion it is assumed that the two vertical lines which form the 'fins' of the illusion have a high contrast ratio and that the test line between these lines has a low contrast ratio. Under these conditions it is reasonable to assume that the deformation of the Euclidean surface is determined by the vertical lines. Let the origin be midway between the two vertical lines and let the x axis lie along the test line. Let $2b$ be the distance apart of the vertical lines. Clearly, h_1 and h_2 are identical to those found for the Poggendorff illusion (apart from a change in the origin), and the parametric equation of the geodesic which lies along the x axis is found in the same manner as the geodesic for the diagonal line of the Poggendorff illusion. In this case p, q, and t are all equal to zero, and r can be set equal to 1. The solution is

$$s = x - \frac{C}{a}\left[(b + x)e^{-(b + x)^2/ab^2} - (b - x)e^{-(b - x)^2/ab^2}\right] \tag{12}$$

Hence the perceived length of a line which extends from $(-x, 0)$ to $(x, 0)$ is

$$s = 2x - 2\frac{C}{a}\left[(b + x)e^{-(b + x)^2/ab^2} - (b - x)e^{-(b - x)^2/ab^2}\right] \tag{13}$$

The equation predicts that short test lines should appear longer than a physically equal line which is not enclosed, and that long test lines should appear shorter than an unenclosed, physically equal one. Fellows (1968) has produced data on the enclosure effect by measuring the length of a free variable line which is judged to be equal in length to an enclosed one, and this data agrees with the prediction made by equation (13). For the test line which goes completely across the gap the equation predicts the normal illusion that the enclosed line appears shorter than an unenclosed one.

Figure 4 shows some data collected from the same subject as in Figure 3 under the same stimulus conditions. In this graph the difference between the perceived length and the physical length of a test line is plotted against the physical length of the line. (The experimental procedure was identical to that used by Fellows (1968).) The theoretical curve, derived from equation (13) with $C/a = 0\cdot69$, and $a = 1\cdot66$, gives a good fit to the data. (See Section 7 for the estimation procedure.) Further, it can be seen that the parameters remain, within acceptable limits, invariant between the two situations. This implies that the geodesic, as defined in terms of direction is consistent at the empirical level with the geodesic as defined in terms of length, and supports the contention made earlier that the illusions can be explained in terms of basic geometric ideas.

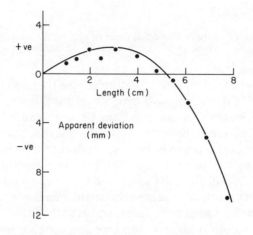

Figure 4. Deviation between the apparent
length and physical length of a line between
the verticals and the Enclosure illusion. The
full curve represents the theoretical predictions based upon equation (13) with $b = 4$ cm,
$C/a = 0.69$, $a = 1.66$

Equation (13) also predicts that the size of the illusion will depend upon the
contrast, and Figure 5 shows the results of an experiment in which a subject
judged the length of the test line under two levels of brightness of the vertical
lines with everything else remaining constant. The range parameter remains
constant at $a = 1.93$, but clearly the size of the illusion is strongly dependent
upon brightness.

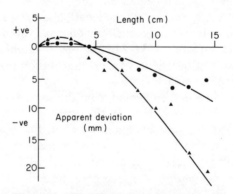

Figure 5. The effect of brightness on the
Enclosure illusion. Low intensity (dots)
condition; theoretical curve based upon
equation (13) with $C = 0.49$, $a = 1.93$,
$b = 7$ cm, and high intensity (crosses)
condition with $C = 1.19$, $a = 1.93$, $b =$
7 cm

3.3 Müller-Lyer Illusion

The lines which define the ingoing arrow-heads of the normal illusion will be assumed at right angles. It will be assumed that the brightness of the arrow-heads is much larger than the test line. Thus the metric is determined by the outline figure. Let the origin lie at the centre of the figure and let the axes be parallel to the arrow-heads which are assumed to extend from minus infinity to plus infinity. If $2b$ is the distance between the parallel lines of the arrow-heads, then h_1 and h_2 are similar to the functions derived for the Poggendorff, and Enclosure illusions, i.e.

$$h_1 = 2\frac{C}{a}\left[\left(\frac{2(b+x)^2}{ab^2} - 1\right)e^{-(b+x)^2/ab^2} + \left(\frac{2(b-x)^2}{ab^2} - 1\right)e^{-(b-x)^2/ab^2}\right]$$

and h_2 is exactly the same except that y is substituted for x.

The parametric equation for the geodesic which lies between the arrow-heads is found by solving equation (5) with h_1 and h_2 as given above and the solution is

$$ns = x - \frac{C}{a}\left[(b+x)e^{-(b+x)^2/ab^2} - (b-x)e^{-(b-x)^2/ab^2}\right]$$

$$ms = y - \frac{C}{a}\left[(b+y)e^{-(b+y)^2/ab^2} - (b-y)e^{-(b-y)^2/ab^2}\right]$$

$$(14)$$

$$n^2 + m^2 = 1$$

where n and m are projection operators. Hence the perceived length of a line which extends from $(-h, -h)$ to (h, h) is

$$s = 2\sqrt{2}h - 2\sqrt{2}\frac{C}{a}\left[(b+h)e^{-(b+h)^2/ab^2} - (b-h)e^{-(b-h)^2/ab^2}\right] \quad (15)$$

From the formula it is predicted that short lines will be overestimated and long lines will be underestimated as in the Enclosure illusion. Further, it can be seen that equation (15) and (13) are similar apart from a $\sqrt{2}$, and this might have been anticipated intuitively, for the Müller-Lyer is (in this case) two Enclosure illusions at right angles to one another.

For the case where the lines of the arrow-heads are finite and end at their point of intersection, then it is obvious that the value of C will be reduced, but otherwise the formula should be still valid. Hence it is predicted that (1), short test lines will be over-estimated, and long test lines will be under-estimated, (this has been found by Oyama (1960), Pollack and Chaplin (1964), and Fellows (1968).) (2), the relative size of the normal illusion (where the test line completely fills the gap between the arrow-heads) should remain approximately invariant and given by

$$s - 2\sqrt{2}h = -4\sqrt{2}h\frac{C}{a}e^{-4/a} \quad (16)$$

(3), the size of the illusion will be dependent upon the brightness of the arrow-heads (Pollack (1970) has produced data confirming this prediction), (4), the size of the arrow-heads will influence the size of the illusion in that C is an integral over the lines. (The data of Erlebacher and Sekuler (1969) confirms this prediction.)

In the case where the lines of the arrow-heads are outgoing, the predictions about the size of the illusion involve assumptions about the position and influence of the boundary. Although the arrow-heads are outgoing from the point of view of the test line, from the arrow-head to the boundary, the arrow-head is ingoing. Therefore, if it is assumed that the boundary is flat or convex then the distance between the arrow-head and the boundary will be contracted (equation (16)). But by Assumption 3 the total distance between the boundaries must remain constant, and therefore the contraction between the arrow-heads and the boundary must be compensated by an expansion in the region between the arrow-heads. Further it is predicted that the expansion will be uniform for all lengths of the test line. This has been confirmed by Oyama (1960), Pollack and Chaplin (1964), and Fellows (1968).

3.4 Ponzo Illusion

Let the two converging lines of the illusion intersect at right angles, let the origin be the point of intersection, let the axes lie along the converging lines, and let the test line run from $(b + h, b - h)$ to $(b - h, b + h)$ as in the normal version of the illusion. In this case there is no convenient symmetry and hence the calculation of the metric becomes difficult, and two approximations will be made depending on the presence or the absence (the illusion can be observed with dots) of the test line. If a test line is present then it will distort the field and act as a major determinant of the field. The range parameter is not a constant but on average should be approximately $\frac{1}{2}b$ if the test line is bright and nearly b if the test line is dim. It will be assumed that the range can be written as tb, where $\frac{1}{2} < t < 1$, and the inhomogeneity will be ignored. Hence, the effect of the converging lines on the test line can be estimated to be

$$h_1 = \frac{\partial^2}{\partial x^2}\left[C(tb)^2(e^{-x^2/a(tb)^2} + e^{-y^2/a(tb)^2})\right]$$

$$h_2 = \frac{\partial^2}{\partial y^2}\left[C(tb)^2(e^{-x^2/a(tb)^2} + e^{-y^2/a(tb)^2})\right]$$

$$(17)$$

The geodesic which approximately follows the test line is found by solving equation (5),

$$ns = x - \frac{C}{a}(b + x)e^{-(b + x)^2/a(tb)^2} + \frac{C}{a}be^{-1/at^2}$$

$$ms = y - \frac{C}{a}(b + y)e^{-(b + y)^2/a(tb)^2} + \frac{C}{a}be^{-1/at^2}$$

$$(18)$$

The origin has been changed to (b, b) for convenience. Hence the perceived length of the test line is

$$s = 2\sqrt{2}h - \sqrt{2}\frac{C}{a}\left[(b + h)e^{-(b + h)^2/a(tb)^2} - (b - h)e^{-(b - h)^2/a(tb)^2}\right] \quad (19)$$

Equation (19) can be assumed only to be approximate in that t has not been specified exactly. However, the ordinal conclusions that can be drawn from equation (19) do not depend critically on t. (The smaller the value of t, the larger the positive distortion becomes, and the smaller the negative distortion becomes. If t is assumed to be some function of position (as it must be), then equation (19) will become distorted, but will retain its general shape. Therefore although equation (19) is only an approximation the expected deviations brought about by more realistic assumptions are not radical, and the equation is not likely to be misleading.) For small test lines the equation predicts that they will be perceived as larger than an equal unaffected line, and this is the usual report. As t gets smaller, i.e. the test line is made brighter, then the illusion should increase. For lines which go almost completely across the gap between the converging lines, the equation predicts that the size of the illusion should decrease and even become negative. (See Figure 8.)

In the case where the size of the illusion is estimated by using dots to define the ends of the 'test line', then the range parameter becomes virtually infinite, and the geodesic can be found by the usual method, and is

$$ns = x - 2\frac{C}{a}\left[1 - \left(\frac{8}{a} - 1\right)e^{-4/a}\right]$$

$$ms = y - 2\frac{C}{a}\left[1 - \left(\frac{8}{a} - 1\right)e^{-4/a}\right]$$
$$\quad (20)$$

Hence it is predicted that the perceived length is

$$s = 2\sqrt{2}h - \sqrt{2}\frac{C}{a}\left[1 - \left(\frac{8}{a} - 1\right)e^{-4/a}\right]2h \quad (21)$$

i.e. the perceived distance between the dots is smaller than the perceived distance between 'free' dots. This has been observed by Morinago and Ikeda (1965).

3.5 Wundt and Hering Illusions

In both cases it is reasonably obvious that the origin of the 'stars' must have a very large intensity effect and hence as one moves out from the centre of the 'stars' the distortion effect will fall off rapidly. Since the geodesic which passes such a radial field is found, by solving equation (5) for a radial field, to be concave with respect to the centre of the 'stars', then any physically straight line passing near to the centre should appear convex with respect to the centre. (Hence we can characterize the effect of the 'star' as 'repulsion'.)

Compounded with this 'repulsive' effect will be a distortion similar to the Poggendorff illusion. As each radial line is encountered the 'probe' line will appear to be more normal to that radial, and hence this angular distortion will increase as the distance from the centre of the 'star' increases, for the distortion is greater for smaller angles of intersection. Hence the 'probe' line will appear to curve round the 'star'.

Thus the two types of distortion act in the same way and produce an effect which distorts the 'probe' line such that it appears to bend around the 'stars'.

3.6 Orbison Illusions

These can be explained in a similar manner as the Hering and Wundt illusions, i.e. as a combination of the 'repulsion' by the centre of a set of radial lines, and a 'Poggendorff' like effect. For example a circle placed off centre from a set of radial lines should appear, due to the 'repulsion' like effect of the 'star', flattened on the side nearest the 'star' centre. Since there are numerous examples of these illusions (see Robinson (1972)), and no mathematical description can be derived for any of them, a detailed analysis is pointless at this stage.

3.7 Zollner Illusion

This can be considered to be a multiple Poggendorff illusion. The vertical straight line(s) can be treated as the diagonal line of the Poggendorff illusion, and each diagonal bar of the Zollner illusion can be considered as one of the vertical lines of the Poggendorff illusion. It has been shown that the extrapolated position of the diagonal line in the Poggendorff illusion does not correspond with the physical position. It has been shown that the physical point should look always as though it is too high on the upper diagonal bar, and too low on the lower bar. Hence the vertical line of the Zollner illusion should appear broken up into segments which should appear to lie more perpendicular to the bars. The extent to which it appears broken up will depend upon the contrast ratio of the diagonal bars, their width, and the angle the bars make with the vertical. As this angle increases (i.e. the bars become more horizontal) there should come a point, depending on the vernier acuity, at which the segments blend together. Since the vertical line(s) is not a geodesic, the tangents to this line do not lie parallel to the line, and hence the line appears to bend without breaking up along its whole length.

Since the Zollner illusion is considered to be essentially similar to the Poggendorff illusion, then the same variables should affect the illusion. This is confirmed to some extent in the literature in respect of the angle between the bars and the vertical line, and the width and density per unit length of the bars, but not all authors agree. (See pages 63–71 in Robinson (1972) for a detailed discussion.) The prediction that the size of the illusion should be dependent upon the brightness of the bars has recently been confirmed by Wallace (1975), and he reports that the size of the illusion is proportional to the log. of the intensity, in remarkable agreement with Figure 2 in which it is shown that the size of the Poggendorff illusion is approximately proportional to the log of the intensity.

3.8 Delboeuf Illusion

This illusion consists of concentric circles but there are numerous variants e.g. concentric squares. If the circles are close together, then it can be assumed that the two circles mutually interact, and neither can be assumed to predominate. In which case the circumferences, which are parallel, are 'pulled' together as in the Enclosure illusion. Therefore it is predicted that the smaller circle should appear larger than a 'free' circle and the larger should appear smaller. As the two diameters become more and more disparate, then the deformation should get larger, for the Enclosure effect is proportional to the distance between the parallel lines. It is obvious, there comes a point at which the interaction between the circles becomes negligible, and therefore the under-estimation of the larger circle should disappear, and the over-estimation of the inner circle should decrease. Hence both the apparent enlargement and reduction should go through a maximum, and this has been found experimentally, and it is known as the 'distance' paradox. (Ikeda and Obonai (1955)).

There are many more illusions than the ones just described. The majority of these are concerned with asymmetry principally between the vertical and horizontal. It is comparatively easy to modify the mathematical formulation to accomodate these effects simply by changing from a spherically symmetric field to an elliptic one. However such a change would greatly increase the mathematical complexity without altering the theory in any essential respect, and therefore this 'improvement' is not included here. Again it could be argued that the asymmetry is due to the usual asymmetry in the field of vision, and would disappear if the illusions were investigated under conditions of symmetry. Therefore the illusions of this type are left unexplained by the current theory.

4. Figural After-effects

The data on the figural after-effects is not as extensive as the illusions, nor are the conditions under which the effects are observed as well documented. There seems to be at least 3 omissions: (1) Whether the after-image is positive or negative, (2) The time at which the observations are made, (3) The period over which the judgement is made. All of these factors could be crucial. Therefore the present 'theory' is more speculative and not so well supported by experimental facts.

Assumption 6. Positive and negative after-images have fields whose effects are opposite. The positive after-image will have a field which is identical to the normal field produced by normal stimulation. The negative after-image will have a field which is negative with respect to normal stimulation.

If this assumption is valid then some of the contradictions in the literature may be resolved.

Assumption 7. The fields will take a finite time to decay. During the fall of the fields, they will remain in quasi-equilibrium.

Here we are making the assumption that the lateral inhibition effects are 'quick' in comparison with the recovery time of the nerves, and the spatial distribution of the fields retain the same form throughout. Hence at any one time equation (4) can be used to make predictions, provided that the value of A is given. In this case A is the brightness per unit area of the after-image and hence it is predicted that the time course of the after-effect should be the same as for the after-image. The evidence for this hypothesis has been reviewed by Ganz (1966). In addition, as with the simultaneous illusions the stronger the after-image, the bigger the effects, and this has been confirmed by Pollack (1958), Oyama (1953), and Ganz (1966).

Assumption 8. The changes in the size of the fields will not be monotonic with time, and oscillations should occur.

Practically all the data collected by microelectrode techniques seem to agree that nerves do not respond smoothly to stimulation and hence we would expect some like effects, although these have not been observed.

Assumption 9. The after-image and its associated field are super-imposed on the current test field, such that any distance is the same for both fields.

Consider the case of two parallel lines. If a negative after-image of the lines is formed, then the perceived distance between the lines is greater than the physical distance, whereas the static condition gives rise to the Enclosure illusion, and the perceived distance is smaller. If the after-image is super-imposed on the 'test field', then both of these conditions cannot coexist. Therefore, either one of two things can happen; (a) Some compromise between the distances can be arrived at. (b) The images are shifted with respect to one another, in such a manner that both the illusions are preserved. This latter hypothesis has been adopted, for it seems to comply (or is implied by) with the well known phenomena that after-effects are dependent on 'apparent' size and not retinal size. (McEwen (1958)).

5. Examples of Figural After-effects

Using the above assumptions a few of the figural after-effects will be discussed. The predictions concerning the sign of the field with changes in the after-image, and the predictions concerning the complex time course of the effects will be dealt with in the experimental section.

5.1 Delboeuf Figural After-effect

This is the only after-effect that has been studied throughly, mainly by Japanese workers, Ikeda and Obonai (1955). The simultaneous illusion has already been discussed. If it is assumed that the stimulus conditions produce a negative after-image (informal observations support the hypothesis) then this negative after-image will produce a field which is opposite to the simultaneous case. Hence when the contours are close together they will appear to have been 'repelled' (rather than 'attracted' as before). Thus if the after-image is smaller than the test circle, then the test circle will appear larger, and if the after-image is larger, then the test circle will appear smaller. Again, as the contours become further apart the distortions should both go through a maximum and then decrease.

In the case where the inducing and test circles have the same retinal size we must use Assumption 9 to predict the outcome. The test circle diameter will be contracted (the Titchener (1901) illusion), whereas the negative after-image circle diameter will be expanded, and hence the field of the after-image will act as if it were coming from a circle of larger diameter than the test circle. Hence the test circle will be 'repelled' and thus appear contracted. This has been confirmed by Ikeda and Obonai (1955).

5.2 The Letter Illusion of Willems

Willems (1967) used as inspection figures various letters with parts missing, and in each case the test figure consisted of that part of the letter which was missing. The part was so placed relative to the fixation point that it fell precisely where, in the inspection figure, the gap had been. In this case the gap can be considered to be the 'gap' between the parallel lines of the Enclosure illusion. Hence in the after-image the gap will be wider than in the figure, and thus the missing part will not appear to fill the gap in the after-image.

5.3 Kohler's Figural After-effects

Under this heading are all the 'repulsion' effects produced by lines and contours. In general these can be treated as 'Enclosure' like illusions. In simultaneous presentation the contours should appear closer together (as measured by comparing a line which goes across the gap with a free line), but in successive presentation (provided a negative after-image is produced) they should appear 'repelled' by one another. Further, since the effect is proportional to the width of the gap then as the width increases so will the size of the effect. However it must be remembered that the size of the effect is dependent upon the after-image brightness which is invariably small and therefore the effect will be subject to interference from other sources as the gap increases, and thus the size of the effect is likely to be decreased. (Kohlers and Wallach (1944)).

6. Experiments

The following experiments were performed with two aims in mind. The first aim was simply to supplement the data from the literature and test some of the conclusions drawn from the theory. The second aim was to investigate a few illusions, principally the Poggendorff, Enclosure, Müller-Lyer, and Ponzo, and see if they bear any relationship to one another, i.e. discover if the constants C and a which occur in equations (9), (13), (15), and (19), remain invariant. The same aim was abandoned in the case of the figural after-effects for reasons which will be apparent when the data is presented.

The apparatus consisted mainly of a 2 m by 1·75 m semi-opaque screen and three 35 mm projectors. The screen was chosen to be as large as possible in order to ensure that the only lines in the visual field of a subject were the lines projected on the screen. (If the lines in the visual field interact, then the outline of the stimulus material will have as much effect as the lines being studied. In addition, it is possible for the subject to use the horizontal and vertical boundaries as a reference frame, and hence yield results which appear to indicate asymmetry especially in the horizontal and vertical directions.)

In order to project white line figures onto the screen, the negatives of photographs of the figures, drawn with Chart-Pak black strip on white paper, were made using the same exposure conditions. The variable line and dot used in most of the experiments were obtained by having variable slits mounted on a projector. A negative of a line was placed across the slits and hence the line image on the screen could be varied from a dot to any desired length. The slits and negative could be traversed horizontally by means of a worm thread. Vertical movement was achieved by raising or lowering the whole projector. On all the projectors the slide holder and lens system could be rotated through 360°. The intensity of the projected image was manipulated by means of a set of neutral-density filters. Three sets of mechanical shutters were placed at the focus of the optical system, and hence figures could be flashed onto the screen.

All the subjects used in any of the experiments quoted herein had no known defects in their vision. The subject sat in an adjustable chair behind the screen so that he could fixate with one eye the centre of the screen. The subject's head was never more than 0·5 m from the screen. It was explained to the subject that he would be asked to make judgements about the equality in the length of two lines, or about the position of a dot with respect to a line. The fixed slide with the illusion or 'inducing' field was presented always on the left side of the screen and the variable 'standard' symmetrically on the right side of the screen. In the case of the Poggendorff illusion the figure was in the middle of the screen but its orientation was randomized between subjects. The subjects were asked in the case of the Poggendorff illusion to make their judgements whilst fixating on the intersection of the 'diagonal' line and the 'vertical' line. (All that is assumed by this is that the subjects refrain from gross eye movements. It was found that gross eye movements do affect the results especially in the vertical and horizontal directions. Indeed it is likely that the supposed asymmetry of the Poggendorff and other illusions may be entirely due to eye movements.) In the other cases the subjects were asked to look at the centre of the line when making a judgement. The method of 'average error' was used and the measurements were made on the projector side of the screen and the results were never revealed to the subject until the end of the experiment. No results were collected until the subject was thoroughly light adapted to the ambient intensity of the laboratory, the waiting time being taken up with practice trials.

7. Discussion of Results

Figures 3 and 4 represent the data collected from the same subject for the Poggendorff and Enclosure illusions respectively. The stimulus conditions were identical in the two experiments (i.e. thickness brightness, distance apart of the vertical lines, the position of the subjects head with respect to the screen, and the background intensity). Hence the parameters C and a should be the same for both illusions. In the case of the Poggendorff illusion the parameters were determined with the aid of equation (9) and (11). (Incidentally, the data represented by crosses in Figure 3 was obtained with one of the vertical lines removed. As predicted the two sets of points agree for $x \ll 8$ cms, the width of the display.) If y_1 is the observed deviation at $2b$ and y_2 is the projected deviation according to equation (11), then

$$\frac{y_2}{y_1} = \frac{\left(\frac{8}{a} - 1\right)e^{-4/a} - 1}{-2e^{-4/a}} \tag{22}$$

and a can be found. ($y_1 = 0\cdot9$ cms, $y_2 = 3\cdot1$ cms, $a = 1\cdot7$). Substituting this value of a into (9) gives a value for C. ($k = 0\cdot89$, b $= 4$ cms, $C = 1\cdot13$). The values of C and a are then used in equation (9) to construct the theoretical curve shown in the graph and it can be seen that the agreement is reasonable.

In the case of the Enclosure illusion the value of C and a were determined with the aid of equation (13). It can be seen from the equation that for some length of test line the distortion should be zero and therefore,

$$(b + x)e^{-(b + x)^2/ab^2} = (b - x)e^{-(b - x)^2/ab^2}$$

With $b = 4$ cms and $x = 2\cdot75$ cms, $a = 1\cdot66$. Given the value of a then C can be found by observing the size of the illusion for $x = 4$ cms, and is found to be $1\cdot14$. These values are then used to construct the theoretical curve which can be seen to agree with the data. Also the parameters are almost the same as the ones derived to fit the data from the Poggendorff illusion. (This has been confirmed by Ridgway (1972) who used 8 subjects and derived the parameters using a minimum Chi-square technique.)

Figure 2 and 5 represent data from experiments designed to test the hypothesis that the illusions vary with the brightness of the defining lines. The results quoted are from individual subjects and only for two illusions, but in terms of the present theory, crucial illusions; the Poggendorff is a directional illusion, and the Enclosure illusion is a distance illusion. However, the results have been confirmed informally for a large number of illusions and subjects. The data in Figure 2 confirms the prediction made from equation (10) that the size of the normal illusion is dependent upon the brightness of the vertical lines, when all else is kept constant (i.e. the size, orientation, and distance from the subject of the stimulus material). It was found, by the above method, that the value of $a = 1 \cdot 7$ (s.d. $= 0 \cdot 02$) does not vary over a sufficiently large range to explain the results, and hence it was concluded that the variation in the size of the illusion was due to changes in the value of C (and hence A, the assumed brightness per unit area of the vertical lines.)

Figure 5 shows the results of a similar experiment using the Enclosure illusion at two levels of brightness, all else being kept constant. The parameters were derived in a similar manner to that just described. It can be seen that the data falls along two curves, given by equation (13), with different values of C but with the same value of a.

Figures 6, 7, and 8 show the results from an experiment on the Enclosure, Müller-Lyer, and Ponzo illusions, using 4 subjects under the same stimulus conditions so that it could be assumed that the value of C and a remained constant. The parameters C and a were derived from an initial experiment on the Poggendorff illusion, and it was found that the parameters were the same for each subject, and hence the results could be pooled. ($C = 0 \cdot 875$, $a = 1 \cdot 75$). It can be seen that the theoretical curves (equation (13) for the Enclosure illusion,

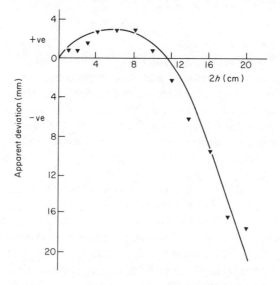

Figure 6. Apparent deviation (average of 4 subjects) in length of a test line of length $2h$ (cm) for the Enclosure illusion. The theoretical curve is based upon equation (13) with $C/a = 0 \cdot 5$, $a = 1 \cdot 75$, $b = 10$ cm

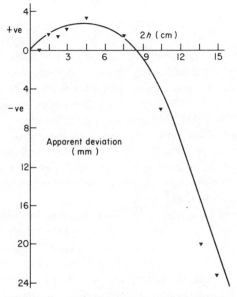

Figure 7. Apparent deviation (average of 4 subjects) in length of a test line of length 2 2*h* (cm) for the Müller–Lyer illusion. The theoretical curve is based upon equation (15) with $C/a = 0.5$, $a = 1.75$, $b = 7.5$ cm

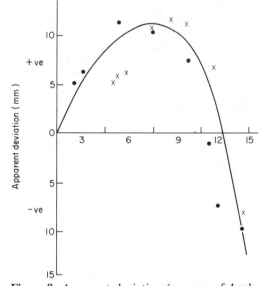

Figure 8. Apparent deviation (average of 4 subjects) in length of a test line of length 2 2*h* (cm) for the Ponzo illusion. The theoretical curve is based upon equation (19) with $C/a = 0.5$, $a = 1.75$, $b = 7.5$ cm, $t = 0.9$. Dots are for the condition where *b* is fixed and *h* varied, and the crosses are for the condition where *h* is fixed and *b* varied (renormalized)

164

equation (15) for the Müller-Lyer illusion, and equation (19) for the Ponzo illusion) pass through the experimental points satisfactorily, except for the Ponzo illusion where perfect agreement was not expected. (Incidentally, the value of t in equation (19) was set equal to 0·9. This figure was arrived at by considering the case of the Enclosure illusion with one of the vertical lines twice as bright as the other. (In the actual Ponzo illusion used here, this was the ratio of brightness of the converging lines to the test line.) The equilibrium position can then be calculated and was found to be 1·8b from the brighter line.) Since none of the presented data was used to estimate the parameters this agreement supports the contention that the subjects were consistent in their judgements of direction and length.

Figures 9, 10, and 11 represent the data collected in order to investigate the assumption that oscillations should occur in the figural after-effect, and also at the on-set of the illusions. Figure 9 shows the results from an experiment on the Enclosure illusion for one subject. The test line and its 'free' comparison line were exposed for 0·2 sec. In the simultaneous illusion the time at which the test line was presented was stepped in intervals of 0·1 sec from the beginning of the presentation of the vertical lines. This time interval was randomized over the 3 sec of observation so that the subject could not anticipate the occurrence of

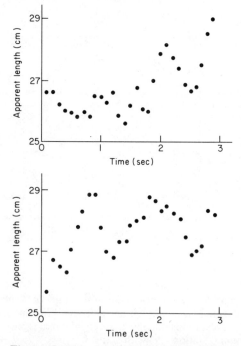

Figure 9. The simultaneous (upper) and successive (lower) Enclosure illusion: Apparent length as function of time for 1 subject

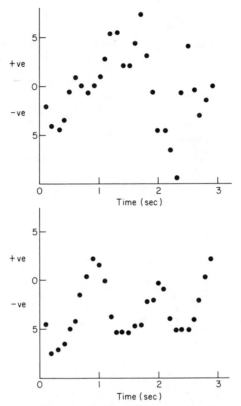

Figure 10. The simultaneous (upper) and successive (lower) Poggendorff illusion: Number of 'positive' and 'negative' judgements as a function of time, average of 5 subjects

the test line. The subject was asked to fixate a point midway between the test line and the 'free' comparison line. The trial rate was kept slow in order to avoid inter-trial interference. In the successive case, the vertical lines were presented for 1·5 sec and then the test line at some time after the end of the inducing field in a similar manner to the simultaneous case. A running average of 0·3 sec was used to smooth the results. The results clearly indicate that oscillations do occur, and equally it is clear that the results are subject to a large amount of noise preventing anything other than ordinal conclusions being drawn from them.

Figures 10 and 11 show the results of an experiment conducted with the aid of an ordinary tachiastoscope. Two illusions were investigated; the Poggendorff and the Müller-Lyer, but in all other respects the experimental procedure was the same, apart from the judgements the subject had to make. In the Poggendorff case the subject had merely to say whether the two short diagonals appeared colinear or if not colinear which way the illusion appeared. The position of the two short diagonals was altered such that the judgements would be *c*. 50% each way. In the Müller-Lyer case he merely had to say which of the two lines

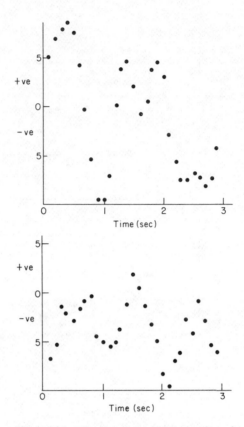

Figure 11. The simultaneous (upper) and successive (lower) Müller–Lyer illusion: Number of 'positive' and 'negative' judgements as a function of time, average of 5 subjects

appeared longest; one line was presented between the 'in-going fins', and the other between the 'out-going fins'. Again the lengths of the lines were altered such that the judgements would be split c. 50% each way. 5 subjects were used in all and the results were pooled and computed by assigning +1 for a report in agreement with the normal illusion, 0 for a equality report, and −1 for an 'opposite' report. In order to smooth the results a running average over 0·3 sec was used. The results show that oscillations occur both at the 'on set' of the illusions and figural after-effects. The periods of the main oscillations were 1·3 sec for the simultaneous illusion and 1·1 sec for the successive illusion, but there is some evidence for oscillations of a shorter period.

Since the results in the two experiments were obtained under different conditions and with different illusions, then some reliance can be placed on them. Hence the hypothesis (Assumption 8) that oscillations should occur i.e. that neural process are responsible for these phenomena, is not unreasonable.

The author has attempted to verify the hypothesis that positive after-images produce the normal illusions, whereas negative after-images produce the opposite effects. In respect of the latter part of the hypothesis this certainly seems to be the case for all the illusions investigated e.g. Poggendorff, Enclosure, Müller-Lyer (both 'in-going' and 'out-going' fins), Ponzo, and Delboeuf illusions. Owing to the difficulties in producing positive after-images and investigating them, only one subject was 'trained' in the 'art'. He confirmed by his own observation that positive after-images do produce the normal illusory effect, the largest effect being observed just before the after-image fades into a negative after-image. The subject was quite naive and volunteered the information without prompting. If these observations can be substantiate by independent workers, then they are likely to prove interesting.

8. Conclusion

In this paper it has been assumed that the visual illusions and figural after-effects are not aberrations or mis-perceptions, but that they are in fact the simple configurations which reveal the non-Euclidean nature of visual space. In all cases of an illusion or after-effect it is suggested that the illusory nature of the configuration is the result of comparing subjective judgements of length, angle, and direction with the known Euclidean measures of these properites. Having argued that visual space is non-Euclidean, a metric equation was constructed which represents the visual space of a subject looking at, or having just looked at, lines on a flat surface. In order to account for the judgements of direction and length made by subjects it is necessary to assume that these judgements are based on the intrinsic properties of the space given by the metric. (i.e. The judgements of direction, straightness, and length are all predictable from a knowledge of the relevant geodesic.) Since the intrinsic properties of the visual space depend upon the configuration of stimulus elements, then the subjective judgements of geometric properties will vary from context to context. Thus most of the geometric illusions and figural after-effects could be explained, and in a few simple cases explicit equations can be derived to predict the size of the illusions and after-effects and their dependence on a few critical variables. Where the literature was lacking in information, experiments were performed to demonstrate the adequacy of the theory, and in all cases the predictions were confirmed.

The theory was presented in an abstract form to avoid dependence upon physiological mechanisms. However, the hypothesized connection between the field effects described by the metric equation and lateral inhibition seem to be compelling, if not conclusive. First, there is the dependence of the illusions and after-effects on the brightness of the outline figures. Brightness contrast effects are observable over large visual angles (Leibowitz, Mote and Thurlow (1953)) and have been attributed to lateral inhibition, and if brightness (i.e. the firing rates of nerves) can be affected over a distance, then it is surely plausible to assume that the firing rates of the nerves associated with spatial perception are

168

affected also. Again if the hypothesis of pairwise interaction is accepted then the distance over which the inhibition effect can be manifest, becomes virtually the whole visual field, and hence inhibition is extensive enough to explain the illusions. Secondly, the dependence of the field on the size of the configuration. This again is in accordance with the hypothesis of pairwise interaction. Thirdly, the correspondence between the region of dis-inhibition and the over-estimation of length, and the region of inhibition and the under-estimation of length. (Given that $a < 2$ then equation (7) for the Enclosure illusion can be seen to be positive over the middle region, and negative at the edges, and these are the regions of over- and under-estimation respectively.) Fourthly, the change in the sign of the field for negative after-images. Fifthly, the occurrence of oscillations at the onset of the illusions and after-effects indicate complex neural processes.

The present theory cannot explain asymmetry, the effects of practice and information feedback, or cultural and individual differences, but it is hoped that these observations can be reconciled at some future time.

References

Bekesy, G. Von. (1967). *Sensory Inhibition.* Princeton: Princeton University Press.

Cornsweet, T. N. (1970). *Visual Perception.* New York: Academic Press.

Creutzfeldt, O. D. (1961). General physiology of cortical neurons and neural information in the visual system. In M. B. A. Brazier (Ed.), *Brain and Behavior.* Washington: American Institute of Biological Sciences.

Eddington, A. S. (1923). *The Mathematical Theory of Relativity.* Cambridge: Cambridge University Press.

Eriksson, E. S. (1970). A field theory of the visual illusions. *Brit. J. Psychol.* **61**, 451–466.

Erlebacher, A. and Sekuler, R. (1969). Explanations of the Müller-Lyer illusion: Confusion theory examined. *J. Exp. Psychol.,* **80**, 462–467.

Fellows, B. J. (1968). The reverse Müller-Lyer illusions and 'Enclosure' *Brit. J. Psychol.* **59**, 369–372.

Ganz, L. (1966). Mechanism of the figural after-effect. *Psychol. Rev.,* **73**(2), 128–150.

Gregory, R. L. (1972). Cognitive contours. *Nature,* **238**, 51–52.

Helmholtz, H. Von. (1962), ed. J. C. P. Southall. *Helmholtz Treatise on Physiological Optics,* Vol. III. New York: Dover Publications.

Ikeda, H. and Obonai, T. (1953). Figural after-effects, retroactive effects and simultaneous illusion. *Jap. J. Psychol.,* **26**, 235–246.

Kohlers, W. and Wallach, H. (1944). Figural after-effects: An investigation of visual processes. *Proc. Amer. Philos. Soc.* , **88**, 269–357.

Leibowitz, Mote, F. A. and Thurlow, W. B. (1953). Simultaneous contrast as a function of seperation between test and inducing field. *J. Exp. Psychol.,* **46**, 453–456.

McEwen, P. (1958). Figural after-effects. *Brit. J. Psychol. Mongr. Suppl.,* **31**.

Morinaga, S. and Ikeda, H. (1965). Paradox in displacement in geometric illusions and the problem of dimensions: A contribution to the study of space perception. *Jap. J Psychol.,* **35**, 231–238.

Oyama, T. (1953). Experimental studies of the figural after-effect. 1. Temporal factors. *Jap. J. Psychol.,* **23**, 239–245.

Oyama, T. (1960). Japanese studies of the so-called geometrical-optical illusions. *Psychologia,* **3**, 7–20.

Pollack, R. H. (1958). Figural after-effects: Quantitative studies of displacement. *Aust. J. Psychol.,* **10**, 269–277.

Pollack, R. H. and Chaplin, M. R. (1964). Effects of prolonged stimulation by components of the Müller-Lyer figure upon the magnitude of the illusion. *Percept. Mot. Skills*, **18**, 377–382.

Robinson, J. O. (1968). Retinal inhibition in visual distortions. *Brit. J. of Psychol.*, **59**(1), 29–36.

Robinson, J. O. (1972), *The Psychology of Visual Illusions*, London: Hutchinson University Library.

Walker, E. H. (1973). A mathematical theory of optical illusions and figural after-effects. *Perception & Psychophysics*, **13**, 467–486.

Wallace, G. K. (1975). The effect of contrast on the Zollner Illusion. *Vision Research*, **15**, 963–966.

Weintraub, D. J. and Krantz, A. (1971). The Poggendorff illusion: Amputations, rotations and other perturbations. *Perception & Psychophysics*, **10**, 257–264.

Chapter 8

Brightness and Contrast*

H. F. J. M. Buffart

Abstract. The human luminance-detection-system comprises three sub-systems:

(a) The retina-system. It transforms lightintensity into neuronal activity in a non-linear way. Then it filters the spectrum of the neuronal activity.
(b) The contrast-detection-system. It is a stochastical system, based on the principle of synergetics, that can detect differences in intensity between adjacent parts of a stimulus field.
(c) The brightness-system. It spreads the brightness across the visual field. This spreading is weighted by the local value of the contrast-detection system.

Threshold measurements are measurements in which the retina-system and the contrast-detection-system are involved. Binocular interaction takes place in the contrast-detection system. For brightness judgement all three systems are used.

Although the contrast-detection system is formulated by a system of coupled differential equations and the solution of it for a stimulus is intricate and laborious, one can infer from it already qualitatively and by approximation some interesting conclusions.

Introduction

From psychophysical and electrophysiological experiments with stabilized retinal images the following conclusions may be drawn (Gerrits and Vendrik, 1970). If a visual pattern is presented, stabilized in relation to the retina, it appears that after the onset of the stimulus:

* This work was supported by the Netherlands Organization for the Advancement of Pure Research (ZWO). The author thanks Dr. Ch. M. M. de Weert for the fruitful discussions.

First of all the electrical activity of the retina, relevant to contrast and brightness perception (spike concentration changes), disappears;

Then the contours (in the cortex) fade away;

Subsequently the colour impression disappears;

And lastly the brightness impression decreases.

We shall leave the colour system out of consideration for the present. Most naïvely we shall now make the assumption that we can subdivide the psychophysical visual system in such a way that it is analogous to the observations regarding stabilized retinal images; thus we have three subsystems, viz.,

The psychophysical retina
The contrast system
The brightness system

From the discussion below it will appear that this subdivision is a good one. The first two systems will be discussed below; the third will be touched upon. Not all the calculations will be presented here: for these, one is referred to Buffart (1978).

1. The Psychophysical Retina

(a) Theory

The system of the psychophysical retina is built up out of two subsystems (Figure 1): a non-linear and a linear system. The perceptual units to be introduced are conceived of as fields on $\mathbb{R}^2$, which are a function of time. A system transforms one field into another field.

The non-linear system is local with respect to the place coordinates on the retina. It is the transformation of the light intensity $L(\vec{r}, t)$ which the retina receives at a certain place $\vec{r}^{(1)}$ and at a certain time $t^{(2)}$ in a dimension-free field $E(\vec{r}, t)$

$$E(\vec{r}, t) = \frac{L(\vec{r}, t) - \tau}{L(\vec{r}, t) - \tau + \delta} \tag{1a}$$

τ and δ are constants which, just as L, are given in cd/m² or td. We require $L(\vec{r}, t)/\tau \geq 1$

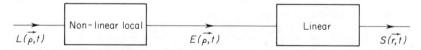

Figure 1. Non-linear, local system and linear system

For a large area, (1a) seems similar to Webers law. By means of it, one can explain various phenomena in the low luminancy area, where the logarithmic transformation does not apply (see also Grossberg, 1978).

The linear system is described by means of a convolution integral (2a)

$$s(\vec{r}, t) = \int_{-\infty}^{\infty} \int\int_{-\infty}^{\infty} s_1(\vec{r} - \vec{\rho}, t - \tau)E(\vec{\rho}, \tau)\,d\vec{\rho}\,d\tau \tag{2a}$$

We require that s_1 is symmetrical in $\vec{r} - \vec{\rho}$.

Of (2a) is required that it satisfies a causality condition.[3] This implies that two 'point-shaped' light stimuli, differing only in their locus on the retina $\vec{r}_1, \vec{r}_2$ will only simultaneously contribute to s at the same coordinates if, for time t, after the beginning of the stimulation it holds that

$$t^2 c^2 \geq \tfrac{1}{4}(\vec{r}_1 - \vec{r}_2)^2 + a$$

where a is a not negative dimensionless constant[1] and c is a positive constant of the dimension 1/time[2].

Moreover, we introduce the hypothesis essential for the theory that the output of the last element of the linear chain of the psychophysical retina is only the first-order time change in the input of this element. This may be compared with the electro-physiological discovery that it is only changes in spike concentration of the on-centre and off-centre cells in the retina that contribute to contrast and brightness perception (Gerrits and Vendrik, 1970). Therefore, formula (2a) may be rewritten as

$$S(\vec{r}, t) = \frac{\partial}{\partial t} \int\int_{-\infty}^{\infty} \int_{-\infty}^{\infty} s_2(\vec{r} - \vec{\rho}, t - \tau)E(\vec{\rho}, \tau)\,d\tau\,d\vec{\rho} \tag{2b}$$

The first two requirements give rise to the formulation

$$s_2(\vec{r}, t) = \theta\left(t - \left[\frac{\vec{r}^2 + a}{c^2}\right]^{\frac{1}{2}}\right) s(\vec{r}, t)$$

where
$$\theta(x) = 0 \text{ if } x < 0$$
$$= 1 \text{ if } x > 0$$

and
$$s(\vec{r}, t) = s(-\vec{r}, t)$$

so that if
$$t' = t - \left[\frac{(\vec{r} - \vec{\rho})^2 + a}{c^2}\right]^{\frac{1}{2}}$$

$$S(\vec{r}, t) = \frac{\partial}{\partial t} \int\int_{-\infty}^{\infty} \int_{-\infty}^{t'} s(\vec{r} - \vec{\rho}, t - \tau)E(\vec{\rho}, \tau)\,d\tau\,d\vec{\rho} \tag{2c}$$

$$= \int\int_{-\infty}^{\infty} \int_{-\infty}^{t'} s(\vec{r} - \vec{\rho}, t - \tau)N(\vec{\rho}, \tau)\,d\tau\,d\vec{\rho} \tag{2d}$$

where
$$N(\vec{\rho}, \tau) = \frac{\partial}{\partial \tau} E(\vec{\rho}, \tau) \tag{1b}$$

If we assume that in general $c/[(\vec{r} - \vec{p})^2 + a]^{\frac{1}{2}}$ is large with respect to the temporal frequencies transmitted by $s(\vec{r}, t)$, then equation (2) may be substituted by

$$S(\vec{r}, t) = \iint_{-\infty}^{\infty} \int_{-\infty}^{t} s(\vec{r} - \vec{p}, t - \tau)N(\vec{p}, \tau)\,\mathrm{d}\tau\,\mathrm{d}\vec{p} \qquad (3)$$

This assumption must be carefully applied, especially if a stimulus contains low spatial and high temporal frequencies.

Let s be normalized, such that

$$\iint_{-\infty}^{\infty} \int_{0}^{\infty} s(\vec{r}, t)\,\mathrm{d}t\,\mathrm{d}\vec{r} = 1 \qquad (4a)$$

We now define
$$c_1(\vec{r}) = \int_{0}^{\infty} s(\vec{r}, t)\,\mathrm{d}t \qquad (4b)$$

$$c_2(t) = \iint_{-\infty}^{\infty} s(\vec{r}, t)\,\mathrm{d}\vec{r} \qquad (4c)$$

We now assume that $c_1(\vec{r})c_2(t)$ is a good first order approximation of $s(\vec{r}, t)$.
Finally, a necessary requirement for perception is

$$S^+(\vec{r}, t) = \frac{S(\vec{r}, t) + |S(\vec{r}, t)|}{2} \geq \sigma_+ > 0 \qquad (5a)$$

$$S^-(\vec{r}, t) = \frac{|S(\vec{r}, t)| - S(\vec{r}, t)}{2} \geq \sigma_- > 0 \qquad (5b)$$

Apart from the threshold τ in (1a), various psychophysical threshold measurements are measurements at the threshold of formula (5).

(b) The Determination of $c_1(\vec{r})$ and $c_2(t)$

The form of $c_2(t)$ may be determined by taking threshold measurements for time-variant contour-free stimuli. The stimuli, however, must be chosen in such a way that one may be certain that the measured phenomena are not a result of the non-linear transformation (1).

The latter also holds for stimuli when determining $c_1(\vec{r})$. Yet $c_1(\vec{r})$ cannot be determined by choosing $L(\vec{r}, t)$ independent of t. In that case of course it holds that $S(\vec{r}, t) = 0$. The only way to eliminate $c_2(t)$ in experiments determining $c_1(\vec{r})$ is to conduct all the experiments with $E(\vec{r}, t) = E_2(t)E_1(\vec{r})$.

In our view, there are two experimental situations in which this is the case, viz., if each stimulus is presented in a flash, $L_2(t) = \theta(t - t_0) - \theta(t - t_1)$ and in the case of contrast threshold measurements with free fixation. In the latter case, the saccadic eye movements ensure stimuli with, in first approximation,

$$L_2(t) = \sum_{i=-\infty}^{n} (\theta(t - t_i) - \theta(t - t_{i+1}))$$

In the case of flashes it holds that

$$S(\vec{r}, t) = (\bar{c}_2(t - t_0) - \bar{c}_2(t - t_1)) \int\int_{-\infty}^{\infty} c_1(\vec{r} - \vec{\rho})E(\vec{\rho}, t_0)\,d\vec{\rho} \qquad (7a)$$

Saccadic eye movements from $\vec{\rho}_i$ to $\vec{r}_i$ at time t_i yields

$$S(r, t) = \sum_{i=-\infty}^{n} \bar{c}_2(t - t_i) \int\int_{-\infty}^{\infty} c_1(\vec{r} - \vec{\rho})(E(\vec{\rho} + \vec{r}_i, t_0)$$

$$- E(\vec{\rho} + \vec{\rho}_i, t_0))d\vec{\rho} \qquad (8a)$$

with $\vec{\rho}_0 = (0, 0)$ and $\bar{c}_2(t) = c_2(t)\theta(t)$
The validity of (3) is assumed.
If $E(\vec{r}, t_0) = A + B \cos(2\pi f x)$—in which f/η is the spatial frequency[1] in cycl/deg—then (7a) becomes:

$$S(\vec{r}, t) = (\bar{c}_2(t - t_0) - \bar{c}_2(t - t_1))(A + B\hat{c}_{11}(f) \cos(2\pi f x)) \qquad (7b)$$

and 8a becomes:

$$S(\vec{r}, t) = \sum_{i=-\infty}^{n} \bar{c}_2(t - t_i)\hat{c}_{11}(f)B[(\cos(2\pi f(x_i - \xi_i)) - 1) \cos(2\pi f(x + \xi_i))$$

$$- \sin(2\pi f(x_i - \xi_i)) \sin(2\pi f(x + \xi_i))] \qquad (8b)$$

where $\hat{c}_{11}(f) = \int_{-\infty}^{\infty} c_{11}(x) \cos(2\pi f x)\,dx$ and $c_{11}(x) = \int_{-\infty}^{\infty} c_1(\vec{r})\,dy$

In order to avoid possible disturbing interactions in systems behind the psychophysical retina, conclusions may be drawn only from contrast-threshold measurements. Davidson (1968) has conducted contrast-threshold experiments with flashes.[4] Subjects were required to indicate whether they saw contrast in the stimulus of the form:

$$E(\vec{r}, t_0) = A + B \cos(2\pi f x).$$

$B = 0$ also occurred and A was a constant in space and time. So

$$S(\vec{r}, t) = (\bar{c}_2(t - t_0) - \bar{c}_2(t - t_1))B\hat{c}_{11}(f) \cos(2\pi f x).$$

In the supposition that systems after the psychophysical retina are able to perceive contrast if

$$\max_{\vec{r}\in R^2}(S^+(\vec{r}, t)) \qquad (\text{or } \max_{\vec{r}\in R^2}(S^-(\vec{r}, t))),$$

with a given A, lie higher than a threshold $\sigma_+(A)$ $(\sigma_-(A))$, it means that B measured as a function of f is proportional to $(\hat{c}_{11}(f))^{-1}$. Many workers have made measurements of the second type. We now make the supposition that, as a result of saccadic movements, it holds that

$$S(\vec{r}, t) = \sum_{i=-\infty}^{n} \bar{c}_2(t - t_i)\hat{c}_{11}(f)2B \sin\left(2\pi f\left(x + \frac{\xi_i + x}{2}\right)\right) \sin\left(\frac{\xi_i - x_i}{2}\right)$$

and

$$\max_{\vec{r}\in \mathbf{R}^2}(S^{\pm}(\vec{r}, t)) = \sigma_{\pm}(A)$$

Once again, with A a constant, B is proportional to $(\hat{c}_{11}(f))^{-1}$.

As far as the spatial part was concerned, Davidson's physical stimulus had the form $\exp(A + B \cos(2\pi fy))$, so that after transformation (1) it, in principle, holds that $E(\vec{r}, t_0) \approx A_1 + B_1 \cos(2\pi fy)$. As a result of the transfer function of the eye-lens B_1, however, is a function of f. B_1 is, considering the nature of the physical stimulus, not linearly dependent on this transfer function. The deviation of a linear dependency increases with an increasing deviation of the transfer function from its values for $f = 0$, i.e. with an increasing f (Campbell and Green, 1965; Westheimer and Campbell, 1962) and with an increasing B. Davidson's data are therefore only reliable for lower f and small B values. The latter is an additional reason for attaching more value to Davidson's threshold data than to his estimation data, though the latter appear to be consistent with the former for $f/\eta < 3$ cycl/deg and for large contrast units even for $f/\eta < 6$ cycl/deg.

Most other authors used a physical stimulus with the form $A + B \cos(2\pi fx)$. The optical transfer function of the eye changes this linearly, yet transformation (1) does not change the stimulus linearly. From all measurements (Van Nes, 1968; Campbell and Green, 1965; Campbell, Kulikowsky and Levinson, 1966; Kelly and Magnuski, 1975) it appears, however, that $\hat{c}_{11}(f)$ decreases steeply for frequencies greater than 7 to 10 cycl/deg. This means that (1) with A constant has a negligible effect on stimuli with frequencies above 7–10 cycl/deg.

In order to determine $\hat{c}_{11}(f)$ we have therefore used data collected by Campbell and Green (1965) in experiments with interference fringes for frequencies larger than 7 cycl/deg. These measurements are not affected by the transfer function of the eye-lens. For frequencies lower than 8 cycl/deg we used Davidson's (1968) contrast threshold data. These are corrected with the optical transfer function of the eye extrapolated to $f = 0$, as measured by Campbell and Green (1965). We assume that from experiments by Campbell, Kulikowski and Levinson (1966) it may be concluded that the fact that Davidson used a vertical contrast and Campbell and Green a horizontal does not affect the results. Both data series are normalized on the extremes found in the $\hat{c}_{11}(f)$. The constants in $\hat{c}_{11}(f)$ are chosen on the grounds of data by Campbell and Green. The direction coefficient in Davidson's data is predicted exactly by means of these. The converse is also true. The idea that low and high frequency behaviour are not independent of each other lies at the basis of methods in which $\hat{c}_{11}(f)$ is theoretically determined. We shall discuss the two methods briefly, especially because the methods may also be applicable elsewhere.

The first method is based on a physical train of thought. In the physical retinal system, interaction occurs between cells. Let us assume that this interaction decreases with distance between the cells. Expressed in our co-ordinates, this means that $c_1(\vec{r} - \vec{\rho})$ is a function that monotonously approaches zero if $|\vec{r} - \vec{\rho}| \to \infty$. If $c_{11}(x) = \int_{-\infty}^{\infty} c_1(\vec{r}) \, d\, y$, the same applies for $c_{11}(x)$. Let us represent $c_{11}(x)$ as $c_{11}(x) = g(|x|, \epsilon)$ where ϵ is determined by the property $g(\epsilon, \epsilon) = \frac{1}{2}g(0, \epsilon)$. ϵ is a measure for the spread of a signal if we assume that $g(|x|, \epsilon)$ is determined by one parameter only, and that $\int_{-\infty}^{\infty} g(|x|, \epsilon) \, d\, x = 1$. In effect, $g(|x|, \epsilon)$ is thus a distribution function. The spread of the signal has the result that contours will be less sharp-cut. Quite contradictory to this is the contour-sharpening mechanism that becomes prominent in the phenomenon of the Mach bands (Cornsweet, 1970; Ratliff, 1965). Contours play an important part in the visual system. It is very conspicuous in binocular interaction (Levelt, 1968). For this reason we hold the supposition that the retina has a contour-sharpening mechanism which eliminates the effects of signal spread. If we presume that, physically speaking, this correction of the spread as well as the spread itself is of a local nature, the most efficient general correction is that which uses $g(|x|, \epsilon)$. If ϵ is small as regards the usual stimulus size, then the more obvious correction is a first-order correction on the size of the spread ϵ. Then $g(|x|, \epsilon)$ changes to $g(|x|, \epsilon) - \partial g(|x|, \epsilon)/\partial \epsilon^{(5)}$ with $\gamma > 0$. On the assumption that $c_{11}(x)$ has this form, we have compared the found measurements with the calculated $\hat{c}_{11}(f)$ of all sorts of possible distribution functions $g(|x|, \epsilon)$. Now $g(|x|, \epsilon)$ appeared to be a Lorentz distribution.[6] (See Figure 2.)

$$g(|x|, \epsilon) = \frac{1}{\pi} \frac{\epsilon}{\epsilon^2 + x^2}$$

The second method is of a strictly mathematical kind and may be regarded as a proof of the completeness of the representation of $c_{11}(x)$ of $\hat{c}_{11}(f)$. We assume these are bound functions—which also appears from the experiments. Now it is always possible to describe $\hat{c}_{11}(f)$ (or $c_{11}(x)$) by means of a system of orthonormal functions $\psi_n(f)$ in which we use the quadratic norm (Wiener, 1970). Thus

$$\hat{c}_{11}(f) = \sum_{n=0}^{\infty} c_n \psi_n(f)$$

We now attempt to find a system of this kind, such that in the sense of the norm c_n is negligibly small for all $n > M$, so that it holds that

$$\hat{c}_{11}(f) = \sum_{n=0}^{M} c_n \psi_n(f)$$

This does appear to hold for one system of functions: the Laguerre functions. We can assume $M = 1$. The test has been conducted up to and including $M = 4$. For $4 \geq i \geq 2$ it holds that $|c_i| \leq |c_{i-1}| 10^{-2}$. It is not probable that the higher order functions play a significant role, for in that case the data (see Figure 2) would have to show more stationary points.

Thus, we propose now

$$\hat{c}_{11}(f) = (1 + \beta \, 2\pi \, \alpha f) e^{-2\pi\alpha f} \sqrt{2} \qquad (9a)$$

and
$$c_{11}(x) = \frac{1}{\pi}\frac{\alpha}{\alpha^2 + x^2} + \frac{\beta}{\pi}\frac{\alpha(\alpha^2 - x^2)}{(\alpha^2 + x^2)^2} \qquad (9b)$$

Representations of these curves may be found in Figure 2. Generalization of formula (9) over the whole retina is not immediately possible. From experiments by Campbell, Kulikowski and Levinson (1966) it appears that there are people in whom α is a function of the orientation angle ϕ. On the fovea, α can be for $\phi = \pi/4$ and $3\pi/4$ 20–25% larger than for $\phi = 0$ and $\pi/2$. Outside the fovea, α is a function of r. Electro-physiological experiments (Fischer and May, 1970)

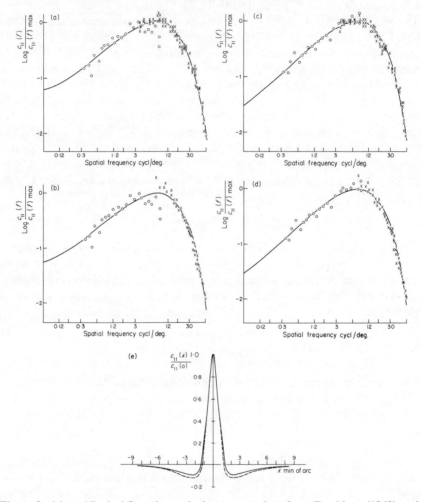

Figure 2. (a) – (d): $\hat{c}_{11}(f)$;—theoretical curve, O data from Davidson (1968) and × data from Campbell and Green (1965); $2\pi\alpha\eta = 0.127$ cycl/deg. (a): O subject LF, × subject DG, $\beta = 10$; (b): O subject LF, × subject FC, $\beta = 10$; (c): O subject BM, × subject DG, $\beta = 56$; (d): O subject BM, × subject FC, $\beta = 56$; (e): $c_{11}(x)$;—$\beta = 10$, ------ $\beta = 56$

suggest that outside the fovea $\alpha(r) = \alpha + \alpha_1 r$. If we restrict ourselves to the fovea, a generalization of 9 yields.

$$c_1(r) = \int_0^{2\pi} \int_0^\infty (1 + \beta\alpha(\phi)\omega)e^{-\alpha(\phi)\omega}e^{i\omega r\cos(\phi-\phi)} \omega d\ \omega d\phi \tag{10}$$

where $\vec{r} = r(\cos\psi, \sin\psi)$. It is not precluded that β too is a function of ϕ.

(c) Results

It follows from formula (1b) that we may distinguish 6 classes of stimuli. These are: Stimulus onset (A); Stimulus offset (B); Moving stimuli (C); and as special cases of these three, Saccade (AB) and Drift (CC). The sixth, stimulus (D) is variant only in time. If $\vec{v}$ represents eye movement, $\vec{w}$ stimulus movement and $\vec{r}_2 - \vec{r}_1$ a saccade then it holds that in the case

$$A : N(\vec{r}, t) = \delta(t - t_0) \lim_{t \downarrow t_0} E(\vec{r}, t)$$

$$B : N(\vec{r}, t) = -\delta(t - t_0) \lim_{t \uparrow t_0} E(\vec{r}, t)$$

$$C : N(\vec{r}, t) = \vec{w} . \vec{\nabla} E(\vec{r} + \vec{w}t, 0)$$

$$AB : N(\vec{r}, t) = \delta(t - t_0) \left[E(\vec{r} + \vec{r}_2, \lambda) - E(\vec{r} + \vec{r}_1, \lambda) \right]$$

$\vec{r}$ is a function of λ, λ is arbitrary.

$$CC : N(\vec{r}, t) = -\vec{v} . \cdot \vec{\nabla} \lim_{t=t_0} E(\vec{r} - \vec{v}(t - t_0), \lambda)$$

$$D : N(\vec{r}, t) = \frac{\partial}{\partial t} E(\vec{r}, t)$$

All other stimulus situations are combinations of these six (or four). In general it holds that

$$N(\vec{r}, t) = \frac{\partial \vec{r}}{\partial t} . \vec{\nabla} E(\vec{r}, t) + \frac{\partial}{\partial t} E(\vec{r}, t) \tag{1c}$$

Apart from stimulus onset and offset $(A$ and $B)$ the cortex only receives information about the contrast in the stimulus. Nearly all threshold measurements are therefore contrast threshold measurements. (See also Section 1 (a)).

The physical stimulus $L(1 + r\sin(2\pi fx))$ with $|r| \le 1$ (sinusoidal grid) transforms under a saccade into

$$N(\vec{r}, t) = 2v \sum_{n=1}^\infty (-c)^n \left[\cos(2\pi nf(x + x_1) - n\pi/2)(\cos(2\pi nf(x_2 - x_1)) - 1) \right.$$
$$\left. + \sin(2\pi fn(x + x_1) - n\pi/2)\sin(2\pi nf(x_2 - x_1)) \right]$$

where $\qquad v = \dfrac{1-a}{(1-r^2a^2)^{\frac{1}{2}}} \dfrac{\delta}{\delta-\tau} \qquad a = \dfrac{L}{L+\delta-\tau} \qquad c = \dfrac{1-(1-r^2a^2)^{\frac{1}{2}}}{ra}$

Using Formula 9 and working out the summation, it follows

$$S(\vec{r}, t) = \frac{1 - a}{(1 - r^2 a^2)^{\frac{1}{2}}} \left[\frac{(1 - R^2)^{\frac{1}{2}}}{1 + R \sin (2\pi f(x_1 + x))} - \frac{(1 - R^2)^{\frac{1}{2}}}{1 + R \sin (2\pi f(x_2 + x))} \right.$$

$$\left. - 2\pi \beta fR \left(\frac{R + \sin (2\pi f(x_1 + x))}{(1 + R \sin (2\pi f(x_1 + x)))^2} - \frac{R + \sin (2\pi f(x_2 + x))}{(1 + R \sin (2\pi f(x + x_2)))^2} \right) \right]$$

where

$$R = \frac{2 c e^{-2\pi a f}}{1 + c^2 e^{-4\pi a f}}.$$

One can prove that $|S(\vec{r}, t)|$ is maximal under the given conditions if $x + x_2 = m/f + 1/4f$ and $x + x_1 = n/f + 3/4f$ where n and m are whole numbers. Thus

$$S_m = \underset{r_1, r_2, r_3 \in \mathbf{R}^2}{\text{maximum}} |S(\vec{r}, t)| = \frac{1 - a}{(1 - r^2 a^2)^{\frac{1}{2}}} \left[\frac{2R}{(1 - R^2)^{\frac{1}{2}}} \left(1 + \frac{2\pi \beta a f}{(1 - R^2)^{\frac{1}{2}}} \right) \right]$$

$$= 4(1 - a) \frac{1 + c^2}{1 - c^2} \frac{ce^{-2\pi a f}}{1 - c^2 e^{-4\pi a f}} \left(1 + 2\pi \beta a f \frac{1 + c^2 e^{-4\pi a f}}{1 - c^2 e^{-4\pi a f}} \right) \tag{11}$$

The solution of the comparison $S_m = \text{minimum} (\sigma_\pm)$

has the form $\displaystyle\sum_{n,m=0}^{\infty} a_{nm}(\mu) \left(\frac{1}{4(1 - a)(2\pi \beta a f + 1)} \right)^{2n+1} e^{2\pi a f(2m+1)}$ \hfill (12)

where $\mu = (2\pi \alpha \beta f - 1)/(2\pi \alpha \beta f + 1)$ and $a_{nm}(x)$ is an nth order polynomial in x. The same applies for the drift component. This means that in a subject's response, a response to the frequency $(2n + 1)f$, where $n \in \mathbf{N}$, is possible. The response to $3f$ has been found by Van Nes (1968).

The weakness of the above approach is that no account is held of the time transfer function. This effect is most certainly present, as appears from experiments by Robson (1966) when contrast threshold measurements were made. Robson used the physical stimulus

$$L(1 + r \cos (2\pi v t) \cos (2\pi f x)).$$

If we only consider the first order term in r, it holds that

$$E(\vec{r}, t) = \frac{L - \tau}{L + \delta - \tau} + \frac{\delta L}{(\delta + L - \tau)^2} r \cos (2\pi v t) \cos (2\pi f x) + O(r^2) \tag{13}$$

It appears that for $v \geq 10$ Hz the contrast sensitive curve is independent of f, except for a factor. Similarly, for $f/\eta \geq 8$ cycles/deg it is, except for a factor, independent of v. Thus formula (10) certainly holds for $v \geq 10$ Hz and $f/\eta \geq 8$ cycles/deg. We now propose formula (10) and $s(\vec{r}, t) = c_1(\vec{r})c_2(t)$ have a general validity so that, if $a = 0$ in formula (3), it holds with $t' = t - |\vec{r} - \vec{\rho}|/c$ that

$$S(\vec{r}, t) = \frac{\partial}{\partial t} \iint_{-\infty}^{\infty} \int_{-\infty}^{t'} c_1(\vec{r} - \vec{\rho}) \, c_2(t - \tau) E(\vec{\rho}, \tau) d\tau d\vec{\rho} \tag{14}$$

Using formula (14) and the maximum contrast principle as used earlier, it follows from formula (13) that

$$S_m(t) \int_{-\infty}^{\infty} \int_{-\infty}^{t-|\theta|/c} c_{11}(\theta) c_2(t - \tau) \cos(2\pi f\theta) \cos(2\pi v\tau) \, d\tau d\theta \, \frac{2\delta L r}{(\delta + L - \tau)^2}$$

$$= \int_{0}^{\infty} \int_{-c\tau}^{c\tau} c_{11}(\theta) c_2(\tau) \cos(2\pi f\theta) \cos(2\pi v(t - \tau)) \, d\theta d\tau \, \frac{2\delta L r}{(\delta + L - \tau)^2}$$

$$(15)$$

where $c_{11}(\theta) = \dfrac{\alpha}{\pi} \dfrac{(\beta + 1)\alpha^2 - (\beta - 1)\theta^2}{(\alpha^2 + \theta^2)^2}$

$$\eta\alpha \approx \frac{0\cdot 13}{2\pi} \text{ cycl/deg approximately constant over all subjects}$$

$$\beta \approx 33$$

$c_2(\tau)$ is a low or bandpass filter (Roufs, 1972). The width of the area $[-c\tau, c\tau]$, for which $c_{11}(\theta)$ contributes to the integral within half a temporal period, decreases inversely with $2v$. This means that the contribution of the negative part of $c_{11}(\theta)$ decreases with increase of v. The result of this is that the suppression of the low spatial frequencies decreases with increased v. This has been found by Robson (1966).

If the contribution of the negative part of $c_{11}(\theta)$ can be decreased by means of a stimulus change in time, it follows that eye movements may also cause this. On the grounds of the principle of maximum contrast one can expect that subjects will make use of this in contrast threshold experiments in order to enhance their sensitivity. The following phenomena may be understood in this light. The change in the effect of the negative part of $c_{11}(\theta)$ by increasing v leads to a situation in which

$$\tilde{c}_{11}(f) = \int_{-c/2v}^{c/2v} c_{11}(\theta) \cos(2\pi f\theta) \, d\theta$$

is an almost constant function of f. According to formula (12) the measured attenuation characteristic will then have the form $e^{-6\pi\alpha f}$. The direct consequence of this is that $e^{-6\pi\alpha f}$ behaviour only occurs when $f < (1/2\pi\alpha)(1 - 1/\beta)$; for this value the maximum of $\hat{c}_{11}(f)$ occurs. Moreover, it can be shown that then f is larger than the frequencies in which there is suppression of the lower frequencies. The measured curves therefore have the following form: for $0 \leq f \leq f_c$ suppression of the lower frequencies; then for $f_c \leq f < (1/2\pi\alpha)$ $(1 - 1/\beta)$, $e^{-6\pi\alpha f}$ behaviour; and finally for $f \geq (1/2\pi\alpha)(1 - 1/\beta)$, $e^{-2\pi\alpha f}$ behaviour in which $0 \leq f_c \leq (1/2\pi\alpha)(1 - 1/\beta)$.

This has been measured by Van Nes (1968). From his measurements it appeared that f_c is a monotonously non-decreasing function of L. This follows from our model of the contrast system (see Section 2), which is a diffusion system. All measurements are carried out with spatially finite stimuli. This means that the cortex also receives information on the contrast at the edge of the stimulus. This contrast is able to suppress the weak contrast $(e^{-6\pi\alpha f})$ if it is sufficiently large. There are two ways in which the effect of this edge contrast on the centre of the visual field may be increased. This can be done simply by increasing the physical contrast, or L, or by changing the contrast barriers between the edge and the field centre. This barrier is the amount of grid contrast between the edge and the centre of the field. If this decreases the influence of the edge contrast on the field centre increases. The function f_c will therefore be a monotonously non-increasing function of the number of cycles between the edge and the field centre. It has been measured by Hoekstra and others (Hoekstra, v.d. Groot, v.d. Brink and Bilsen, 1974). It follows from formula (11) that $r(f)$ curves, which may be determined in threshold measurements, become smaller with increasing L and close themselves, until for some L values they coincide; this appears also from data obtained by Van Nes, 1968. Finally, with yet more increasing L, $r(f)$ will again increase. From measurements by Van Nes it follows from formula (11) that for δ in formula (1), the δ must lie between 20 and 100 cd/m². Finally, it may be remarked that the non-linear transformation in formula (1) of the stimulus $L(1 + r \cos(2\pi f x))$ has the consequence that the lighter parts of the stimulus appear wider than the darker parts. This effect increases with the increase of rL. The lighter parts have a width of $\approx 1/2f$, the grey bands $\approx 1/12f$ and the dark parts $\approx 1/3f$.

Our conclusion is that the proposed theory, consisting of a non-linear transformation of the form (1), followed by a local spatial interaction (2), while the output of the system represents only first order changes in intensity, satisfactorily explains the obtained experimental results. Transformation (2) is naturally the cause of the Mach 'band phenomenon (Ratliff, 1965) and the brightness illusions (Cornsweet, 1970); however, these can only be fully understood in relation to the contrast system.

2. Contrast of Weighting System

(a) Theory

De Weert and Levelt (1974) have shown that measurements of binocular brightness combination lead to the conclusion that a psychophysical model of the binocular brightness combination makes use of brightness weighting factors. They also show that a sufficient form for this is:

$$\mathfrak{B} = W_L(L_L, L_R) f(L_L) + W_R(L_R, L_L) f(L_R) \tag{16}$$

where $W_L(L_L, L_R) + W_R(L_R, L_L) = 1$, $\mathfrak{B}$ the binocular brightness and L_L, L_R the luminances of the left and the right eye. A psychophysical mechanism such as this may be thought to be built up neurophysiologically as follows. A unit (7) in the cortex is activated into a certain state, either by a signal from another cortical unit or by a signal originating in the retina, such that it will transmit this signal. The time that is needed in order to effect this state is a monotonous function of the strength of the signal. The average behaviour of all units in a limited area results in the psychophysical response as a weighting system. We wish to generalize this notion of weighting coefficients for the whole brightness system.

Gerrits and Vendrik (1970) among others have conducted various experiments to look into the so-called filling-in process. A subject is given stimuli stabilized on the retina. When, after stimulus onset, the image is no longer perceived, a part of the stimulus is moved with respect to the retina. Depending on the nature of the movement and the stimulus, brightness and darkenss spread over parts of the total field. A L(ight)–D(ark) contrast in the direction of movement (see Figure 3) results in a darkness spread from this transition in all directions except that of the movement vector perpendicular to the contrast. For a D–L contrast, the same applies for the brightness spread. Darkness (brightness) never spreads further than an activated D–L (or L–D) transition. The spread is decremental.

Gerrits and Vendrik conclude that the cortex has four mechanisms, viz., brightness spread, darkness spread, brightness barrier and darkness barrier, and that they are all coupled to stimulus contrast. The results of these experiments may, however, be explained by the notion of weighting coefficients, coupled to the output of the psychophysical retina. We assume that a monocular brightness-unit has two states: a darkness and a brightness state. If the unit follows the darkness state it will transmit a darkness signal. A darkness signal is a signal originating from another unit in the darkness state or an off-signal from the retina. The same applies, *mutatis mutandis* for brightness.

If, after a stimulus onset, a unit is in a brightness state, then stimulus offset means that the unit must receive a darkness signal in order to change from the brightness to the darkness state. A darkness signal cannot, however, be applied to maintain a state of darkness in units. In this case, the strongest signal would continually determine the state of all the units in the area, so that only

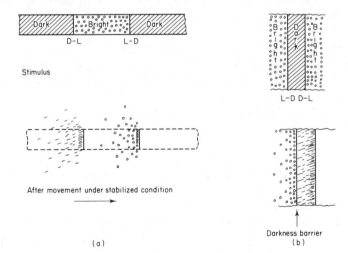

Figure 3. Darkness and brightness spread by movement under stabilized condition
From Gerrits and Vendrik (1970)

black or white but no grey can be perceived. It would then be impossible for Mach band phenomena in an increasing step-wise stimulus $(L(x) = \sum_{i=1}^{3} A_i(\theta(x - x_i) - \theta(x - x_{i+1})))$ to occur in cases where the contrasts are not equal $(A_3/A_2 \neq A_2/A_1)$. Therefore we assume that the following rivalry hypothesis holds. If a unit is in the brightness state, a darkness signal will affect the state of the unit; a brightness signal will not. The same will hold, *mutatis mutandis* for a unit in the darkness state. As regards weighting coefficients, this implies that a darkness signal reduces the brightness weighting coefficient when this is not zero, and *vice versa*. The argument presented above results in the following equation:

$$\frac{\partial}{\partial t} \begin{bmatrix} W_D(\vec{r}, t) \\ W_B(\vec{r}, t) \end{bmatrix} = \mu \vec{\nabla}^2 \begin{bmatrix} W_D(\vec{r}, t) \\ W_B(\vec{r}, t) \end{bmatrix} + \rho \begin{bmatrix} S^-(\vec{r}, t)\, W_B(\vec{r}, t) \\ S^+(\vec{r}, t)\, W_D(\vec{r}, t) \end{bmatrix} - \rho \begin{bmatrix} S^+(\vec{r}, t)\, W_D(\vec{r}, t) \\ S^-(\vec{r}, t)\, W_B(\vec{r}, t) \end{bmatrix} \tag{17}$$

In this expression, $W_D(\vec{r}, t)$ is the darkness coefficient and $W_B(\vec{r}, t)$ is the brightness coefficient.

The rivalry principle formulated here has been found by Levelt (1968) in the process of binocular rivalry. Levelt shows that a contrast change in one eye only affects the dominance time of the other. This can immediately be explained by means of the notion that a binocular unit has two states, one on the left and one on the right. If a unit is in the state 'left', only a signal 'right', originating in the right eye or other units in the state 'right', can affect the state of the unit. In rivalry experiments it can be seen that the change in eye dominance spreads out from the contrast over the whole field. This behaviour of diffuseness, the fact that only contrast, i.e. $S(\vec{r}, t)$, affects rivalry and Levelt's discovery that rivalry is not always complete give cause to ascribe to binocular interaction an analogue two-state system as in equation (17). However, it is then impossible to recognize what the difference is between binocular rivalrous and fusing stimuli. To do so, the system must explicitly use the feature—antagonistic or not—of the stimuli on both eyes. To that end we assume that a unit has four states: brightness-left, brightness-right, darkness-left and darkness-right. We assume that for the system 'left' as well as for the system 'right' equation (17) is valid. The question that now remains is whether brightness-left rivals with brightness-right and/or with darkness-right. In the latter case, an overall rivalry between non-antagonistic stimuli would be possible. Because this is not the case, we conclude that brightness-left rivals with brightness-right and that darkness-left rivals with darkness-right. The equation therefore becomes

$$\frac{\partial}{\partial t} \begin{bmatrix} B_R \\ D_R \\ B_L \\ D_L \end{bmatrix} = \mu \vec{\nabla}^2 \begin{bmatrix} B_R \\ D_R \\ B_L \\ D_L \end{bmatrix} + \rho \begin{bmatrix} S_R^+ D_R - S_R^- B_R \\ S_R^- B_R - S_R^+ D_R \\ S_L^+ D_L - S_L^- B_L \\ S_L^- B_L - S_L^- D_L \end{bmatrix} + \kappa \begin{bmatrix} S_R^+ B_L - S_L^+ B_R \\ S_R^- D_L - S_L^- D_R \\ S_L^+ B_R - S_R^+ B_L \\ S_L^- D_R - S_R^- D_{L'} \end{bmatrix} \tag{18}$$

$B_R = B_R(\vec{r}, t)$, etc., is the weighting coefficient of brightness-right.

It goes without saying that in a theory wholly based on local interactions one would assume that binocular disparity perception within this system must take place locally. This can easily be accomodated. Since at each disparity 2Δ fusion can occur, we assume that in principle there is an equation such as equation (18) for each separate Δ. We must then introduce for every disparity value 2Δ four weighting coefficients:

$$B_R(\vec{r}, \Delta, t), D_R(\vec{r}, \Delta, t), B_L(\vec{r}, \Delta, t) \text{ and } D_L(\vec{r}, \Delta, t).$$

We must then assume that

$$\int_{-\infty}^{\infty} \left[B_R(\vec{r}, \Delta, t) + D_R(\vec{r}, \Delta, t) + B_L(\vec{r}, \Delta, t) + D_L(\vec{r}, \Delta, t) \right] d\Delta = 1 \quad (19)$$

Apart from a rivalry between these four systems for each Δ we must also assume a rivalry between the systems with different disparity. If a binocular stimulus with various disparities is presented to a subject, then, with the normal conditions for fusion, fusion occurs for each disparity separately (Julesz, 1971). Seeing that these separate fusions can occur at the same time, the mechanism that is responsible for the rivalry between parts of the system with a different disparity must be the same as that responsible for the fusion. This means that the rivalry between the systems with a different disparity is described by a generalization of the last term of (18). From experiments by Fender and Julesz (1967) it appears that the system tends toward the solutions with $\Delta = 0$ if the eyes do not receive any stimulus. To take this behaviour into account, a term, describing it, must be introduced into the equation. The simplest is the operator $(\partial/\partial\Delta)\Delta$.

The equation now becomes:

$$\frac{\partial}{\partial t} \begin{bmatrix} B_R \\ D_R \\ B_L \\ D_L \end{bmatrix} = \mu \vec{\nabla}^2 \begin{bmatrix} B_R \\ D_R \\ B_L \\ D_L \end{bmatrix} + \nu \frac{\partial}{\partial\Delta}\Delta \begin{bmatrix} B_R \\ D_R \\ B_L \\ D_L \end{bmatrix} +$$

$$+ \rho \begin{bmatrix} S_R^+(x - \Delta, y, t)D_R - S_R^-(x - \Delta, y, t)B_R \\ S_R^-(x - \Delta, y, t)B_R - S_R^+(x - \Delta, y, t)D_R \\ S_L^+(x + \Delta, y, t)D_L - S_L^-(x + \Delta, y, t)B_L \\ S_L^-(x + \Delta, y, t)B_L - S_L^+(x + \Delta, y, t)D_L \end{bmatrix} \quad (20)$$

$$+ \kappa \int_{-\infty}^{\infty} d\lambda f(\Delta - \lambda) \times$$

$$\times \begin{bmatrix} S_R^+(x - \Delta, y, t)B_L(x - \Delta + \lambda, y, \lambda, t) - S_L^+(x - \Delta + 2\lambda, y, t)B_R(x - \Delta + \lambda, y, \lambda, t) \\ S_R^-(x - \Delta, y, t)D_L(x - \Delta + \lambda, y, \lambda, t) - S_L^-(x - \Delta + 2\lambda, y, t)D_R(x + \Delta + \lambda, y, \lambda, t) \\ S_L^+(x + \Delta, y, t)B_R(x + \Delta - \lambda, y, \lambda, t) - S_R^+(x + \Delta - 2\lambda, y, t)B_L(x + \Delta - \lambda, y, \lambda, t) \\ S_L^-(x + \Delta, y, t)D_R(x + \Delta - \lambda, y, \lambda, t) - S_R^-(x + \Delta - 2\lambda, y, t)D_L(x + \Delta - \lambda, y, \lambda, t) \end{bmatrix}$$

where
$$\vec{\nabla} = \left(\frac{\partial}{\partial x}, \frac{\partial}{\partial y}\right)$$

$f(x)$ is some symmetric function which is monotonous, not increasing for $x > 0$ and $\int_{-\infty}^{\infty} f(x)\,dx = 1$. $D_R = D_R(x, y, \Delta, t)$ etc.

If $L_L(x - \Delta, y) = L_R(x + \Delta, y)$, the coefficients $B_R(\vec{r}, \Delta, t)$, $D_R(\vec{r}, \Delta, t)$, $B_L(\vec{r}, \Delta, t)$ and $D_L(\vec{r}, \Delta, t)$ form the stable solution of equation (20). If $f(x) \neq 0$ for $x_0 > x \geq 0$ for some x_0 then the solution of (20) approaches this stable solution for $t \to \infty$. In other words, equation (20) yields solutions for the problem of depth vision. The function $f(x)$ in fact determines the area over which fusion can occur in the case of disparity. $f(x)$ thus determines Panum's area. The exact form of $f(x)$ is difficult to establish, especially because eye movement also plays a role in experiments on depth perception. The function $f(x)$ may, however, be regarded as a characteristic function:

$$f(x) = \frac{1}{2x_0} \text{ if } |x| < x_0 \text{ and } f(x) = 0 \text{ if } |x| > x_0.$$

In the case of experiments by Kaufman and co-workers (Kaufman, 1973) where the essential inner squares of a stereogram are expressed as follows:

$$L_L(x, y) = F(x - \Delta, y) + F(x + \Delta, y) \quad \text{and}$$

$$L_R(x, y) = aF(x - \Delta, y) + (2 - a)F(x + \Delta, y), \quad \text{where } 0 \leq a \leq 2$$

the stable solution is a coupled solution of the expressions

$$\{B_R(\vec{r}, 0, t), --\} \quad \text{and} \quad \{B_R(\vec{r}, \Delta, t), --\}.$$

There is also a solution possible if 2Δ is greater than Panum's area. This does not arise as a result of local rivalry within the expressions

$$\{B_R(\vec{r}, \Delta, t) ---\} \quad \text{and} \quad \{B_R(\vec{r}, 0, t), --\}$$

but by means of a local rivalry between these expressions. The result is that up to twice Panum's area a stable solution exists, albeit that the rivalry between the expressions gives rise to a brightness acquisition. This is exactly what Kaufman and co-workers found. They did not, however, report a brightness acquisition but a grey lustrous veil: possibly this is the same.

Fender and Julesz (1967) have measured the fall-off of the disparity. They did this by applying to the subject a large disparity, switching off the stimulus and after a short while switching the stimulus on again with the same disparity. The maximum time for stimulus-absence was then determined such that the subject could immediately perceive the binocular test stimulus. The perceived fall-off in disparity is described by the solution of (20), where $S_L^{\pm} = S_R^{\pm} = 0$. If the stimulus off-set takes place on $t = t_0$ with $\Delta = \Delta_0$ and the on-set on $t = t_1$, then it follows from (20) that at $t = t_1$, $\Delta = \Delta_0 e^{-\nu(t_1 - t_0)}$. The simple assumption that the subject can perceive the depth in a stereogram if the difference between the stimulus disparity and the value of 2Δ is less than or equal to the width of Panum's area—P—leads to $2\Delta_0 - 2\Delta_0 e^{-\nu(t_1 - t_0)} \leq P$. So, the formula that,

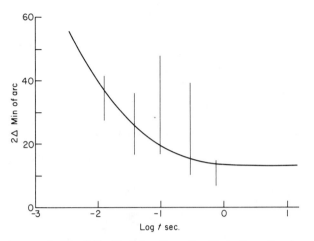

Figure 4. The fall-off of the disparity. Data from Fender and Julesz (1967). Theoretical curve with $P\eta(1) = 14$ min of arc and $v = 60$ Hz

following the theory, describes the finding of Fender and Julesz is $2\Delta_0 = P/(1 - e^{-v(t_1 - t_0)})$. This curve fits—see Figure 4—in with their data.

In apparent motion there is stimulation onset-offset of an area R_1 at time t_1 and $t_1 + \Delta t_1$, followed by a stimulation onset-offset of an area R_2 at time t_2 and $t_2 + \Delta t_2$. In our opinion, apparent motion means that $B(\vec{r}, t) \neq 0$ for $\vec{r}$ in the area between R_1 and R_2 and $t \in [t_2, t_2 + \Delta t_2]$. In this case brightness-spread between R_1 and R_2 is possible. Although it is not yet clear in what way this complicated process exactly develops, it may be concluded that the diffusion part of equation (20) determines the behaviour of the weighting coefficients in the non-stimulated areas. This implies that the course in time of the apparent motion is largely determined by a formula of the form:

$$\frac{e^{-a/(t-t_0)}}{t - t_0}.$$

These are the well-known U-shaped curves. Many experimentalists has carried out measurements of apparent motion. In our view, the perceived intensity of the first stimulus is largely co-determined by the value of $B(\vec{r}, t_2)$. In fact this represents the strength of the brightness coefficient at the place where the second stimulus would appear if presented. Because $B(\vec{r}, t_2) + D(\vec{r}, t_2) = 1$ holds, $B(\vec{r}, t_2)$ is determined by the darkness spread which is the result of the offset of the first stimulus at time $t_1 + \Delta t_1$. This spread is given by $P_e^{-p/(t-t_1-\Delta t_1)}/(t - t_1 - \Delta t_1)$, so that $B(\vec{r}, t_2)$ has the form

$$Q - \frac{Pe^{-p/(t_2 - t_1 - \Delta t_1)}}{t_2 - t_1 - \Delta t_1}.$$

In Figure 5 this curve is plotted and the data obtained by Meyer (1976) are also given. She established by means of a dichoptic brightness matching procedure

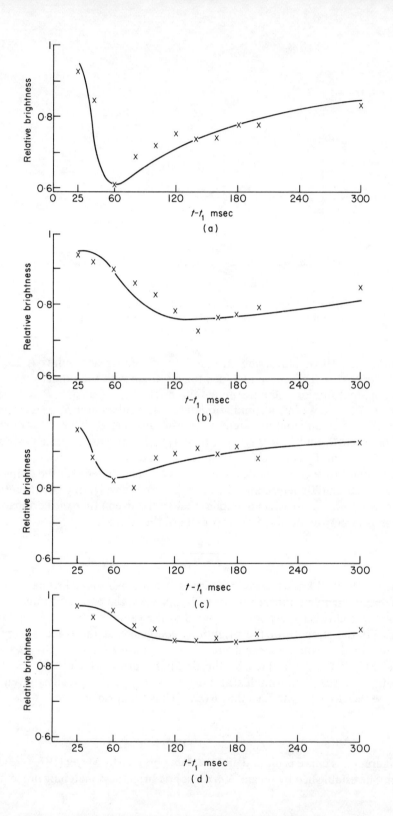

the brightness of the first stimulus as a function of $t_2 - t_1$. Although the concept of apparent motion has not yet properly been worked out, the conclusion is justified that the above data support the theory of diffusion.

In the case of binocular rivalry, the alternating frequency is in first order proportional to κ times the sum of the contrasts. Levelt (1968) has carried out an experiment on this. He used three different contrasts in the left eye:

$$c_1 = \frac{710}{\delta + 710} - \frac{85}{\delta + 85}$$

$$c_2 = \frac{100}{\delta + 100} - \frac{85}{\delta + 85}$$

$$c_3 = \frac{100}{\delta + 100} - \frac{85}{\delta + 85}$$

and in the right eye always the same contrast:

$$c = \frac{100}{\delta + 100} - \frac{5 \cdot 75}{\delta + 5 \cdot 75}$$

For the frequencies he found 9·6, 6·4 and 10·9 alternations per minute, respectively. If $\delta = 55$ cd/m^2 and $\kappa = 0 \cdot 18$ Hz, the calculated frequency series will be 9·4, 6·4 and 11·0 alternations per minute. We note that $\delta = 55$ cd/m^2 lies within the area that we determined in section 1 from data obtained from van Nes.

Finally, we wish to remark that the weighting coefficients are possibly the source of the geometrical illusions. In this context we would refer to work by Watson (1978). His force fields have the form of our weighting coefficients. If the weighting coefficients with different Δs affect each other, they do not on account of the diffusion term. So, it would in that case be impossible for binocular elements in random dot stimuli not having the same disparity to give rise to geometric illusions. This is confirmed by Julesz (1971) in his experiments with geometric illusions in random dot stereogrammes. Moreover, if eyemovements are changed by cognitive factors the weighting coefficients and so the perception of the illusion can be influenced by cognitive factors.

3. The Brightness System

(a) Theory

Completely in agreement with what was proposed in the previous section, there are no equations for brightness and darkness spreading. This spreading is in fact the spreading in the weighting system. Now the brightness impression arises because the units, having been activated into a certain state, can[8] adopt

---

Figure 5. Brightness matching in meta-contrast. Data from Meyer (1976) with $\Delta t_1 = 25$ msec. (a) subject R.S., $Q = 0 \cdot 95$, $P = 0 \cdot 34$, $p = 35$ msec; (b) subject R.S., $Q = 0 \cdot 95$, $P = 0 \cdot 19$, $p = 115$ msec; (c) subject N.M., $Q = 0 \cdot 97$, $P = 0 \cdot 14$, $p = 35$ msec; (d) subject N.M., $Q = 0 \cdot 97$, $P = 0 \cdot 10$, $p = 115$ msec

and transmit the strongest signal that they receive proper to this state. Thus a unit in the state of darkness-right transmits the strongest darkness-right signal received.

It is very well possible that the build-up of the brightness reproduction proceeds according to a build-up in time. This, however, we do not know at the moment. Should experimental evidence for it be found, it can always be fitted in afterwards.

Let x be a function of $\vec{r}$ and t. Let $\theta(x, \vec{r}, t) \in \mathbf{R}^2 \times \mathbf{T}$. θ is defined by the property $(\vec{\rho}, \tau) \in \theta(x, \vec{r}, t)$ if there is a continuous mapping $(\vec{\rho}_0, \tau_0)$ of $[0, 1]$ on $\mathbf{R}^2 \times \mathbf{T}$, where $(\vec{\rho}_0, \tau_0)(0) = (\vec{r}, t)$ and $(\vec{\rho}_0, \tau_0)(1) = (\rho, \tau)$ and $x(\vec{\rho}_0, \tau_0)(\lambda) \neq 0$ for all $\lambda \in [0, 1]$. θ indicates the domain of units from which the unit at $(\vec{r}, t)$ can be reached by a signal proper to its state. Let $\vec{\Delta} = (\Delta, 0)$

$$\text{Let } \mathfrak{B}_{LD}(\vec{r}, \Delta, t) = D_L(\vec{r}, \Delta, t) \max_{(\vec{\rho}, \tau) \in \theta(D_L(\Delta), \vec{r}, t)} (S_L^-(\vec{\rho} + \vec{\Delta}, \tau))$$

$$\mathfrak{B}_{LB}(\vec{r}, \Delta, t) = B_L(\vec{r}, \Delta, t) \max_{(\vec{\rho}, \tau) \in \theta(B_L(\Delta), \vec{r}, t)} (S_L^+(\vec{\rho} + \vec{\Delta}, \tau))$$

$$\mathfrak{B}_{RD}(\vec{r}, \Delta, t) = D_R(\vec{r}, \Delta, t) \max_{(\vec{\rho}, \tau) \in \theta(D_R(\Delta), \vec{r}, t)} (S_R^-(\vec{\rho} - \vec{\Delta}, \tau))$$

$$\mathfrak{B}_{RB}(\vec{r}, \Delta, t) = B_R(\vec{r}, \Delta, t) \max_{(\vec{\rho}, \tau) \in \theta(B_R(\Delta), \vec{r}, t)} (S_R^+(\vec{\rho} - \vec{\Delta}, \tau))$$

Then the brightness impression $\mathfrak{B}$ will be given by

$$\mathfrak{B}(\vec{r}, t) = \int_{-\infty}^{\infty} [\mathfrak{B}_{RB}(\vec{r}, \Delta, t) + \mathfrak{B}_{LB}(\vec{r}, \Delta, t) - \mathfrak{B}_{RD}(\vec{r}, \Delta, t) - \mathfrak{B}_{LD}(\vec{r}, \Delta, t)] d\Delta \tag{21}$$

The entire presented theory has implications for the measuring procedure in brightness experiments. Two principally different procedures may be distinguished. In the first there is a simultaneous presentation of a matching field and a test field. In most of the investigations a fixation point is given. The theory is that such a procedure never yields direct results since there are interactions between the test fields and matching fields. Moreover the possibility of interaction between these fields and the fixation point should not be ignored. Moreover, in many studies employing a fixation point, the fields are presented partly in an extra-foveal way so that Troxler's effect plays a role.

A variant of this procedure is that in which the test and matching fields are not presented simultaneously but sequentially and at the same place. However, the temporal aspects of this procedure are manipulated by the experimenter. Consequently, on the grounds of the theory is valid in this case also that the results can never be directly interpreted. Two fields to which subjects ascribe an equal brightness will have this property partly on the grounds of temporal and spatial interactions which are determined not by the variables of the objective, but by the methodological variables. The spatial interactions have the largest effect.

In order to be able to conduct direct measurements in the sense of the theory, we assume that a subject has a good memory for brightness *casu quo* relative brightness[9]. The hypothesis is not completely unreasonable, for subjects responded consistently in experiments testing these. The second method is based on this hypothesis. It then becomes possible to conduct experiments, free from spatial and temporal interactions between test and matching stimulus, with a reasonably loose fixation; in binocular experiments fusion must of course be guaranteed. In these experiments, test and matching fields hardly differ in place and the subjects themselves determine the temporal alternation in such a way that the test and matching stimuli are perceived as being stationary.

(b) Results

In connection with the theory in the preceding section it is possible to explain by means of the above the brightness illusions. Amongst others, Cornsweet (1970), Ginsburg (1974) and Ratliff (1965) have shown that a low pass or a band pass filter applied to 'illusory' stimuli produce excess contrasts that coincide with the contours of the perceived illusions. The psychophysical retina postulated by us is a band pass filter. With Equation (17) it produces a spread of B and/or D coefficients between these contrast lines. This area is subsequently filled with the highest value of the brightness or darkness signal. If the last statement of the preceding section is true, then geometric illusions can also appear as a result of brightness illusions. This has indeed been observed. The Poggendorf illusion occurs at a Kaniza triangle.

Applying a monocular matching procedure, Jameson and Hurvich (1960) asked for brightness judgements on the squares in the stimulus, represented in Figure 6a. The stimulus is presented in three different light intensities, such that the ratios of the different illuminations of the six parts of the stimulus is always the same. (The ratio between the background and the squares is unknown. That of the squares with respect to each other is $L_1:L_2:L_3:L_4:L_5 = 27:21 \cdot 5:10 \cdot 8: 2 \cdot 5:1$). The most important results of the experiments are the following: that brightness in such a complicated stimulus neither varies according to a power law nor is it a function of the physical contrast within a stimulus; that the 5th square decreases in brightness if the illumination increases; that the brightness of the 4th square remains constant – possibly decreasing slightly and subsequently rising – and that the brightness of the remaining three squares increases with increasing illumination.

The matching stimulus—see Figure 6b—differs from the test stimulus in form, spatial proportions and average illumination. Moreover, the subject has to carry out a spatially complicated action in order to switch from the test stimulus to the matching stimulus and *vice versa*; he has to turn round. The theory does not deal with such complicated transformations. Indeed, quantitatively, the results are at first sight difficult to interpret, but in the supposition that the reported brightness is a monotonous function of the perceived brightness, they may be satisfactorily interpretable qualitatively. The theoretically occurring constants have been arbitrarily determined. In equation (17), $\rho = 1$ is proposed.

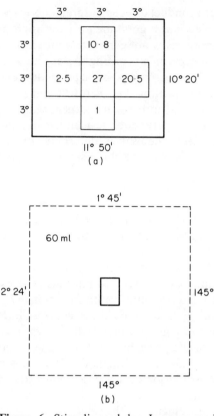

Figure 6. Stimuli used by Jameson and Hurvich (1960). (a) test stimulus, (b) matching-stimulus

The diffusion within squares is supposed optimal. For δ in equation (1), the mean value calculated from Levelt's (1968) brightness experiments (see below) and from his rivalry experiments (see above) has been chosen. The illumination of the background in the test stimulus supposed to be equal to the mean illumination of the five squares.

Two results are presented in Figure 7a. Qualitatively, the theory successfully predicts the effects observed by Jameson and Hurvich. In order to try to treat the experiment of Jameson and Hurvich quantitatively we suppose that the subjects did not report brightness but lightness.[9] If lightness is defined as relative brightness of adjacent fields and if a subject can only make a real lightness comparison if the contrast direction between the test field and its surroundings is the same as that between the matching field and its surroundings, one gets the results presented in Figure 7b. No constant has been fitted to the data. The constant δ come from other experiments and other subjects—Levelt (1968)—, and again $\rho = 1$ is proposed.

In Figure 7c the calculated brightness is plotted as a function of the illumina-

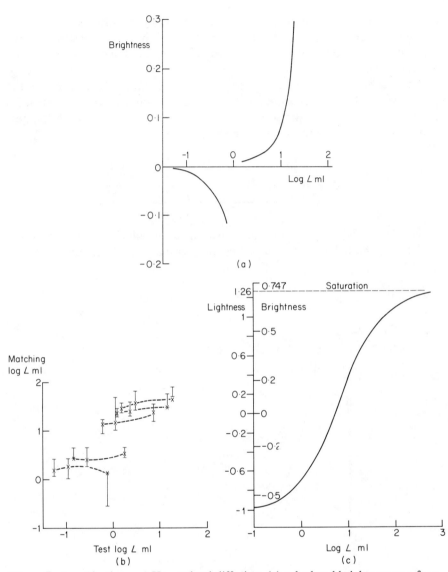

Figure 7. $\delta = 12$ ml, $\rho = 1$ Hz, optimal diffusion. (a) calculated brightness as a function of luminance for the brightest and the darkest square. (b) Lightness-matching. Data from Jameson and Hurvich (1961). The theoretical results of the brightest square are not from lightness-matching, because the calculated lightness exceeds the highest possible lightness in the matching stimulus. A brightness match of this square would give results below the match of the other squares, so he also can not make a brightness match for it. Therefore, he is forced to match the inner square above the outer squares and not too far above 60 ml, because such a match is conflicting with a lightness matching. So we have set the theoretical match such that the relative difference between this value and the match of the right square is equal to the relative difference between the chosen value and the maximum possible lightness. But it is an arbitrary choice. (c) calculated brightness and lightness of the matching stimulus

tion of the matching stimulus. The theory does not deal with the problems of assigning a number to the perceived brightness of the matching stimulus, but again it predicts qualitatively these measurements of Jameson and Hurvich satisfactorily.

If the effect of eye movement on the determination of the output of the psychophysical retina is estimated as being constant, then it follows with equations (20) and (21) that the perceived brightness in binocular brightness combination is provided by the formula:

$$\mathfrak{B} = \rho \frac{\left(\dfrac{L_L - \tau}{\delta + L_L - \tau}\right)^2 + \left(\dfrac{L_R - \tau}{\delta + L_R - \tau}\right)^2}{\left(\dfrac{L_L - \tau}{\delta + L_L - \tau}\right) + \left(\dfrac{L_R - \tau}{\delta + L_R - \tau}\right)}$$

From this immediately follows the measured equi-brightness curves measured by Levelt (1968). These are the curves that, with a given L, satisfy.

$$\mathfrak{B} = \rho \frac{L - \tau}{\delta - \tau + L}$$

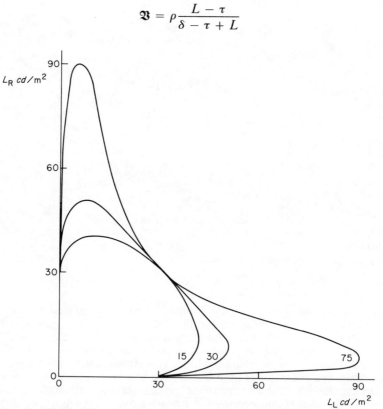

Figure 8. Binocular equi-brightness curves without disturbances. The curves have been normalised to $L = 30 \, \text{cd/m}^2$. The curve $L = 75 \, \text{cd/m}^2, \delta = 25 \, \text{cd/m}^2$ has been represented as $L = 30 \, \text{cd/m}^2$, $\delta = 10 \, \text{cd/m}^2$ and the curve $L = 15 \, \text{cd/m}^2 \, \delta = 25 \, \text{cd/m}^2$ as $L = 30 \, \text{cd/m}^2$, $\delta = 50 \, \text{cd/m}^2$

Three theoretical curves have been plotted in Figure 8 with $\delta = 25$ cd/m^2 and $\tau = 0$.

The equi-brightness formula does not contain a correction for eye dominance. If we suppose that eye dominance means, that the signal from one eye is[10] stronger—say a coefficient μ—than that from the other eye, then $(L_L - \tau)/(L_L + \delta - \tau)$, or respectively $(L_R - \tau)/(L_R + \delta - \tau)$ must be multiplied by μ and $\mathfrak{B}$ must be multiplied by $(\mu^2 + 1)/(\mu + 1)$. Levelt has done measurements on equi-brightness with extra contour information—with the same physical contrast—in one of the eyes. Following the theory this influences only the weighting coefficients by some coefficient say v. If extra monocular contour information is presented to the right eye and if the right eye is dominant to the left eye, the equi-brightness formula becomes

$$\frac{\mu^2 v + 1}{\mu v + 1} \frac{L - \tau}{\delta + L - \tau} = \frac{\left[\dfrac{L_L - \tau}{\delta + L_L - \tau}\right]^2 + v\mu^2 \left[\dfrac{L_R - \tau}{\delta + L_R - \tau}\right]^2}{\dfrac{L_L - \tau}{\delta + L_L - \tau} + v\mu \dfrac{L_R - \tau}{\delta + L_R - \tau}}$$

If the left eye is stimulated by the extra contour information instead of the right eye, v must be replaced by $1/v$. In Figure 9 four examples are given.

The first-picture represents Levelt's data with equal contour information in both eyes. So, in the theoretical curve we have set $v = 1$. In the theoretical curve we have chosen $\delta = 25$ cd/m^2, $\tau = 0$ and $\mu = 1 \cdot 14$. These values are the same in the next three pictures. Figure 9b represents Levelt's data with extra contour in formation in the right field. From this we have calculated v. In the third picture Levelt's data with extra contour information in the left field are represented, and the theoretical curve with v replaced by $1/v$ has been plotted. In Figure 9d the equi-brightness curve—Levelt's data—for $L = 20$ cd/m^2 without monocular contour information and the theoretical curve and plotted. The data at the flanks of the curves seem to be too high in relation to the theoretical prediction. This happens systematically. We impute it to the experimental procedure, because de Weert (private communication) has made other measurements in which the data were systematically too low.

De Weert and Levelt (1974) have shown that the curve in which $L = 30$ cd/m^2 can also be described by the equation:

$$\mathfrak{B} = \frac{L_L^{0 \cdot 66} + L_R^{0 \cdot 66}}{L_L^{0 \cdot 33} + L_R^{0 \cdot 33}}$$

The curves for larger and smaller L (see Figure 8) can also be described by means of a power function. For a larger L the coefficient becomes smaller and for a smaller L it becomes bigger. This indeed is one of the well-known phenomena in Steven's Law. The suggestion is implied that the proposed weighting coefficients system together with the psychophysical retina can explain the measured results, known as Steven's Law. De Weert (in a private communica-

196

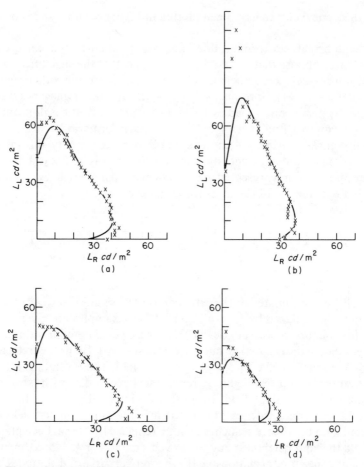

Figure 9. Equi-brightness curves. Data from Levelt (1968) subject
W. L. $\delta = 25$ cd/m^2, $\mu = 1 \cdot 14$
(a) matching stimulus (ms) = 30 cd/m^2, $v = 1$; (b) ms = 30 cd/m^2, $v = 1 \cdot 37$; (c) ms = 30 cd/m^2, $v = 1/1 \cdot 37 = 0 \cdot 73$; (d) ms = 20 cd/m^2, $v = 1$

tion) has indeed measured the above predicted effect of the course of the equi-brightness curves in lower and in higher luminescence.

Summary

A contrast-brightness theory is proposed in which there are three subsystems. The theory is able to explain various different phenomena both quantitatively and qualitatively. The starting-points are very simple. The theory is built up on the basis of the idea that all the phenomena are a result of local interactions and that every subsystem is linear but for one transformation.

This non-linear transformation is the first in the system. It explains the non-linear phenomena in contrast threshold measurements at sinusoidal grids and forms the basis for the phenomena in brightness perception. The proposed retinal filter describes the obtained data and is a first step in the generation of the brightness illusions. The contrast system is able to explain the phenomena of binocular rivalry and depth vision and possibly also apparent motion. Binocular and monocular brightness perception can be explained by the contrast system and the brightness system.

Notes

(1) We use the convention $\vec{r} = (x, y) \in \mathbb{R}^2$. If $\vec{r}$ is a parameter of a physical quantity, $\eta\vec{r}$ indicates a place on the retina. $\eta|x|$ is then the distance along the horizontal axis from the centre of the fovea ($\vec{r} = (0, 0)$) and $\eta|y|$ is the distance along the vertical axis. The vectors with $|x| = x$ seen from the subject's position lie to the right of the line $x = 0$; those with $|y| = y$ lies above the line $y = 0$. Depending on the choice of η, $|x|\eta$ and $|y|\eta$ are expressed in degrees (visual angle) or millimetres (distance on the retina).

(2) Time t is in principle, also in psychophysical experiments, a measurable magnitude because the reaction times of subjects is a measurable magnitude. t therefore has the dimension time also in perceptual magnitudes.

(3) This is really a sort of maximum velocity principle and arises from the fact that the perceptual magnitude s_1 is a representation of a physical process. c may be regarded as a maximum velocity. The constant a can be unequal to zero since the physical process takes place in three dimensions.

(4) The duration of the flashes has been chosen such that Bloch's law is valid. As a result one may consider $\theta(t - t_0) - \theta(t - t_1)$ substituted by a Dirac-delta function $\delta(t - (t_0 + t_1)/2)$; for Bloch's law implies that $L(\vec{r}, t) = L_1(\vec{r})[\theta(t + h) - \theta(t - h)]/2h$ is independent of h if $h \lesssim 30$ msec (Barlow, 1958). If $h\downarrow 0$ then it holds that $L(\vec{r}, t) = L_1(\vec{r})\delta(t)$, so that on account of Bloch's law, $[\theta(t + h) - \theta(t - h)]/2h$ may be substituted by Dirac's delta function.

(5) A Taylor-development of $g(|x|, \epsilon - \gamma)$ towards γ yields $g(|x|, \epsilon - \gamma) = \sum_{n=0}^{\infty} (-\gamma(\partial/\partial\epsilon))^n/n!\ g(|x|, \epsilon)$. A complete correction is $g(|x|, 0) = \lim_{\gamma \to \epsilon} (g|x|, \epsilon - \gamma)$, so that $g(|x|, \epsilon) - \gamma(\partial/\partial\epsilon)g(|x|, \epsilon)$ is a first-order correction.

(6) The two-dimensional generalization of $(1/\pi)\ \alpha/(\alpha^2 + x^2)$ is $(1/2\pi)\ \alpha/(\alpha^2 + r^2)^{3/2}$ ($\vec{r} = (x, y)$). Both are distribution functions with an infinite spread. This has consequences for the theories on the build of the retina. The two distribution functions may be conceived of as those of the 'average' of an infinite number of stochastic variables of which the spread is not, however, constant or bound. In that case, this 'average' would have followed the Gauss or normal distribution (central limit theorem). Cells are apparently mutually connected, also over long distances, with a chance (Lebesque measure) greater than zero. Two stimulated areas on the retina will show less interaction the longer the distance between them becomes; yet one should be very careful in interpreting the measured results if one is to regard the areas as independent. The following picture of the retina is thrust upon us. There is a great density of cells. Even over a large distance the units show a not negligible interaction. This interaction is given a first-order correction locally.

It is plausible to treat the retina, psychophysically viewed, as a field. The stationary field equation is, then, the equation

$$\left(\frac{\partial^2}{\partial x^2} + \frac{\partial^2}{\partial y^2} + \frac{\partial^2}{\partial z^2}\right) R_1(x, y, z) = E_1(x, y)\delta(z)$$

The general solution is

$$R_1(x, y, z) = \iint \rho(x - \xi, y - \eta, z)E_1(\xi, \eta)\mathrm{d}\xi\mathrm{d}\eta$$

where ρ satisfies the Laplace equation. The sought-for solution is that for which holds $z = \alpha(\vec{r}, \varphi)$ (see equation (10)) and $\lim_{|x| \to \infty} \rho(x, y, z) = \lim_{|y| \to \infty} \rho(x, y, z) = 0$ and which satisfies the boundary conditions that determine where the on-off transitions—the lines $R_1(x, y, \alpha) = 0$—are.

(7) A unit must not be regarded as a cell. A unit is some construct in relation to contrast interaction. How this is physiologically realized is not relevant. Possibly it is realized by means of a functional cluster of cells. This cluster can exist in relation to the interaction but in another sense these cells can be mutually quite independent. One might compare this with a little Weiss area, of which the atoms, as regards magnetism form a cluster, but at the same time in another sense—e.g. in electric conduction—act quite independently.

(8) We intentionally speak of 'can' since it is not certain that other mechanisms, e.g. attention, do not co-determine this brightness spread.

(9) A better name for relative brightness is perhaps lightness. The sensations white, grey and black are not originating from the total brightness level but from the brightness differences in the field. Therefore, it is possible that many brightness-experiments are in fact lightness-experiments.

(10) One can devise another obvious model for the eye dominance. Then it is supposed, that eye dominance only affects the weighting coefficients. This means that κ in formula (20) is not equal for both eyes. So, extra monocular contour information in one of the eyes has the same effect as eye dominance. But then, a consistent fitting of data and theory as described below is impossible.

References

Barlow, H. B. (1958). Temporal and spatial summation in human vision at different background intensities. *Journal of Physiology*, **178**, 477–504.

Buffart, H. F. J. M. (1978). *Contrast, brightness and cyclopean perception* (in preparation).

Campbell, F. W. and Green D. G., (1965). Optical and retinal factors affecting visual resolution. *Journal of Physiology*, **181**, 576–593.

Campbell, F. W., Kulikowsky, J. J., and Levinson, J. (1966). The effect of orientation on the visual resolution of gratings. *Journal of Physiology*, **187**, 427–436.

Cornsweet, T. N. (1970). *Visual perception*. Academic press, New York.

Davidson, M. (1968). Perturbation approach to spatial brightness interaction in human vision. *Journal of the Optical Society of America*, **58**, 1300–1308.

De Weert, Ch. M. M., and Levelt, W. J. M. (1974). Binocular brightness combinations: additive and non-additive aspects. *Perception and Physiophysics*, **15**, 551–562.

Fender D. H., and Julesz, B. (1967). Extension of Panum's fusional area in binocular stabilized vision. *Journal of the Optical Society of America*, **57**, 819–830.

Fischer, B., and May, H. U. (1970). Invarianzen der Katzen Retina: Gesetz-mässige Beziehungen zwischen empfindlichkeit, Grösse und Lage receptiver Felder von Gangliënzellen, *Exp. Brain Research*, **11**, 448–464.

Gerrits, H. J. M. and Vendrik, A. J. H. (1970).
—Simultaneous contrast, Filling-in process and information processing in men's visual system. *Exp. Brains Res.*, **11**, 411–430.
—Artificial movements of a stabilized image. *Vision Research*, **10**, 1443–1456.

Ginsburg, A. P. (1975). Is the illusory triangle physical or imaginary? *Nature*, **257**, 219–220.

Grossberg, S. (1978). This volume.

Hoekstra, J., van der Groot, D. P. J., van den Brink, G., and Biben, F. A., (1974). The influence of the number of cycles upon the visual contrast threshold for spatial sine wave patterns. *Vision research*, **14**, 365–368.

Jameson, D., and Hurvich, L. M. (1961). Complexities of perceived brightness. *Science*, **133**, 174–179.

Julesz, B. (1970). *Foundations of cyclopean perception*, The University of Chicago press, Chicago, London.

Kaufman, L., Bacon, J., and Barosso, F. (1973). Stereopsis without image segregation. *Vision research*, **13**, 137–147.

Kelly, D. H., and Magnuski, H. S. (1975). Pattern detection and the two-dimensional fourier transform: circular targets. *Vision research*, **15**, 911–915.

Levelt, W. J. M. (1968). *On binocular rivalry*, Mouton, The Hague.

Meyer, P. C. A. (1976). *Uni-lateral inhibition in apparent motion*, University paper. University of Nijmegen 76 FU 13.

Ratliff, F. (1965). *Mach bands: quantitative studies on neural networks in the retina*, Holden-day inc. San Francisco California.

Robson, J. G. (1966). Spatial and temporal contrast-sensitivity functions of the visual system. *Journal of the Optical Society of America*, **56**, 1141–1142.

Roufs, J. A. J. (1972). Dynamic properties of Vision-I: Experimental relationships between flicker and flash thresholds. *Vision research*, **12**, 261–278.

Van Nes, F. L. (1968). *Experimental studies in spatio temporal contrast-transfer by the human eye*, Thesis, University of Utrecht. See also Van Nes, F. L., and Bouman, M.A. (1965). The effects of wavelength and luminance on visual modulation transfer. In: *Performance of the eye at low luminances*, Excerpta Medica International Congres Series **125**, 183. Van Nes, F. L., and Bouman, M. A. (1966). Analysis of spatial modulation transfer in the human visual system. In *Proc. of the 2nd international biophysics congres*, Vienna, 1966. Van Nes, F. L., and Bouman M. A. (1967). Spatial modulation transfer in the human eye. *Journal of the Optical Society of America*, **57**, 401.

Watson, A. S. (1978). This volume.

Westheimer, G., and Campbell, F. W. (1962). Light distribution in the image formed by the living human eye. *Journal of the Optical Society of America*, **52**, 1040–1045.

Wiener, N. (1970). *Extrapolation, interpolation and smoothing of stationary time series*. M.I.T. Press, Cambridge, Massachusetts.

Part II

Coding Theories of Complex Patterns

Introduction

As indicated in the Preface of this volume, the content of the papers to follow has in comparison to the foregoing a greater relevance to the perceptual features represented in the codes of more complex patterns. The emphasis of the subject matter lies on the results of the perceptual process rather than on the process as such. On the basis of process results, may be deduced which are the characteristics of the perceptual codes or the coding processes of patterns.

In the first three papers (Julesz, Pommerantz, Frith) texture patterns have been studied. In general, propositions are tested by means of discrimination tasks using texture patterns. New arguments have been put forward for the hypothesis that the order of statistics is decisive for discrimating texture patterns (Julesz). Pommerants draws attention to the crucial role that special relationships (intersections) between primitive features (Hubel, Wiesel) play in these discrimination tasks. Frith too stresses the specific meaning of contour and the position of details, symmetrized in various ways, in similarity judgements.

A distinction is always drawn between texture perception and form perception. This distinction is related to the distinction between pre-attentive and focal perception. To what extent these differ from each other essentially or only in degree remains an open question. Since in texture perception some 'structural' code elements first appear (Pommerantz), the conjecture remains that the texture perception rules are induced by a part of the 'focal form perception' rules. The remaining focal-form rules, in this view, have not yet come into play in texture perception, on account of the overloading of the perceptual capacity.

The authors that follow (Restle, Johannson, Leeuwenberg) direct their attention to the focal perception of the 'single' form. It is not so much their coding systems that receive discussion—these, after all, have been published elsewhere—as the implications of structural information theories on various aspects of perception. Restle discusses a quantitative specification of the effect of context on the perception of a figure. The repeated subdivision of a figure into figure and background features in his analysis. According to the structural information theory, the hierarchic relationships constitute the elements of a pattern. A specified series of elements describes the perceived figure.

Very convincing is Johannson's demonstration of such elements in the analysis of movement perception. He regards as quite inadequate conceptions in which movements are represented in terms of independent cues. The code elements of movements resemble those of static patterns. With regard to these,

Leeuwenberg has measurements for figural salience, transparency and similarity, in terms of such structural information units.

The following authors (Geissler, Klix, Scheidereiter and Simon) again deal with coding systems as such. Their contributions are not only concerned with the form of codes for sequential structures, but also with the manner in which these are generated. Amongst others, Geissler, Klix and Scheidereiter have directed their attention to the definition of structural information. Experiments gave rise to a distinction between two process stages in the recognition of sequential structures.

Simon has also conducted an analysis of sequential structures. In his search for invariants in a sequential structure, he has formulated theoretically possible cognitive strategies. These he has subsequently related to experimental results. In research into coding systems, it is important to obtain an accurate picture of the effect of context and previous knowledge.

Chapter 9

Perceptual Limits of Texture Discrimination and Their Implications to Figure–Ground Separation

Bela Julesz

Abstract. Some interesting questions have been raised regarding the conjecture that humans are unable to discriminate between textures that agree in their second-order (dipole) statistics (Julesz, 1962; Julesz, Gilbert, Shepp, and Frisch, 1973; Julesz, 1975). These are discussed in this paper. Particularly insightful is the observation that for two-tone textures the dipole statistics determine the autocorrelation functions and power spectra. Thus the conjecture can be restated such that the human visual system cannot discriminate between textures with identical power spectra or, in other words, ignores the phase information. However, with scrutiny it is possible to discriminate between forms, even if the autocorrelation functions agree. Therefore, autocorrelation models can be useful for texture perception, but cannot account for form perception.

I accepted the invitation to this prestigious meeting with the proviso that although I was glad to give a detailed talk on my research in texture discrimination, I would keep the written material intended for the Proceedings at a minimum. It is my view that the reprinting of already published research—even in modified form—unnecessarily clutters the literature, for which there is no excuse. On the other hand, even the best symposium-proceeding is not the proper forum for important new ideas and findings. These should be published in the usual scientific journals that are available in libraries and are printed with minimum delay.

Fifteen years ago, I proposed a conjecture on the limitations of human texture discrimination (Julesz, 1962). Recently, I have confirmed that conjecture. I would ask the interested reader (who did not hear my talk and see the many demonstrations) to get hold of two recent publications of mine: Julesz (1975) and Julesz, et al. (1973) in which I report the confirmation. In this brief article I want to give the essence of these studies that occupied me for so long, and clarify some problems that were raised by other workers who became interested in these recent findings.

Definition of Texture Discrimination

We will restrict ourselves to two-dimensional textures (i.e. textures without relief). Textures are an aggregate of elements (that occur either at random or semi-regular locations). The global perception of a texture is different from the local scrutiny of its elements. This is demonstrated by Figures 1 and 2. In Figure 1 one can perceive effortlessly, even within a brief flash of presentation that one quadrant of the texture differs from the rest. I defined this effortless, spontaneous, and rapid performance of differentiating juxtaposed textures as visual texture discrimination (Julesz, 1962). On the other hand, in Figure 2 considerable effort and deliberation is needed to discern a unique square-shaped area in one quadrant. As a matter of fact, the quadrant can be found only by scrutinizing each element individually. Each n must be distinguished from the background of u's. In Figure 1, one texture was derived from the other by a 90° rotation, while in Figure 2 this rotation was 180°. Figure 1 will be regarded as an example for texture discrimination since the textures can be easily discriminated in a tachistoscopic flash (followed by a masking stimulus). However, in Figure 2 texture discrimination fails for tachistoscopic presentation times that yield good discrimination for Figure 1. Hence, Figure 2 will be regarded as a nondiscriminable texture.

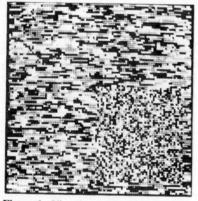

Figure 1. Visual texture discrimination is studied by tachistoscopically presenting images with controlled statistical properties and asking the subject if he can see an area of one texture embedded in an area of similar but different texture. Here the two textures have identical first-order but different second-order statistics. The difference in textures can be perceived without effort. (Julesz, et al., 1973)

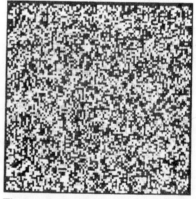

Figure 2. Example of a nondiscriminable texture pair. Here the two textures have identical second-order statistics (hence identical first-order statistics), but different third- and higher-order statistics. Here discriminating between the two textures requires deliberate effort. (Julesz, et al., 1973)

Description of Texture

An elegant way to describe textures with increasing complexity is to use the methods of random geometry (Julesz et al., 1973). In this method n-gons of arbitrary shapes are thrown in a random way on the texture. The statistics are obtained by counting the number of instances that all the n vertices of the n-gons land on the same color of the texture. For example on a two-colour (say, black and white) texture the 1-gons (confettis) determine the proportion of black and white areas. For both Figure 1 and Figure 2 the luminance proportion is the same for both the test square and background textures. In Figure 1, the 2-gon (or dipole) statistic for the test square is different from the background texture. However, Figure 2 maintains the same dipole statistic for the test square and background texture, but varies the 3-gon (triangle) statistic (Julesz, et al., 1973).

Conjecture

In the paper (Julesz, 1962) I posed the general question whether one could find ways to generate texture pairs that were identical in their $(n - 1)$-gon statistics, but differed in their (n)-gon statistics, and if so, what would be the highest n that still yielded texture discrimination. Rosenblatt and Slepian (1962) invented one-dimensional Markov processes which allowed for manipulation of first, second, and nth order statistics. (This procedure requires at least three colours.) To my surprise I found that these Markov textures with identical dipole statistics but different 3rd-and higher-order statistics could not be discriminated (Julesz, 1962). However, Markov textures are one-dimensional. But vision is inherently 2-dimensional. The various scanning paths of the texture dots yield very different resultant textures even when using the same underlying Markov process. Therefore, in 1962 I could not, in general, propose that the human visual system is incapable of breaking camouflage which varies only beyond the second-order statistic. I did not know how to generate non-Markov textures in two dimensions with identical first and second order statistics but different third-(and higher-) order statistics. The breakthrough came many years later when Ed Gilbert, Larry Shepp, and Harry Frisch became interested in this problem and helped me to find ways to generate such texture pairs.

Non-Markov Textures with Same Dipole Statistics

At the moment we have three methods to generate textures that agree in their second-order statistics but differ in third-or higher-order statistics (Julesz, et al., 1973). The first method yielded Figures 1 and 2. One can easily prove that if a texture is composed of identical elements (not permitting rotation) thrown at random, then another texture composed of the same elements but rotated by some constant amount will, in general, yield the same first-order but different second-order statistics. The only exception is when the rotation of the elements is 180° as shown in Figure 2. For 180° rotation, regardless of what the texture elements portray, the dipole-statistics agree with those of the texture consisting of the original elements, but the 3-gon, 4-gon, etc. statistics are very different. The finding that Figure 2 cannot be discriminated is thus in accordance with the conjecture. The lack of discriminability is astounding to us, since u's and n's are very familiar letters.

The second method we used to generate 2-dimensional textures with identical second but different higher order statistics uses mirror images between the test and background patterns. The original texture consists of identical elements thrown at random locations and random orientations while the corresponding texture partner consists of the same elements, but mirrored. An example, using as element the letter R and its mirror image for the partner texture is demonstrated in Figure 3. One has to scrutinize each element individually to gradually locate the square-shaped area in one quadrant which is composed of the mirrored R's. The preservation of the dipole statistic for mirrored images is easy to prove (Julesz, et al., 1973), provided one assumes ergodicity. It is surprising that textures composed of a familiar letter of the alphabet cannot be discriminated from a texture that is composed of a letter that is not a member of the alphabet. Again, the evidence supports my hypothesis, and not simple intuition.

Let me give a final demonstration, based on our third method (Julesz, et al., 1973). Here the two texture elements (a closed and an open figure composed of four equisized discs) have again the same dipole statistics (when thrown in all

Figure 3. Non-discriminable texture pair generated by the mirror-image method. The texture in the large square is composed of identical R's in random orientations, whereas the texture in the small square consists of mirror-image R's. (Julesz, et al., 1973)

Figure 4. Method of generating micropatterns that yield texture texture pairs with identical second order statistics begins with the construction of a triangle of arbitrary dimensions, KLM. At the midpoint of one side, say LM, a line is drawn perpendicular to OK, and on it points P and Q are placed so that PO equals QO. Five non-overlapping disks are drawn with centres at K, L, M, P and Q. The three central discs and disc Q form the micropattern a; the same central discs and disc P form the micropattern b. The micropatterns have identical second-order statistics because any dipole whose ends touch any two disks in micropattern a can be matched by a dipole of equal length touching two discs in micropattern b. If micropatterns are also randomly rotated, a dipole of given orientation will touch pairs of discs with equal frequency in each micropattern. The micropatterns differ in third-order statistics, however, because a triangle, for example KLQ, can be placed on micropattern a in a manner that cannot be duplicated on b

possible orientatiớns) but different 3-gon (triangle) statistics, as described in the caption of Figure 4. These two elements appear very different, and even an octopus would be able to discriminate between them when viewed in isolation (Sutherland, 1964). Yet when they form a texture, as shown in Figure 5, discrimination becomes very difficult, if not impossible.

I restricted myself only to these three demonstrations and the interested reader could find several other surprising cases in Julesz, et al. (1973) where each element pair looks very different, yet when the corresponding texture pair is briefly presented, they appear indistinguishable. As of now, we found practically no counterexample. As a matter of fact, we found some texture pairs where even the dipole statistics *differ*, (the first-order statistics are identical) yet one *cannot* discriminate between the texture pairs. Because of such examples, I am more confident that discrimination of textures varying only in their third and higher order statistics is impossible. Consequently, if counterexamples were to be found, they might turn out to be rather weak. After all, if there are even cases for which we are unable to discriminate between textures with differing dipole statistics, then the conjecture that textures with identical dipole statistics are undiscriminable is perhaps not so far-fetched.

Implications to Figure–Ground

These demonstrations imply two important aspects of the texture processing system. One is that for global texture processing the many hierarchical feature

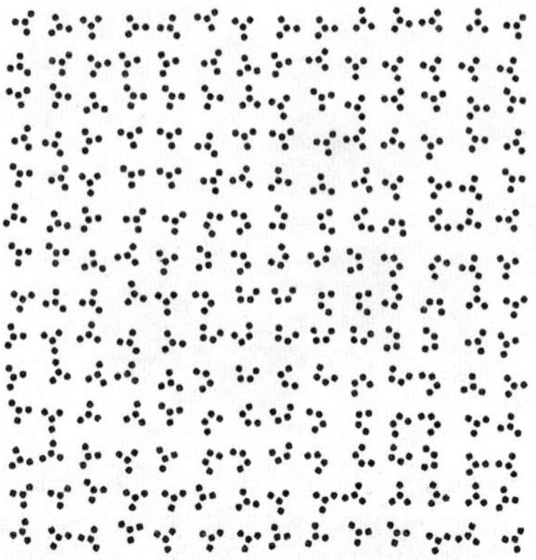

210

Figure 5. Texture pair generated by the method described in Figure 4. While the closed and open texture elements (composed of the four equisized discs) in isolation appear very different, the two textures formed by them are very difficult to discriminate if at all. (Julesz, et al., 1973)

extractors discovered by the neurophysiologists, particularly by Kuffler (1953) and Hubel and Wiesel (1962) may not be used. The feature extractors may only be useful for local element (figure) perception. Indeed, almost the simplest feature extractors could differentiate between the elements shown in Figure 5, and yet we experience great difficulty in discriminating between an aggregate of these elements. Thus the texture processing system seems to occur at a very early (peripheral) level of processing and applying perhaps only the receptors or some Kuffler units. The second implication is that the outputs of *only two* such units are evaluated by the next hierarchical stage. I am not claiming that *anatomically* only two synapses exist on the second neural units, but I state that *functionally* only two input units are processed by each successive neuron, otherwise they could compute higher than dipole statistics.

The difference between local scrutiny and global texture discrimination is illustrated in Figure 6. I stressed in my 1975 paper that these two different systems might reflect the difference between figure and ground perception. Traditionally, psychologists have focused on the rules governing figure perception and have ignored ground perception. It was assumed that all those areas that fell outside the limelight of our attention constituted the ground. In the light of this research, however, we can say the first concrete things about ground perception. It is my belief that ground perception can be considered to be the equivalent to texture discrimination. It serves as an early-warning system. If the many interposed or adjacent objects have the same surface texture (i.e. have the same dipole statistics) we do not stop to inspect them

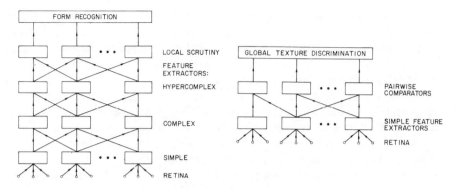

Figure 6. Neurophysiological models for form recognition or local scrutiny (*left*), and global texture discrimination (right). In form recognition visual information passes through a hierarchy of feature extractors, culminating in recognition. Global discrimination seems to employ only simple feature extractors whose outputs are evaluated only in pairs by the next neural units. (Julesz, et al., 1973)

separately. We are satisfied to regard them as the same object with the same surface texture. Only if the first or-second-order statistics change do we notice that certain areas differ in their tonal (colour) quality or granularity. Then, and only then do we have reason to slow down and inspect such areas in great detail. For example, few people, if any, would have noticed without prior warning the area composed of mirrored R's in Figure 3.

Alternative subdivisions of vision have been discussed before. One school distinguishes between peripheral and foveal vision. The peripheral system with its motion sensitivity and low form resolution serves as the early-warning system that triggers eye-movements in order to bring the moving object into the centre of our fovea for detailed inspection. Note, however, that the dichotomy I am posing is not for moving versus static objects, and not between peripheral and foveal vision. The figure-ground system pertains to static objects alone. The figure-ground system works equally for the fovea or parafovea, wherever spatial resolution of objects is possible. Yet, there is some analogy between the two dichotomies. The periphery as an early-warning system cannot resolve figure details, only their movement. The texture discrimination system similarly ignores figure details, serving as an early-warning system. Its primary task is to discern textural parameter changes determined by first- and second-order statistics. Both early warning systems are necessary in our daily lives to focus our attention on sudden changes in position or surface texture. This allows one to ignore the huge amount of trivial information in the ground.

Some Comments

These recent developments are important, since these are the first texture pairs that are non-Markovian which have identical dipole statistics, but differ in higher-order statistics. Unlike the Markovian textures, these textures are two-dimensional and are of only two colours (while the Markovians require at least three colours). These enable us to use texture elements of white and black clusters similar to the patterns which maximally excite receptive fields studied by the neurophysiologists. We can, therefore, evaluate the role of these feature extractors in global texture discrimination.

Of course, the conjecture—if proved valid—does not mean that the full dipole statistic is used by the texture processing system. The conjecture regards the complete dipole statistic as a sort of upper bound on texture discrimination. As I mentioned before, there are instances where we are unable to discriminate between textures that differ in their dipole statistics. David Marr, who became interested in this research from an artificial intelligence point of view (Marr, 1975), regards these instances as a 'failure' of our 'dipole model'. While his work is very interesting and thought provoking, I think he misunderstood one aspect of our work. We do not use a dipole model in the usual sense to predict performance. We, instead, have a *negative* model that has no prediction about dipoles, but rather about *n*-gons that are higher than dipoles (such as trigons, etc.) and even for these the prediction is a negative statement. No difference in trigon, or higher *n*-gon statistics can yield texture discrimination. Therefore, those instances where even differences in dipole statistics produce indistinguishable textures are not counter-examples but, on the contrary, yield strong support for our conjecture.

Let me note that the structural diagram of the texture discrimination process in Figure 6 should also be regarded as only a possible complex version of the mechanism and not the actual one. As we noted in Julesz, et al. (1973), it might be that only some first-order statistics of some simple dipole parameters (such as their length, orientation, and width) are utilized by the texture processor. Whatever the crucial parameters of the dipole statistics are, such research will eventually lead to the true dipole model.

Finally, I wish to emphasize the importance of this type of conjecture for psychology. It is analogous to the 'existence proofs' in mathematics, as opposed to the more common 'constructive proof' analogies. Indeed, most theories in the life sciences and in artificial intelligence are based on a detailed knowledge of the building blocks (algorithms) and their interconnections. For instance, Marr's attempts to simulate texture discrimination on a computer resulted in cascaded complex algorithms whose description fills a large monograph (Marr, 1975). While his work is very ingenious, the complexity and ad hocness of his approach cautions me. In contrast, the assertion of a human inability to discriminate textures with the same second-order statistics is easy to grasp, and describes a huge repertoire of findings in one sentence.

Ways to Break Camouflage Beyond Second-order

If our conjecture is upheld, then we have an obvious example of how to construct automata that are 'better than human'. For instance, a machine that notices differences in trigon statistics of textures, performs better than humans do—both quantitatively and qualitatively. However, an increase from second-order evaluation, to third- or higher-order, increases the computational complexity exponentially. Probably this enormous increase of required nuerons made such an advancement impractical in human evolution.

On the other hand, breaking animal camouflage must have had great importance for predators. Furthermore, if evolution stumbled upon a solution, then this solution is often used for a more difficult problem, provided it requires only a small modification. We have discussed how the texture discrimination system must have neurons that compare the output of, at most, two simple input units. If these two inputs are in the same retina (monocular vision) then they cannot break camouflage of third-order. However, if the two input units are placed in the left and right retina and the next unit to which they connect becomes a binocular cortical neuron, then the situation changes. If one takes two such binocular units (and assumes that owing to binocular disparity the two binocular units get different outputs) then the 4th-order unit to which the two binocular disparity units are connected is a local stereopsis unit. A gamut of such units gives rise to global stereopsis as exemplified in the fusion of random-dot stereograms (Julesz, 1960). Such a random-dot stereogram is shown in Figure 7. If viewed monocularly, the arrays appear as a uniform random texture. Yet when binocularly fused, a centre area (whose binocular disparity differs from its surround) jumps out in vivid depth. As I speculated in my book (Julesz, 1971) the main reason for the emergence of stereopsis was to break camouflage of motionless prey.

Let me note that monocular movement parallax can be used also to break camouflage. Indeed, if a patch of random texture is placed over a background of the same texture the patch cannot be seen. However, if the patch moves with respect to the background, it becomes apparent. Even flies can orient themselves to such moving textures. From Reichardt and Poggio's (1976) beautiful work, we know that the local feature extractors of the fly's visual system are of fourth

Figure 7. A typical random-dot stereogram (Julesz, 1960). The left and right images contain a texture pair with identical statistics. Therefore monocularly no texture discrimination can be possible. However, there is a phase (location) shift between the left and right images which can be easily detected by stereoscopic fusion (stereopsis).

order. They used Volterra expansions and showed that the basic elements are built up from two second-order Volterra elements.

However, for monocular vision and for motionless scenes, it remains to be seen whether there exist organisms that surpass us in penetrating camouflaged surface textures for patterns which vary beyond dipole statistics.

The Role of Autocorrelation in Perception

Two-tone images (such as textures with two colours) have an interesting, not generally known, property (see, for instance, Frisch and Stillinger, 1963): The dipole statistics uniquely determine the autocorrelation function and thus the power spectrum. So, for all black-white texture pairs which have identical dipole statistics, their power spectra are also identical.

Therefore, the three indiscriminable texture pairs described previously have identical power spectra, as well as identical dipole statistics. Since these textures cannot be discriminated from each other, *differences in phase spectra cannot be processed by the texture discrimination system.* In this way, the visual texture discrimination is similar to the auditory system which also ignores the phase information. Of course, this insensitivity to phase is only valid for stationary textures. Similarly, the human ear is sensitive to phase for auditory textures that are not stationary. (For instance, a sharp click sounds very different from white noise, although both have the same flat power spectrum.) Texture may be characterized by its stationarity. That is, it lacks preference for any position (phase). It is not surprising that our global texture processing system capitalized on this property and developed to ignore phase information.

The equivalence of dipole statistics and the autocorrelation function for two-tone images has far reaching consequences for several theories of psychology. In fact, these consequences are not limited to two-tone images, since any half-tone image (with many shades of gray between black and white) can be adequately approximated by two tones (with the use of the screen technique). Many psychologists believe the autocorrelation function is an important component for form perception. The interested reader is referred to a recent book by Uttal (1975) entitled *An Autocorrelation Theory of Form Detection.* Our results indicate the importance of autocorrelation in texture discrimination and specifically, in *ground* perception. What we have shown is that autocorrelation is not only a good descriptor for texture discrimination, but is also a *sufficient* one, since no higher-order autocorrelation functions can be utilized by our ground perception system.

However, the situation is very different for *form* perception. Since one is able to scrutinize and subsequently discriminate between the *elements* of texture pairs having identical autocorrelations, the figure system can process visual information much beyond the autocorrelation level. (Note that Uttal is concerned only with the first-order autocorrelation, while the higher-order autocorrelation functions, as developed by Wiener (1958), are not considered.) Since scrutiny allows one to discriminate between the elements in Figure 2, any autocorrelation theory of form cannot survive. The autocorrelation is the same both for the texture pairs and for their individual elements in this figure. A 180° rotation of any figure preserves unchanged the dipole statistics, and thus the autocorrelation and power spectrum. Indeed, the autocorrelation for u and n, or d and p, respectively, is the same, yet we can easily discriminate between them.

The situation is somewhat different for the examples given in Figures 3 and 5. Here the autocorrelation is different for a *selected* pair of texture elements. The autocorrelation functions differ because the two individual elements occupy two fixed orientations while the elements of the textures occupy *all* orientations. However, this difference in autocorrelation between any two elements is the same regardless whether the two elements belong to the same texture, or to two different textures. So again, an autocorrelation function would not be sensitive to a difference between two individual elements embedded in either texture, or in two different textures of Figures 3 and 5. Yet with scrutiny we can easily discriminate between the elements, and thus tell the textures apart.

In summary, autocorrelation seems to be the right theory for texture perception, but the wrong one for figure perception. One might ask whether global stereopsis—a task more complex than texture discrimination, but much simpler than figure perception—could be explained by some correlation model. (Obviously, in this case, correlation means crosscorrelation between the left and right images of a stereopair.) The answer is an emphatic no! Global stereopsis is a highly nonlinear, cooperative phenomenon. The spring-coupled magnet model of stereopsis (Julesz, 1971)—although easily understood—is much more complex than a crosscorrelational model. However, it is possible to study stereopsis of a single depth plane and study binocular fusion or binocular rivalry in this one depth plane as a function of binocular correlation (Julesz and Tyler, 1976; Tyler and Julesz, 1976). In this situation, it is easy to detect a sudden change from high binocular correlation to reduced correlation. But a change towards increased correlation by the same amount is much more difficult to detect.

While crosscorrelation between the dynamic noise in the left and right arrays uniquely describes the stimulus, the large difference in perceptual performance in favour of change from order to disorder indicates that a simple crosscorrelational model does not work, not even for perceiving *binocular correlation.*

I hope that some of these remarks might clarify a few problems. Of course, most of these comments depend on the validity of the conjecture I posed. Since in the sciences one can never prove a hypothesis, only disprove it, these speculations can only gain some respectability with time, but one cannot ever be sure. Yet I have found the existing examples so astonishing and counter-intuitive that I think it is worth sharing them with my colleagues.

References

Frisch, H. L. and Stillinger, F. H. Contribution to the statistical geometric basis of radiation scattering. *J. Chem. Phys.*, 1963, **38**, 2200.

216

Hubel, D. H. and Wiesel, T. N. Receptive fields, binocular interaction and functional architecture in the cat's visual cortex. *J. Physiol.*, 1962, **160**, 106.

Julesz, B. Binocular depth perception and pattern recognition. *Bell System Tech. J.*, 1960, **39**, 1125–62.

Julesz, B. Visual pattern discrimination. *IRE Transactions on Information Theory IT-8*, 1962, 84–92.

Julesz, B. *Foundations of Cyclopean Perception*, 1971, Chicago: University of Chicago Press.

Julesz, B. Experiments in the Visual Perception of texture. *Scientific American*, 1975, **232**, 34–43.

Julesz, B., Gilbert, E. N., Shepp, L. A., and Frisch, H. L. *Perception* 1973, **2**, 391–405.

Julesz, B. and Tyler, C. W. Neurontropy, an entropy-like measure of neural correlation, in binocular fusion and rivalry. *Biol. Cyb.* 1976, **23**, 25–32.

Kuffler, S. W. Discharge patterns and functional organization of mammalian retina. *J. Neuro. Physiol.*, 1953 **16**, 37–68.

Marr, D. Early processing of visual information. Artificial Intelligence Lab., MIT, Memo No. 340, to be published in *Phil. Trans. Roy. Soc.*, **B** (in press).

Reichardt, W. and Poggio, T. Visual control of orientation behaviour of the fly. *Quart. Rev in Biophysics*, Aug. 1976.

Rosenblatt, M. and Slepian, D. Nth order Markov chains with any set of N variables independent. *J. Soc. Indust. Appl. Math.*, 1962, **10**, 537–49.

Sutherland, N. S. The learning of discrimination by animals. *Endeavour*, 1964, **23**, 148–52.

Tyler, C. W. and Julesz, B. The neural transfer characteristic (neurontropy) for binocular stochastic stimulation. *Biol. Cyb.*, 1976, **23**, 33–37.

Uttal, W. R. *An autocorrelation theory of form detection.* (L. Erlbaum Assoc., Hillsdale, N.J.).

Wiener, N. *Nonlinear Problems in Random Theory.* New York: John Wiley & Sons. 1958.

Chapter 10

Are Complex Visual Features Derived from Simple Ones?*

James R. Pomerantz

Abstract. Several experiments have been reported in recent years showing that line slope differences are detected very rapidly by the visual system. This evidence would support a model of pattern coding in which the primitive unit was the sloped line segment, coded perhaps by cortical line or edge detectors. This paper presents evidence that slope differences are not detected rapidly by the visual system, but that differences in line arrangement or configuration are registered quite rapidly. Thus it appears that configural features such as angles and intersections may be the primary units of visual pattern analysis, and that these higher-order features are not derived from line slope information but rather are encoded directly from the visual array.

How are simple visual shapes coded in the human visual system? This is surely a complex, multifaceted problem. Among the most important facets is the question of what primitives are employed in the analysis of form. Except for certain wholistic (or template) theories of pattern recognition, all models assume that shapes are identified by analysing them into components of some sort; from the particular set of components registered plus the interrelations among them, the identity of the pattern in question can be deduced. (For recent reviews of the pattern recognition literature, see Dodwell, 1975; Sutherland, 1973; Reed, 1973).

Assuming that this line of reasoning is sound, it is proper to ask what components are actually analysed in shape perception. A short list of possibilities would include: (1) simple, local parts such as straight line segments in various orientations; (2) more complex local features such as angles, vertices and inter-

* This research was supported by a grant from the National Science Foundation (BNS76-01227). I gratefully acknowledge the help of Randi Martin on the section of this paper dealing with textural analysis. We are currently preparing a detailed report of some experiments we have completed recently testing the importance of statistical operations in texture discrimination.

sections; (3) global geometric properties such as symmetry and convexity; and (4) other global features such as spatial frequency components and autocorrelation statistics. Among these several alternatives, the first (line segments) seems to have gained the greatest popularity, perhaps because of the wealth of neurophysiological evidence for cortical detectors of lines and edges in the mammalian visual system (Hubel and Weisel, 1962, 1965, 1968; for a recent review see Robson, 1975).

Coding by Sloped Lines

Consider a model of shape coding in which lines of varying orientations are used as primitives. How, under such a system, might a triangle be recognized? When a triangle falls on the retina the first process relevant to form recognition is the abstraction of its three component line segments. The mere detection of three differently oriented lines is clearly not sufficient to code the presence of a triangle. The segments must meet one another to create angles, but must not pass through one another to create intersections. Thus, it would appear that we need angle or vertex detectors too. Without much difficulty we can (at least in principle) create such higher order detectors out of simple line detectors by properly concatenating the outputs of line detectors in a logical hierarchy (Lindsay and Norman, 1972; Milner, 1974). The mere detection of three angles, however, may still be insufficient to code the presence of a triangle. The letters F and Y, for example, each contain three line segments and three angles by one reasonable criterion, yet neither is a triangle. More conditions must be satisfied, such as a restriction that no two line segments be parallel or that the three angles must sum to exactly 180 degrees, or that the vertices of the three angles lie in different locations, or that the figure be closed. But once again these analyses can be based upon an appropriate integration of the output of simple line detectors. In any case; the basic structure of the line-based shape recognizer is a hierarchy of detectors, with information from the simplest detectors for lines flowing in a 'bottom up' fashion into detectors for more abstract properties (Norman and Rumelhart, 1975; see Suppes and Rottmayer, 1974, or Reed, 1973, for an introduction to formal grammatical approaches to visual pattern recognition based upon straight line segments as the primitive).

Evidence from Pattern Discrimination Experiments

While the main impetus for a line-based model of shape coding has come from neurophysiological findings on lower animals, corroboration has come from behavioural experiments on human perception. Quite a wide range of evidence has been brought to bear on this matter, including studies on the disappearance of stabilized images (Pritchard, Heron and Hebb, 1960), on the McCollough effect (McCollough, 1965), on adaptation to bar gratings in specific orientations (Blakemore and Campbell, 1969), and even on the 'fortification images' experienced by migraine headache sufferers (Richards, 1971).

The kind of evidence I would like to consider in this paper comes from studies of visual pattern discrimination in humans. In particular, the line of research begun by Beck (1966) and continued by him (Beck, 1967, 1972; Beck and Ambler, 1973) and by Olson and Attneave (1970) appears to have given strong support to the importance of line slope in primitive perceptual processes. Figure 1(a) and (b) (adapted from Olson and Attneave) illustrates one of the major findings of this research. The subject is presented with an array of elements and is asked to locate the portion of the array that differs from the rest. In Figure 1(a), it is the lower right quadrant that is disparate; it differs from the rest in the slopes of the line segments it contains. In Figure 1(b), by contrast, the disparate quadrant contains the same slopes as the rest but differs in the arrangements of these sloped lines; the angles formed by the sloped lines point in a different direction in the odd quadrant.

Olson and Attneave's experiment showed that the disparate quadrant is detected much faster in Figure 1(a) than in 1(b). In fact, the subject's task is so much easier in Figure 1(a) that Olson and Atteave claimed the odd quadrant here is segregated from the rest of the array automatically, perhaps by those immediate perceptual processes which are responsible for perceptual organization and figure ground segregation (Neisser, 1967; Julesz, 1975). Locating the disparate quadrant in Figure 1(b), Olson and Attneave claimed, proceeds by a qualitatively different process resembling a slow, serial search.

These results would be expected if the unit of analysis in the visual system were the sloped line. With Figure 1(a), the odd quadrant would stimulate a different population of line detectors than would the remaining three quadrants, while with Figure 1(b) all four quadrants would stimulate identical populations. Thus, with Figure 1(a), a decision could be made at the level of the primary detectors, while subsequent, additional processing would be required for Figure 1(b). Further experiments by Beck (e.g., Beck and Ambler, 1973) have demonstrated similar effects. For instance, a 'T' figure is more discriminable from a tilted ⅄ ⅄) than it is from an L presumably since the former discrimination involves a difference in line slope while the latter involves only a difference in line arrangement.

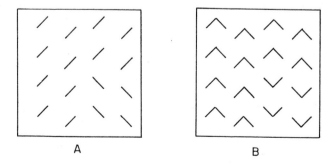

A   B

Figure 1.

Contrary Evidence

Recent experiments I have performed with my collaborator, Lawrence Sager, suggest that these conclusions may be in error. Consider the array shown in Figure 2(a), which is basically a simplification of Figure 1(a). The task is the same, that is to locate which quadrant (in this case which element) of the array differs from the rest. Here once again it is the lower right quadrant that is disparate, since it differs in slope from the other three. Next consider Figure 2(b). Again the lower right quadrant is odd, but here the discrepancy involves not line slope but line arrangement, since all four quadrants contain the same horizontal, vertical and diagonal lines. In this respect it is analogous to Figure 1(b). Two facts are apparent from these arrays. The first is that locating the odd quadrant in Figure 2(a) is rather difficult, requiring subjects in one of our experiments an average of 1884 milliseconds (msec). The second fact is that the task is much simpler with Figure 2(b), requiring subjects in the same experiment an average of only 759 msec. For comparison, a control condition in which the disparate quadrant differed only in brightness (i.e. three quadrants black, one white or vice versa) required 724 msec.

There is a clear discrepancy between Figures 1 and 2: the former shows that differences in line slope are more salient perceptually than differences in line arrangement, while the latter indicates the exact opposite. Reconciling this discrepancy and determining the implications of these findings for theories of visual pattern coding will be the primary goals of this paper.

If the sloped line detector were the fundamental unit of shape processing, then locating the disparate element in Figure 2(a) should be simple. Two types of line detectors would be activated by this array, since just two slopes are represented. The visual system would only have to compute which slope was in

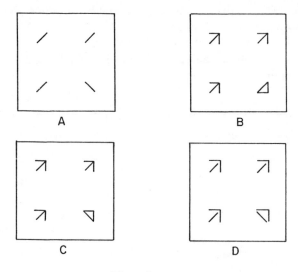

Figure 2.

the minority and where this slope was located within the array in order to perform the task. With Figure 2(b) on the other hand, three different kinds of line detectors would be activated (since three slopes are represented). But since each of the four quadrants contains exactly the same slopes, the visual system would have to do some further computations to determine which quadrant is the disparate one. One solution would be to derive what kinds of angles and vertices are present in each quadrant, using available information about what slopes are present and where particular line segments terminate. Since the 'triangle' and 'arrow' configurations differ in terms of the vertices they contain (see Guzmán, 1969, for an analysis of forms by vertices), a response could be based on this level of analysis. If this line of reasoning were correct, it would immediately follow that responses to Figure 2(a) should be faster than to 2(b), since the decision for 2(a) can be based on an earlier, more primitive level of analysis. The fact that the opposite is true, (i.e. that responses are dramatically faster to 2(b) than to 2(a)) implies that this reasoning is wrong.

Figure 2(c) strengthens this conclusion further. Here the disparate quadrant differs from the others in line slope as well as in line arrangement, since the diagonal line is oriented differently in the lower right quadrant. If line slope mattered in this task, then responses should be faster with this array than in Figure 2(b) where no line slope cues are present. In fact, responses to Figure 2(c) averaged 749 msec, an insignificant 10 msec improvement over Figure 2(b). Evidently, absolute line slope is irrelevant; what is critical are the angles and vertices that emerge where the lines meet. This finding, I believe, poses a strong challenge for line-based models of visual pattern recognition.

Comparing Figure 2(a) and (c), it is clear that they are identical except for the addition of the horizontal and vertical line segments in 2(c). These segments are identical for all four quadrants, so they do not by themselves provide any additional cues to help the subject isolate the disparate quadrant. Nevertheless, their presence is quite helpful, cutting reaction times nearly in half. The reason they are helpful, I would argue, is that they interact with the diagonal line segments to create emergent features such as angles and vertices, as discussed above. However, the data indicate that these emergent, higher-order features were not derived from sloped line detectors, since they were responded to faster than the sloped lines. The conclusion is that these angle and vertex features are encoded directly. In other words, these findings imply that features of a higher order than line slopes are true primitives of the pattern recognition system.

These findings do not force us to conclude that sloped line detectors do not exist in the human visual system. These simple detectors could serve an important function in vision, since straight lines and edges are critical in their own right in analysing scenes. Furthermore, it is difficult to see how straight lines could be encoded directly by angle detectors. My point is that angles and vertices, which are at least equal in importance to lines and edges, are not derived from line detectors but are recognized directly, say by templates.

Before we accept this conclusion too quickly, are there any alternative interpretations that could explain the results from Figure 2 without abandoning the sloped line detector as the building block of the recognition process? The answer is yes. It is conceivable that higher-order features are derived from lower-order ones in the perceptual process, but that the subject is not able to make responses on the basis of lower-order feature detectors. That is, line detectors may input directly and automatically into angle detectors, where information regarding absolute slope is discarded. When the subject must respond on the basis of slope information alone, as in Figure 2(a), his task is a difficult one since the critical information he needs has been lost. He must therefore find a way to 'work backwards' and reconstruct slope information from the output of angle detectors. My term for this notion is the 'sealed channel' hypothesis, since it posits that information is extracted from the stimulus that cannot exit from its processing channel until it has been transformed. While the sealed channel hypothesis is a logically acceptable interpretation of the results from Figure 2(a) and 2(b), there are several difficulties with this interpretation. In the first place, this explanation is both unparsimonious and ad hoc. It would seem uneconomical for the visual system to go through the process of abstracting line segments from the visual array only to discard these units before they could be put to any useful purpose. If pattern processing is based on angles and vertices, it would be simpler for these units to be encoded directly by the process of template matching. Secondly, this explanation may be untestable. If we argue that lines are extracted but are recoded before they can be responded to, it is difficult to see how we could prove they were ever extracted in the first place. The third and most telling objection to this interpretation is that it undermines the meaning of the concept of perceptual units. One might, for the sake of argument, claim that each successive synapse in the visual system represents a separate stage or unit of processing. By this reasoning, the primitive of pattern processing is the pointillistic representation given at the level of individual retinal receptors; lines then would not be the building block of perception but rather the points from which they are constructed. Clearly, however, this is not what most of us mean when we refer to the unit of analysis in perception. A true perceptual unit is one that plays an important functional role in processing, such as providing information on which response can be based, or providing critical transformations of the stimulus on which later decisions can be based. Under the sealed channel hypothesis, line detectors serve neither of these functions, since responses cannot be based upon their output and since they are not in principle an indispensable stage in the extraction of angles and vertices.

Explaining Earlier Observations

If the sloped line detector is not the building block of the visual pattern recognition system, then how can the observations of Beck and of Olson and Attneave be explained? To be more specific, how can the apparent ease of locating the disparate quadrant in Figure 1(a) be reconciled with the apparent difficulty in Figure 2(a)? It should be noted first that there are no firm data confirming that the task in Figure 1(a) is any easier than that in 2(a), since the two have never been compared directly in the same experiment. Nevertheless, the difference between the two seems obvious enough to warrant explanation. The most plausible reason why the task is so easy in Figure 1(a) is the emergence of angle features along the imaginary border which separates the disparate quadrant from the others. Along this border, the sloped line segments of the disparate quadrant approach those of the remaining quadrants in a perpendicular manner, suggesting right angles (albeit incomplete ones). These partial angles may be complete enough to trigger angle detectors along this border. Nowhere else in the array do these right angles occur, so the output of our hypothetical primitive, the angle detector, would indicate the boundary of the disparate quadrant.

This argument is made more plausible by considering the array shown in Figure 2(d). This array is identical to that in Figure 2(c) except that the horizontal and vertical line segments do not quite touch the diagonal ones. Nevertheless the disparate quadrant still stands out perceptually, presumably because the angle detectors can be stimulated by angles that are not complete. Certainly as the angle becomes more incomplete by widening the gap, the task will become harder (Pomerantz and Schwaitzberg, 1975).

Another example of emerging features is shown in Figure 3. In these arrays the task is the same, namely to decide which quadrant is different. Here the elements used to construct the arrays are not straight line segments but curves, which differ in their direction of curvature. Figure 3(a) represents a baseline or control condition. In Figure 3(b), an identical curved segment has been added to each quadrant; since they are all identical, these added segments provide in themselves no additional cue for performing the task. Nevertheless our experiments have shown that the disparate quadrant is located much more rapidly in arrays like Figure 3(b) than like 3(a) (1450 vs 2400 msec). In Figure 3(c), on the other hand, the added curved segments only make the task harder (2950 msec). Evidently, features are emerging from Figure 3(b) that are especially easy for the visual system to detect. As in the case of Figure 2(d), these features cannot be local in the strict sense of the word, since the added segments do not overlap with the original segments to form angles or intersections. Instead, the symmetrical pattern, (), seems to close perceptually to form an oval or a circle while the assymmetrical pattern,)), fails to close. Whether it is this property of closure that the visual system uses to isolate the target in Figure 3(b) is hard to say; constructing a detector for a global property like closure may be more difficult than building detectors for more local features like angles (Minsky and Papert, 1972). Alternatively, it is possible that the way in which the curved segments of the () pattern approach one another is such that an angle detector is stimulated here, but not when the pattern is)). While this possibility would be quite consistent with the angle-based coding system for patterns presented here, it must remain for the moment as speculation.

Why, according to the theory being advanced, is the task so difficult with Figure 1(b)? Phonomenally, no striking features appear at the border of the dis-

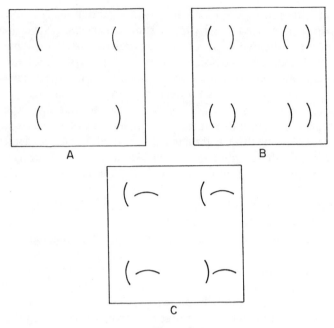

Figure 3.

parate quadrant in this array. Nevertheless it is possible that right angle features do in fact emerge at the border, but such features would help little in isolating the disparate quadrant since right angles occur throughout the display, not just along the border.

Finally, how can we explain the finding of Beck mentioned above that it is easier to discriminate a T from a tilted T (⅄) than from an L? According to the theory proposed here, the following explanation seems to be called for. A T is so easily discriminated from a tilted T not because the two differ in line slope but because they differ in their component angles. This would be true if angle detectors were orientation-specific, that is, if any given angle detector was sensitive to: (1) the kind of angle or vertex presented (Guzmán, 1969); (2) the size of the angle, in degrees; *and* (3) the orientation of the angle (i.e. the orientation of the axis bisecting the angle). Both the T and the tilted T contain simple right (i.e. 90 degree) angles, but these angles (not the line slopes) are oriented along the diagonals for the normal T and along the horizontal and vertical for the tilted T. In the case of T and L, on the other hand, the angles in both are simple right-angles oriented along the diagonals. Convincing arguments have been offered by Attneave (Attneave, 1969; Olson and Attneave, 1970) that angles are perceived with a definite orientation.

It might strike some readers as odd to propose orientation-specific angle detectors. Some theorists (e.g., Milner, 1974) have held that orientation information should be discarded quickly in a pattern recognizer in order to account for orientation invariance, i.e. our ability to recognize visual stimuli regardless of the orientation in which they are presented. In point of fact, however, orientation invariance does not seem to be a basic characteristic of the visual system. It takes longer to determine the identity of an object when it is presented in an unexpected orientation than in an expected one (Rock, 1973; see also Cooper and Shepard, 1973). A wide variety of shapes ranging from simple geometric forms to complex stimuli like faces and outline maps of continents are difficult to recognize in novel orientations (Yin, 1969). Thus, it is far from clear that orientation invariance is desirable as a fundamental property of a pattern recognizer. Rather, it may better be added on in a *later* stage of processing where, perhaps, forms are rotated into new orientations so they can be recognized.

Texture Perception

The discussion so far in this paper has been based on an implicit assumption, namely that the task of localizing the disparate quadrant in the various arrays is performed by assessing and comparing the features present in the four quadrants. The question up to this point has been whether these features are lines or angles. The possibility has been ignored that these arrays have been processed not as 'three identical quadrants plus a fourth disparate one' but rather as 'a uniform texture with a break in it'. Perhaps it is easiest to see Figure 1(a) and (b) as textures, although the other Figures can be seen this way with some effort.

Julesz (1975) has proposed that when people are presented with textures like those in Figure 1, they detect differences in textures on the basis of certain statistical properties. Julesz has shown, for example, that textures made from micropatterns of black grain on a white background can be described in terms of order statistics. The first order statistic of a texture corresponds to its average density or brightness, and can be assessed by measuring the probability that a point thrown randomly on the texture will land in a black region. Second order statistics correspond to the spacing of black and white regions within the texture, and can be assessed by determining the probability that a randomly thrown *pair* of points (at a given separation and orientation) will both land on black. Third order statistics in turn can be assessed by throwing triplets of points (i.e. triangles of fixed size, proportion and orientation), and so on. Based on his work with specifically constructed textures, Julesz has advanced the principle that humans can readily and effortlessly discriminate textures that differ in their second (and hence higher) order statistics but cannot discriminate those that are the same in their second order statistics (differing only in third and higher orders), except with great effort and scrutiny. (Although Julesz has not claimed so himself, it would be possible to derive the second order statistics of textures such as those considered here by using the output of sloped line detectors. Similarly first order statistics could be computed from the outputs of units sensitive simply to brightness levels. It is harder to imagine how the visual system would compute third order statistics, but since humans are apparently insensitive to them, this problem is not a pressing one.)

Let us suppose that when we look at the figures in this paper we treat them as textures, where the disparate quadrant represents a break in an otherwise uniform texture. How well can Julesz's principle describe the various findings that I have summarized? Looking first at Figure 1(a), it can be shown that the disparate quadrant of this array differs in its second order statistics from the remaining three quadrants, while in Figure 1(b) all four quadrants have identical second order statistics. Thus, Julesz's principle would predict that the disparate quadrant should stand out perceptually in Figure 1(a) but should be apparent only with great difficulty in 1(b). This is, of course, in perfect agreement with the findings presented earlier.

Skipping ahead to Figure 3(a), all four quadrants in this array show identical second order statistics, while in Figure 3(b) the disparate quadrant differs in this respect from the other quadrants. Thus, Julesz's principle again predicts correctly that Figure 3(b) should be easier than 3(a). Difficulties begin to arise, however, when we consider Figure 3(c). Here, as in 3(b), the disparate quadrant differs from the rest of the array in second order statistics; but as I pointed out earlier, the disparate quadrant is harder to locate here than in Figure 3(a) where all four quadrants agree in second order statistics. This represents a violation of Julesz's principle.

Similarly, Figure 2(a) presents difficulties for the texture explanation. The disparate quadrant of this array differs from the others in second order statistics, yet it is hard to locate this quadrant. In other words, Julesz's principle encounters the same difficulty as the sloped line detector theory did: why should Figure 2(a) yield different results from Figure 1(a)? As a final example, consider Figure 4. This Figure is a simplification of an array tested by Olson and Attneave (1970). Our tests with this array have shown, in agreement with Olson and Attneave, that the discrimination is a hard one, yielding the same order of difficulty as Figure 2(a). Yet the stimulus in the disparate quadrant differs from the others in second order statistics. Furthermore, Olson & Attneave showed that the discrimination in Figure 4 becomes much easier if the entire array is rotated 45 degrees, either clockwise or counterclockwise. (See their paper for their explanation of this phenomenon.) Since rotating an array would leave its statistical characteristics unchanged, this presents still another problem for the texture hypothesis. In summary, it appears that Julesz's principle does not do a

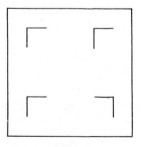

Figure 4.

good job of explaining the phenomena at hand. Perhaps these figures are not perceived as textures at all, and so their textural statistics are not important in this setting.

Conclusions

The point of this paper has been to present evidence that the sloped line detector, of the variety discovered in the mammalian cortex by Hubel and Weisel, is not the primitive of the human visual pattern recognition system. In particular, I have shown that (1) discriminations based upon line slope alone are often difficult, that (2) discriminations based upon angles and vertices are relatively easy, and that (3) angle discriminations are equally easy regardless of whether the component line segments of these angles do or do not differ in slope. Taken together, these findings suggest first that angle and vertex detectors be considered as alternative candidates for pattern primitives, and second, that these higher-order units are detected directly rather than being computed from sloped line detectors. It is interesting to note that these conclusions are in agreement with some recent physiological data, summarized by Stone (1972), that simple, complex and hypercomplex cortical cells receive input directly and in parallel from the lateral geniculate rather than following a strictly serial, hierarchical organization. Parenthetically, it might well prove informative to attempt experiments on cats and monkeys (for whom direct evidence of sloped line detectors exists) similar to those reported here.

It should be made explicit that adopting the angle of vertex as the unit of pattern recognition does not provide a panacea for theories of visual perception. The principal difficulty of feature-analytic theories of perception, which the Gestalt psychologists repeatedly emphasized, remains: namely, a pattern is more than a listing of its component parts. A complex stimulus is not simply a collection of angles any more than it is merely a collection of lines. Rather, the structural relations among these angles can be critical in differentiating between different shapes, and the human visual system is clearly sensitive to these relations.

It is possible, however, that early processing in the visual system is concerned only with the detection of primitive features, while later processing computes the structural relations among the features detected. Many theorists (Neisser, 1967; Julesz, 1975; Beck, 1972; Olson and Attneave, 1970) have distinguished between immediate perceptual process that are automatic, parallel and effortless, and secondary processes that are slow, serial and effortful. Neisser has identified these stages as 'preattention' and 'focal attention' respectively. The role of the preattentive system is to structure the perceptual field into figure and ground, and to direct attention to the specific units or figures which it isolates. The role of focal attention is to perform detailed analysis on isolated units in order to identify them. It is possible that the illustrations given in this paper demonstrate the capacities only of the preattentive system. The task with these arrays is, after all, only to isolate *where* the disparate portion of the array is located and not to identify *what* is in the array. The preattentive visual system requires some unit upon which to base its crude analysis of shape. Angles, vertices and intersections seem likely candidates for that unit.

References

Attneave, F. Triangles as ambiguous figures. *American Journal of Psychology*, 1968, **81**, 447–453.

Beck, J. Perceptual grouping produced by changes in orientation and shape. *Science*, 1966, **154**, 538–540.

Beck, J. Perceptual grouping produced by line figures. *Perception & Psychophysics*, 1967, **2**, 491–495.

Beck, J. Similarity grouping and peripheral discriminability under uncertainty. *American Journal of Psychology*, 1972, **85**, 1–19.

Beck, J. and Ambler, B. The effects of concentrated and distributed attention on peripheral acuity. *Perception & Psychophysics*, 1973, **14**, 225–230.

Blakemore, C. and Campbell, F. W. On the existence of neurones in the human visual system selectively sensitive to the orientation and size of retinal images. *Journal of Physiology*, 1969, **203**, 237–260.

Cooper, L. A. and Shepard, R. N. Chronometric studies of the rotation of mental images. In W. G. Chase (Ed.), *Visual information processing*. New York: Academic Press, 1973.

Dodwell, P. C. Pattern and object perception. In E. C. Carterette and M. P. Friedman (Eds.), *Handbook of Perception*, Volume 5. New York: Academic Press, 1975.

Guzmán, A. Decomposition of a visual scene into three-dimensional bodies. In A. Grasselli (Ed.), *Automatic Interpretation and Classification of Images*. New York: Academic Press, 1969.

Hubel, D. H. and Weisel, T. N. Receptive fields, binocular interaction and functional architecture in the cat's visual cortex. *Journal of Physiology*, 1962, **160**, 106–154.

Hubel, D. H. and Weisel, T. N. Receptive fields and functional architecture in two nonstriate visual areas (18 and 19) of the cat. *Journal of Neurophysiology*, 1965, **28**, 229–289.

Hubel, D. H. and Wiesel, T. N. Receptive fields and functional architecture of monkey striate cortex. *Journal of Physiology*, 1968, **195**, 215–243.

Julesz, B. Experiments in the visual perception of texture. *Scientific American*, 1975, **232** (April), 34–43.

Lindsay, P. H. and Norman, D. A. *Human Information Processing*. New York: Academic Press, 1972.

McCollough, C. Color adaptation of edge-detectors in the human visual system. *Science*, 1965, **149**, 1115–1116.

Milner, P. M. A model for visual shape recognition. *Psychological Review*, 1974, **81**, 521–535.

Minsky, M. and Papert, S. *Artificial intelligence progress report* (Memo No. 252). Massachusetts Institute of Technology, January, 1972.

Neisser, U. *Cognitive Psychology*. New York: Appleton-Century-Crofts, 1967.

Norman, D. A. and Rumelhart, D. E. *Explorations in cognition*. San Francisco: W. H. Freeman and Co., 1975.

Olson, R. K., and Attneave, F. What variables produce similarity grouping? *American Journal of Psychology*, 1970, **83**, 1–21.

Pomerantz, J. R. and Schwaitzberg, S. D. Grouping by proximity: selective attention measures. *Perception & Psychophysics*, 1975, **18**, 355–361.

Pritchard, R. M., Heron, W. and Hebb, D. O. Visual perception approached by the method of stabilized images. *Canadian Journal of Psychology*, 1960, **14**, 67–77.

Reed, S. K. *Psychological Processes in Pattern Recognition.* New York: Academic Press, 1973.

Richards, W. The fortification illusions of migraines. *Scientific American*, May, 1971.

Robson, J. G. Receptive fields: neural representation of the spatial and intensive attributes of the visual image. In E. C. Carterette and M. P. Friedman (Eds.), *Handbook of Perception*, Volume 5. New York: Academic Press, 1975.

Rock, I. *Orientation and form.* New York: Academic Press, 1973.

Sutherland, N. S. Object recognition. In E. C. Carterette and M. P. Friedman, (Eds.), *Handbook of Perception*, Volume 3. New York: Academic Press, 1973.

Stone, J. Morphology and physiology of the geniculocortical synapse in the cat: The question of parallel input to the striate cortex. *Investigative Ophthalmology*, 1972, **11**, 338–346.

Suppes, P. and Rottmayer, W. Automata. In E. C. Carterette and M. P. Friedman, (Eds.), *Handbook of Perception*, Volume 1. New York: Academic Press, 1974.

Yin, R. K. Looking at upside-down faces. *Journal of Experimental Psychology*, 1969, **81**, 141–145.

Chapter 11

The Subjective Properties of Complex Visual Patterns

C. D. Frith

Abstract. To what extent is it possible to relate the subjective properties of complex visual patterns to the many possible objective descriptions that are available? Subjective properties of patterns can be inferred from judgements of the similarity of pairs of patterns and from the ability to distinguish structured from random displays. The patterns consisted of matrices of black and white squares and were constructed with certain predetermined attributes which were amount of information content (in the sense of contextual constraint), amount of contour (length of edge between black and white areas) and type of symmetry (reflection, rotation and counter-change). The many other properties of the patterns were not controlled and were therefore a function of the random number generator used in their construction. The extent to which the controlled properties of the patterns fail to relate to our subjective perception of them will indicate the importance of these various uncontrolled properties.

Our subjective perception of these complex patterns seems to be least influenced by information content and most influenced by amount of contour. Paradoxically patterns with less constraint (more information) appear more similar to one another than those with more constraint. This might be because we perceive a complex pattern as a collection of features of various shapes from a rather limited set and do not code very precisely the relationships between these features. Symmetry type also strongly influences perception, but this is clearly not due to the perception of the symmetry rules themselves, but to the kinds of shapes and frameworks which these rules tend to produce. This was well known to the Islamic designers who were such masters of the art of geometric ornament. For rather than designing a subunit with certain properties and then applying symmetry rules to it as in my procedure they developed their patterns by fitting particular shapes into particular frameworks.

What is the mental representation of a complex pattern? The answer to this question is only of interest when we reach some level of representation where the correspondence with the objective pattern is not one to one. Certainly that representation of the pattern which reaches consciousness, does not have a one to one correspondence with the objective pattern. It is this relationship between the subjective and objective properties of a stimulus that the classical methods of psychophysics were designed to study. The only essential difference between the subjective perception of intensity studied by Weber and the study of the subjective impressions of complex patterns is that the patterns vary along many dimensions rather than one. In such a situation there are essentially two ways in which recoding of the objective variables into subjective variables may take place. Firstly some variables may be given less weight than others. Indeed in extreme cases they may be completely ignored. Secondly, as in the Weber-Fechner law, a single variable may be transformed or, in the multivariate case a set of variables may be transformed into a different, but equivalent set (as in orthogonal polynomials). I have concentrated on the first type of recoding, trying to discover which variables in a design are ignored and which attended to.

One major criticism of any attempt to study the perception of patterns in term of their objective properties (the criticism is usually levelled at information theoretic approaches although it applies in general) is that whenever we specify the basic units of which the pattern is composed we do this arbitrarily and can never know what units the perceiver uses. With a real life stimulus this is an insoluble problem since we genuinely do not know its composition. However, if we have constructed the stimulus we know exactly what its components are. Even if the observer does not perceive the stimulus in terms of this set of components the set he does perceive must be some kind of transformation of this original set. It is this recoding of the objective properties of a pattern into subjective properties that I shall talk about.

It is usually introspectively fairly obvious how we perceive a complex stimulus. However there are also various simple techniques available for putting these introspective speculations on a firm empirical basis. Perhaps the most convenient is to ask people to indicate the relative similarity of different patterns. This tells us something about the relative weight applied to the different objective components of the patterns. If two patterns are perceived as similar then any objective properties on which they differ must receive relatively little attention. There are other even stronger ways of showing that certain properties are not perceived which I shall describe later.

The patterns I have studied consist of matrices of 80×80 squares each of which can be black or white. However, before I can start to specify the colours of all these squares I have to make some sort of guess about which of the many possible objective properties of such a pattern are likely to be perceived by an observer. For rather than specifying exactly every square in the matrix I specified a certain number of properties and left the rest to chance. The first properties I tried were based on Information theory which has probably more influence than any other in the study of complex patterns. I took as the basic

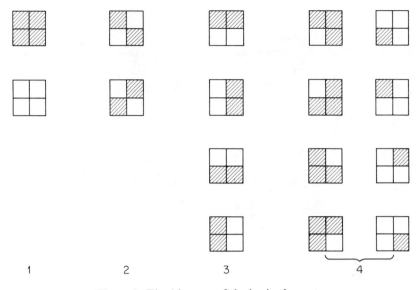

Figure 1. The 16 states of the basic elements

elements from which the stimuli would be built clusters of four adjacent squares. Since each square could be either black or white this gave a total of 16 possible basic elements. To reduce the amount of information present in the total matrix we cause some elements to occur more frequently than others. In terms of the individual squares this is equivalent to contextual constraint. Figure 1 shows the 16 basic elements divided into four classes. The members of these classes are equivalent since they are all the same configuration of squares either complemented or rotated. If we want to make patterns in which the ratio of black to white squares is 1:1 then we must ensure that complementary elements occur equally often. Equating the frequency of rotated elements ensures that the resulting pattern has no obvious 'right way up' in terms of its basic elements. Figure 2 shows some patterns constructed from these elements. Figure 2(a) has a great preponderance of elements which are either all black or all white. Figure 2(b) has a preponderance of elements which have horizontal or vertical edges. In Figure 2(d) all the elements occur with equal frequency. All the figures also have mirror symmetry, but this is just to make them easier on the eye. The only property of these figures that was predetermined was the proportion of the various basic elements. Any other properties they have are due to the operations of the pseudo random number generator used. In terms of information content Figure 2(a) and (b) has the least amount of information since it is composed of a great preponderance of one type of element. Figure 2(c) has an intermediate level of information and Figure 2(d) has the most information. However, I hope you will agree with my subjects that in terms of subjective perception Figure 2(b) is very like Figure 2(d) and not at all like Figure 2(a). Thus it seems that information content is not a major

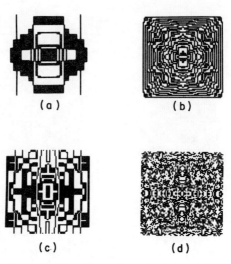

Figure 2. The effects of varying information content and type of predominant element

determinant of the subjective appearance of these patterns. The type of predominant element is clearly determining their appearance to some extent, but if
this was of major importance we might expect (b) and (d) of Figure 2 to look
more different than they do. In fact there is another simple property of the
stimuli that has been controlled almost inadvertantly which is partly independent of information content and the type of predominant element. This is the
amount of contour; that is the number of times a black square is next to a white
square or the total length of edge. Parts (b) and (d) of Figure 2 have a large and
roughly equal amount of contour and in terms of this property therefore are
similar. Figure 2(a) has very little contour. In an experiment I carried out with
David Nias we found that we could predict the subjective similarity of a number
of patterns like this very well from this simple measure of the amount of contour.

In many experiments on information content and perception amount of contour and information content have been confounded. This is obviously the
case if information content is varied by altering the number of black or white
squares in a matrix. The results of our experiment in which contour and information were partially separated suggest that in these earlier experiments it
may have been the contour rather than the information content of the stimuli
that was determining the results. This strong effect of amount of contour or
amount of edge on perception has of course been observed and commented on
before and in many species other than man. Sutherland for example has found
this effect in the rat and the octopus and Warren has observed it in cats.

I believe that this result is equivalent to Restle's finding that the basic perceptual element of binary sequences is the 'run' of identical elements. Amount
of contour, which is the number of times there is a change from one element
to another, is clearly identical to the number of 'runs'. Figure 2(b) and (d) have

a large number of such runs even though one has little and the other a lot of information. The two-dimensional equivalent of a run is a black area surrounded by white or vice versa. I would like to call it a 'detail' since I think it is the basic unit from which our perceptions of complex patterns are built. Whereas the 'run' can only vary in length the detail is much more complex since it can vary in shape.

The next figure demonstrates something about how we perceive these details. The patterns in the top row all have many details (high information, high contour). Those in the bottom row have few details (low information, low contour). Any differences between the stimuli in a row are due to the random number generator used in their construction. I hope you will agree with my subjects that those in the top row look very similar to one another whereas those in the bottom row are clearly different. You would have great difficulty in remembering an individual member of the top row. In many ways this result is paradoxical. Compared to the patterns in the bottom row those in the top row contain more information and are less constrained. This means that they are members of a much larger set of patterns. One might expect that a few patterns selected at random from a larger set would be more different from one another than patterns selected from a smaller set. Furthermore if we select two small corresponding areas from a pair of high information patterns these areas are much more likely to be different than for the low information patterns. Two small areas in the low information patterns are likely to be all black or all white which ever pattern we choose them from. Apparently this difference between corresponding areas of the high information patterns does not help our perception of them at all. This strongly suggests that we do not recognize areas as corresponding. One possibility is that we perceive such patterns in terms of a number of component details, but do not retain the absolute or relative positions of these details. Only a limited number of different details can occur and the high

Figure 3. Examples of displays characterised by high and low detail density

information patterns have so many details that all possible kinds are present and so the patterns are nearly indistinguishable. In the low information patterns only a few details are present and so they tend to be different and therefore distinguishable. This effect is exaggerated in these particular patterns due to the method of construction.Since each pattern is composed of the same total number of squares the many small details in the high information patterns are each composed of a rather small number of squares and therefore have a much more limited range of shape than the large details in the low information patterns which are made of many squares.

I have investigated this property of these patterns more directly in an experiment in which subjects had to find small discrepancies between patterns. This technique provides a more exact measure of the similarity of the designs. As you see in Figure 4 the subject was shown three patterns one of which differs slightly from the other two. Because of their mirror symmetry the centre of the designs forms a particularly outstanding detail and provides an anchor point for the eye. If the discrepancy is near the centre of the design then it is rapidly observed whether in a high contour or a low contour design (Figure 4(a) and (c)). If the discrepancy is away from the centre (the discrepancy consisted of a small area which was complimented with respect to the original design and was symmetrically placed somewhere on the diagnosis of the design) then it is much easier to find in a low contour than in a high contour design (Figure 4(b) and (d)). In fact, as Figure 5 shows, the time taken to find the discrepancy depends not on the absolute distance from the centre of the design to the discrepancy, but on the number of details (i.e. changes from black to white) intervening between the centre and the discrepancy. However there was another factor which effected the difficulty of finding discrepancies which was not under experimental control. Frequently, and this was more noticeable in the high contour patterns, there would be an outstanding detail somewhere in the design by chance. If the discrepancy involved this outstanding detail it would be easy to see wherever it was. There seem to be two reasons for a detail being outstanding in these designs. One is that the detail has a familiar and possibly verbally codeable shape. An example is the small black cross in Figure 4(d). Had the discrepancy involved this small cross it would have been much easier to find. It is no problem to scan through the three patterns and note whether or not the 'cross" is present in each. Another reason for a detail being outstanding is that it is much larger than the rest of the details in the design. In other words it is an area of low contour in a high contour design. This too can sometimes occur by chance. The operation of the mirror symmetry tends to produce such areas of low contour in the centre of the high contour designs as in Figure 4 (c). As a result the centre of this design is much more noticeable than that of Figure 4 (d).

So far then I would conclude that the patterns I have constructed are perceived as consisting of collections of details some of which may be particularly outstanding. The only subjective property of these designs that I have managed to control is the number of details of which they are composed which is a func-

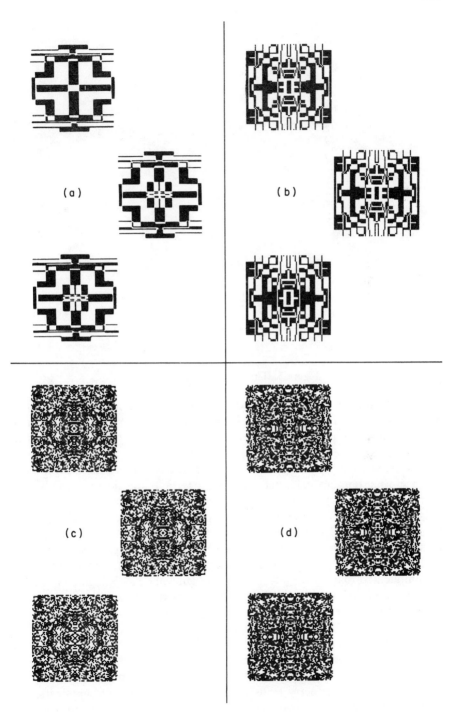

Figure 4. Searching for discrepancies

238

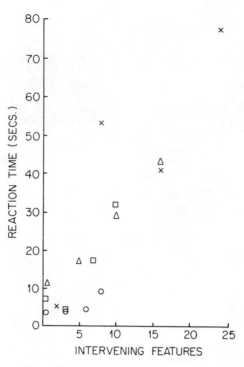

Figure 5. Time to find discrepancies.

tion of information content and amount of contour. Perhaps it is not so surprising that by controlling these properties I control so little about the subjective appearance of the patterns. For apart from these rather simple properties all other aspects of the desgins were left to chance.

This excessive influence of chance in the construction of these designs leads me to another paradoxical aspect of them. In terms of the most frequently used definition of complexity that is the information content, the most complex of these designs is the one that is most left to chance. For me a complex pattern should be one which has a very intricate structure which it is difficult to see. This is different from the random design which has no structure at all. Subjectively, of course, the two types of design will overlap since if the structure is so complicated that we cannot see it the design will be indistinguishable from one which has no structure. I therefore attempted to make patterns in which rigid structures were present and much less was left to chance.

To see a structure we must see the parts that make up the whole and the rules by which the parts are joined together. Frequently a structure is made of one part which is repeated and transformed according to various rules. Such structures based on the rules of symmetry have been widely used as decorative ornaments. Since the symmetry transformations involve the rigid application of simple geometry they are easily applied to the computer constructed patterns I have been discussing. There are three transformations which are used in generating symmetry in two dimensions in addition to the basic operation of

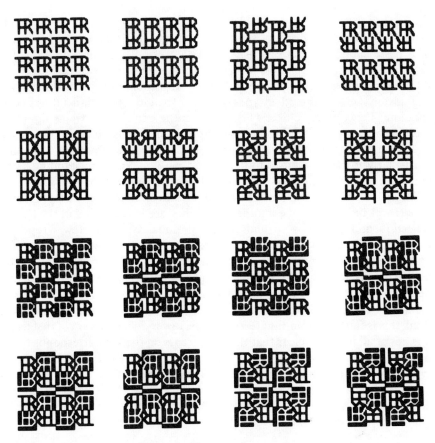

Figure 6. 16 types of symmetry

spatial translation. These are reflection, rotation and counterchange. These are illustrated in Figure 6. Mirror reflection is the most well known form of symmetry. It can appear in various forms depending upon the underlying lattice it is associated with. Four types of rotation are possible; 30°, 60°, 90° and 180°. Counterchange involves changing black areas into white and vice versa giving a chess board effect. Many of these transformations can occur in combination with one another. Figure 6 illustrates all possible types of symmetry except those involving 60° and 30° rotations which cannot be based on the rectangular lattice which is so convenient for programming. In order to construct symmetrical designs I first generated a random subunit just as in the designs I have already talked about which could have various amounts of information and contour. I then applied one of the symmetry rules. All the patterns in Figure 6 are based on the same initial subunit.

I first investigated the extent to which people could distinguish these symmetrical structures from displays generated at random. Subjects were presented with displays which had three random quadrants and one symmetrical quadrant. They had to pick out the structured quadrant. They did not have to know what the structure was to do this. As has been found in many previous experiments mirror reflection was much easier to find than simple repetition of a basic subunit. Rotations of 90 or 180° were of intermediate difficulty. However when counterchange was added to these basic transformations a very different picture emerged. Mirror reflection with counterchange no longer had any advantage over the other types of symmetry and was as difficult to find as rotation plus counterchange. This result can be explained if we assume that these designs too are seen as being composed of 'details'. It seems introspectively, that the way we solve this problem of which quadrant has structure, particularly if the problem is difficult, is to pick out some outstanding detail and search for repetitions of that detail. The quadrant that contains such repetitions is the structured one. With simple mirror reflection these repeated details will be close to one another when they are in the region of the axes of reflection and thus easy to find. With rotational symmetry fewer repeated details will be close together, those close to the axis of rotation. When the basic subunit is merely repeated without any other transformation all the repeated details will be relatively far apart. This analysis implies that we recognize details as repeated even if they have been rotated or reflected. However it seems we do not recognize details as repeated if they have been counterchanged. I think this is fairly clear in Figure 7(b). In the lower right quadrant of that figure it is not at all instantly clear that the black cross on the left corresponds to the white cross on the right. The close repeated details on each side of the axis of symmetry can no longer easily be recognized because of the operation of counterchange. The only repeated details that can still easily be recognized are those that result from the rotational symmetry that is a secondary consequence of the bilateral mirror reflection, for this is not destroyed by the counterchange. As a result mirror reflection with counterchange is as difficult to recognize as rotation with counterchange. Thus it appears that we recognize symmetrical structures by finding repeated details. Since we do not seem to attend very closely to the exact position of these details it also seems likely that we would accept as symmetrical designs that are only approximately so. Furthermore using only this very primitive method of analysis we would not be able to say what kind of symmetrical structure it was that we had recognized. In fact it is quite apparent with some designs I shall show you later

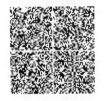

4 repeats
high contour
90° rot. + counterchange

4 repeats
high contour
mirror refl.+ counterchange

Figure 7. Searching for structure

(Figure 11) that it is easy to perceive that they are structured, but extremely difficult to discover the underlying principle of the structure in terms of the basic subunit and the symmetry rules applied.

So far then I have shown that people perceive symmetrical designs in terms of component details and can recognize them as structured if some of the repeated details are close together. This explains why some kinds of symmetry are easier to see than others. However does controlling the symmetry rules of a design also control any important subjective properties of that design? The symmetry rules certainly determine the distance apart of repeating details, but this seems to be of relatively little importance in our perception of the design as a whole. If the basic subunit and its transformations are repeated a great many times as in some decorative design for a textile or a tiled wall then it is immediately obvious that the design is structured however complex are the symmetry rules that have been applied. With 80 × 80 matrix designs I can achieve many repeats by using a much smaller basic subunit. This technique also increases the influence of the symmetry rules and reduces the effect of chance on the final result since chance plays a part only in the construction of the original subunit.

I have constructed a number of such designs using all the 16 types of symmetry already illustrated (Figure 6) and have asked people to rate them for similarity. With patterns based on high contour subunits there was considerable agreement between subjects as to which patterns were similar to one another and these groups of patterns were largely composed of a particular type of symmetry. With low contour subunits there was less agreement between subjects and the grouping of the designs was less clear cut. Nevertheless the groups that did emerge were also largely composed of particular types of symmetry. This difference between the low and high contour designs was presumably because as we have already seen the high contour subunits looked more similar to each other even before the symmetry rules were applied. The principal groups of designs were: those with 90° rotations with or without other transformations present, mirror reflections without counterchange, mirror reflections with counterchange, 180° rotations, and simple repetitions. However even though these rules would describe the majority of the designs in a particular group there were always a few striking exceptions. Figure 8 shows a particularly clear cut group of high contour designs which in general are characterized by 90° rotations. However Figure 8(a) is constructed from mirror reflection and counterchange. All subjects agreed that this design was very similar to the 90° rotation designs rather than to the other designs based on mirror reflection and counterchange. This strongly suggests that subjects do not perceive these designs as similar because they detect the 90° rotations in them, but because the 90° rotation tends to produce a particular shape or framework. However it is possible, given the appropriate basic subunit, for other symmetry rules to produce the same characteristic shape or framework. For example with this set of designs we may perceive them as consisting of roughly circular medallions with a rotating quality in a square framework. Figure 9 shows another pair of patterns that were judged similar even though

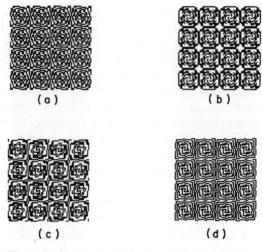

Figure 8. Similar designs with different symmetry

Figure 9. Similar designs with different symmetry

they are composed from different symmetry rules that do not normally produce similar patterns. Both are low contour designs one constructed from 180° rotations and counterchange and the other with simple repeats and counterchange. Clearly the unifying aspect in this case is the strong diagonal component. Our perception of the two designs as similar does not seem to be much effected by the fact that the repeating detail in one is symmetrical whereas in the other it is not.

I must conclude therefore that by controlling the symmetry of these designs I am still not directly controlling any major subjective properties of them. For these designs it seems that the shapes of the major details and the frameworks in which they appear are the important subjective properties of the designs and these are only indirectly determined by the symmetry rules. Particular symmetry rules tend to produce particular shapes and frameworks, but major deviations can result from the particular random subunit from which the design happens to be constructed.

I think it is now time to show some real decorative symmetrical designs instead of these ersatz computer generated versions. Perhaps the most intricate and varied decorative geometric designs were produced by Islamic artists from about the 12th century onwards. These designers produced patterns which rigidly followed the various symmetry rules even though the geometric principles underlying these rules were not yet understood. It is quite clear from their designs and their working drawings that they did not start with some basic subunit which was then repeated with the appropirate symmetry transformations. Figure 10 shows two designs that have been developed by the Persian master, Mirza Akbar, from the simple lattice shown above them. The original lattice is rich in symmetry. It has horizontal, vertical and diagonal mirror planes in addition to axes of 90° rotation. The developments reduce the richness of the symmetry, but make the structure considerably more complex. In both designs only the diagonal mirror planes have been retained and half the 90° axes have been reduced to 180° rotational axes. In the design on the left this has been achieved by the simple method of removing alternate crossing points in the original lattice. Furthermore although the symmetry of the design is clearly complex the design is in one sense simple since it contains only two details, the black windmill motif and the white dumbbell. Nevertheless the design is subjectively fairly complex probably because there is a figure-ground conflict between these two features. The design on the right has been developed from the one on the left by inserting black squares in the dumbbell figure and remov-

Figure 10. Decorative designs derived from a simple lattice

244

ing a black square from the windmill, while retaining the same symmetry principles. This effectively prevents one from perceiving the two original details and increases the number of details in the design so much that we no longer see any outstanding detail, but rather a structured texture. The large number of details probably makes this design subjectively rather complex also. In both designs we are also aware of strong diagonal components. These designs seem to have been developed by manipulating the details of which they are composed; altering their shape and size. Thus we see that the professional designer of decorative displays works in terms of the principle subjective units of these displays: the component details and the framework in which they are arranged. In some cases the designer has deliberately chosen a particular detail and exercised great ingenuity in fitting it into a symetrical framework. Islamic designers were very keen to have five- and ten-pointed stars in their displays. This is a difficult requirement since a lattice based on a five fold rotation cannot exist. However this geometrical limitation was not proved until quite recently. Figure 11 shows two ingenious solutions to this problem in which the ten pointed star is in fact incorporated into a diamond lattice with vertical, horizontal and diagonal mirror planes. There is however no axis of five or tenfold rotation although the illusion of such an axis is created.

My aim in this talk has been to describe how the objective properties of certain designs get recoded into subjective perceptual properties. I have tried to define two basic types of objective property: those which produce an obvious perceptual change when they are varied and those which do not. I assume that

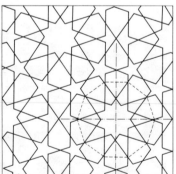

Figure 11. Decorative designs incorporating ten pointed stars

those objective properties which do affect perception in some way correspond to the subjective properties of the designs. Figure 12 shows a list of the properties that I have either directly or indirectly varied and their effects on perception. Some of the results are very clear cut. It seems that the position of a detail is not an important subjective property of a design whereas the shape of a detail is. Also whereas repeated details are readily perceived if they are rotated or reflected, they are not easily perceived if they are counterchanged. Other results are less clear. Changing the information content of a design may produce a large perceptual change, but in certain circumstances does not. This is because this objective property of the design indirectly effects another property, the amount of contour. This latter property which is equivalent to the number of details in a design strongly effects our perception and probably directly corresponds to a subjective property. Similarly changing the symmetry of a design usually produces a change in our perception of the design, but does not always do so. Once again this is because the type of symmetry only indirectly affects those objective properties that correspond to subjective properties. The properties that symmetry seems to be indirectly controlling are the framework or lattice on which the design is based and possibly the shapes of some of the details.

I would conclude then that any coding scheme for describing complex patterns, must, if it is to correspond to the code actually used by people in their perception of the pattern, retain information about the details in the design: the density of the details, their shape and their 'outstandingness'. The code must also allow for the fact that only certain kinds of repeated details will be recognized and must preserve the distinction between figure and ground. Finally the code must retain information about the framework or lattice (if any) within which the details are arranged.

OBJECTIVE PROPERTIES VARIED	EFFECTS ON PERCEPTION
Information content	+ −
Type of predominant element	+ −
Contour (number of details)	+ +
Position of details	−
Shape of details	+
Shape of outstanding details	+ +
Structural complexity (symmetry)	+ +
(equivalent to separation of repeated details)	
Repeated details reflected	+ +
Repeated details rotated	+ +
Repeated details counterchanged	−
Symmetry type	+ −
Framework or lattice	+ +

Figure 12

246

Bibliography

Christie, A. H. (1969). *Pattern design*. New York, Dover.

Deregowski, J. B. (1971). Symmetry, Gestalt and information theory. *Quarterly Journal of Experimental Psychology*, **23**, 381–385.

Frith, C. D., and Nias, D. K. B. (1974). What determines aesthetic preferences? *Journal of General Psychology*, **91**, 163–173.

Julesz, B. (1971). *Foundations of Cyclopean perception*. Chicago: University of Chicago Press.

Restle, F. (1966). Run structure and probability learning: Disproof of Restle's model. *Journal of Experimental Psychology*, **72**, 282–289.

Sutherland, N. S. (1960). Visual discrimination of shape by Octopus: Open and closed forms. *Journal of Comparative and Physiological Psychology*, **53**, 104–112.

Warren, J. M., and McGonigle, B. D. (1969). Perimeter, complexity and generalization of a form discrimination by cats. *Psychonmic Science*, **17**, 16–17.

Weyl, H. (1952). *Symmetry*. Princeton: Princeton University Press.

Chapter 12

Relativity and Organization in Visual Size Judgements

F. Restle

Abstract. A version of Adaptation-Level theory has been used to account for some of the illusions in visual size perception, using a general principle of relativity or contrast. One particular kind of experimental result is reviewed, which seems not to agree with this sort of theory. A model using a weighted-average formula for adaptation-level, but asserting that the weight of an object in the field depends on the size of that object, is formulated and shown to agree closely with the data. It corresponds closely to Sarris' formulation. The more general question is then asked, What controls the weights in such a field? Two general theories are outlined, one based on set-theory and probabilities, the other based on an hierarchical model. The two theories represent extremes of the degree of organization of the perceived field.

The purpose of this paper is to develop certain conceptions of visual perception in the form of a mathematical model. Some of the formal structures invoked have been used in mathematical learning theory, and in fact they have been the basis of the perceptual theory in discrimination learning. The present development is concerned, not with learning or the solution of a conceptual problem, but instead with the subject's effort to make size judgements.

As you all know, one great difficulty in formulating a mathematical theory of perception is that there is a huge literature about perception, and within it are many studies to disprove almost any theory one might formulate. In particular, it is difficult to formulate a simple theory that says anything in particular about detailed perceptual data, and is not also disproved by many well documented observations. One reason may be that our theories are too simple, and we must take more factors into account, perhaps in a more complicated way, than we have in the past. If so, this is a justification for the mathematical approach. Another possibility is that we have not developed our theories far enough and made sufficiently serious efforts to fit the detailed quantitative results of experiments.

This paper will continue a series of studies we have been presenting, based upon Helson's Adaptation-Level theory and applied to size judgements, especially to judgements within various contexts that give rise to optico-geometric illusions. First I shall outline our version of Adaptation-Level (AL) theory and derive the basic equations needed for our later analysis. Second, I shall show some of the indications that the weights in the adaptation-level formula are not constants, but instead are dependent variables. Third, I shall develop a rather simple set-theoretic treatment of these weights, and indicate several predictions that can be made. Fourth, I shall develop the hypothesis that a simple set-theoretic model cannot handle highly organized fields, and I shall introduce an hierarchical approach to such problems.

The Role of Weights in Adaptation-Level Theory

The adaptation-level theory says that the judgement of a test stimulus of size X will be given by

$$J(X) = X/A \qquad (1)$$

where A is the adaptation level. Suppose that the situation contains several background elements of size B_1, B_2, etc., which are varied by the experimenter, and then some aggregation of other factors having a net magnitude of K. Then the adaptation level is the weighted geometric mean of all of these factors;

$$A = \left[B_1 \; w_{B_1} \cdot B_2 \; w_{B_2} \cdot K^{w_k} \right] 1/(w_{B_1} + w_{B_2} + w_{B_3}) \qquad (2)$$

Here it is to be understood that A is the adaptation-level for the stimulus X, and that each weight depends upon the relationship between X and the stimulus having that weight.

If we take logarithms and combine Equations 1 and 2,

$$\log J(X) = \log X - \frac{1}{w_{B_1} + w_{B_2} + w_K} \left[\sum w_{B_i} \log B_i + w_K \log K \right] \qquad (3)$$

where the summation is over the two background stimuli. Equation (3) states that $J(X)$ is a decreasing power function of each of the variable background elements B_i.

This theory predicts that if the w_{B_i} are constant, $J(X)$ will decrease as each of the background elements is increased, and the decrease will follow a negative power function.

When the observer is instructed to judge the length of a line, his first question must be, 'With respect to what'? A relativistic theory of perception assumes that any judgement must be relative to something. Instructions in these experiments do not specify any particular stimulus as the sole frame of reference, so the observer or set of observers exhibit some distribution of attention over background objects. That is to say, the observer compares the test shaft with these various objects, and there is a probability or relative weight for each such object. The weight of each object B_i is w_{B_i}, in this model.

In the first experiment we did, Restle and Merryman (1969) tested this hypothesis by having subjects judge the length of a horizontal test shaft with a square box at each end. The shaft length X ranged from 4 to 14 cm, and the boxes took a similar range. Generally speaking, an increase in box size led to a lower judgement of the test shaft $J(X)$, and the whole body of data could be described by the model given above. We estimated that the boxes constituted about ·10 of the total attention—this came from the observation that $J(X)$ was a power function of B, and the power was about − ·10.

Our interpretation is that perception of the length of the line is not distorted in this experiment, but that the nearby boxes serve an important role in the frame of reference. The estimated weight of the boxes, w_B, varied from ·093 to ·138 depending upon how we handled the data. In the particular experiment, the projection screen was quite large (130 cm on a side) and the room was dimly illuminated without salient features. As a result, we believe that the observers were forced to rely upon the boxes for about 10% of their frame of reference, even in the face of the obvious fact that the boxes varied in size from trial to trial and therefore did not constitute a stable frame of reference. The other 90% of the weight must, by equation (2), be the parameter w_K, which is the weight of the constant factors in the field—the screen, door, wall, etc. Also included in these constant factors would be memories of past stimuli, if those enter into the judgements. All such factors are constant or randomly variable from trial to trial and therefore contribute to veridicality of judgement.

Merryman and Restle (1970) studied the Baldwin figure, consisting of a line having a large box at one end and a small box at the other, and a hashmark near the middle. Following Baldwin's (1895) approach we hypothesized that each half line would be affected primarily by the box nearer it, so that the half-line near the larger box would have a higher adaptation level and would appear shorter. The result would be that the hashmark would appear displaced nearer the larger box, because the distance is judged smaller. A highly consistent illusion was found, in that the hashmark was consistently displaced toward the larger box, and the magnitude of the illusion depended directly upon the ratio of sizes of boxes. Furthermore, if we take parameters from the first experiment and apply them to this one, we can predict the actual small magnitude of the illusion almost exactly.

These preliminary results merely give the outline of the old, simple AL theory and some simple experimental results that agree with it quite well.

Factors Influencing the Weights w_{B_i}

The theory says that the parameters w_{B_i} constitute a distribution of attention across various parts of the figure. In fact, however, we have merely plotted $J(X)$ as a function of B_i, in log-log coordinates, and estimated the slope of the line. We need some further basis to substantiate the idea that these slopes have anything to do with attention. Let us consider how we might influence the subject to use a certain part of the field B_i in judging test shaft X.

First, one can get a subject to use B_i by moving it close to the end of the test line, and one can reduce his tendency to use it by moving it farther away. Restle and Merryman (1968) had observers judge the length of a test line with boxes that were right at the ends of the test shaft, or were separated from it by small gaps. The figures were judged by the rating-scale method. It was expected, from the attention interpretation, that w_{B_i}, the weight of the box, would decrease with d, the distance the box was from the ends of the test line. We used test shafts of 13, 16, or 19 cm, and boxes of size 6·4, 13, or 19 cm. The gap between test line and box was 0, 1·6, 3·2, 6·4, or 13 cm. Each configuration was judged 65 times by nine experienced observers. It was found that the estimated w_{B_i} decreased as the gap increased, taking values ·089, ·052, ·055, ·043, and ·032 for the five increasing gaps. This result coincides with our expectation, based on the hypothesis that less attention was given to boxes farther from the end of the test shaft.

A second way to vary the subjects' attention to a context figure is to make it more or less similar to the test object. Coren and Miller (1974) tested the apparent size of a test circle surrounded by small or large inducing figures. The inducing figures could be circles, hexagons (which appear quite similar to the circles), triangles which appear quite dissimilar, or jagged 'random' shapes that were rated as very dissimilar to the test circles. Using their data we obtained rough estimates of w_B, the weight of the four surrounding figures on the test circle. The four shapes had equally-spaced values of rated similarity from an earlier experiment, and the estimated values of w_B were ·055, ·044, ·021, and ·009. Clearly, dissimilar objects get less attention, and furthermore, the trend is smooth and may perfectly well be a linear function of judged similarity.

A third way to affect the weights of various parts of the field, according to the attention hypothesis, is merely to instruct the observer to use one part of the field as his frame of reference, and to ignore another part. Other subjects are given the switched instructions, being told to use the cues that were to be ignored by the other group. Although this experimental approach seems almost brutally direct, it has the advantage that the weight of part of the field is changed without any change in the stimulus display. This eliminates any hypothesis that the change in weight depends upon some subtle change in the display. When subjects were told to use part of the field as frame of reference, its weight was ·18. When they were told to ignore it, its weight was only ·05. (Restle, 1971).

These early experimental results make it clear that the adaptation-level is not some absolute constant, but instead depends upon the conditions of the experiment in such a way that one can think of the AL as the main dependent variable. Furthermore, the weights of each of the parts of the field are not constants, but instead depend on the arrangement of the field, on general properties such as similarity, and on cognitive and intentional factors that can control the process of sampling.

What Happens When Weight Depends upon Magnitude of the Stimulus

The above results are all established by simple experiments, and although they can be denied by simply denying the theory, there is no ambiguity of interpretation given that the general framework of the theory is accepted. The reason is that in the above cases, there was a way of varying propinquity, similarity, or instructions independent of other stimulus properties. However, it also seems possible that small stimuli may generally get small weights and large stimuli may get large weights. If this is true, then two quite different theoretical quantities, B and its weight w_B, may vary at the same time and cannot be extricated. In studies using anchoring stimuli (which do in fact avoid the confounding mentioned above) Sarris showed that an anchor is most effective if it is approximately the same size as the test stimulus, and is less effective if it is either much larger or much smaller.

This seems like a possiblity, and one that should not be too complicated to understand. Unfortunately, at least for our rather simple theoretical program, the Sarris hypothesis can cause a lot of trouble. In the experiments described above, we estimated the weight w_B by varying the size of the stimulus B and then plotting $\log J(X)$ as a function of $\log B$. Theoretically, the slope of that function is $-w_B$. However, the validity of such an estimation method depends upon the assumption that w_B is a constant with respect to variations in B. If we consider conditions in which w_B depends upon B, then the slope is no longer constant, and is not a valid estimate of w_B (which is of course not a constant, either).

Our investigation of this problem began with receipt of a manuscript by John Clavadetscher and Norman H. Anderson (1977) in which they critically analysed several predictions of the AL model. In one of their experiments they studied the judgement of a test shaft with a square box at each end, and varied the box sizes over a wide range, from very small to quite large. They found an 'inverted-U' function, in that $J(X)$ increased with box size up to a certain value, about one-fourth of the length of X, and then decreased with further enlargement of the boxes. In fact, the line with boxes was generally judged longer than a comparable comparison line without boxes. Thus, as they correctly noted, the result is doubly incompatible with a simple contrast theory. First, boxes at the end do not decrease, but instead increase the apparent length of the test shaft. A contrast theory should say the opposite. Second, at least when the box is small, increasing the size of the box causes the test shaft to increase, not decrease. This trend is in the wrong direction for any contrast theory. In fact, the results are generally in agreement with an 'assimilation' interpretation, except that the large boxes apparently cause the shaft to look small.

We have looked into this possibility rather closely, Restle (1977). The Clavadetscher and Anderson result, which is superficially a disproof of the principle of relatively used in AL theory, is certainly reproducible, and we have repeated it with several variations in our laboratory. We have found that on closer consideration, this result is quite understandable from our AL point of view. First, consider the basic formula for adaptation-level when there are no boxes at all. The only factor is K, and therefore

$$A = K$$

which is the special case of equation (2) when B_1 and B_2 do not come into consideration. However, another way of thinking of the same display is of a line having boxes of length zero, that is to say, setting $B_1 = B_2 = 0$. However, in equation (2), this would immediately set $A = 0$. The only way out of this conclusion is to say that when the boxes B_i go to zero, their weights w_{B_i} also go to zero.

Now consider an experiment like that of Clavadetscher and Anderson, in which very small values of B are employed. If $J(X)$ is a continuous function of the background magnitude B, then in the limit as B approaches 0, its weight also approaches 0. This suggests that in general, and at least for small values of B,

$$w_B = f(B)$$

with the bounding condition that $f(0) = 0$.

Following Sarris (1975) we suppose that when B is smaller than X, the weight of B is a function of B/X; when B is larger than X, it is a function of X/B. Working from this hypothesis, with various technical specifications, we were able to calculate the inverted-U function obtained by Clavadetscher and Anderson, and similar functions obtained by us. We have obtained very good agreement between theory and data, but the project of simplifying the theory and optimizing the fits, and then of developing statistical evaluations of the fit, is not completed. However, I may say that we have found it quite possible to fit the obtained data quite exactly to the eye, getting maxima in the right location and of the correct magnitude, while using parameters that have reasonable values.

The result of this last set of calculations is an interesting reversal. The data appeared, at first, to disprove AL theory. When we were able finally to calculate good fits to the data, we found that the model illustrates a characteristic of AL theory in our investigations, namely that the AL depends upon the weights of many factors in the field, and these weights depend on all sorts of experimental manipulations; at least, now, we know that they depend upon propinquity, similarity, intention, and on the magnitude of the stimulus itself. Such results make it somewhat more complicated to establish the validity of the AL model, but they make it an interesting instrument for designing and analysing experimental data.

Theory of Weights in the Adaptation Level

Adaptation-Level theory gives a systematic and quantitative way of relating judgements to the stimuli in the field and their weights, but in itself it provides no theory of what the weights will be. AL theory can 'fit' a rather wide variety of data, provided that one allows the weight parameters w to vary appropriately. Actually, AL theory makes predictions only in conjunction with some theory of the weights. The standard assumption has been that these weights are constant within the given experiment. This assumption is tenable if the experimenter is careful to use very simple and standardized displays, and to vary his stimuli only within a narrow range. In general, however, the assumption of constant weights is suicidal, and in conjunction with this hypothesis the AL theory makes many wrong predictions. An alternative approach would be to say that the weights w can vary as a function of various parameters of the experiment. The trouble with this alternative is that it permits the AL theory to fit nearly anything, and so weakens its predictions that it becomes almost untestable, and certainly uninteresting. Using this approach, the experimenter merely uses AL theory to reduce his data.

It seems, at least at this point in the history of the study of perception, that it will be extremely difficult to make predictions of weights in a completely *a priori* fashion, but it may be possible to predict the systems of weights in a certain set of fields if we have already measured weights in related fields. The general purpose of a theory of this kind is to permit predictions of the weights in a complex field, given that the weights of components in simpler fields have already been estimated. If successful, such a theory can be of great practical and experimental value, for it permits the investigator to take his desired measurements in simple and convenient settings, and then to predict performance in more complicated and important, but perhaps inaccessible, situations.

The Set-Theoretic or One-Level Model

One approach to this problem of predicting weights is to employ a mathematical approach from learning theory. In Estes' stimulus-sampling theory, the stimulus situation is conceived of as a set of elements. In hypothesis-sampling theory of discrimination learning (Restle, 1961; Trabasso and Bower, 1968; Levine, 1966) the subject is confronted with a set of hypotheses or possible modes of action. In learning theory, simple set theory was used to make many predictions of rate of learning, transfer-of-training, and related phenomena.

By analogy, let us formulate a set-theoretic model of a subject who is trying to judge test-shaft X in a given context. He has about him (and perhaps in his memory) a set of stimuli with which X might be compared, and each of these is an element of the situation. The total situation can be partitioned into subsets B_1, B_2, etc., with a residual K. We assume that there is a measure function m on the subsets of stimuli.

If we assume that separate context stimuli correspond to disjoint sets of stimulus elements, then we can make exact predictions regarding additivity of stimuli. Consider an experiment with one background stimulus, for example, a box at one end of a test shaft. By varying box size we carefully estimate its weight, and obtain a value w_{B_1}. With equal care we estimate the weight of a box at the other end of the line, w_{B_2}. Each of these is, of course, a relative weight. If we assume that the measure of $\mathbf{B}_1$ is $m(\mathbf{B}_1)$, and the measure of the constant factors is $m(\mathbf{K})$, then the experiment has estimated

$$w_{B_1} = m(\mathbf{B}_1)/(m(\mathbf{B}_1) + m(\mathbf{K}))$$

and

$$w_{B_2} = m(\mathbf{B}_2)/(m(\mathbf{B}_2) + m(\mathbf{K})).$$

Now suppose that we put boxes at both ends of the test shaft and estimate the weight of the concatenated boxes. This third experiment has a set of stimuli B given by

$$\mathbf{B} = \mathbf{B}_1 \cup \mathbf{B}_2$$

and if we can assume that $\mathbf{B}_1$ and $\mathbf{B}_2$ are disjoint, then

$$m(\mathbf{B}) = m(\mathbf{B}_1) + m(\mathbf{B}_2)$$

This means that the relative weight of these boxes is $m(\mathbf{B})$ relative to $m(\mathbf{K})$, that is,

$$w_B = m(\mathbf{B})/(m(\mathbf{B}) + m(\mathbf{K})) = (m(\mathbf{B}_1) + m(\mathbf{B}_2))/(m(\mathbf{B}_1) + m(\mathbf{B}_2) + m(\mathbf{K}))$$

A little algebra shows that

$$w_B = \frac{w_{B_1} + w_{B_2} - 2w_{B_1} w_{B_2}}{1 + w_{B_1} w_{B_2}}$$

which is a prediction of the estimated weight of two boxes together, given weights for each separately. Notice that this model does not predict that the raw illusions will add, nor even that the numerical weights of the two boxes add directly. In fact, the predicted weight will be somewhat smaller than the sum of the separate weights. For example, if each weight is estimated at $\cdot 05$, then the two boxes together will have a relative predicted weight of $\cdot 0952$, slightly smaller than the sum of the weights, $\cdot 10$.

The experimental problem with testing this prediction centres around the difficulty of estimating w_B with sufficient accuracy, in this case, so as to discriminate a discrepancy corresponding to 1/20th part of the estimate itself. We have not yet carried out this experiment, though it is feasible.

A second related application of the theory would study the effect of competition of two different sources of cues. For example, one can study the effect of boxes at the ends of the test shaft in two situations; one having a framework drawn around the whole field, the other not. By varying the size of the framework we can gain an estimate of its weight when it is present, and we assume zero weight when it is absent.

In effect, we then compare the weight of the boxes when there is a frame, w_{B_F} with the weight of the same boxes when there is no frame, $w_{B_{\bar{F}}}$. Both involve the same $m(\mathbf{B})$ and $M(\mathbf{K})$, but they differ with respect to whether they contain reference to $m(\mathbf{F})$. In simple form,

$$w_{B_F} = m(\mathbf{B})/(m(\mathbf{B}) + m(\mathbf{K}) + m(\mathbf{F}))$$

and

$$w_{B_{\bar{F}}} = m(\mathbf{B})/(m(\mathbf{B}) + m(\mathbf{K}))$$

The qualitative prediction, of course, is that the box will have greater weight without the frame than with it. The quantitative prediction becomes possible when one has already evaluated the weight of the framework by performing experiments varying F and having no box present, for they permit estimating

$$w_F = m(\mathbf{F})/(m(\mathbf{F}) + m(\mathbf{K}))$$

With this information it is a matter of elementary algebra to compute exact predictions for w_{B_F} given $w_{B_{\bar{F}}}$:

Somewhat more experimental leverage is obtained by using a more complex situation in which a number of stimuli can be combined, instead of only two. An example is the figure sometimes called Titchener's circles, in which a test circle is surrounded by a ring of other circles, for in such an experiment one can vary the number of surrounding circles. Furthermore, the symmetry of the display suggests that all the surrounding or inducing circles will have much the same weight, so one can make a simplifying assumption that all surrounding circles have weight $m(\mathbf{C})$. Then by varying all of n circles together, one can see the power of the illusion increase, and by varying one independently of the others one can observe its influence wane the more competitors are introduced.

If there are n circles each having a measure of $m(\mathbf{C})$, then the total relative influence or weight of all of them is given by

$$w = \frac{n\, m(\mathbf{C})}{n\, m(\mathbf{C}) + m(\mathbf{K})}$$

If we measure the weight of just one of the circles by varying it independent of the others, we expect that

$$w = \frac{m(\mathbf{C})}{n\, m(\mathbf{C}) + m(\mathbf{K})}$$

From an experiment with a single circle one can measure the weight of that circle, which is $m(\mathbf{C})/(m(\mathbf{C}) + m(\mathbf{K}))$. Knowing this weight, it is possible to calculate the numerical weights expected for configurations with more circles.

It may be expected that the above predictions will hold provided that accurate estimates of the weights can be obtained. Obviously, if the experimental parameters vary over a wide range, it must be expected that the corresponding weights will vary, and therefore that simple estimation methods will be inadequate. The only method currently available is to restrict the ranges of stimulus parameters to the middle values, so that the measures are at least almost constant.

Hierarchical Theory of Weights

The set-theoretic model given above is not perfect. One major difficulty with it is that it takes no account of the three-dimensional character of the visual world, and merely operates in terms of a single set of 'cues'. The theory does not tell us to use distal measurements (i.e. that the subject is looking at a 4-cm line) or proximal ($2°$ of visual angle). This can make quite a difference if different parts of the field are at different distances. One might say that objects at different distances constitute separate subsets, but this would mean that the power of the analysis would reside, not in the formal operations of the set-theoretic model, but in various subtleties of its interpretation.

However, the problem is not concerned only with distance—the set-theoretic analysis simply takes no serious formal account of the organization of the visual field. By having all information enter into the set of stimulus elements in the same way, such an approach does not make use of what is known about perceptual organization. However, organizational theories are notoriously unable to integrate themselves with methods of detailed quantitative analysis.

The effort in this section of the paper is to carry ideas from learning theory, more accurately, from cognitive psychology, into the problem of perception of organized fields. The central idea is that perception will depend upon a cognitive structure or organization, and that the various stimulus elements in the field act only through their logical place in that structure.

Although there are many forms of cognitive structure, one of the most widely studied is that of an hierarchical structure, and particularly the tree structure. By this I do not mean that we shall divide the stimulus elements into two halves, and then each of these halves into smaller parts, etc. This would result in a kind of tree structure but it would not be truly hierarchical, since the elements at the top of the tree are very much like the elements at the bottom. Instead, I shall use an approach in which the highest hierarchical level is occupied by the most general and profound distinctions, whereas lower levels are occupied by surface classifications.

First, consider the organization of a plane display, of the sort usually considered by Gestalt Psychology and of the sort used in studies of geometric illusions. First, such a display can generally be divided into figure and ground, and this is a relatively general and profound analysis. Therefore, at the top of the hierarchical analysis, we set the division into figure and ground.

Before I go into other levels of organization, let me make two comments about the use of the figure-ground distinction in this paper. First, I am not offering at this time a theory of what the subject will consider figure and what he will treat as ground. It is true that small, compact, highly contrasting, symmetrical figures tend to be seen as figure more than their opposites. However, as is well known, one can intentionally reverse figure-ground relationships and 'look at' what would otherwise be the ground. The theory put forward here attempts to specify the consequences of a given cognitive structure—if the figure-ground organization is such-and-so, then the system of judgements of X will vary in a certain way. Second, I am not able to give a complete and general specification of all of the consequences of a given figure-ground analysis, and I feel that this is a special theoretical question. My point is that figure-ground analysis has priority and is at the top of the cognitive structure or hierarchy of analysis of a plane visual display.

A figure, in turn, may be divided into two aspects, its contour and its area. In the case of a circle drawn on a piece of paper, for example, the contour is the line and the area is merely the space within the line. The two are different in that a person may be asked to judge how large the circle is, or to judge the curvature of its contour. Sometimes the analysis of a figure may involve application of such a principle in a rather indirect way. Consider, for example, a display consisting of a row of ten circles in a circle. This whole group of circles may be the figure, in which case its contour is made up of the little circles, and its area is the space within. Obviously, in a case like this, the contour can be further analysed into its parts.

Is it always true that a figure can be analysed into contour and area? Perhaps not, particularly if the figure is merely a loose cluster of little stimuli, with no clear contour, or if it is effectively a point or dot with no contour and no inner area. The point is not that every figure can always be analysed into contour and area, but that such an analysis is commonly applicable, and if it does apply, it of course applies just after or just below the figure-ground analysis. In fact, one may ask if all displays can be analysed into figure and ground, and must agree that a ganzfeld, or a featureless field of grass, may in a sense lack a figure-ground analysis.

Let us consider the contour of a figure. In the typical line drawing, this contour may consist of straight line segments, corners, and curves. The approach by which such elements may be combined, hierarchically, into a complex contour, has been elucidated by Leeuwenberg (1971). Some contours, like that of a circle, are very simple for they lack segments and corners, and have only a single degree of curvature. Squares, triangles, and other equilateral polygons are made up of a set of equal segments and equal bends. Figures that are convex may have complex contours, but at least they have relatively simple and easily identified areas. There is now considerable information available about the complexity of various 'random' shapes, and this complexity depends upon the number of line segments and bends, on the degree to which they are unequal, on the variations in curvature, etc.

The ground, in many displays, can be characterized by its orientation and its texture. It is believed, at least by Gibson, that grounds in such displays have the character of surfaces, and the orientation and texture of a surface are important properties. From this statement it is obvious that the area of a figure, that which is enclosed by the contour, is often characterized by its orientation and texture, and therefore has the same analysis as a ground.

Furthermore, a figure may be analysed into a set of elements, provided that the figure in a display is not singular but multiple, as in the example of a circle of small circles. In general, whenever the figure in a drawing is a family, a bunch of flowers, etc., the analysis should identify the figure but then analyse it into a set, which in turn can be analysed into its elements.

It was mentioned above, in the circle of circles, that a contour can also be analysed into a set. The property of 'good continuation' in Gestalt psychology arises whenever a contour exists in the cognitive structure, but is made up of a set of elements.

In addition, the texture of a surface or ground can in many cases be analysed into the set of elements that make it up, as the texture of a field of wheat can be analysed into individual plants, or a stippled background into its dots or clusters of dots.

A similar analysis can be made of displays in three dimensions—the figure-ground analysis remains essentially the same, and the ground remains a surface, but the figure may in this case be analysed not into contour and area, but rather into surface and contents. Also, of course, the arrangement of parts may include relationships of being behind or in front, rather than just above, below, and to the side. Development of such cognitive structures for visual displays is, however, beyond my powers at this time, though I believe it may be an important and unsolved problem.

In the above analysis, the reader may have noticed that I have introduced only metric properties—I have not mentioned the colour of surfaces, or such optical properties as transparancy, or such physical properties as the substantiality of a pig of iron as contrasted with a fog. The reason is that my goal, in sketching this theory of organization, is to relate it to the problem of optical illusions.

The first thing the reader may notice is that the hierarchical approach to cognitive structure supplements the set-theoretic model in useful ways. To keep the weights constant, in set-theoretic analysis, we had to keep the dimensions of the figures within a rather close range. Why? Obviously, one reason is that when a figure is changed drastically, as when one changes from very small boxes to very large boxes at the ends of a test shaft, one may easily induce a change in the organization of that display. In one display the shaft may be seen as figure with the boxes part of the surround, and in another display the shaft plus boxes may be the figure.

Also, in experiments in which parts of the display are removed, as in the additivity experiments, it is possible that the organization of the whole display may change. For example, consider Titchener's circles, a test circle surrounded by either small or large circles. One experiment suggested above would change the number of surrounding circles, and measure the effects on the illusion. However, if one has less than three surrounding circles, and particularly if there is only one, it can hardly be said to 'surround' the test circle. When there are seven or eight surrounding the test circle, the property of surrounding is very strong. In the analysis given above, the ring of seven inducing circles itself constitutes a circle whose contour is made up of the individual inducing circles. This means that the test circle lies within the area of this ring. When one drops down to only one or two inducing circles, then at most the inducing circles might form a line, but certainly not a ring—that whole element of the analysis is missing. This means that the test circle cannot be thought to be within this area.

Thus, the hierarchical analysis of visual displays can at the least serve as a complete theoretical basis for a system of 'bounding conditions' on the set-theoretic model. It is reasonable to suppose that the set-theoretic model will hold, at least to a close approximation, if the experimental variations do not require a change in the observer's cognitive structure. Also, then, one would expect observers to give comparable results when judging such a display, provided that they have equivalent cognitive structures.

If the bounding conditions are violated, experimental results may be obtained that appear paradoxical, and such paradoxes, until resolved, tend to paralyse the development of quantitative theory. I have recently studied the effect of figure-ground organization in the display called, by Morinaga, his 'Paradox of Displacement'. The display consists of pairs of wings pointing in and out, alternately, as in the famous Müller-Lyer arrow-head illusion, in which the shafts are missing. This, it is well known, does not decrease the Müller-Lyer illusion. An example of the display is shown as Figure 1.

If one looks at this and compares the distance between points of the angles, it seems that when the angles point outward they are also farther apart, and when the angles wings point inward, they seem close together. Then, one can shift his attention and look down the row of apexes of the angles, and see if they appear to be aligned. The answer is that they do not, and by a substantial constant error. However, surprisingly, it turns out that the angles appear to overlap, somewhat like clenched teeth. Careful consideration shows that this is exactly the opposite of the illusion seen when the distance between angles was compared. Thus, exactly the same display produces two opposite illusions, depending upon how the observer views it.

We developed the hypothesis that the difference between the two modes of viewing was the result of different figure-ground organizations of the same display. In the case of the Müller-Lyer organization, the subject interprets the display of consisting of four subfigures each consisting of an opposite pair of wings, paired horizontally. The subject judges the length of one subfigure and

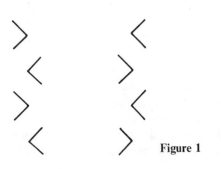

Figure 1

then another, and compares the lengths. When the subject is then asked whether the apexes of the angles are vertically aligned, the display is divided into two subfigures, one on the left and the other on the right. Then one of these sub-configurations is analysed into figure and ground. The figure is a pathway down the figure, between the angles. This figure is bounded by the angles. When the points of the angles are actually aligned perfectly, the pathway must bend back and forth and the observer sees the angles as overlapping slightly.

Our experiment Restle (1976) showed that this second illusion occurs in full force when only the left half of the figure is displayed, and the illusion when measured by the method of adjustment is quite substantial in magnitude, near one-fourth of the length of the wings.

To verify our idea that the Morinaga displacement effect depends upon organizing the figure as a vertical pathway, we modified the display by adding stems to the angles so that each would look like the letter 'Y' lying down. This display effectively disrupts the organization, and one can no longer see a pathway bordered by wings. We thought that this might reduce or remove the illusion, and in fact it completely obliterated and partly reversed the Morinaga displacement effect in our data.

In summary, the hierarchical model provides an account of the organization of the visual field. This in turn permits us to predict certain situations in which the set-theoretic model will not be successful, and gives some ground for understanding paradoxical effects. It is true that we need more than this—we need some way to go from the organization of a field to experimental data. It would appear, for example, that the size of a test shaft or test circle is judged mainly with respect to other figures that lie above it in the hierarchical cognitive structure—that a part is judged with respect to the whole more than the whole is judged with respect to its parts. It would appear that a test object is judged with respect to properties just above it in the tree rather than things which are over in some remote branch of the cognitive structure. Unfortunately, though these conjectures lead toward a quantitative theory of the weights in a field as a function of the hierarchical cognitive structure, I have not been able to formulate such a theory.

Relation of the Two Theories of Weights

The set-theoretic model projects an image of the visual field as completely without organization, and the hierarchical model described above describes a field with a single, unified, and rather rigid structure. However, most visual displays do not show a perfect hierarchical organization, at least to most viewers most of the time, nor are they entirely without structure. The set-theoretic and the hierarchical models both seem, at least to my intuition, too extreme to be realistic for the analysis of most of the experimental data on perception we may find in the literature or collect in our laboratories.

If we follow the scientific methodology currently in vogue we must attempt to decide between the two theories, or find a third theory preferable to both.

However, I should like to put forward the position that the set-theoretic and the hierarchical models represent two theoretical descriptions of seeing, and in fact two modes of visual perception. The problem is not so much one of deciding between the two theories as it is one of integrating them, so as to have a more complete understanding of visual perception.

The conflict is not merely one between two arcane mathematical models of psychophysical judgements, or two theories of geometrical illusions. In one mode of perception, where the observer has a very clear idea of what he expects to see, every piece of visual information fits into a well-organized cognitive structure. Subjects are relatively quick to recognize objects, and can make very fine and consistent discriminations. Their one weakness is that they are vulnerable to various tricks and illusions, for they will tend to force ambiguous stimuli into congruence with their organized structure. It is difficult, in this mode, to see the unexpected, and any change in organization is accompanied by massive restructuring. This is the mode of perception associated with Gestalt psychology.

In another mode of perception the observer is searching, and is willing to take in any information available, but in consequence he has poor sensitivity, his responses are unstable, and he often gains a poorly organized concept of what he has seen. In this relatively disorganized and receptive state there is a great deal of averaging over the field, and the set-theoretic model applies.

The visual field is not highly organized (Gestaltist) at all levels, nor is it disorganized (Elementarist) at all levels. It is quite possible for a display to be organized at a low level but quite disorganized at a high level, and in fact it seems likely that all possible combinations may occur. If this is true, then we shall have serious theoretical difficulties in deciding between, or in striking a compromise between, the set-theoretic and hierarchical models.

My proposal for solving this problem is analogous to the approach used in formulating the hypothesis theory of learning. In that theory the set-theoretic model is used, but the elements of the theory are not simple stimulus elements. Instead, each element is itself an organization, and may be either a very simple organization corresponding roughly to a stimulus element, or may be a highly organized and complex system of hypotheses. It is assumed that the subject has some set of elements, corresponding to his various hypotheses however complicated, and that his choice among these hypotheses follows the set-theoretic model, therefore is probabilistic. Given any hypothesis, however, the behaviour may be perfectly deterministic.

To apply this same theoretical formula to the two theories of visual perception, we should say that when faced with a display the subject has various possible ways of organizing it or organizing parts of it. Each of these is a cognitive structure. However, it is only an extreme special case if the entire display is organized into a single unified and exclusive hierarchical structure. More often there will be some ambiguity, and during inspection the subject may organize the visual in several different ways.

Consider the figure consisting of a test shaft with boxes at each end. In one hierarchical organization, the test shaft may be seen as figures and the boxes as ground. In that case, one might expect that the boxes would mainly serve in the AL for the test shaft, and increases in the size of the boxes would make the shaft be judged shorter. In another hierarchical organization, the shaft plus boxes might be seen as a single figure. This figure has a length equal to the length of the shaft plus both boxes, and the subject might therefore make judgements depending on that total length, or that total length might enter into the adaptation level. In a third organization, if the boxes are small, they might be interpreted as large 'dots' which mark the ends of the test shaft, so that judgements might depend upon the distance between the centres of the boxes.

To apply the theory I am suggesting, we should first have to lay out the set of possible hypotheses that subjects might use, and then to discover the judgements that would be made in the event that each organization is used. Then the hypotheses or sub-structures would be gathered into sets, so that the structures within a set all give rise to the same experimental responses. These sets, then, would be entered into the set-theoretic model, and we would attempt to estimate their measures.

In this approach, the quantitative mathematical structure used within the set-theory model can be used, and we can make good use of probability theory, develop methods of parameter estimation, and even hope for a rational theory of the variability of response. At the same time, since this approach includes the possibility of complex cognitive structures, we would not be forced into the over-simplified interpretations hitherto required to apply adaptation level or other mathematical theories of perception.

Conclusions

In this paper I have attempted to formulate a theoretical problem within the theory of perception, namely, the question of specific judgements of size and extent and how they depend upon the whole visual field as well as instructions and general perceptual organization. It appears to me that this problem cannot be considered solved except within a quantitative theory.

The approach that I have suggested in this paper is derived, in a general way, from theories developed and tested in learning theory and cognitive psychology. In the areas of concept learning, memory, skilled performance, attention, and others, we always seem to come up against the same theoretical dilemma; we can use probability theory to develop a good quantitative theory, and we sometimes can develop an organizational theory to give an intuitive account of the higher processes, but we find it very difficult to get a viable quantitative theory that involves the higher processes.

One method of resolving this dilemma, which was worked in concept formation and to a degree in some studies of the learning of serial patterns, is to employ probability theory and set theory as the fundamental structure, but to distribute the probability not over a set of simple elements, but instead over a set of complex cognitive structures.

This general theoretical strategy is not a theory—it is more like a piece of advice. Like advice in general it may be very difficult to use. In recent months I have been deeply involved in a series of detailed quantitative experiments on the Müeller-Lyer illusion and have attempted to employ this general theoretical strategy. In the analysis of the specific experiments, however, the general strategy is not very useful, and one must solve a great many special and specific problems before the data can be understood.

Nonetheless, the general theoretical structure has been useful in our research in four ways. First, we start with the quantitative model expressed in equations (1) and (2) above, and therefore can make use of the quantitative details of our data at all stages of the investigation. Second, because we can use ideas about overall organization, we are not paralysed by an unexpected finding but instead are motivated to discover some specific cognitive structure that subjects might use to produce such results. Third, this sort of theory encourages us to perform our experiments with more and more precision, and we hope that even if the theoretical enterprise falters we shall be able to contribute precise data from which others may work. Fourth and last, we find that the presence of this sort of theoretical strategy gives us both special models to fit the data and a general direction for correcting our previous errors of interpretation, and therefore has a beneficial effect on the morale of our research group.

References

Baldwin, J. M. The effect of size contrast upon judgments of position in the retinal field, *Psychological Review*, 1895, **2**, 244–59.

Clavadetscher, J. E., and Anderson, N. H. Comparative judgment: Tests of two theories using the Baldwin figure. *Journal of Experimental Psychology: Human Perception and Performance*, 1977, **3**, 119–135.

Coren, S., and Miller, J. Size contrast as a function of figural similarity. *Perception & Psychophysics*, 1974, **16**, 355–357.

Leeuwenberg, E. L. J. A perceptual coding language for visual and auditory patterns. *American Journal of Psychology*, 1971, **84**, 307–349.

Levine, M. Hypothesis behavior by humans during discrimination learning. *Journal of Experimental Psychology*, 1966, **71**, 331–338.

Merryman, C. T., and Restle, F. Perceptual displacement of a test mark toward the larger of two visual objects. *Journal of Experimental Psychology*, 1970, **84**, 311–318.

Restle, F. *Psychology of Judgment and Choice*. New York. Wiley, 1961.

Restle, F. Instructions and the Magnitude of an illusion: Cognitive factors in the frame of reference. *Perception & Psychophysics*, 1971, **9**, 31–32.

Restle, F. Morinaga's paradox and figure-ground organization. *Perception & Psychophysics*, 1976, **20**, 153–156.

Restle, F. Assimilation predicted by Adaptation-Level Theory with variable weights. In N. J. Castellan and F. Restle (Eds), *Cognitive Theory*, Vol. 3. Hillsdale, New Jersey. Lawrence Erlbaum Associates (In Press, 1977).

Restle, F., and Merryman, C. T. An adaptation-level account of a relative-size illusion. *Psychonomic Science*, 1968, **12**, 229–230.

Sarris, V. Effects of stimulus-range and anchor value on psychophysical judgment. In H. -G. Geissler and Yu.M. Zabrodin (Eds.), *Advances in Psychophysics*. Berlin. V E B Deutscher Verlag der Wissenschaften, 1976.

Trabasso, T., and Bower, G. H. *Attention in Learning*. New York. Wiley, 1968.

Chapter 13

About the Geometry Underlying Spontaneous Visual Decoding of the Optical Message

Gunnar Johansson

1. Introduction

It was Berkeley who in his famous *A New Theory of Vision* (1709) introduced the discussion about the visual decoding of the images projected from the environment onto the retina. He naturally founded his analysis on the Euclidean geometry—the only geometrical system known at that time and then regarded as a Law of Nature. Strange enough, von Helmholtz without any questioning accepted Berkeley's type of analysis and in a forceful way further developed the cue concept as an essential part of the theory. The acceptance of a set of additional cues as extra sources of information about space must be regarded as a necessary theoretical complement when Euclidean congruence forms the basis for determining perceptual similarity contra dissimilarity.

Due to a strong tradition, this geometric-congruence approach has been determining for most part of the theoretical work on space vision up to the present time. Still most of us tacitly, and without questioning, accept as something like an axiom that the primary neural analysis of the optical message inhering in the retinal image is carried out by processes representing Euclidean measurement and comparison of distances and angles in this image. The formulation of the traditional problems of shape and size constancy afford striking examples of this approach ('How can retinal images of different size or form bring about perception of equal objects?').

We are all familiar with the treatment of the problems of space perception within the framework of Euclidean geometry and cue theory. These theoretical constructs primarily have been applied to static perception, i.e. the perception of a static space, static objects etc. observed by a fully stationary subject. When it is a question of motion perception this traditional theory has demonstrated serious deficiencies. In these connections we cannot be satisfied with a comparison of different images, but are enforced to ask: how can a continuous transformation of a retinal pattern be interpreted as moving object with constant size and shape? Thus, in this case we have to deal with continuous transformations in a flow rather than discrete transformations of images. Furthermore, static perception in fact is a very special case. Generally the retinal message has the character of a continuous flow.

During my studies of visual motion perception I have become more and more convinced that the traditional assumption that the visual system in its analysis of the optical message primarily acts as a congruence decoder is fundamentally wrong. Furthermore, in my opinion it has a serious blocking effect on our endeavour to gain a better understanding about the functioning of visual space perception. Strange enough, there hardly exists much systematic research about these problems but they certainly are possible to deal with experimentally. During the last years I have therefore started some research in this field. This work has brought me to accept—at least in a tentative way—some basic principles of projective geometry as a useful analogue to the visual decoding of the optical flow over the retina.

Briefly my arguments run as follows:

The geometers (following Felix Klein in his famous *Erlangen program* of 1872) classify the set of geometries as groups of figural transformations under which certain figural properties are preserved, i.e. stay invariant. With respect to the number of invariances in the different transformation groups we get a receding series, starting with the congruence geometry where, as is well known, all figural properties except localization remain invariant. The affine geometry and the projective geometry are geometries with fewer invariants and lacking the absolute metric which is typical for the congruence geometry. These geometries are of special interest because they specify the theoretical foundations for parallel and central projection respectively.

Optically the vertebrate eye with its refracting positive lens is functioning in accordance with the principles for central projection. Therefore, the transformations in the optical message transmitted from the environment onto the retina, preserve only those invariances in figural properties which specify the projective geometry. Consequently it is very nearby to assume that the visual system is tuned for a search for projective invariants rather than for orthogonal ones. In fact, as soon as the problem has been put in this way it seems very artificial, to say the least, to assume that the organism would have developed a neural system for decoding figural transformations in accordance with the Euclidean principles for congruence (which are principles for measurement but certainly no 'Law of Nature'). In everyday life of animal and man, transformations of the retinal patterns satisfying the demands for congruence must be regarded as rare exceptions. Ordinarily transformations in the projections from rigid objects in motion (Euclidean form change) or motion of the eye relative to the environment result in form and size change when described in Euclidean terms but as invariant figures when described within the framework of projective geometry. Thus, while a hypothetical (technical or sensory) decoder constructed for orthogonal pattern analysis would treat all such projections as figural changes, a similar decoder tuned for abstraction of projective invariances would like the perceptual system report relative motions of an invariant spatial structure.

As I pointed out above, the question whether the visual system acts as a Euclidean or projective decoder of the optical message can in a more or less critical way be answered experimentally. Already many old experiments on perceptual object constancy during motion, in which a shadow caster technique was applied, yield good experimental support for the projective alternative. Still more decisive in this respect are the results from a number of experiments which I recently have carried out, experiments intended to be as critical as possible for the question brought forward (see e.g. Johansson, 1974). At the conference a film with some of the experimental material used in this research was shown. In the following I will briefly describe some of these experiments.

The basic experimental material to be referred to consists of electronically generated and computer controlled displays with a few spots or lines in motion or simple geometrical figures slowly changing form and size. In the experiments the displays were presented to Ss through a collimating optical system, which a.o. reduces the physiological cues for equidistance and fronto-parallel orientation and which removes the information about a frontal screen. The rationale for this methodological approach is the assumption that under such impoverished but correct conditions the perceptual outcome will reveal some fundamental principles of stimulus decoding, hard to manipulate under full-cue conditions.

2. Relativity: A General Principle for the Visual Decoding of the Optical Flow

As pointed to above the proposed change from the traditional type of stimulus analysis to a model of type projective geometry implies accepting an anchorage in relational invariance rather than in absolute metric properties. Therefore, I regard this way of analysing the stimulus flow as one of the fundaments of what could be termed a relativistic theory of visual perception. I need to mention here also a second major component in this theoretical structure namely the *perceptual vector analysis* in motion perception. This principle says that the stimulus flow always is perceptually interpreted as hierarchical sets of equal relative motion units. Thus, motion of an object or of a simple element in the visual field is always seen as motion relative to other motions in the field.

Classically motion of simple optical elements like dots, lines, surfaces etc. was thought of in terms of their physical paths over the static background. Already Rubin (1927), Duncker (1929) and Johansson (1950) demonstrated experimentally that this is at variance with the spontaneous functioning of the visual system. These investigations demonstrated that a visual element perceptually can take part in two or more motions simultaneously. Johansson studied this effect in a great number of experiments and has demonstrated that this is a general rule (Johansson, 1950, 1958, 1964, 1973, 1974a,b, 1975, 1976). A most simple but informative type example of such vector analysis, adapted from Johansson (1950) is shown in Figure 1.

In this pattern of 'physical' motion of three 'elements': A, B, C, over the background there exists a component vector representing the motion of the element B relative to A and C. With this vector subtracted from the physical motion of B there remains a component equal to the motion of A and B. As Figure 1 illustrates this analysis corresponds to the percept. Perceptually A, B and C forms a system in horizontal motion, while B moves vertically within the system. This principle is fully general. An optical flow pattern is always and initially analysed in common and relative component vectors in a way which is principally correct from mathematical point of view.

The combination of the projective model proposed and the principle of perceptual vector analysis is essential because (1) both are founded on re-

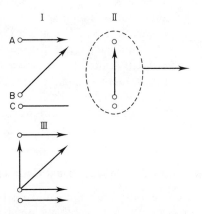

Figure 1. Example on perceptual vector analysis. The three bright (dark) dots, A, B, C are seen in motion on a homogeneous bright (dark) frontal screen. These elements describe sinusoidal motions with the same frequency (·5–2 c/s) and phase as diagrammed in Figure 1:I. Figure 1:II represents the percept of this motion pattern, which is a vertical line formed of the three dots moving to and fro horizontally while the dot B moves up and down along the line. Figure 1:III shows how the percept is a correct vector analysis of the stimulus motion **B** in one component of motion relative to A + **B** and another component equal to the motion of these elements

cording of relations and (2) because the generalization of the vector analysis to comprehend also motion in other directions in space than along the fronto-parallel one holds true only in the framework of projectively invariant relations. Cf Johansson (1974a).

3. Experimental Support of the Relativistic Model

3.1. Perception of Translation in Depth.

First a couple of words about the model. Its basic structure is well known from the theory of central projection and perspective drawing. Let me remind the reader of the following most central concepts: (1) the figure plane = the plane of the figure to be projected, (2) the picture plane = the plane on to which the figure is projected, here representing the retina, (3) the station point (= the centre of projection), not on either plane, here represented by the nodal point of the lens of the eye. Figure 2 is a diagram of this model.

We may also remember that in the framework of central projection we meet with the concepts of points and lines at infinity. The horizon in a photograph or a perspective drawing is a pictorial representation of the line at infinity of the figure plane. We also know that in perspective pictures parallel lines meet at a point at infinity on the horizon of the plane of the lines (see Figure 2). The motion tracks of the optical elements of a figure in translatory motion of course are parallel and therefore their projections on the picture plane generally are converging toward a point at the horizon. Furthermore, they will move with proportionally equal velocity relative to this point. Inversely, any two or more

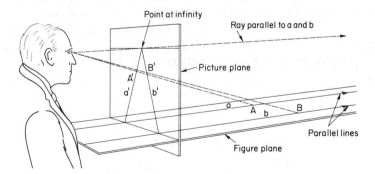

Figure 2. The basic principle of central projection from one plane, the *figure plane* to another plane, the *picture plane*. Motions of the two elements A, B along parallel tracks (a, b) on the figure plane are projected onto the picture plane to motions along the tracks a', b' which are concurrent at the projection of the line at infinity for the figure plane. In accordance with the model the event on the picture plane is a representation of the optic flow over the retina. (From *Scientific American* with due permission)

rectilinear element motions on a picture plane, moving along tracks converging toward a point on the horizon with proportionally equal velocity, represent translation of a rigid object. This last sentence can be regarded as a formulation of the projective model for visual decoding of translatory motion.

A set of experiments reported in Johansson (1964) yield good support for this model, while their results hardly can be explained in terms of the cue theory. The basic and most simple display in this series of experiment was a slowly shrinking–growing homogeneous, bright square as shown in Figure 3(a). The continuous and periodical size change followed a triangular function. Under the experimental conditions mentioned above this display is always perceived as a fronto-parallel square moving back and forth in sagittal direction.

Some readers probably think of previous experience as possible explanation of this effect. Therefore I like to mention that this explanation hardly is possible with reference to the more complex changes of the square also studied in this set of experiments. In these experiments change of shape and size brought about perception of translation in depth simultaneously with change of form of the figure. The same holds true for a variant of the display pictured in Figure 3. In this case only four bright spots representing the corners of the shrinking square were displayed. They of course moved in exactly the same way as the corners of the square. This variant gave exactly the same perception of motion as the basic one. Ss reported seeing the bright corners of an invisible rigid square moving sagittally in depth.

It is easily seen that the percept description is in accordance with the model sketched above. If Figure 3 is regarded as a perspective drawing of the motion of a sagitally moving square the diagonals of the square represent the parallel tracks of its corners, concurring toward the point (P) at infinity. All four spots move with proportionally equal velocity relative to the point P and thus they represent a rigid figure moving in depth. Figure 3(b) shows the same square with the corner tracks directed toward another point on the horizon line and with another slope of the plane of motion. This should represent motions in oblique direction relative to the optical axis of the eye and this also always was the percept.

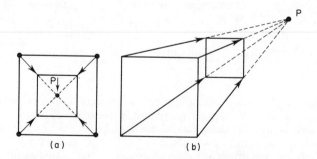

Figure 3. Proximal stimulus patterns yielding perception of (a) a frontal square moving sagitally in depth and (b) the same square moving obliquely upward. See text.

3.2 Perception of Rotation

The writer recently has reported some experiments with a few elements tracing conic sections (Johansson, 1974c). These experiments, which were designed exclusively in order to test and develop the projective model, will give the material to this section.

As is well known, because of the metric of the Euclidean geometry we meet in this system with three classes of conic sections as an effect of the direction of the plane intersecting the double cone. Furthermore, no two sections within each category result in similar figures. For instance in the family of ellipses each individual ellipse is specified by its degree of eccentricity.

In terms of projective geometry on the other hand all conic sections are equivalent because certain relations, their projective properties, stay invariant under central projection. Thus, a circle is projectively equivalent with any other conic section, and therefore also all members of the family of ellipses are equivalent with the circle.

Now, it has been experimentally found that an ellipse with continuously changing eccentricity always is perceived as a circle continuously changing its slant. This is also nicely demonstrated in an educational film (Maas, 1971) or can easily be studied by means of a couple of function generators and an oscilloscope. Thus, it must be accepted as an empirical fact that under good experimental conditions every ellipse (perceived with central vision) changing its shape in any random but continuous way (between the extremes formed by the circle and the line) is perceived as a circle changing its slant. This means that (1) the projectively invariant relations under continuous transformation of an ellipse have as a direct perceptual counterpart an invariant shape in motion and (2) that the perceived figure always has the shape of the most symmetric form of a conic, namely the circle.

These facts about perceptual as well as projective equivalence of ellipses were chosen as starting point for the experiments (Johansson, 1974c). It was hypothetized that also under the condition of relative motion of elements tracing different types of static or moving ellipses circular tracks in various slants should be seen. From this reason a computer controlled display was set up with a few (1, 2–10) bright spots tracing ellipses with different eccentricities, constant or changing. Figure 4 illustrates how the optical projection of this type of display is treated as a case of central projection of a conic from a figure plane to the picture plane (retina) via the lens. In this figure the conic on the picture plane is regarded as a section at right angles to the central axis of a circular cone with an oblique central axis. Thus hypothetically the percept should bring about information about the circular base as well as the slope of the central (optic) axis to the base plane.

The basic experiment was carried out with one, two, three and four spots tracing a set of stationary ellipses with different eccentricity. Figure 5 shows the arrangements of these spots. They moved, as seen in the figure, in the same

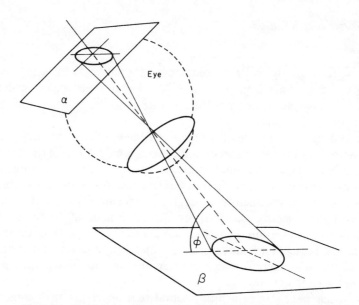

Figure 4. Section in a circular cone with inclined central axis and the sectioning plane α normal to the central axis. This forms a model for projection from the proximal pattern to the percept. The rationale for his model is the theoretical supposition that every proximal conic section is perceived as a circle. α = the picture plane, β = the figure plane

elliptic path and their speed was computed to represent a central projection from a motion with constant speed in a circular path.

The result from these experiments was convincing. With only one spot displayed Ss reported seeing a spot tracing an ellipse, but as soon as one or more spots were added Ss always reported seeing a rigid or semirigid figure (a line, a triangle or a square) rotating on a plane with a specific slant. Subjectively it is hardly possible to see the track as an ellipse in these cases with more than one spot moving.

In order to relate the perceived slant of the circular track to the computed one a special experiment was carried out. In this experiment Ss were asked to indicate the slant of the perceived plane of rotation of two spots by adjusting the slant of a board movable about a horizontal axis. The result demonstrated a fairly good correspondence between the computed and the perceived slant.

Figure 5. Typical element arrangements in the experiments with 2–4 bright spots tracing the same ellipse

Still more interesting was the outcome of the next variant of this experiment, where the liminal time of presentation for evoking perception of slant of the circle was sought for.

The rather astonishing result of this still unpublished experiment was that seeing the pattern (with its cycle time of 4 sec) during a small fraction of a second was enough for semicorrect slant perception. Figure 6 shows the individual data from one S. We must conclude that the perceptual organization in terms of central projection seems to be an initial act. Cf similar result in Johansson (1976).

Figure 7 shows two paths representing rotation on a plane oscillating with twice the frequency of rotation (the spots are tracing an ellipse with changing eccentricity). Also in this case the percept was in accordance with the projective interpretation in almost all Ss. 'A pencil hanging in a string, fixed at its centre of gravity, is swinging up and down while it rotates as if the string had been twisted' was an illustrative description.

Finally, I like to mention an experimental result from this series which I regard as the most critical one to the questions whether the visual system applies a Euclidean or a projective type of analysis. In this case two spots were tracing a rectangle rather than an ellipse. When only one spot was displayed a rectangular path was of course clearly seen. However, as soon as a second spot is added diagonally most Ss again see a rigid 'rod' rotating and simultaneously describing a pendulum motion about its centre.

The main difference as compared with the experiment just described was that the oscillation was seen as forced and very unnatural with sudden, jerky shifts of direction for each 90° of rotation. See Figure 8 which illustrates the percept in accordance with the descriptions and the projective model.

Thus, instead of simply reporting a frontal rectangular track of two spots as predicted from the Euclidean model the perceptual system performs a highly complex vector analysis in a framework of projective geometry.

Discussion

The experimental data referred above are just some selected examples of experimental support for a geometric model for visual stimulus decoding of type projective geometry. There exists in fact a large number of a little more indirect indications in the same direction. Our examples have been chosen because I have found them rather convincing or critical for the choice between the traditional congruence model and a model built on relational invariances. If we go to the literature on visual space and motion perception we over and over again find such indirect indications. We need only remember the large number of experiments with shadow casters displaying moving stimulus patterns. These arrangements automatically generate continuous perspective transformations under polar (or semiparallel) projection. For a thorough analysis see the chapter 'Spatial Constancy and Motion in Visual Perception', by Johansson in Epstein (1976).

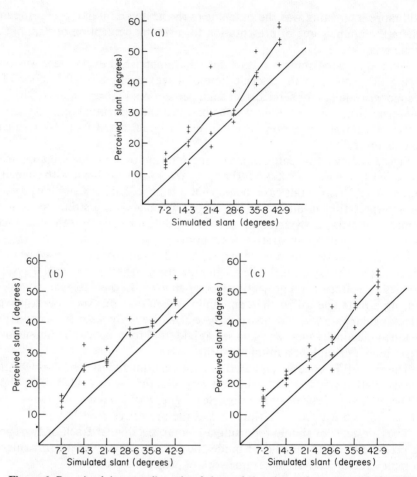

Figure 6. Perceived (reported) angle of slant of the plane of rotation as a function of simulated angle in accordance with the projective model. Three exposure times, five iterations, data from one S. Stimulus: two bright spots tracing three ellipses with different excentricity. Exposure times: (a) ·2 sec, (b) ·5 sec, (c) ·7 sec.

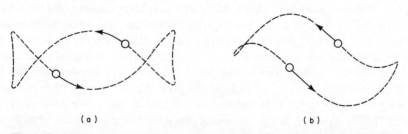

Figure 7. Motion paths of two spots tracing a circle on a slanted oscillating plane. The frequency of oscillation is twice that of rotation and the Figures represent two different phase relations between rotation and oscillation

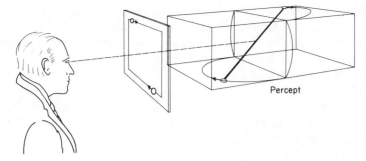

Figure 8. Two spots tracing a frontal rectangle as shown is prefer-
ably seen as a rigid 'rod' carrying out a guided motion like rotation
in a box under continuous contact of the ends of the 'rod' with the
sides of the box

All this evidence makes it consequent to leave the traditional cue theory for
visual space perception and apply a relational type of theory in the research in
this field. Also the recent applications for various purposes of visual decoding
characteristics in technical simulations of visual space by means of computers
and graphic displays give good support for this position. To my knowledge has
in this work in no case technical considerations along the line of the cue theory
been determining for the programming. Instead computations in strict accordance with the principles of perspective transformations under central projection have been the general principle in this highly successful branch of computer
science. With this background it seems strange, to say the least, to find that
many theorists in the field of space vision still persevere in their application of
an evidently very ineffective or defective theory worked out during the eight-
eenth and nineteenth century.

However, accepting relational invariance in accordance with perspective
transformations as a model for visual decoding does of course not necessarily
imply the assumption that the visual system in its data processing follows
exactly those principles for analysis which are determining for the stating of
perspectivity in projective geometry. To put it in another way: the fact that
continuous perspective transformations in proximal stimulus yield perception
of rigid motion in 3-space does not necessarily imply that the visual system
really works in direct accordance with the basic principles of projective geometry. Therefore, we can not stop our experimental analysis with an acceptance of the principles of perspective transformation as a model for the process
of visual decoding. In fact, I have found good empirical evidence that the visual
system in its interpretation of simple transformation patterns applies certain
essential restrictions which go far beyond the mathematical principles for
determining invariance under central projection. More specifically, it seems as
if the visual system follows some special rule saying that a perspective transformation (spatial object rigidity + motion) shall be indicated whenever con-
tradication to this is lacking. An example can make this more clear. Geo-

metrically there does not exist under central projection sufficient information about invariant spatial relations between two points changing their distance along a line which simultaneously changes its direction. Four points with invariant cross ratio during the transformation are needed. It has been found, however, that under the first mentioned conditions (proximal change of length and angle on a straight line seen against a dark background) a line with constant length, moving on a plane with mathematically correct slant relative to the visual axis is perceived (Johansson and Jansson, 1968). Further studies of the principles underlying the visual decoding of the optical flow will be an interesting task in the future.

References

Duncker, K. Ueber induzierte Bewegung. *Psychologische Forschung*, 1929, 12.

Johansson, G. and Jansson, C. Perceived rotary motion from changes in a straight line. *Perception & Psychophysics*, 1968, **4**, 165–170.

Johansson, C. *Configurations in event perception*. Almqvist & Wiksell, Uppsala, 1950.

Johanssson, G. Rigidity, stability and motion in perceptual space. *Acta Psychologica*, 1958, **14**, 359–370.

Johansson, G. Perception of motion and changing form. *Scandinavian Journal of Psychology*, 1964, **5**, 181–208.

Johansson, G. Visual perception of biological motion and a model for its analysis. *Perception & Psychophysics*, 1973, **14**, 2, 201–211.

Johansson, G. Projective transformations as determining visual space perception. *Perception: Essays in Honor of J. J. Gibson*, (ed R. B. MacLeod and H. L. Pick Jr.) Cornell University Press, Ithaca, New York, 1974a.

Johansson, G. Vector analysis in visual perception of rolling motion. *Psychologische Forschung*, 1974b, **36**, 311–319.

Johansson, G. Visual perception of rotary motion as transformations of conic sections. *Psychologia*, 1974c, **17**, 226–237.

Johansson, G. Visual motion perception. *Scientific American*, June 1975, 76–88.

Johansson, G. Spatio-temporal differentiation and integration in visual motion perception. *Psychological Research*, 1976.

Maas, J. B. Motion perception II (film). Houghton Mifflin, New York, 1971.

Rubin, E. Visuell Wahrgenommene wirklische Bewegungen. 1927. *Zeitschrift für Psychologie*, **I**, 103.

Chapter 14

Quantification of Certain Visual Pattern Properties: Salience, Transparency, Similarity

E. Leeuwenberg

Abstract. Some measures for pattern properties are proposed in terms of their structural information. The goal is to predict the salience of and the similarity between patterns on the basis of these measures over a wide range of mainly visual patterns. A comparison between the theoretical values and the empirical data reveals the perceptual relevance of structural information measures. Experimental data show, moreover, that predictions can be made with sufficient accuracy on figure-ground relations, on transparacy in visual and auditory patterns, on the 'Ehrenstein' and 'neon' (Van Tuijl) illusions and on masking phenomena. The general conclusion is that most of these pattern properties are not based on the primary perception processes, but rather on the results of these processes, i.e. the pattern codings.

Introduction

At the beginning of the present century, innumerable visual phenomena have been remarked upon, amongst other by Koffka (1935), Wertheimer (1912), Metzger (1930), Gottschaldt (1929), being incompatible with a simple theory based on 'direct' figure characteristics. One striking feature brought forward was that patterns as we see them break down into specific subparts. Thus Figure 1 is generally given the A interpretation and less frequently the B, C or D interpretation.

These investigations were interested in the roles played by regularity, continuity, similarity and commonfate of figure background configuration. These features are given the collective term 'figural goodness'. According to Hochberg (1953) this figural goodness may be reduced to figure simplicity, which in effect implies that perceptual interpretation is guided by the 'minimum principle'. We too are in agreement with this principle. However, the task remains to specify this minimum principle more exactly.

278

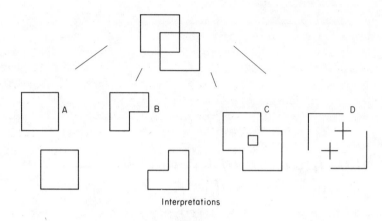

Interpretations

Figure 1.

Various investigations of perception (Attneave 1954, Fitts 1956, Quastler 1955, Klemmer 1953, Garner 1962, Hake 1951) have resorted to the selective information theory proposed by Shannon (1949). However, the many attempts to determine by means of this theory a perceptually relevant measure for figure simplicity (or complexity) strengthened the conviction that it was necessary first to specify the perceptual 'descriptive elements' by which patterns were described. As has been suggested by Attneave (1959) and Oldfield (1954) in particular, these descriptive elements are closely related to the sources of figure regularity such as similarity and repetition. The number of descriptive elements for a given figure corresponds to its 'structural information' (MacKay 1950). Only at a much later date have structural coding theories been produced, namely by Simon (1963), Restle (1970), Vitz (1969) and Leeuwenberg (1968). Even though these theories have been developed for different types of patterns, e.g., letter sequences, tonal series and two and three dimensional patterns, they display (Simon 1972) noticeable agreement. Here we shall examine the theory that specifically deals with the description of visual patterns (Leeuwenberg 1971).

Before explaining the latter theory, however briefly, we shall first make a few general statements about where it stands and what its claims are.

(a) The theory does not in fact deal with the perceptual process, though the suggestion may be otherwise, but with the result of this process, which is the memory code.

(b) Structural information relates to the structural aspects of figures only, and not to quantitative (metrical) variations which do not essentially determine the 'structure'. For example, two completely different right angles have the same amount of structural information. The perceptual length and breadth assessment may be described better in terms of selective information.

(c) The system is applicable to stimuli in as far as they enjoy 'focal attention' in contrast to 'ambient attention'. Although a clear-cut criterion for this difference is yet unknown by us, an indication of the two forms of attention can be given. Focal attention appears to be directed more to the information that emerges as a pattern is sequentially scanned. Ambient attention, on the other hand, concentrates on the simultaneous acquisition of basal features. The latter form of attention would be more prevalent e.g., where large numbers of separate patterns are present (texture) (Beck 1966, Julesz 1977). It is not impossible in our view that in texture stimuli information processing of each of the many patterns at least begins in a sequential manner, but, due to overloading it does not proceed further than the first overall features of each of the many texture patterns.

(d) The coding system is only applicable to the structures of patterns in as far as these are not loaded with associations and meanings. It is presumed that a basal, autonomous system of information storage exists and also that it constitutes however the basis for generating context-dependent 'chunks' and learning-dependent distinctive features as code elements (see at the end of this paper).

Coding Theory

The coding system we are discussing is based on the description of regularities in patterns. Thus a linear figure is first described as a sequence of extremely small lengths of line, which we call 'grains'. The patterns are completely described by indicating the points of furcation and the relative angles between the successive grains. A description such as this of a pattern is called a 'primitive code' of that pattern. Naturally, one stimulus may have several primitive codes, but for each primitive code there is only one pattern (Buffart 1973).

The rewriting of a primitive code is carried out by means of the three operators (see Figure 2) that the system includes. Each of these operators corresponds to a recognizable source of figure regularity.

The sum of the number of operators employed and the number of relative angles which are not eliminated in coding is taken as equal to the structural information of that coding. In fact it represents the number of elements that have to be remembered for a certain coding—or interpretation—of a pattern.

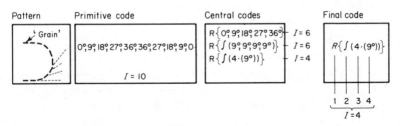

Figure 2.

In general we consider the structural information of a pattern equal to that of the shortest code which is the 'final code'.

Figure 2 will serve to illustrate the role of the three operators referred to above.

This figure is subdivided into straight lengths of line, which for the sake of simplicity will be considered in this example as the already mentioned elementary 'grains'. The primitive code consists of the series of relative angles between the successive grains. This primitive code is characterized in the first place by symmetry. If we let the symbol R mean: 'repeat the next series and mirror it', then the primitive code can be rewritten in a reduced form (see Figure 2). The rewriting of the latter code may be realized by means of the symbol i. This symbol means, 'Regard the angles that follow upon $\int$ as the succession of differences that each coded angle has with the preceding angle'. This code, obviously, may be simplified further. The structural information of this last central code is the least. It is therefore the final code. It should be noted that a different rankorder of operators in a code usually refers to a different pattern.

We shall summarize the chief rules and add to these some subsidiary rules that will arise when working out some examples.

1. reversal: $R\{a, b\} = a, b, b, a$
2. integration: $\int (1, 3, 2) = 0, 1, 4, 6$
3. iteration: $3 \cdot \{a, b\} = a, b, a, b, a, b$
4. alternation: $(a, b)(c, d, e) = a, c, b, d, a, e, b, c, a, d, b, e$
5. chunking: $(a, b)(\{c, d\}, e) = a, c, d, b, e$
6. enlarging: $2 \cdot (a, b) = a, a, b, b$
7. left-right: $\pm (a, b, c) = +a, -b, +c, -a, +b, -c$
8. to–fro: $\underset{\leftrightarrow}{a}$:
9. pivot point: $R\{a, b/c\} = a, b, c, b, a$
10. continuation: $\{a\}$:
11. vanishing: $0, \overline{0}, 0$ — —
12. furcation: $0, a$: $\underset{b}{}$

We shall elucidate the above rules as follows.

(sub 4) The symbols enclosed in the brackets are run through cyclicly and alternatingly until an identical period is about to follow. In general holds for all the bracket signs, that they are not informative.

(sub 5) The symbols enclosed by { } remain together as if they comprised one symbol (see also rule 3).

(sub 6) The symbols enclosed in ( ) are iterated one by one.

(sub 7) Positive angles are left-turning; negative angles are right-turning. The ± symbol counts as one information unit.

(sub 8) A certain angle is added, but at the same time an identical angle is constructed in the opposite direction. The ↔ symbol counts as information.

(sub 9) The pivot around which the symbols are symmetrically arranged is specifically indicated (in this case, c).

(sub 10) The symbols (angles) are repeated over and over again until the angle series thus constructed meets that part of the figure that has already been constructed according to the rest of the code. This continuation symbol is not informative.

(sub 11) The figure is first constructed according to the code (without vanishing sign), and after this the indicated parts are made invisible.

(sub 12) The parallel structure in the code refers to angles successively emanating from one single point. It should be noted that all the rules for serial structures, such as the alternation rules, are also valid for parallel-furcation structures.

This whole system of rules, of which only a small part is indicated here, has been rearranged by Buffart (1973), so that the ad-hoc character that it undoubtedly now has is greatly diminished.

Many types of experiments have been carried out in order to demonstrate the perceptual relevance of our coding language. Only a few of them will be summarily indicated here. First of all correlations were worked out between subjective 'complexity' and the calculated structural information of a great number of pattern series. For two and three dimensional patterns and auditory tone sequences the correlations appeared to be ·97, ·94, and ·84 respectively. These were higher than could be calculated on the lines of other theories for the same patterns (Leeuwenberg 1971).

More important evidence follows from the agreement between the theoretical subdivision of a pattern on the one hand and the experimentally obtained subjective subdivision of the same pattern on the other (correlation = ·95).

The code that is obtained by minimalizing I (Information content) is often composed of several distinct part-codes. These each appear to correspond with exactly one of the part-figures that the subject conceives of in the total figure, as is illustrated in the example of Figure 3.

Review of Figure Properties

We shall now make some general remarks on the main concepts to be discussed in the present paper. There are two main types of salience, viz. (i) constraint salience, and (ii) distinctive salience (S. Evans, 1967). Constraint salience occurs if a certain figure *interpretation* stands out in contrast to the expectation, which is, in effect, an alternative *interpretation*. The second type, distinctive

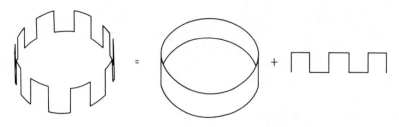

Figure 3.

salience, is the resultant of the contrast between the features of a certain *pattern* with respect to those of the background *patterns*. There is no question of there being a conflict of interpretation. Seeing this type of salience can in practice be reduced to 'dissimilarity', we shall discuss this type of salience when we come to the theme of 'similarity' (see below).

Until now, the meaning of salience has been reduced to a contrast, either between interpretations or between 'patterns'. In our opinion, salience in this meaning of contrast, can also be seen in a different light as determined by the quantity of arguments in favour of a certain impression. The arguments are to be found, not principally in the determinants of the impression itself, but rather in the relationship of the impression to its alternative, background or contrasting interpretation. Salience has been therefore presented in such a general sense that concepts such as strikingness and interestingness may also be classed under the heading 'salience'.

Beside strikingness and interestingness, on which some comments will be made below, other meanings of '*constraint salience*' may be distinguished. Amongst these are constraint salience in a strict sense of redundancy; i.e. Constraint (C); and further, Prominency (P) and Transparency (T). We shall propose a general formula for the three meanings in which the difference between the three meanings can be reduced to the differences in the task that an observer meets.

It should be realized that the close relationship (see below) between the meaning of constraint salience and the meaning of similarity (G) imposes restrictions on the form of the specification of constraint salience. A diagrammetric outline is given opposite:

At the end of this article in Table 1 the formulas of all these pattern-properties are presented.

Constraint : C

If the set task is to represent a pattern clearly by means of basic image elements, then the amount of these must be maximalized. For example, a square expressed in 1000 dots is clearer than a square represented by seven dots. The deviation of the pattern interpretation from the interpretation: that the dots are randomly arranged, determines the clarity of the pattern. A connection

Diagrammatic outline:

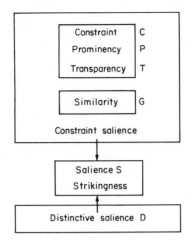

could be laid with a measure of redundancy, well-known in selective information theory. Translated into terms of structural information (I), the formula will be:

$$\text{Redundancy} = \frac{I_{max} - I}{I_{max}}$$

This measure, however, has two objections. Firstly, there are many patterns for which the redundancy is virtually equal to 1, in spite of the fact that the patterns vary widely in subjective regularity; and secondly, the redundancy measure does not play a consistent role in the description of the pattern aspects that build up from it, such as prominency and similarity.

In order to meet these objections, we suggest the formula for Constraint (C) as follows:

$$C_\alpha^a = {}_2\log\frac{Ie}{I\alpha}$$

In this formula, e equals the number of elementary lengths of line from which pattern a is built up. The absolute length of these pieces of line we regard as irrelevant. $e(e)$ in fact stands for the number of initial directions of the above mentioned lines; 1, $I(e)$ refers to these pieces of line as if separately considered (so $Ie = e$). The α symbol stands for a certain interpretation of the figure.

C_α^a represents the clarity with which a certain regularity-containing interpretation α may be seen in a particular figure: a.

The symbols that we have all introduced so far are

C constraint	e elements
α interpretation	I structural information
a concrete figure	

The reason for choosing the logarithm is chiefly prompted by the experience that for the measures deduced from C, of prominency and especially of similarity, proportions rather than differences are determinant. Furthermore, the logarithm covers the decrease in effect with increased difference between Ie and $I\alpha$.

As an example we shall take Figure 4(a). The cross-shaped figure α may be coded as $\{90, -90, -90\}$. $Ie = 12$, so that

$$C_\alpha^{4a} = {}_2\log\frac{12}{3}.$$

We have to keep in mind that Ie in the numerator also corresponds with an interpretation, namely that given by an observer who is quite oblivious to any relationships. In other words it is a 'random-interpretation'.

For the random structure of Figure 4(b) we may write the equation $C_\beta^{4b} = {}_2\log\frac{12}{12} = 0$. In this case it is not more efficient to choose a certain regularity-containing interpretation in preference to the random interpretation of Figure 4(b).

In the case where the actual pattern displays random deviations (f), in respect to the ideally chosen fundamental structure α, the formula for C becomes somewhat more complicated (see Figure 4(c)). Let it be noted at once that in principle α can be chosen arbitrarily, but that, where no further explanation is given, α is regarded as the interpretation with the least amount of information. As denominator, the choice would obviously be $I(\alpha) + I(f)$, for just as $I\alpha$ includes memory-loading information, so $I(f)$ includes the loading information, of which the processing has to be realized in order to give access to interpretation α. However, it is erroneous to assert that just as 'f' indicates deviations, so 'α' shows similar deviations, for 'f' refers to deviations from α, not the converse. Figure 4(c) is probably viewed as a perfect cross, from which some pieces of line have *afterwards* been removed. We can regard the construction of a pattern interpretation in a similar manner. First, a memory code for the ideal interpretation α, is constructed. Next, this hypothetical α is matched with the stimulus. To this end, the concrete figure is again reconstructed in the imagination from the memory code: α. For the cross-shape of Figure 4(c) this requires the construction of $\{-90, 90, 90\}$, which are three acts of the imagination (w), and subsequently the fourfold repetition of these chunks which in total requires $w = 7$. The reconstruction in the imagination is compared with the actual Figure 4(c). This actual figure matches the ideal cross-shape, except for three elements ($f = 3$), which still have to be coped with. The reconstruction in

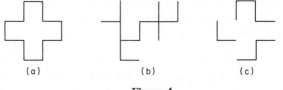

(a)   (b)   (c)

Figure 4.

the imagination of the actual figure thus requires $w = 7 + 3$. Comparison of the actual imagination load with that of the ideal hypothetical interpretation finds expression in the fraction $(7 + 3)/7 = w(\alpha + f)/w(\alpha)$. The bigger the fraction, the bigger the imagination-load that is needed in order to see the ideal figure in the given figure. If we now 'add' the relative 'imagination-load' to the memory load $I\alpha$, the formula for constraint will be:

$$C_\alpha\backslash^a = {}_2\log \frac{Ie}{I\alpha \times \dfrac{w(\alpha + f)}{w(\alpha)}}$$

using the equation $a = \alpha + f$, the expression will be:

$$C\backslash_\alpha^a = {}_2\log \frac{Ie \cdot w\alpha}{I\alpha \cdot wa}$$

The following example will clarify the specification of w:

$$\text{if} \qquad \alpha = 3 \cdot \{R \quad \{2 \cdot \{a, \quad b, \quad c\}\}\}$$
$$\text{then } w(\alpha) = 3 + 2 + 2 + 1 + 1 + 1$$

From this example it should be clear that the imagination-load w includes the quantities corresponding to each operation in the central code. This is in agreement with the image grammar (Moran, 1968), which possesses both features of the central code and those of the primitive code.

The term $W\alpha/I\alpha(=(\overline{W}\alpha))$ may be viewed as a 'measure of the average imagination load' per information unit of the α interpretation.

The rewriting of C in these terms leads to:

$$C\backslash_\alpha^a = {}_2\log \frac{Ie}{I\alpha + \dfrac{f}{\overline{w}\alpha}}$$

This formulation indicates that f is weighted with the inverse of the average imagination load of the hypothetical α. Application of a formula in which f is absent, or in which f is not weighted, or in which f is weighted with the inverse of $I\alpha$ or e, or $e_{(\alpha)}$ or $e/I\alpha$ or $e^{(\alpha)}/I(\alpha)$, etc. leads for various patterns to absurd results. With all these variations, a formula in which $Ie_{(\alpha)}$ appears in the nominator, (instead of Ie) similarly leads to perceptually irrelevant predictions.

Alongside arguments such as these for introducing an imagination load measure, Neisser's (1967) explanation of Sternberg's (1967) search experiments can be put. During the perceptual process, according to Neisser, a pattern wrapped in noise is first of all stripped of this noise. The remaining pattern, in his view, is that which plays a part in the subsequent information processing. In other words, only the perceptual reconstruction of the stimulus is remembered or recognized or involved in a comparison. Congruent with this view, only the ideal hypothetical construct (as for instance the cross shape in Figure 4(c)) is expressed in structural information units, as proposed in the constraint formula.

As has been said, this structural information refers to the memory load. On the other hand, the constructive perceptual activity, involved in subtracting noise, corresponds to the imagination load measure w. This perceptual activity virtually only occurs while the stimulus is present.

If $C_a^\chi = 0$, there must be a stimulus for which the random interpretation is as valid as a meaningful interpretation. It must then hold that

$$e_{c=0} = \left(\frac{w(\alpha) + e(\alpha)}{w(\alpha) + I(\alpha)}\right) I(\alpha)$$

Applied to Figure 5(a) this gives:

$$e_{(c=0)} = \frac{(13 + 52)}{(13 + 7)} \cdot 7 = 22$$

where $\alpha : \{-90, \quad R \{ 2 \cdot (90, -90), 90, -90\}\}$

$$I\alpha : \Big| \quad 1 + 1 + 1 + 1 + 1 + 1 + 1 = 7$$
$$w(\alpha): 4 + 1 + 2 + 2 + 1 + 1 + 1 + 1 = 13$$

$$e_\alpha = 52$$

In Figure 5(a), the 22 elementary grains present in Figure 5(α) are given at random. If these elements are not indicated randomly, i.e. if an order had afterwards been demonstrated, then the configuration would certainly not have conjured up any ambiguous, vague impression. However, has this been the case it would have been catered for by the 'prominency' measure to be discussed below.

For the stimulus Figure 5(β_1), the maximal common lengths of line must be regarded as grains, with the result that $e = 12$. If in this Figure the half-lengths of the maximal lines are taken as grains, then instead of the code $\{+90, -90, -90\}$, the code of Figure 5(β_1) would be $\{(+90, -90, -90)(0)\}$. This code is longer and for that reason not acceptable.

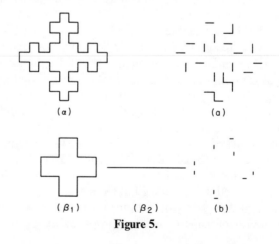

(a)   (a)

(β_1)   (β_2)   (b)

Figure 5.

However, in Figure 5(β_1) acts as the ideal figure basic to the description of Figure 5(b), then necessarily, in respect to the description of deviations, a choice will have to be made for the most efficient and, at the same time, the largest common grain length. This grain length will be a sixth of the size of the maximal length. Thus the code will be for Figure 5(β_1): $\{(+90, -90, -90)$ $\{5 \cdot (0)\}\}$ $I = 5$. A second code of the ideal figure underlying Figure 5(b) is, how-ever, possible, containing the same amount of information. This code consists in an invisible cross, with the maximal length of line as grain (so that $e = 12$). This cross is subsequently hemmed in (see for ⓧ: Leeuwenberg 1971) with a chain of grains which are 6 times as small as those of the cross (indicated as $\frac{1}{6} \cdot (0)$): $5 (\beta_1) + 5(\beta_2) = \{+90, -90, -90\}$ⓧ$\{\frac{1}{6} \cdot (0)\}$; $I = 5$. Even though both interpretations have an equal information content, there is a preference for the latter interpretation, since this results in a higher constraint value. Not only in determining the constraint, but also in determining the similarity, a choice has to be made for the form which in the specific case yields the maximal similarity (see below). Proceeding from the latter code, the determination of the number of grams that must be visible in order that the boundary between random pattern and cross shape may be attained is as follows:

$$I_\alpha = 5$$

$$w_\alpha = 4 + 1 + 1 + 1 + 6 \times 12 + 1 = 80$$

$$e_a = 6 \times 12 = 72$$

$$e_{(c=0)} = \left(\frac{80 + 72}{80 + 5}\right) \cdot 5 = 9$$

Only a relatively small number (9) is needed in order to give a pattern contain-ing many constituent elements an equal clarity ($c = 0$). A similar tendency is present in a pattern made up of many sub-patterns. In other words, the number of visible grains needed for the perceptual impression of 10 crosses is on average far less per cross than the number of visible grains needed for the representation of a single cross.

Undoubtedly, a considerable number of perceptual effects will not be accomodated in this way. An example we could mention is the pronounced pre-ference for seeing three-dimensional structures rather than planes and, in turn, the preference for planes rather than line patterns. A number of these effects too may be deduced from the above method of calculation. Another type of 'effect' which up till now could not be accomodated will be looked at more closely below.

Prominency : P

In our examples we have often used the cross shape. However, we should in principle have set out from the pattern interpretation that yields a maximal constraint. For example, Figure 6(a), regarded as a twofold zig-zag structure whose code is $3 \cdot \{90, -90\}//3 \cdot \{90, -90\}$) has a constraint: $C_\alpha^{\backslash e} = \log \frac{14}{6} = \log 2 \cdot 33$. The same Figure 6(a) considered, however, as the incomplete Figure 6(β) (whose code is $\{90, 3 \cdot \{90, -90\}\}/f = 14$) has a constraint: $C_\beta^{\backslash e} = \log (14 \times 10)/(4 + 24) = \log 1 \cdot 46$. The degree to which, nevertheless, interpretation 6(β) is recognized in Figure 6(a) is indicated by the measure of prominency:

$$P_\beta^{\backslash \alpha} = C_\beta^{\backslash a} - C_\alpha^{\backslash a} = \log \tfrac{146}{233}$$

Prominency describes the contrast between two divergent *central* interpretations (α and β) of the same pattern. A constraint measure, on the other hand, describes the contrast between one primitive interpretation (e) and one central interpretation (e.g. α). Here it must be noted that in the latter case the primitive interpretation 'precedes' the central interpretation. A subordinate relationship such as this between the two interpretations e and α is not, strictly speaking, present in the P description. In other words, the interpretations α and β are completely separate. Prominency, regarded in a wider sense, contains the measure of constraint:

$$C_\alpha^{\backslash a} = C_\alpha^{\backslash a} - C_e^{\backslash a} = P_\alpha^{\backslash e}$$

In order to illustrate a few calculation rules, we shall take the example of Figure 6(c). The interpretation with the least information: 6(γ) comprises two triangles: $\{a\}//\{a\}$. In this case, the common length of line, which at the same time is the most efficient for determining the information content, is chosen as the basic grain that may then be disregarded. A second property of the given code is that it may be incomplete and in the present example it actually is. In other words, the code does not yield an unambiguous reconstruction of Figure 6(c). The relation between the triangles $\{a\}$ and $\{a\}$ is not described. We propose the rule that the sub-patterns, into which a pattern is divided according to a certain interpretation, should each be completely described in the code, but that the mutual relationship should only be involved if in this way the code becomes shorter.

A second, relatively simple interpretation of Figure 6(c) is indicated in Figure 6(δ). This consists of a lozenge shape: $\{a, b\}$ and four triangles $\{a\}//\{a\}//\{a\}//\{a\}$.

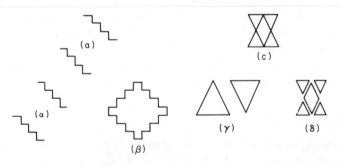

Figure 6.

$(I = 6)$. However, in this case it is more efficient to describe these triangles dependent of the lozenge:

$$\{a\hat{b}\} \quad (I = 5).$$
$$\overline{\underset{\leftrightarrow}{C\{a\}}}$$

For Figure 6(c) we calculate, on the basis of the above information values, $P_\gamma^{\backslash\delta} = {}_2\log\frac{5}{2}$. This does not mean that the γ interpretation will always be chosen. It is better to state that the strength of the preferences for the γ interpretation above the δ interpretation is indicated by P, according to our theory, by approximation. Clearly, many more interpretations of Figure 6(c) may be given than are presented here. The presumption will obviously be that the probability of the occurence of an interpretation is proportional to the inverse of that interpretation. It appears, however, from judgements, that only the few interpretations that have very little information content are given by subjects. This gives rise to the suggestion that virtually only the contrast between at most a few low information-value interpretations serves to determine the strength of one of the interpretations.

Predictions based on the prominency formula were tested in which 42 subjects could choose between two alternative interpretations of 21 patterns, like the one in Figure 6(c). The alternative interpretations of each pattern consisted of two possible subdivisions, i.e. the theoretical most efficient and the one less efficient subdivision.

There were only three patterns which were judged otherwise than was predicted. Further research on this topic is done in our laboratory by van Tuijl, and will be reported soon.

Transparency

One of the forms in which prominency is most easily testable is where there is Transparency. This form of prominency arises where two structures (α and β), in spite of their overlap are yet perceptually clearly discernible. As a demonstration of T, we shall present the reports of three little experiments.

(i) Metelli figures. In as far as the T effect is determined by fairly 'sensory', qualities such as colour, this has been worked out by Metelli (1974). To the extent that T is determined by structural form aspects we propose:

$$T_{\alpha+\beta}^{\searrow\gamma} = P_{\alpha+\beta}^{\searrow\gamma}$$

where γ corresponds to the shortest code of the pattern which includes neither the code of α nor that of β.

Fourteen figures, similar to Figure 7(a) (b), composed of the same two subpatterns, were rank-ordered by 40 subjects according to their perceived transparency. For this series, a rank order correlation coefficient was obtained between the average transparency judgements on the one hand and the com-

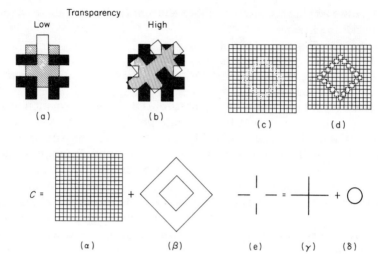

Figure 7.

puted transparency values on the other ($r = \cdot86$). It should be noted that we have here, at the same time, a measure of *camouflage and masking* (M) which is the converse of the amount of $T(M = -T)$. It will doubtless be clear that camouflage in the case of two subpatterns is greater to the extent that the contours of the subpatterns coincide. However, this property had already been accounted for implicitly, because the more coincidence there is the simpler the alternative coding.

(ii) The 'Neon' illusion. A very striking illusion has recently been discovered by van Tuyl (1975, 1977), a member of our research team. The 'Neon' effect, as has been demonstrated in various pattern examples, may also be described in terms of our T formula. If some line elements of a black matrix grid are replaced by coloured elements, e.g., blue lengths of line, such that the blue constitute one single pattern, the impression can be gained that the blue colour pervades the immediate environment of these blue line elements, forming a 'simple' pattern which is actually not present. In Figure 7(c) the blue line elements are represented in light grey. Figure 7(c) demonstrates the 'Neon' phenomenon much more convincingly than Figure 7(d). The strength of the phenomenon may be described by the prominency of the interpretation, in which the pattern is regarded as the sum of a complete black grid (α) and a superimposed blue diamond-shaped pattern (β). This interpretation can be contrasted with the interpretation in which the pattern is regarded as consisting of the actually present blue squares in the configuration of a diamond (γ) plus the adjacent black lines of the grid (δ).

$$T_{\alpha+\beta}^{\gamma+\delta} = \log\frac{I(\gamma) + I(\delta)}{I(\alpha) + I(\beta)}$$

The experimental results, obtained for many patterns, proved, in our view, to be very adequately described by the T formula ($r \approx \cdot95$). (See Van Tuÿl, 1977). Ehrenstein illusions also have been similarly 'explained' (Van Tuÿl $r \approx \cdot95$). An example of this is given in Figure 7(e). It is the degree of effort needed to see a cross (γ) with a superimposed disc (δ) as compared with the effort—or, specifically, the amount of structural information—spent on the assimilation of the four given lengths of line, that determines the strength of the Ehrenstein illusion.

(iii) The 'Cocktail-Party' phenomenon in music. In the experiment using music stimuli, a series of tones is presented dichotically to the left and to the right ear in an alternating fashion. The series of tones presented to the left ear will be called the A series; that to the right ear, the B series. The complete series of tones is called the C. We predict that the degree to which a listener will hear the tones in his left and right ear as one single integrated melody is negatively related to $T_{A+B}\backslash^C$; and that the degree to which the two series of tones are perceived as two separate, though intermingled melodies is positively related to the T measure.

The T measure was correlated ($r = \cdot86$) with the degree of recognition by 19 subjects of the afterwards separate presented A and B melodies.

Similarity : (G)

One of the most interesting, yet most contested pattern features is similarity between patterns. Also with respect to this concept, we set out from the very basic structural aspects of patterns, on the grounds of which subjects are very definite and consistent in their similarity judgements. There are similarity-criteria which have arisen out of learning processes or which are determined by specific meanings. These are, for the time being, left out of consideration.

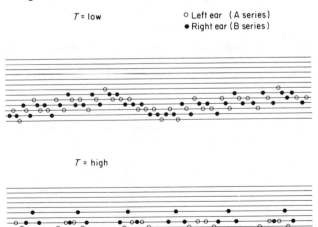

Figure 8.

It almost goes without saying that the manner in which patterns are interpreted is determinant for the degree to which patterns are related to each other (This will become apparent in examples). For this reason a measure of similarity (G) will have to be expressed in terms of prominency. On the other hand, a straightforward relation between similarity and constraint may be given, for the constraint of a pattern can be conceptually considered as being determined by similarity between parts of that pattern. Conversely, similarity between the parts (a and b) of a specific pattern may be, to some extent, regarded as the constraint of the whole pattern ($\alpha \cup \beta$). It is then necessary to abandon the internal constraint inherent in both the subpatterns ($C\alpha + \beta$). Thus the similarity between two patterns can be conceived of as their interpattern constraint. Thus $G_{ab} = C(\text{total}) - C(\text{intra-pattern})$

or $\quad G_{ab} = C\alpha \cup \beta - C\alpha + \beta$

or $\quad G_{ab} = P^{\frac{\alpha+\beta}{\alpha \cup \beta}}$

The latter formula displays close agreement with the measure of masking (T^{-1}); however, the relationship cannot be rediscovered if one looks at the difference between the situations in which T and in which G are applied. T or M are applicable to one pattern, if this pattern can be broken down into two overlapping subpatterns, and these can only be recognized in retrospect. G is applicable if there are two separate, already specified patterns.

It is important to note in this context that the twofold nature of e.g., two identical patterns is a given datum and is therefore not included as information in the determination of $C\alpha \cup \beta$. Thus it holds for identical patterns that

$$G_{ab} = C\alpha \cup \beta - C\alpha + \beta = C\alpha \cup \alpha - C\alpha + \alpha$$

$$= C\alpha - C2\alpha = {}_2\log \frac{I(2a)}{I(a)} = 1$$

Two types of G may be distinguished.
(a) The first occurs if the common structure ($\alpha \cap \beta$), shared by two figures a and b according to the shortest code of their total ($a \cup b$), also occurs in the code of both figures separately ($a + b$). From this it follows that, for the hypothetical structure aspects,

$$\overline{w}(\alpha \cup \beta) = \frac{w(\alpha \cup \beta)}{I(\alpha \cup \beta)} = \frac{w(\alpha \cap \beta)}{I(\alpha \cap \beta)} = \frac{w((\alpha \cap \beta) + (\alpha \cap \beta))}{I((\alpha \cap \beta) + (\alpha \cap \beta))}$$

$$= \frac{w(\alpha + \beta)}{I(\alpha + \beta)} = \overline{w}(\alpha + \beta).$$

For the similarity formula this means:

$$G_{a,b} = C\alpha \cup \beta - C\alpha + \beta = {}_2\log \frac{I(e) \cdot \overline{w}(\alpha \cup \beta)}{w(\alpha \cup \beta)} \cdot \frac{w(a + b)}{I(e) \cdot \overline{w}(\alpha + \beta)}$$

and so

$$G_{a,b} = {}_2\log \frac{w(a + b)}{w(a \cup b)}$$

We shall present an example to illustrate this.

The codes of Figures 9(a) and (b) taken separately are 3. $\{90, -90\}$ and 6. $\{90, -90\}$, respectively. The code of $a \cup b$ is $(2 \times 3)\{90, -90\}$ in which, as has been said, the citation of the code of a is not additionally counted:

$$G_{ab} = {}_2\log \frac{5 + 8}{8} = {}_2\log 1{\cdot}60$$

In the Figures 9(c), (d) the cross shape is hypothetical structure $= \{90, -90, -90\}$ $(w = 4 + 3 = 7)$. The number of deviations from this equals 5 both in Figure 9(c) and in Figure 9(d).

Therefore: $G_{c,d} = {}_2\log \left(\dfrac{7 + 5 + 7 + 5}{7 + 5 + 5} \right) = {}_2\log 1{\cdot}42$

Should Figure 9(e) be regarded as a cross, then the following formula would hold:

$$G_{c,e} = {}_2\log \frac{7 + 5 + 7 + 5}{7 + 5 + 7} = \log 1{\cdot}37$$

Worth noting is that if a naive similarity measurement were applied, according to which similarity would be equal to the literally primitive agreement (0), divided by the number of difference elements (d), then Figure 9(c) and (e) would clearly look similar:

$$\frac{0}{d_{(c,e)}} = \frac{4}{3}$$

whereas Figures 9(c) and (d) would display only a weak mutual similarity:

$$\frac{0}{d_{(c,d)}} = \frac{2}{10}$$

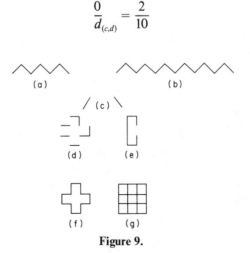

Figure 9.

In other words, it is essential for the determination of similarity to set out from the interpretation of the given stimuli. In the example given above, the cross shape plays an intermediary role with respect to similarity determination.

(b) A second mode of occurrence of G is if two patterns (a and b) display common features which though they appear in the total code ($a \cup b$) do not occur in the codes of the patterns taken separately. In other words, here it is more efficient to code each of the figures without making use of the common features. If we now consider the case that: $f_a = f_b = 0$, then

$$\alpha + \beta = a + b$$

The deviations from the common features which will have to be indicated in $a \cup b$ cannot therefore be regarded any longer as secondary information in relation to the common basic structure which could be used as a matter of fact in both patterns. Because of this, the hypothetical information ($\alpha \cup \beta$) will now embrace not only the common information ($\alpha \cap \beta$) but also the deviations (F) from these.

Therefore $\alpha \cup \beta = \alpha \cap \beta + F = a \cup b$

The similarity formula is thus simplified:

$$G_{a,b} = {}_2\log \frac{I(a + b)}{I(a \cup b)}$$

An example is presented in Figures 9(f) and (g). The codes of these patterns are $\{90, -90, -90\}$ and $\{90, 2.(0)\}$ respectively. The code of Figure 9(g), in

$$\underbrace{90, \{0\}}$$

which the cross shape has been taken as common basic structure is:

$$\frac{\{90, \underbrace{-90} \underbrace{-90\}}}{\underbrace{0} \quad \underbrace{0, -90}}$$

This code applies also to $f \cup g$ because, as has been said, the repetition of the common cross form has to be disregarded. Now it holds that:

$$G_{f,g} = {}_2\log \frac{3 + 4}{6} = {}_2\log 1{\cdot}17$$

Distinctive Salience : D

It is trivial to remark that dissimilarity may be described as $-G$. The degree to which pattern a contrasts with background b, c ... is determined, amongst other things, by the dissimilarity of a with respect to b and c. However, this type of salience D is likewise determined, to no small extent, by the similarity between the parts of the background, b, c. Thus distinctive salience may be described:

$$D = G_{b,c} - G_{a,(b,c)}$$

Salience : S

It is likewise obvious that the two forms of salience, constraint and distinctive salience, contribute to the total salience.

$$S = C + D$$

The constraint, that has been dealt with up to now, is determined by the number of primitive elements on the one hand and the smallness of the structural information of the final-code on the other. Expressed in general terms we can say that the greater the number of arguments (primitive elements) and at the same time the simpler the object to which these arguments are related, the greater the constraint. In a broader and analogous sense the size of the constraint may be regarded as the number of interpretations which are related to but one single structure. This form of constraint occurs for instance in a situation in which several mnemonics are applicable to one single content. The role of distinctive salience is related to the degree to which these interpretations diverge, i.e. they are not related to each other. This is the case if interpretations or aspects correspond to different dimensions. A colour photograph is more easily assimilated than a black and white photograph. A three-dimensional image is generally better remembered than a two-dimensional image. Let it be noted that this role which the various divergent dimensions play in this may just as well be performed by different levels of hierarchy (Leeuwenberg 1971, 1973).

Even the aesthetic value of structures can be regarded, if only in part, as deriving from the salience size, in a wider sense. Notable is that in structures that appeal to a sense of aesthetics there are often several interpretations which on the one hand are related to a single image, yet which on the other hand widely diverge. In music, for instance, there is often a main melody and an accompaniment, usually in the lower register. The accompaniment on the one hand is largely harmonically attuned to the main melody and on the other hand the accompaniment has often its 'own melody'.

Analyses of some of Bartok's (single melodies) in terms of these structural operations have shown that two interpretations can be given. One corresponds to a structure that is obvious if a short preview is allowed. The other requires a larger span and corresponds with the bar. The analyses have only dealt with the numeric melody structure and no use is made of metric-accentuation cues. Although the two interpretations were largely divergent, the amount of structural information of the two were virtually equal.

In conclusion, a review of the formulas will be given.

Context and Memory

Some observations, finally, may be made on the subject of the position of learning process in our coding theory. With this in mind it is useful first to examine the role played by context in figure codes. A demonstration is pre-

Table 1

1. Constraint Salience (C)		$C_\alpha^{a} = \log \dfrac{I(e)\cdot w(\alpha)}{I(\alpha)\cdot w(a)}$
2. Prominency (P)		$P_\alpha^{\beta} = C_\alpha^{c} - C_\beta^{c}$
3. Transparency (T)		$T_{\alpha+\beta}^{\gamma} = P_{\alpha+\beta}^{\gamma}$
4. Masking (M)		$M = -T$
5. Similarity (G)		$G_{a,b} = P_{\alpha\cup\beta}^{\alpha+\beta}$
a) if: $I(a) = I(\alpha\cap\beta + fa)$ and: $I(b) = I(\alpha\cap\beta + fb)$		$G_{a,b} = \log \dfrac{w(a+b)}{w(a\cup b)}$
b) if: $Ia < I(\alpha\cap\beta + fa)$ or: $Ib < I(\alpha\cap\beta + fb)$		$G_{a,b} = \log \dfrac{I(a+b)}{I(a\cup b)}$
6. Distinctive Salience (D)		$D_a^{bc} = G_{b,c} - G_{a,(b,c)}$
7. Salience (S)		$S = C + D$

I = structural information
f = deviations
α = hypothetical structure
w = Imagery strength
e = primitive elements
$a = \alpha + f$ = concrete pattern

sented in Figures 10(a) and (b). Figure 10(a) may be described simply as two rectangles. Figure 10(b) is but an extension of Figure 10(a) with two diamonds. However, it appears to be simpler to describe Figure 10(b) as three diamonds with some additions, rather than as two rectangles plus two diamonds. The surplus of Figure 10(b) with respect to Figure 10(a) (the two diamonds) may be regarded as context information of Figure 10(a). It appears then that this context completely alters the figure interpretation of Figure 10(a).

Instead of a given context, a certain pre-knowledge can induce an effect of this kind on a figure interpretation. The pre-knowledge only needs registration as a single chunk in the code of a figure. This chunk then contains only one unit of information, in the same way as the reference to a previously coded partial structure only contains one information unit. If it were possible that one had a subject's memory content completely available, one could calculate adequate figure codes. The whole memory content plus the given stimulus figure may be regarded together as the structure to be coded. Naturally, loss of memory must also be taken into account.

As has been said above, a partial structure once coded in detail (chunk) needs only one information unit if it recurs. This rule is implicit in the coding system. Therefore it is in agreement with this system that where partial structures repeatedly recur, the coding language seems superficially to 'change'. In other words, the basic operators of this coding system are gradually replaced by the above mentioned chunks (features). This phenomenon also occurs in human perception. It is known that a certain set of stimuli induce the specific

(a)   (b)

Figure 10.

features (chunks) that belong to the set. Because it is practicably impossible to determine what is contained in memory, the testing of the coding system must be conducted with figures which are not, or only very slightly, known.

References

Attneave, F. (1954). Some informational aspects of visual perception. *Psych. Rev.*, **61**, 183–193.

Attneave, F. (1959). *Applications of information theory to psychology*. New York, Chicago, London.

Beck, J. (1966). Perceptual grouping produced by changes in orientation and shape. *Science*, **154**, 538–540.

Berlyne, D. L. (1973). *Pleasure, reward, preference*, (ed) Berlyne-Madsen, Academic Press, New York, London.

Buffart, H. F. J. M. (1973). A coding language for patterns *73 FU 07* (University paper, Nijmegan).

Evans, S. (1967). Redundancy as a variable in pattern perception. *Psych. Bulletin*, **67**, 113.

Fitts, P. M. (1956). Stimulus correlates of visual pattern recognition. *J. exp. psych.* **51**, 1–11.

Garner, W. R. (1962). *Uncertainty and structure as psychological concepts*. Wiley, New York, London.

Geissler, H. G. (1975). Towards a new reconciliation of Stevens and Helson's approaches to psychophysics. *Acta Psych.*, **39**, 417–426.

Goldmeier, E. (1972). *Similarity in visual perceived forms*. Vol. VIII, No. 1, monograph 29, Academic Press, New York.

Gottschaldt, K. (1929). Über den Einfluss der Erfahrung auf die Wahrnehmung von Figuren. *Psych. Forsch.*, **129**, 1–87.

Hake, H. W. and Garner, W. R. (1951). The effect of presenting various numbers of discrete steps on scale reading accuracy. *J. exp. psych.*, **42**, 358–366.

Hochberg, J. and McAllister, E. (1953). A quantitative approach to figural 'goodness'. *J. exp. psych.*, **46**, 361–364.

Julesz, B. (1977). Perceptual limits of texture discrimination and their implications to figure-ground separation. In: *Formal theories of visual perception* (Ed.) Leeuwenberg, Buffart. Wiley, New York, London.

Klemmer, E. T. and Frick, F. C. (1953). Assimilation of information from dot and matrix patterns. *J. exp. psych.*, **45**, 15–19.

Klix, F. (1971). *Information und Verhalten*. Berlin.

Klix, F. (1975). Der Gestaltbegriff und Aspekte der kognitiven Strukturbildung in der Wahrnehmung. Aus: *Gestalttheorie in der modernen Psychologie*, (Ed.) Ertel/Kemmter/Stadter, 187–199.

Koffka, K. (1935). *Principles of Gestaltpsychology* New York: Harcourt, Brace & World.

298

Leeuwenberg, E. (1969). Quantitative specification of information in sequential patterns. *Psych. Rev.*, **76**, 216–220.

Leeuwenberg, E. (1971). A perceptual coding language for visual and auditory patterns. *Amer. J. of psych.*, **84**, 3, 307–349.

Leeuwenberg, E. (1973). Meaning of perceptual complexity. In: *Pleasure, Reward, Preference*, (Ed.) Berlyne, D. E. Academic Press. New York, London, 99–113.

MacKay, D. (1950). Quantal aspects of scientific information. *Phil. Mag.*, **41**, 289–301.

Metelli, F. (1974). The perception of transparency. *Scient. American*, **230**, 4, 91–98.

Metzger, W. (1934). Beobachtungen über phänomenale Identität. *Psych. Forschung*, **19**, 1–60.

Moran, T. (1968). The grammar of visual imagery. *University Paper*, Carnegie-Mellon University, Pittsburgh.

Neisser, U. (1967). *Cognitive psychology*. New York, Appleton Century Crofts.

Oldfield, R. C. (1954). Memory of mechanisms and the theorie of schemata. *Brit. J. psych.*, **45**, 14–23.

Quastler, R. (1955). *Information theory in psychology*, Glencoe, Illinois, Free Press.

Restle, F. (1970). Theory of serial pattern learning: structural trees. *Psych. Rev.*, **77**(6), 481–495.

Scheidereiter, U. (1974). Zur beschreibung strukturierter Objekte mit kontextfreien Grammatiken. Aus: *Organismische Informations-Verarbeitung* (Ed.) Klix, F. Berlin, 131–135.

Simon, H. and Kotovsky (1963). Human acquisition of concepts for sequential patterns. *Psych. Rev.*, **70**, 534–546.

Simon, H. (1972). Complexity and the representation of patterned sequences of symbols. *Psych. Rev.*, **79**, 369–382.

Sternberg, S. (1967). Two operations in character recognition. *Percept. & Psych. Phys.*, **2**, 45–53.

Van Tuyl, H. (1975). A new visual illusion: Neonlike color spreading and complementary color induction between subjective contours. *Acta. Psych.*, **39**, 441–445.

Van Tuyl, H., and Leeuwenberg, E. (1977). Structural descriptions and visual illusion strength. University paper: *Report 76Fu10* Nijmegen, submitted to *Perc. & Psych. Phys.*

Vitz, P. and Todd, T. (1969). A caded element model of the perceptual processing of sequential stimuli. *Psych. Rev.*, **76**, 433–449.

Wertheimer, M. (1912). Experimentelle Studien über das sehen von Bewegung. *Z. psychol.*, **61**, 161–265.

Chapter 15

Visual Recognition of Serial Structure: Evidence of a Two-stage Scanning Model

H.-G. Geissler, F. Klix, and U. Scheidereiter

Abstract. A concept of structure is defined formally to represent perceptual and memory codes of so called sequential patterns which can be conceived of as sequences of patterns out of a set of pattern primitives. A measure of structural information of sequential patterns is defined and possible alternatives are discussed. In the experimental part of the paper data from two structure recognition tasks are considered:

(1) In a number of experiments pattern recall (reproduction) after repeated tachistoscopic presentation was required. The number of presentations necessary for full reproduction is strongly correlated to the degree of structural information assigned to the patterns. There are, however, strong dependencies on special components of structural information, indicating that the overall effect results from a mixed influence of different components, for instance, from the interruption of coding at different processing levels, depending on time characteristics of sensory buffers, short-term and long-term retention.

(2) To analyse the coding process in more detail an order detection procedure was designed. In three different pre-information conditions Ss had to decide whether a pattern subsequence was repeated within a pattern presented or not. Reaction time was recorded and analysed under the hypothesis that only serial scanning takes place. The model obtained identifies two general serial scanning processes working in parallel. Scanning turns out to be self-terminating, sensitively depending on the pre-information condition.

1. Introduction

The precise definition of the concepts of structure and of structural information ranges among the top priorities of cognitive psychology. In general, a structure can be defined by a set of elements and a set of relations on it (cf. Klix and Krause 1969), aspects of structural information content being conceived as measures on both sets.

The crucial psychological problem is the empirically valid specification of these general definitions in accordance with the particular area under consideration.

For perception and memorization of complex patterns various formal coding systems have been developed, which either have been used directly or after supplementation by rules for calculation of information content (cf. Restle 1970, Vitz and Todd 1969, Leeuwenberg 1968, 1971, Böhm 1970, Klix 1974a, b). The coding systems differ mainly in the relations admitted. Our attention has been focused on a family of sequential patterns with nominal elements, i.e. patterns restricted to the identity and successor relation (cf. Klix 1974b).

The preliminary goal in defining measures of structural information has been to use them as *a priori* predictor variables, considering any regular empirical relation as a desired outcome. This, of course, is not the last resort of applying such measures in psychology. Thorough analysis of the issue inevitably leads to the question of how in detail structural information is related to the underlying information processing.

A first step in this direction has been the attempt to split up a previously defined measure (Böhm 1970) into its proposed components, each serving as an independent predictor variable. More recent work (cf. Weiland 1976) has revealed some limitations of this approach. The present paper aims to tackle the problem more from a principal angle providing for a reanalysis of earlier results by means of the information measure and for direct confrontation with reaction time data obtained for another recognition task.

2. Structural Information and Recognition of Structure Revisited

2.1 Prerequisites

To facilitate understanding a few remarks should be made on the so-called lattice procedure for coding and calculating information content, which in our work served as point of departure.

For simplicity we restricted ourselves to sequences which exhibit two simple types of regularities: repetition and inverse (mirrored) repetition of substrings.

By way of an example, the sequence a b a b c d is an admissible string with the repetitive substring a b. This can be marked by brackets resulting in (a b)(a b) c d. This and equivalent notations will be called 'marked strings'. In general, more than one marked string can exist for a given string. The so-called lattice assigns a distinct code label to each distinct pair of the string, thus producing a second row above that of the string originally represented. This procedure is in turn applied to the newly obtained sequence and so repeatedly on until a row appears that contains but different labels. In the above example using digits for labelling elements of the pair coding rows the following lattice is obtained:

$$1\ 2\ 3\ 4$$
$$1\ 2\ 1\ 3\ 4$$
$$a\ b\ a\ b\ c\ d$$

The aim of employing the lattice procedure is twofold: the derivation of marked strings and the establishment of the lattice measure. We are commenting now only on the latter aspect.

An *a priori* measure should include the following structural attributes:

(1) length of string, i.e. number of elements in the string
(2) number of repetitions of elements
(3) repetition and inverse repetition of substrings, length of repetitive substrings.

The measure actually used accounts for these variables by four components:[1]

I_1—number of different elements
I_2—number of different pairs
I_3—number of repetitive strings
I_4—number of mirrored repetitions.

The overall measure has been defined as the sum

$$I = \sum_{v=1}^{4} I_v \tag{1}$$

or the weighted sum

$$I = \sum_{v=1}^{4} g_v \cdot I_v \tag{2}$$

of the components.

Maximum information I_{max} has been defined by

$$I_{max} = \text{supr}\,(I), \tag{3}$$

which is obtained if all elements of the string are distinct.

With l being the length of the string,

$$I_{max} = l + (l - 1) \tag{4}$$

holds after (1).

Furthermore, redundancy is defined by the equation

$$R = I_{max} - I. \tag{5}$$

Thus after (3), R is not defined with regard to the modified definition (2) of I.

---

[1] In earlier versions a correction term I_5 was introduced, which proves necessary only if I_2 is restricted to ordered pairs.

2.2 Empirical Evidence against the a priori Information Components

For the present purpose some facts have briefly to be reviewed, which defy strong empirical validation of the above-defined measures though their heuristic value is undoubted. The arguments here are restricted to results of a special recall procedure (cf. Leeuwenberg 1968). After short presentation of visual patterns Ss were required to reproduce the patterns according to a given code for the elements. The notes taken by Ss were taken away after each trial. The mean number of presentations $\overline{N}$ necessary until complete reproduction served as indicator variable.

Three major points are to be made:

(1) As Klix, Veličkovskij, and Weinrich (1972) have pointed out, there is considerable interaction of I and I_{max} in determining $\overline{N}$, thus indicating that I

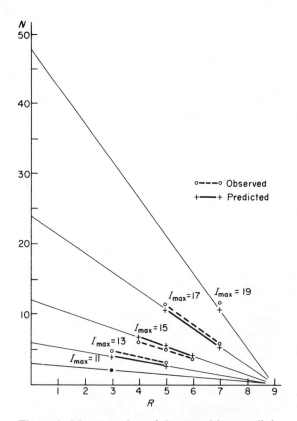

Figure 1. Mean number of ·5 s expositions until the first error-free reproduction is a linear function of redundancy R of sequential patterns for each value I_{max} (cf. equations (1) and (5)). The predicted data are described by equation (6). Data were taken from Weiland (1976)

either acts as an independent variable or is not adequately incorporated in measure (1).

Most clearly this is seen from the R-plot of $\bar{N}$ (Figure 1). Including the points for $I_{max} = 11$ and $I_{max} = 19$, the results can be well approximated by a linear fan converging at R_0 according to equation

$$\bar{N} = A^{I_{max}} \cdot (R_0 - R), \qquad (6)$$

where $R_0 \approx 9$.

(2) In experiments with patterns of constant I_{max}, Weiland (1976) did not obtain a monotone dependence on I. Even the correlations to the individual components were found to be relatively weak. Instead, a strong dependence of $\bar{N}$ on the length and number of the repeated strings was shown, once again indicating either independent action or underestimation of a structural variable by the measure and its components (Figure 2).

(3) Weiland (1976) in an experiment with two-dimensional checkerboard-like patterns obtained similar results. But the functions turned out to be much more stable and smooth when the calculation was based on scanning strategies suggested by the individual protocols than when based on *a priori* ones. This clearly suggests the relevance of the actual recognition strategy.

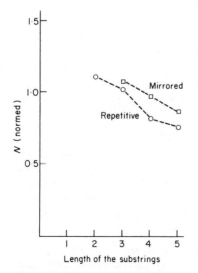

Figure 2. Mean number of ·5 s expositions until the first error-free reproduction standardized for each S is a linear, decreasing function of the length of repetitive and mirrored substrings. Data from Weiland (1976)

2.3 Process-oriented Measurement of Structural Variables.
Some Considerations

There is no reason to conclude that the checked scaling of structural information is lacking in strong empirical relevance. However, at the present stage of investigation there is a strong change in emphasis towards the demand for scales representing relevant dimensions of structure, which are invariant under given changes of conditions, e.g., of the presentation mode, of the task and of the indicator variables chosen. This is a goal which poses many more thorny problems than the construction of *a priori* scales and no one-step solution can be expected. Thus the subsequent assertions should be only considered as a reasonable starting-point.

The following considerations link up with the quoted empirical evidence and a reanalysis of the lattice measure. In accordance with further evidence presented below two general stages of processing for a great variety of recognition tasks are assumed: first, a stage of structure recognition and coding; second, a stage of sequential transfer into memory. (The question of the different memory stages involved is omitted in this context.) The first stage results in a 'marked string' representation which in the second stage is fixed and organized in correspondence with given response requirements.

From this basic assertion three conclusions can be drawn:

(1) It is the marked string representation itself that is relevant to valid information measures.
(2) At any given moment the depth of structural analysis determines the empirical marked string as memory input.
(3) The number of trials N, necessary for complete memory storage, can be a nonlinear monotone function of a linear combination of the structural information components defined on the empirical marked string.

The components $I_1, \ldots, I_4$ as defined above clearly do not meet requirements 1 and 2. This is already seen from the case of ideally marked strings, i.e. strings with complete labelling of repetitive substrings. Here the length of the repetitive strings is a structural variable of a representational unit. This attribute is to some degree reflected only by I_2, the number of pairs. But for three reasons this reflection is unsatisfactory: (1) A decrease in I_1, the number of different elements, automatically reduces the number of possible pairs, although the length of repetitive strings may remain unchanged. (2) The length of the repetitive substrings can be changed without changing I_1 and I_2, which is readily shown by way of an example:

$$1\ 2\ 3\ 4\ 5\ 1\ 2\ 6\ 7$$
$$\wedge\ \wedge\ \wedge\ \wedge\ \wedge\ \wedge\ \wedge\ \wedge\ \wedge$$
$$\text{(a b c)e c(a b c)d e,} \qquad (7a)$$

$$\overset{\overset{1}{\wedge}\ \overset{2\ \ 3}{\wedge\wedge}\ \overset{4\ \ 1}{\wedge\wedge}\ \overset{5}{\wedge}\ \overset{6\ \ 7}{\wedge\wedge}\ \overset{3}{\wedge}}{\text{(a b) (e c) (a b) c d (e c)}}.\tag{7b}$$

The latter string (7b) is derived from the preceding one by adding the first c to the end of the string. (3) The mixture of different 'natural' variables of structure in I_2 prevents the weight of repetitive string length from being separately changed by means of a weighting factor. Thus, only the simple measure (1) can be considered a reasonable approximation of an overall measure for structural information.

Bearing these deficiencies in mind, it is not difficult to suggest alternatives that avoid them. One way is to consider substrings as higher-order elements and to sum up the information content of pairs with different weights depending on the order of the elements combined.

In (7a), for example, we obtain for the pair component of information

$$I_p(\text{A e c A d e}) = w_{21} \cdot I_p(\text{A e}) + w_{11} \cdot I_p(\text{e c}) +$$
$$w_{12} \cdot I_p(\text{c A}) + w_{21} \cdot I_p(\text{A d}) +$$
$$w_{11} \cdot I_p(\text{de}) + I_p(\text{A}),\tag{8}$$

where $I_p(\text{A})$ denotes the pair information term for A, calculated in the usual way.

Alternative variants could start from a grammatical representation as suggested by Geissler and Scheidereiter 1973, Scheidereiter 1974 (cf. also Klix 1974, Thiele 1974).

Next we should look for ways of how to meet requirement 2 (p. 6). With regard to the application of a procedure for the calculation of information no special problem arises. We have just to distinguish between ideal and actual (effective) representations. If, for instance, order has not yet been recognized, string representations are not marked at all. Thus on the pair level, analogous to (8), any pair contributes separately to the total information content.

Actual calculation of this 'effective information' I_{eff} is, in general, of course a complex task. Much simplification, however, tends to arise in the experimental situation, leaving only two or three alternative marking variants appearing in an all-or-none fashion and in predictable order.

Using information from protocols and possibly from further indicators, such as eye movement recordings, a solution seems possible.

Finally, we have to discuss the third conclusion from the basic assertion. Let $\overline{I}_{\text{eff}}$ be the vector of the components of effective structural information, then $\overline{N}$ is assumed to be a function $f_{ij}(\overline{I}_{\text{eff}})$ of the vector which depends on task and individual, labelled by i and j.

As a first approximation we can assume that $\overline{N}$ depends only on the marked string representation at the terminal trial. Assuming but two states of recognition—'not recognized', 'recognized',—with the corresponding effective overall values I_{eff_0} and I_{eff_1}, we get, on average, a function of the form

$$\overline{N} = G \cdot f(I_{\text{eff}_0}) + (1 - G) \cdot f(I_{\text{eff}_1}), \quad G < 1.\tag{9}$$

From the data of Klix, Veličkovskij and Weinrich it can be inferred that $f(\cdot)$ takes an approximate exponential form.

Taking the lattice measure as a reasonable approximation in the case under consideration, (9) changes into

$$\bar{N} = G_1 \cdot C^{l_{max}} + G_2 \cdot C', \tag{10}$$

where G_1, G_2 and C denote constants.

This is equivalent to

$$\bar{N} = G_2 \cdot C^{l_{max}} \cdot \left(\frac{G_1}{G_2} + C^{-R} \right). \tag{11}$$

A fit by straight lines in a given interval leads to a relation of the form (6). This seems to support our view.

3. A Two-stage Reaction Time Model for the Recognition of Sequential Structure

3.1. Experimental Design

An approach as above developed has to be additionally supported by evidence on the temporal structure of processes of structural analysis and retention. A basis for this is provided by chronometric methods as they were initiated by Sternberg (e.g., 1969).

It suggests itself to extend the so-called Sternberg paradigm to structures as are here considered. The experimental paradigm has been developed by Scheidereiter and was called 'detection of structure'. Basic to its definition is the response mode: Ss have to respond with one of two alternative responses if a given attribute of order is found in a pattern presented. Otherwise, the complementary response is required.

The specific task was to detect repetitive substrings within sequences of relatively complex visual pattern primitives. In a factorial design the following conditions were varied:

(1) length of strings, $l = 8, 10, 12$
(2) length of repetitive substrings, $m = 1, 2, 3, 4$
(3) distance of repetitive substrings, a, defined by the difference of the sequential position indices of the corresponding elements of the substrings, $a = 1, 2, 3, 4$ with restriction $a \geq m$
(4) position of substrings, which has been randomly selected from the set of possible positions as restricted by l, m and a
(5) task by varying the information given in advance (preinformation). The conditions can be described as follows (Figure 3):

Series A: The occurrence of repetitive strings within a given pattern is to be indicated without any further information being given.

Series B: Same as *A*, but in addition the length of a possible repetitive string is marked by a sequence of blank squares at the bottom of the slide.

Series C: Same, but with the possible repetitive string notified at the bottom.

Length of the additional sequences in series *B* and *C* is referred to as 'length by instruction'.

One fourth of the trials were blank trials, i.e. the patterns presented contained no repetitive strings. Ss had to respond with 'Yes' and 'No' by pressing one of two buttons, respectively. In series *A* after responding information on length of the repetitive string detected was asked of the Ss. In a more recent investigation, this condition was dropped without essential changes in the results.

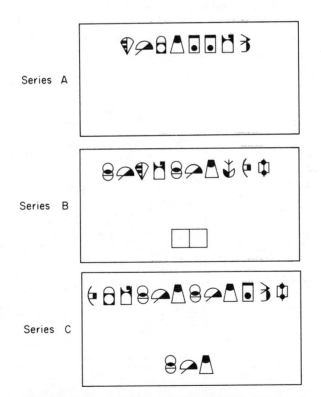

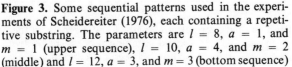

Figure 3. Some sequential patterns used in the experiments of Scheidereiter (1976), each containing a repetitive substring. The parameters are $l = 8$, $a = 1$, and $m = 1$ (upper sequence), $l = 10$, $a = 4$, and $m = 2$ (middle) and $l = 12$, $a = 3$, and $m = 3$ (bottom sequence)

3.2. Results and Model

In Figure 4 the broken lines represent the mean reaction time for series *A*, *B* and *C* plotted against length of substrings *m*. The parameters of the families of functions obtained are substring distance *a* and the response (negative or positive).

The most striking features as well as a few preliminary interpretational remarks shall be briefly summarized:

(1) Not only does reaction time for positive responses depend on substring length, but in addition that for negative responses depends on 'length by instruction'. This suggests a strategy of information processing resulting from experience in the whole set of strings, accumulated during the experiment.

(2) Series *A* and *B* exhibit a closely similar pattern of data, thus suggesting that neither length nor preinformation changes the processing strategies in an essential manner.

(3) As compared to series *A* and *B*, the trend in the series *C* outcome is reversed and flatter. Furthermore, mean reaction times are much shorter and the family of empirical functions is much more 'compressed' than in *A* and *B* cases. This indicates an essential change in the processing strategy.

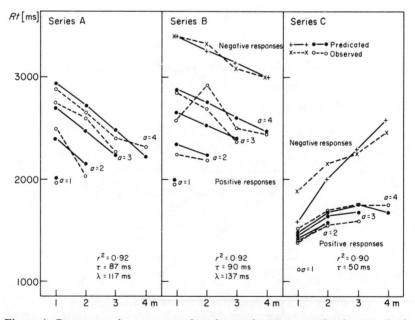

Figure 4. Rts averaged over pattern length. τ and λ represent the time required for one step in the first and second scanning process, respectively, and r^2 the squared correlation between data and model

(4) Reaction time depends nonlinearly on substring distance a, thus excluding a simple linear strategy in performing the recognition task.

The model designed by Scheidereiter and Geissler and further elaborated by Scheidereiter (1976) can here be described only in its basic assumptions. On top of the list stands the proposition taken from Sternberg's serial scanning model, that only serial scanning occurs. Since only few parallel processing models have been checked and disproved the seriality assumption might be considered with some suspicion. However, as serial scanning models render possible the understanding of many detail effects (otherwise completely unconnected) in terms of information processing categories, the general assumption seems to be indirectly validated.

From many considerations follows under the assumption of serial scanning at least two-stage information processing until specific decision and response generation occurs, which corresponds to a third, separate stage. The first stage can be interpreted as responsible for search and marking of repetitive strings, the second as a kind of recoding stage providing for the production of a new representation in memory with the repetitive strings as higher-order units. So the fact that no second stage can be separated under the conditions of series C may result from the knowledge of the possible repetitive string from the very beginning of each trial.

From among the set of models that do not violate the qualitative properties (1) to (4), different implementations are possible. The main assumptions for one specification of the first stage are illustrated by Figures 5 and 6. Figure 5 shows the type of serial pattern analysis assumed for series A: Two internal representations of the string are compared by laying them alongside each other and subsequent exhaustive comparison of the elements lying one upon the other. The relative position of the two string copies is assumed to change step by step from a shift of one element until a match occurs, the match terminating further shift and resulting in a marked string by labelling of the substring.

By applying this strategy to the conditions in series A and B one obtains for the number of comparison operations

$$k = \sum_{i=1}^{i=a} l - i \equiv a \cdot l - \frac{a(a + 1)}{2}, \tag{12}$$

if the comparison for each shift is assumed to be exhaustive. This is in good accordance with the approximate paraboloid a-trend observed. The predicted $a \cdot l$ interaction could not be verified with the present data. A good fit has been obtained by setting l constantly 8.

The strategy applies to series C in a modified way (Figure 6). Instead of a copy of the whole string a representation of the displayed substring is put alongside. Furthermore, the data provide evidence for an even subtler change: since the length of the possible repetitive string is known, $m - 1$ elements can be skipped when shifting after the first match.

310

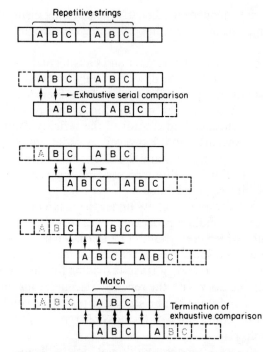

Figure 5. Schematic representation of the detection of repetitive substrings in series *A* and *B* by a number of exhaustive serial comparisons

For negative cases the assumption is successful that serial comparison is terminated on a shift which is the highest to be expected under the particular preinformation conditions. This is demonstrated by Figure 7, where reaction time for different *l* values is plotted against the 'virtual' maximum *a*-value to be expected from the 'length by instruction'. The figure exhibits a fairly smooth continuation of the data for positive responses with 'real' *a*-values.

In all series the entire process can equivalently by represented by diagonal scanning of different identity matrices (cf. Figures 8, 9).

This first stage of order recognition and marking the string representation can already explain the wide differences between mean reaction time levels for series *A* and *B* on the one hand, and series *C* on the other. But the first stage model alone does not account for the trend reversal.

The latter property is provided for if assuming a second scanning applied to the marked string representation. To get a fit it is necessary to assume that in this scanning the scan of the marked string takes a constant period of time.

So the model explains the negative slopes of the curves in series *A* and *B* in terms of a saving of operations within this stage, the flatter course in series *B* being attributed to the identification of the preinformation. For the present implementation of the model the best fit is obtained for each series separately

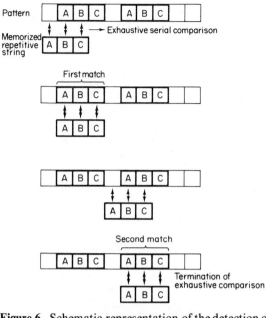

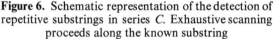

Figure 6. Schematic representation of the detection of repetitive substrings in series *C*. Exhaustive scanning proceeds along the known substring

if the second scanning is assumed to proceed in parallel to the first scan (cf. Figure 4). Thus, after terminating the first process, different additional time spans are necessary for the second process.

A slightly worse quantitative fit is obtained under the assumption of full independence of the first and second stages, but in this case the model exhibits a high degree of parameter invariance. The parameter estimates for series *A*, *B* are 62 ms each, for series *C* 63 ms and 54 ms for positive and negative responses, respectively.

It remains to be pointed out here that further data obtained under stronger task variation (Meyer 1976) support the two-stage view. But at the same time, as for the present case, the high adaptivity and flexibility of the internal organization (scanning strategy, termination) of the stages and their interaction are to be emphasized.

4. Conclusions

Our theoretical considerations and the empirical evidence presented lead us to the following hypothetical conclusions:

(i) In the tasks considered the recognition of sequential order of nominal elements is linked with two processing stages, the first leading to a primary coding of order resulting in a marked string representation, the second serving sequential transfer of marked string components into

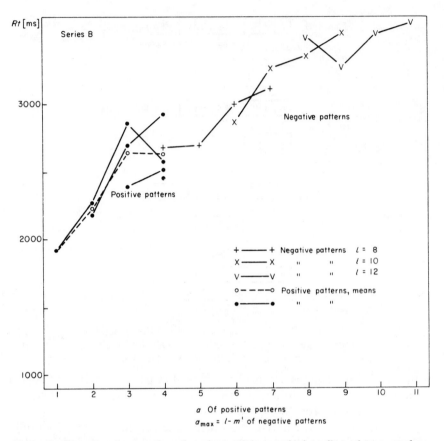

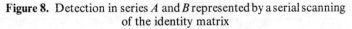

Figure 7. Reaction time as plotted against a-values and 'virtual' maximum a-values to be expected from the 'length by instruction'. Parameter: length of the entire strings, l

memory. At least with regard to the particular task of order detection this type of processing involves redundant operations. Thus it seems effective only if viewed on the background of a large-scale task variation within more natural situations, where contextual information changes often unexpectedly.

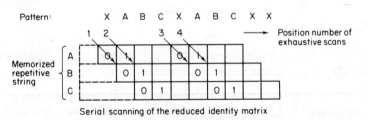

Figure 8. Detection in series A and B represented by a serial scanning of the identity matrix

313

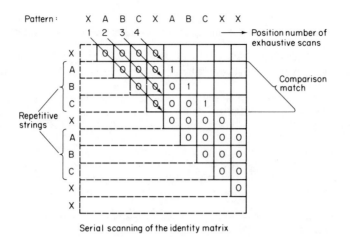

Serial scanning of the identity matrix

Figure 9. Detection in series *C* represented by serial scanning of the reduced identity matrix

(ii) Information measures describing recognition performance have to meet certain requirements which follow from the fact that they presumably refer to structural attributes of marked string representations.

(iii) The two general stages are adaptively organized as depending on the specific task performed. This adaptivity corresponds to a flexible combination rule of relevant information components.

From the last conclusion it might seem as if measures of structural information are at the most variables of secondary concern as compared to a detailed systems analysis of recognition processes. This, however, is not true. Flexible changes of recognition procedures presuppose internal criteria for comparison of possible alternatives. Thus the search for stable overall measures remains a goal for further research. Such measures should, however, include task-related information components.

References

Böhm, H. Das Gittermodell—ein Beitrag zur Analyse und Benschreibung von Strukturbildungsprozessen in der Wahrnehmung. Diploma thesis (unpubl.), Berlin, 1970.

Geissler, H.-G. and Scheidereiter U., Information content and the result of perception (in Russian), Moscow, 1973.

Klix, F. Struktur, Strukturbeschreibung und Erkennungsleistung. In: Klix, F. (Hrsg.) *Organismische Informationsverarbeitung*. Berlin, 1974a.

Klix, F. Interrelationships between information content, fixation of memory traces and internal activation state. In: *Cybernetics and Bionics. Proceedings of the 5th Congress of Deutsche Gesellschaft für Kybernetik*, held at Nuremberg, March 28–30, 1973. München, 1974b.

Klix, F. and Krause B., Zur Definition des Begriffes 'Struktur', seinen Eigenschaften und Darstellungsmöglichkeiten in der Experimentalpsychologie. *Z. Psychol.* **173**, 1969.

Klix, F., Veličkovskij B. and Weinrich, L. Strukturgehalt geometrischer Muster und seine Widerspiegelung im psychologischen Verhalten bei Rekonstruktionsanforderungen. Unpubl. Berlin 1972.

Leeuwenberg, E. *Structural information of visual patterns.* Den Haag, 1968.

Leeuwenberg, E. A perceptual coding language for visual and auditory patterns. *Am. J. Psychol.*, **84**, 1971.

Meyer, L. -U. Reaktionszeitanalysen bei der Strukturentdeckung in visuellen Mustern. Diploma thesis (unpubl.), Berlin, 1976.

Restle, F. Theory of serial pattern learning: Structural trees. *Psychol. Rev.*, **77**, 481–495, 1970.

Scheidereiter, U. Zur Beschreibung strukturierter Objekte mit kontextfreien Grammatiken. In: Klix, F. (Hrsg.) *Organismische Informationsverarbeitung.* Berlin, 1974.

Scheidereiter, U. Die Entdeckung von Strukturen in visuellen Mustern. Zur Systemanalyse von Erkennungsprozessen. Diss. (A), Humboldt-Universität zu Berlin, Berlin, 1977.

Sternberg, S. The discovery of processing stages: Extensions of Donders' method. *Acta Psychologica*, **30**, 1969a, 276–315.

Thiele, N. Zur Definition von Kompliziertheitsmaßen für endliche Objekte. In: Klix, F. (Hrsg.) *Organismische Informations-verarbeitung.* Berlin, 1974.

Vitz, P. C. and Todd, R. C. A coded element model of the perceptual processing of sequential stimuli. *Psychol. Rev.*, **76**, 433–449, 1969.

Weiland, C. H. Analyse von Strukturerkennungsprozessen—die psychologische Relevanz eines Ansatzes zur Bestimmung des strukturellen Informationsgehaltes sequentieller Muster. Diss. (A), Humboldt-Universität zu Berlin, Berlin, 1976.

Chapter 16

Induction and Representation of Sequential Patterns

Herbert A. Simon

Abstract. A small set of formalisms has been shown to be sufficient to describe the ways in which human subjects encode patterned sequences of digits or letters, and also more complicated sequential patterns like musical patterns. However, there are usually a number of alternative ways of representing any particular pattern, and the actual encoding will vary as a function of a subject's previous experience and the strategy he adopts for performing a particular task. Detailed characteristics of the task presented to the subject may also, by affecting the lead on short-term memory or in other ways, influence what encoding he uses. Hence, the pattern-encoding language, but not the patterns themselves, may be regarded as a psychological invariant.

The central goal of cognitive psychology is to discover and describe the invariant structures and processes of the human information processing system. A serious difficulty in achieving this goal is that the information processing system is adaptive: it does not behave in any unvarying, inflexible way, but molds its behaviour in any particular task environment to the requirements of the task confronting it (Simon, 1969). The system's flexibility is, of course, not unlimited. Given a sufficiently difficult task, it will simply fail to perform it; and even with tasks it can handle, it will not always find the most efficient route to their accomplishment.

A closely related difficulty that interferes with finding invariants in human information processing is that many, if not most, cognitive tasks can be performed in a wide variety of different ways, using different programs. Not only does the system often fail to find the most efficient of these programs, as suggested above; in most cases it does not even search for the most efficient, but settles upon a satisficing or 'good enough' program. Many features of the context in which the task is performed, as well as experiences in the previous history of the system, combine to determine which of the satisficing programs is employed for a particular task at a particular time. In the context of problem

316

solving, Allen Newell and I have put the matter this way (Newell and Simon, 1972, pp. 788–9):

(1) A few, and only a few, gross characteristics of the human IPS are invariant over task and problem solver.
(2) These characteristics are sufficient to determine that a task environment is represented (in the IPS) as a problem space, and that problem solving takes place in a problem space.
(3) The structure of the task environment determines the possible structures of the problem space.
(4) The structure of the problem space determines the possible programs that can be used for problem solving.

In this passage, 'problem space' means the way in which the problem is represented internally by the problem solver. The adjective 'possible' in the third and fourth propositions emphasizes that the task environment does not determine the problem space uniquely, nor the problem space the program.

The plasticity of the information processing system may exhibit itself at three levels. First, there is the underlying physiological system, analogous to the 'hardware' of a computer system. The physiology of the nervous system may change in the course of maturation, or through senile deterioration, or by trauma. Second, there are the stored contents of the system, the memory, which undergoes continuing, major change through the processes we call learning, analogous to changes in data and program in a computer memory.[1] Third, the programs stored in memory are themselves adaptive, the behaviour they produce being highly contingent on the specific situation in which they are operating. Programs are adaptive because they contain numerous branch points that make the sequences of processes responsive to tests on information derived from perceptions or held in short-term memory. All of these sources of variability complicate the task of identifying and characterizing the underlying invariants of the human information processing system. Yet it is these invariants that are the proper subject matter of psychological theory.

Programs as Invariants

If cognitive behaviour were mainly the product of a relatively small number of specific adaptive programs, then the task of psychological theory would be relatively clear. In that case, cognitive theory would consist of descriptions of these programs, combined with demonstrations showing how, in interaction

[1] Of course, the changes produced in learning are also physiological changes—of a mostly unknown nature—but it is useful, in discussing the brain as in discussing a computer, to distinguish between 'hardware' and 'software'. Learning in the brain is best compared with change in the data and program stored in the computer memory. Memory changes in a computer are, after all, also changes in the physical state of the machine. These changes are different, however, from the more permanent changes that might be made in the computer's wiring diagram.

with the stimuli in particular task environments, they could account for task performance in these environments. The programs themselves would be the invariants of the theory. Moreover, since each program would contain mechanisms for orienting behaviour to goals, it would account for adaptive behaviour over a range of task environments.

The content of such a theory might consist of one, or a few, programs for solving problems; one or several programs for handling induction tasks; a program for perceptual recognition of patterns, and for learning to recognize new patterns; one or more programs for storing semantic information in long-term memory, and for accessing such information; and so on. In its overall shape, such a body of theory would resemble theory in a field like physiology or biochemistry. A large part of the theory of physiology consists of descriptions of circulatory mechanisms, of the mechanisms of digestion, of respiratory mechanisms, and so on. An information processing theory of an analogous kind would look like a physiology of the mind, its primitives consisting of elementary information processes instead of chemical reactions, and its programs describing the major components of the cognitive system.

In the past twenty years, substantial progress has been made toward building an information-processing theory of human cognition along these lines. The General Problem Solver (GPS), for example (Newell, Shaw and Simon, 1960; Ernst and Newell, 1969; Newell and Simon, 1972), is a program capable of simulating a good deal of human problem-solving behaviour, employing a form of means-ends analysis as its central mechanism of adaptation. The EPAM program (Feigenbaum, 1961), an organization of rote learning processes, accounts for many of the known phenomena of human rote verbal learning (Simon and Feigenbaum, 1964; Gregg and Simon, 1967) and of perceptual recognition of simple patterns (Simon and Gilmartin, 1973).

Of more direct relevance to the particular phenomena to be considered in this paper, a program constructed by Simon and Kotovsky (1963; also Kotovsky and Simon, 1973) simulates some of the processes used by human subjects to extrapolate sequential patterns of the sort found in the Thurstone Letter Series Completion Test. (This program was, somehow, never baptized with an acronym. To remedy this lack, we will call it here, SEREX, for SERies EXtrapolation.)

A number of other programs can be mentioned that have had some measure of success in accounting for significant aspects of human cognition: a whole spate of programs, beginning with the work of Quillian (1968), for simulating long-term memory organization, the parsing of natural language input for storage in long-term memory, and accessing of long-term memory (see, e.g., Bobrow and Collins, 1975); the UNDERSTAND program for simulating the processes for generating new problem representations (Hayes and Simon, 1974); and many others.

While these broad-purpose programs have had substantial success in explaining some of the principal mechanisms of human cognition, they have also encountered some serious problems that derive from the plasticity, discussed earlier, of the human cognitive system. The first of these problems stems from the ample evidence of individual differences among subjects in performing cognitive tasks. If the General Problem Solver is an accurate description of the processes used by some particular person, call him X, to solve problems, then it is not a completely accurate description of the processes used by persons who do not solve problems in exactly the same manner that X does (i.e. almost all other persons). At best, the General Problem Solver is a description of the 'representative subject', a blood brother to the 'representative firm' of classical economic theory.

There is a further, and equally serious, difficulty with GPS. From the empirical evidence, it appears doubtful that a human subject has a single general problem solving program that he applies to all of the problem environments in which he finds himself. Instead, it may be that he generates a new program for each task environment (or retrieves it from long-term memory, if the environment is a familiar one); and that his behaviour is to be explained in terms of a large repertory of such programs, each adapted to a narrow range of tasks. Each of these programs, though independent, might consist of an organization of GPS-like processes (Simon, 1975). Another possibility, for which some evidence exists in the task environment of chess playing (Chase and Simon, 1973, 1974), is that problem-solving skill relies heavily upon learned capabilities for recognizing a very large number (tens or hundreds of thousands) of specific patterns corresponding to equally specific classes of problem situations, associated with which in memory are responses that are appropriate to these patterns.

These same difficulties of constructing a single general theory arise in the domain of pattern extrapolation, the domain for which SEREX was constructed. Here again, significant individual differences are observable among subjects, so that it cannot be claimed that SEREX describes more than a representative subject (or perhaps even the representative college sophomore). Moreover, recent empirical and theoretical work by Restle (1976), Jones and Zamostny (1975), Greeno and Simon (1974), and Gerritsen, Gregg and Simon (1975) shows that, if subjects actually possess a SEREX-like program for extrapolating sequences, then this program can be modified by changes in task instructions, and by relatively small changes in the nature of the patterned sequences that are presented to the subjects.

The remainder of this paper is devoted to reassessing the status of a program like SEREX as a theory of serial pattern induction (or induction in general), and drawing from this reassessment some conclusions about the appropriate form for theories of human cognition.

Invariants in Pattern Induction

A substantial number of information-processing explanations of the methods that people use to discover patterns in sequences of digits or letters have been put forward in the past two decades.[2] The theories have made use of several different formalisms, for example, phrase-structure grammars (Restle, 1967), and computer programming languages (Simon and Kotovsky, 1963).

Typical stimuli for tasks in this domain would be sequences like: ABMCDM. . ., or 123 321 456 654. The stimuli are constructed from an alphabet (ordered set) of symbols: the digits (or some subset of them), letters of the Roman alphabet, simple geometric figures (square, triangle, circle), the scales of musical notes, and so on. The stimuli consist of sequences of these symbols, which may continue indefinitely (as in the first example above), may be finite in length (as in the second example), or may be periodic (the second example, continued simply by repeating it). The stimuli are usually constructed in a patterned fashion: that is, so that they can be recoded more or less succinctly in terms of a small number of relations. In the first example above, for instance, every third symbol is an 'M', the remaining symbols are simply the letters of the alphabet in their usual order. The second example consists of the first three digits, in order, then the same digits in reverse order, then the next three digits, and so on.

Since the symbols used in the sequences are most often drawn from an ordered set, they come with two ready-made relations defined on them: the relation of *identity* (or *same*), and the relation of *successor* (or *next*). These are, in fact, the relations we used in describing the patterns of the two examples. In some research that has been carried out using integers, the relations of *sum* and *difference* have also been employed. For example, the sequence 1 1 2 3 5 8 1 3 . . . can be encoded by representing each symbol as the sum of the two that preceded it.

Patterns may be *hierarchic* in structure. For example, 123 321 456 654 may be encoded as two six-digit sequences, one beginning with 1, the other with 4. Each six-digit sequence, in turn, may be encoded as two triads, and each triad as a sequence of three digits—a hierarchy of three levels.

Essentially, these are the materials out of which all of these stimuli are constructed: ordered sets of stimuli, the relations of same and next (and occasionally sum and difference), and hierarchy. Quite complex patterns can be generated from this rather parsimonious set of raw materials, and indeed it has been argued (Simon and Sumner, 1968) that nothing more is needed to describe the patterns in the musical works of Bach, Beethoven, Schoenberg, or the Beatles.

In some of the experiments that have been carried out with patterned sequences, the subject's task is to extrapolate sequences of which initial segments are given as stimuli. In other experiments, the subject's task is to memorize a set of finite sequences. In still other experiments, his task is to judge the relative complexities of different sequences. I will also discuss an experiment in which the subject's task is to construct sequences, given their patterns.

---

[2] For a review, and references to the literature, see Simon (1972) and Jones (1971).

The SEREX Program

SEREX is a computer program that purports to be a theory of the processes that human subjects use to perform the first of the tasks listed above: to extrapolate sequences from given initial segments. As a matter of fact, SEREX is not a single theory, but a whole collection of closely related theories, for the program exists in a number of variants. In making detailed comparisons between the programs and the behaviour of human subjects, Kotovsky and Simon (1973) took a particular version of the program, Variant C, as *the* theory.

Processes

The SEREX program operates in two main segments. First, it induces from the given initial segment of the sequence a pattern capable of generating it. Then an interpretive process uses this pattern to extrapolate the sequence as far as is desired. The pattern-generating component of the program is divided, in turn, into two parts. The first of these seeks to discover the periodicity of the sequence (the period is three in both of our examples); the second induces a pattern description using this periodicity to guide its search and its organization of the description.

We may outline the structure of SEREX thus:

Induce Pattern
   Determine Period
   Describe Pattern
      Find Relations
      Assemble Pattern Description
Extrapolate Pattern
   Initialize Symbols
   Compute Successive Symbols

SEREX, viewed as theory, asserts that human subjects will use the same processes as these, organized in the same way, to perform the series extrapolation task. SEREX can be tested in a variety of ways. For example, since it can solve certain extrapolation problems but will fail on others, it can be used to make predictions of problem difficulty. It can also be tested more directly by comparing the program trace with thinking-aloud protocols or other evidence of the successive processes used by human subjects while solving extrapolation problems. The protocols, and other data on subject behaviours, permit inferences to be drawn not only about processes, but also about the representations that subjects use in order to organize the induced pattern information and to hold it in memory. The subjects' pattern representations can then be compared with those induced by SEREX.

The next three sections of this paper will illustrate these three methods of testing the validity of the program as a theory: first, analysing measures of problem difficulty; next, examining evidences of problem-solving processes; finally, comparing the pattern representations arrived at by program and subjects, respectively.

Testing the Program: Problem Difficulty

Testing SEREX as a theory of human behaviour in this task raises all of the questions, discussed earlier, about the variability of human behaviour. This can be seen in the data on problem difficulty. The program succeeded in solving 7 of the 15 problems presented to it, failing to find solutions for the remaining 8. The difficulty of these same problems for groups of human subjects was measured by the percentage of the subjects who found solutions. In one group of subjects, for example, the percentage of problems solved correctly ranged from 40 to 100, and averaged 9·25. The point biserial correlations between the program's behaviour and problem difficulty for two sets of subjects were ·58 and ·62, respectively, while the rank-order correlation of problem difficulty between these same two sets of subjects was about ·87. Thus, although the program's predictions of problem difficulty do not correlate with difficulty measured in human subjects quite as well as difficulty correlates between two groups of subjects, yet the former correlations are substantial; the program and subjects rank problems by difficulty in roughly the same way.

It is also instructive to compare the program's behaviour with that of a subject who solved the same number of problems as it did. Subject 9 in the group of 12 was the only one who solved exactly 7 problems, as Version C of the program did. On five problems, both subject and program found the correct answer, on six problems, both were wrong; on two problems, only the subject was correct, on two problems only the program, yielding a tetrachoric correlation of about ·7. This is equal to the correlation between Subjects 7 and 8, each of whom solved 8 problems, and subjects 10 and 11, each of whom solved 6. By this test, the program agrees with subjects in assessment of relative problem difficulty as closely as individual subjects agree with each other.[3] From these data, it is not unreasonable to regard the program as a representative subject having a problem-solving ability comparable to Subject 9.

Testing the Program: Information Processes

But in this kind of theory construction, we are interested not merely in making predictions of problem difficulty. We would like to test also whether or not there is close agreement between the processes used by the model and the processes used by the human subjects. In doing this, we test the important assumption that, while there are differences among the programs used by different subjects, these differences mainly relate to details of the programs, and

---

[3] These comparisons are derived from the data reported in Simon and Kotovsky, 1963, Table 3, and Kotovsky and Simon, 1973, Table 2.

that their basic structures and organization are relatively invariant, at least over the subculture from which the subjects were drawn. If the program representing the theory also shares these same basic structures and organization, then it can legitimately be regarded as a representative subject. The structures and organization that are common to the programs of (almost) all subjects, and that are shared by the simulation program are the psychological invariants we are looking for.

This general point of view was adopted by Kotovsky and Simon (1973) in testing the SEREX program. The basic structures and organization in terms of which they described the program were these:

(1) The program had mechanisms for recognizing the relations of *same*, *next*, and *predecessor* on familiar ordered lists (e.g., the Roman alphabet and the digits).

(2) The program had mechanisms to induce a new ordered list ('alphabet') from a given sequence, and to apply the *next* relation to extrapolate with it. (Example: given a triangle followed by a circle, followed by a square, the program could treat circle as 'next' to triangle, square 'next' to circle, and triangle 'next' to square.

(3) The program had mechanisms for generating and fixating a pattern description of a sequence, using the mechanisms listed above.

(4) The program had mechanisms for extrapolating a sequence by interpreting the pattern description it induced from it.

(5) In inducing a pattern from a sequence, the program first discovers the periodicity in the sequences, then induces the full pattern using this periodicity.

(6) When extrapolating a sequence, the program first initializes the pattern (marks its place on certain lists), then uses the relations listed above to extrapolate.

The empirical task, then, is to show that these characteristics of the program are also present in the programs of the human subjects. The test can go a little farther. It can also attempt to account for individual differences among subjects in terms of variations in their programs that do not affect the structural and organizational invariants listed above. It may also endeavour to make qualitative predictions about likely sources of error among the human subjects—essential components may be missing from a subject's program (e.g., he may have an inadequate repertory of relations), he may be confused by spurious relations (relations that are present in the sequence but irrelevant to the pattern), or he may be unable to organize and record the relations he detects in a coherent pattern description.

A number of forms of evidence are available for testing hypotheses and predictions of these kinds. Simon and Kotovsky (1973) have confirmed the main features of the SEREX program, as described above, principally from thinking-aloud protocols, and timing information obtained from responses in the sequence extrapolation task. It can be asserted with considerable confidence that human subjects possess the mechanisms that constitute the first four items in the description, and that they carry out the pattern induction and extrapolation in the order indicated by the fifth and sixth items.

The regularities that have been observed might, of course, disappear if subjects from a quite different culture than that of American university students were tested, although the only obviously culture-dependent component of the SEREX program is the set of ordered lists that are assumed to be familiar to subjects. (Subjects brought up without benefit of the Roman alphabet would have difficulty with a sequence like AMBCDM . . .).[4]

Testing the Program: Pattern Encodings

At the heart of the sequence extrapolation process is the pattern encoding that describes the regularities in the sequence. What can be said about the specific encodings that subjects use to represent patterns?

For a subject to encode the pattern of a sequence means for him to store in memory knowledge that permits him to generate each successive symbol of the sequence from information about a subset of the symbols that precedes it. In the simplest case, a subject who has stored the knowledge that each member of a particular sequence is the successor digit to the preceding member can continue the sequence 1 2 3 4 . . . . Similarly, the knowledge that each symbol is the sum of the two preceding it permits him to extrapolate 3 5 8 13 . . .

The pattern of a sequence is precisely this knowledge which permits extrapolation. To a considerable extent, the information that a subject must store in order to extrapolate a particular sequence is dictated by the sequence itself, as is shown by the two examples above. To handle the first example, he must employ the successor relation on the digits, and to handle the second one, he must employ the relation of sum. Even for these simple sequences, however, there exist alternative encodings. The first sequence can also be described as an alternation of the sequence of odd numbers and the sequence of even numbers—each number being regarded, in this interpretation, as the successor (on the alphabet of odds or evens) of the second number preceding it. In the second example, the ith symbol, s_i, can also be represented as $s_i = s_{i-3} + 2S_{i-2}$.

To the extent that the encoding of a sequence is determined by the sequence itself, the simple fact that a subject can extrapolate the sequence correctly (i.e. in the manner intended by the experimenter) demonstrates that he is able to detect the relevant relations among symbols, to recognize the alphabet to which the symbols belong, and to store the information about relations and alphabets in an appropriate organization in memory. To the extent that there

[4] A scientific mission to the People's Republic of China, in which I participated, unintentionally but thoroughly confused our hosts by listing our names alphabetically. Our hosts evidently did not doubt that the list must be ordered by some principle; but the only principle they could discover was a perfect (and entirely accidental) inverse relation between age and 'rank' in the delegation–an ordering not easily reconciled with the Chinese ethos.

are alternative ways of describing a sequence, additional information is needed about the subject's behaviour to determine how he has encoded it. In practice, it is not difficult to obtain this information experimentally. Kotovsky and Simon (1973), for example, were able to determine with at least moderate certainty how subjects had encoded sequences in about 85% of more than 200 cases they examined. In 58% of these successful cases, the encoding agreed in detail with that predicted by SEREX, and in another 10% it varied only in minor details from the prediction. Among 14 subjects, only five of the 15 sequences tested had a unique coding (four of the five identical with the coding predicted by SEREX). The remaining 10 sequences were encoded in at least two different ways by different subjects.

In the case of sequences that are encoded differently by different subjects, we are back to the position of requiring of a theory only that it be representative of subject behaviour. Thus, in the case of seven of the ten problems for which subjects offered more than one encoding, SEREX agreed with a plurality (and usually a majority) of the subjects. In the case of sequences that are encoded in a unique manner, it is not clear whether the program's success in prediction means that it has captured a psychological invariant, or merely that it is responsive (but perhaps using different processes than were used by the human subjects) to the demands of the task environment. In this case, data on the processes used to induce the pattern are essential for testing the veridicality of SEREX as a theory of behaviour.

In recent years, Jones (e.g., Jones and Zamostny, 1975) has studied the adaptation of subjects' pattern encoding to the structure of the sequences presented. In particular, she has used 'hierarchic' patterns (e.g., 345 543 432 234), where the second half of the pattern has a structure similar to the first half, and 'linear' patterns (e.g., 345 123 234 456), where each triad is obtained by some operation on the preceding one. The subjects were shown to use encodings appropriate to the structure of the patterns. Again, the principal source of variance is the structure of the stimulus material, and the main psychological phenomenon demonstrated by the experiments is that the subjects are, in fact, adaptive in their encoding behaviour.

It is important that we not confuse the subject's representation of a pattern with the particular notation *we* use to describe that representation. A number of alternative notations have been offered by various investigators.[5] Some of these notations are quite general; others apply only to particular kinds of sequences. However, in all cases where the notations are applicable, there is a very high correlation (usually $\cdot 8$ to $\cdot 9$) between the number of symbols required to describe patterns in one of the notations, and the number required in any one of the others. The reason for this, of course, is that the various coding schemes are not unrelated but are all based on the same set of relations, on notation for iteration, and on notation to indicate nesting or hierarchy. Thus, if we measure the complexity of a pattern by the number of symbols required to describe it in a

---

[5] Some of these are reviewed in Simon, 1972.

particular notation, the relative complexities of different sequences do not depend very much on which notation we use for the measurement. This is fortunate, for it gives us some confidence in predicting that the patterns will order themselves according to complexity in the same way when they are expressed in the internal notation used by the subject's brain in storing them. The relatively high correlations that obtain among complexity of the encoded pattern, judged complexity of sequences, and difficulty of problems lends support to this hypothesis (Simon, 1972).

Summary

In the three kinds of tests that have been sketched out here, SEREX has stood up well as a theory of the representative subject. We are justified in thinking that the basic invariants, at the information processing level, underlying the performance of this task are pretty well identified and described by the program. The discrepancies of behaviour between program and subjects are of no greater magnitude than the differences between subjects, or than the changes in subject behaviour that can be induced by changing the nature of the stimulus material.

If we wish to pay particular attention to the adaptiveness of the human information processing system, rather than to its invariance (whether this invariance is 'intrinsic' or due to invariant requirements of the task environment), then we must seek experimental means for manipulating the behaviour, while keeping the task stimuli fixed. In the final section of this paper, an example of this kind of experimental manipulation will be examined.

Alternative Strategies for Extrapolation

Most experiments on patterned sequences have presented the subject either with the task of discovering the pattern in the sequence and then extrapolating it, or of learning the sequence (which is usually accomplished by first discovering the pattern, then memorizing the pattern rather than the raw sequence). The somewhat different task we shall discuss here is extrapolating the sequence on the basis of a given description of its pattern (Gerritsen, Gregg and Simon, 1975). Experiments with this task show that a subject may use a number of quite different processes to carry out the extrapolation of a pattern, and that the processes can be identified from latency and error data.

The pattern consists of a digit followed by three, four, or five letters, as in the following example:

1 TRM

The letters designate operators: T for 'transpose' (successor), R for 'repeat' (identity), and M for 'mirror' (7's complement, in this experimental situation). Thus, to transpose a digit means to increase it or decrease it by one; to mirror a digit means to take its 7's complement. The application of these operators in the example is to be interpreted as follows: T applied to 1 gives 2; R applied to the sequence, 1 2, gives 1 2 again; M applied to the sequence, 1 2 1 2, gives 6 5 6 5. Hence, the entire sequence obtained from 1 TRM is:

12126565

In this interpretation of the formula, each operator is applied, in turn, to the entire sequence of digits produced by the previous operators. Hence, three operators produce a sequence of 8 digits from an initial digit; four operators, 16 digits; and so on. In the above example, applying T increased the digit by one. If T is applied, however, after an odd number of M's have been applied, the rule is that it decreases rather than increases the digit.

The process just described is one way to produce the sequence from the pattern, a way that has been called the Doubling method (Greeno and Simon, 1974). It can be depicted graphically as in Figure 1(a). The arrows show the input, output, and operator for each successive digit in the sequence.

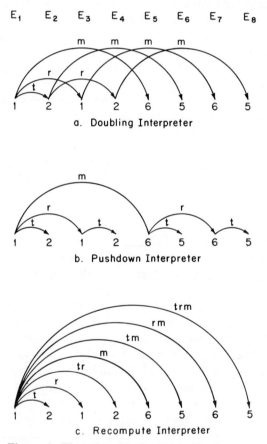

a. Doubling Interpreter

b. Pushdown Interpreter

c. Recompute Interpreter

Figure 1. Three interpretive processes for producing a sequence from 1 TRM. The arrows show the inputs, outputs, and operators for each successive digit in a three-operator problem. (Adapted from Greeno and Simon, 1974, p. 192)

A second interpretive method for generating the sequence, called the Pushdown method, is shown in Figure 1(b). Each response is obtained by applying one operator.to some previous response. The arrows in the figure show which previous response: the first, then the second, then the first, then the fourth, and so on. Applying this method requires that certain of the responses be retained, to be used later as inputs to operators for obtaining subsequent responses. One possible method for holding them in memory is on a 'stack' or pushdown list, organized so that each new response, as it is made, is retained at the top of the stack and, when no longer needed, removed from the top. The Pushdown method will always produce exactly the same sequence from a pattern as the Doubling method.

A third method, which will also always generate the same sequence is called the Recompute method. It is depicted in Figure 1(c). In this method, each digit is computed directly from the intial digit by applying one or more operators: the first, then the second, then the first and second, then the third, then the first and third, and so on.

Latencies for carrying out the extrapolations using these three different methods can be estimated from models of the processes used by each method if the time requirements of each process are known. For example, suppose that it is known that it takes 500 ms to make a response, 1000 ms to retrieve an operator from memory, and 1000 ms to retrieve a symbol from memory. The average latencies for successive quadruples of responses on these assumptions are shown in Figure 2. The Doubling method becomes gradually faster,

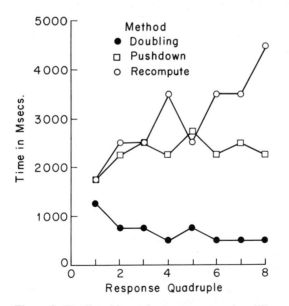

Figure 2. Predicted latencies per response, in milliseconds, for three methods. (Average for quadruples of responses in five-operator problems)

328

for fewer and fewer operation retrievals are required per symbol produced. The time per response with the Pushdown method remains relatively constant; while the time increases rapidly with the Recompute method as the number of operator retrievals per response increases.

These predictions of the model can be tested by training subjects in each of the three methods and measuring their performance latencies. Since subjects using each method can be expected to make errors that are characteristic of that method and different in distribution from the errors associated with the other methods, an independent check is available to verify that the subject is actually using the method in which he was trained. Figure 3 shows the response latencies of three highly trained subjects performing the task with each of the three methods. It can be seen from the figure that the predictions of the model are borne out, at least qualitatively, by the data. It can also be seen from Figure 3, however, that there are substantial differences in the response patterns of different subjects. While the model accounts for gross characteristics of the response, there is much fine detail that is not captured, and this detail reflects important differences among individuals. Not all of the methods were equally easy for the subjects to apply. The Doubling method was the easiest, and subjects had to guard themselves against a tendency to 'backslide' to that method from either of the others.

The data from this experiment underline the central theses of this paper. The behaviour of the subjects was generally what would be predicted from a knowledge of the task environment (adaptiveness) and the specific instructions as to the method to be applied (learning). Insofar as there were departures from the behaviour predicted from the model, they were mostly idiosyncratic, differing greatly from one subject to another. Hence, what the experiment mainly teaches us about the human information processing

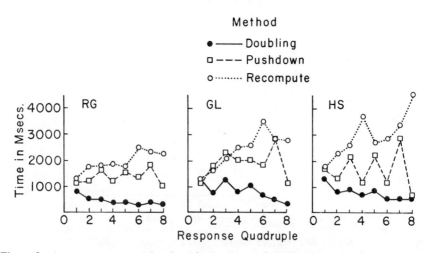

Figure 3. Averages, over quadruples of responses, of median latencies for each of three methods—three experienced subjects

system is: (a) that it is able to adapt to the requirements of this particular task, and (b) that it is able to learn these particular methods of task performance.

There is one other characteristic of the human information processing system that one could hope to determine with the help of an experiment like this one: the basic process times for elementary information processes. If an operation like 'retrieve an operator from memory' or 'retrieve a symbol from memory' were a truly elementary process, then we would expect consistency in the times required for the operation, not only while working on a given task, but even in going from one task to a different but similar one. In the experiments we have carried out so far, there was not sufficient cross-task consistency in the estimated times of the basic processes to allow them to be treated as elementary in this sense. We were unable to obtain consistent estimates of unit processing times that were invariant over the different extrapolation methods.

Again, the models we constructed for the three different processes played the role of a representative subject, reflecting and predicting characteristics of behaviour that the subjects had in common, but not matching, of course, the deviations from these norms exhibited by individuals.

Conclusion

The goal of cognitive psychology is to find invariant characteristics of the human information processing system. Because the system is adaptive to its task environments, and because it can learn, this is an undertaking of great subtlety. In designing experiments to investigate cognition, we must overcome two difficulties:

(1) We must design tasks in which the behaviour is not so constrained by the task environment that we could predict it in detail from the characteristics of that environment without knowing anything about the information processing system.
(2) In interpreting our findings, we must distinguish between those invariants we discover that are genuinely 'psychological' (i.e. built-in properties of the human information processing system) and those that are 'sociological' (i.e. learned behaviours and capabilities acquired through exposure to a particular culture).

Constructing computer programs to model subject behaviour in cognitive tasks is a powerful method for learning (and testing) what capabilities must be attributed to the information processing system in order for it to perform successfully in a particular task environment. The SEREX program provides us with a quite detailed picture of the mechanisms subjects use to perform sequence extrapolation tasks, and a formal description of the encodings they use to represent the patterns that they induce from the sequences. The simulation approach does not offer us, however, an automatic means for determin-

330

ing which components of the computer programs are 'psychological' and which 'sociological' in the senses just defined. For that, we must experiment with subjects drawn from different cultures, or test our ability to modify behaviour through instructions and training.

At best, any single computer simulation (or any other cognitive theory) will describe a representative subject; it cannot account for individual differences. To the extent that behaviour is in fact variable, it is Quixotic to seek universal invariants. The next step beyond a theory of the representative subject is the study of individual differences and their etiology. Such an investigation calls for the construction of multiple simulation programs to account for the differences.

References

Bobrow, D. G., and Collins, A. (Eds.) (1975). *Representation and Understanding*. New York, Academic Press.

Chase, W. G. and Simon, H. A. (1973). Perception in chess. *Cognitive Psychology*, **4**, 55–81.

Chase, W. G., and Simon, H. A. (1974). The mind's eye in chess, in W. G. Chase (Ed.) *Visual Information Processing*. New York, Academic Press.

Ernst, G. W., and Newell, A. (1969). *GPS: A Case Study in Generality and Problem Solving*. New York, Academic Press.

Feigenbaum, E. (1961). The simulation of verbal learning behavior. *Proceedings of the Western Joint Computer Conference*, **19**, 121–132.

Gerritsen, Rob., Gregg, L. W. and Simon, H. A. (1975). Task structure and instruction-induced strategies as determinants of latencies. *C. I. P. Working Paper 292*, Carnegie-Mellon University, Department of Psychology.

Glanzer, M., and Clark, W. H. (1964). The verbal-loop hypothesis: conventional figures. *The American Journal of Psychology*, **77**, 621–626.

Greeno, J. G., and Simon, H. A. (1974). Processes for sequence production, *Psychological Review*, **81**, 187–198.

Gregg, L. W. and Simon, H. A. (1967). An Information-processing explanation of one-trial and incremental learning. *Journal of Verbal Learning and Verbal Behavior*, **6**, 780–787.

Hayes, J. R., and Simon, H. A. (1974). Understanding written problem instructions, in L. W. Gregg (Ed.) *Knowledge and Cognition*. Potomac, Maryland, Lawrence Erlbaum Associates.

Jones, M. R. (1973). Higher order organization in serial recall of digits, *Journal of Experimental Psychology*, **99**, 106–119.

Jones, M. R., and Zamostny, K. P. (1975). Memory and rule structure in the prediction of serial patterns, *Journal of Experimental Psychology: Human Learning and Memory*, **104**, 295–306.

Kotovsky, K., and Simon, H. A. (1973). Empirical tests of a theory of human acquisition of concepts for sequential patterns, *Cognitive Psychology*, **4**, 399–424.

Newell, A., Shaw, J. C., and Simon, H. A. (1960). Report on a general problem solving program, in *Proceedings of the International Conference on Information Processing*. London, Butterworth's.

Newell, A., and Simon, H. A. (1972). *Human Problem Solving*, Englewood Cliffs, N. J., Prentice-Hall.

Quillian, M. R. (1968). Semantic memory, in M. Minsky (Ed.) *Semantic Information Processing*. Cambridge, Mass., M.I.T. Press.

Restle, F. (1967). Grammatical analysis of the prediction of binary events, *Journal of Verbal Learning and Verbal Behavior,* **6**, 17–25.

Restle, F. (1970). Theory of serial pattern Learning: structural trees. *Psych. Rev.,* **77**, 481–495.

Restle, F. (1976). Structural ambiguity in serial pattern learning. *Cognitive Psychology,* forthcoming.

Restle, F., and Brown, E. R. (1970). Serial pattern learning, *Journal of Experimental Psychology,* **83**, 120–125.

Restle, F., and Burnside, B. L. (1972). Tracking of serial patterns, *Journal of Experimental Psychology,* **95**, 299–307.

Simon, H. A. (1969). *The Science of the Artificial.* Cambridge, Mass., The M.I.T. Press.

Simon, H. A. (1972). Complexity and the representation of patterned sequences of symbols, *Psychological Review,* **79**, 369–382.

Simon, H. A. (1975). The functional equivalence of problem solving skills, *Cognitive Psychology,* **7**, 268–288.

Simon, H. A., and Feigenbaum, E. A. (1964). An information-processing theory of some effects of similarity, familiarization, and meaningfulness in verbal learning. *Journal of Verbal Learning and Verbal Behavior,* **3**, 385–396.

Simon, H. A., and Gilmartin, K. (1973). A simulation of memory for chess positions. *Cognitive Psychology,* **5**, 29–46.

Simon, H. A., and Kotovsky, K. (1963). Human acquisition of concepts for sequential patterns, *Psychological Review,* **70**, 534–546.

Simon, H. A., and Sumner, R. K. (1968). Pattern in Music, in B. Kleinmuntz, (Ed.), *Formal Representation of Human Judgement,* New York, Wiley.

Vitz, P. C., and Todd, T. C. (1967). A model of learning for simple repeating binary patterns, *Journal of Experimental Psychology,* **75**, 108–117.

Index

342

344